You're Reading in the Wrong Direction!!

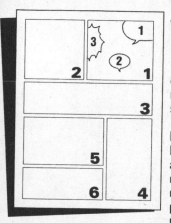

Whoops! Guess what? You're starting at the wrong end of the comic!

...It's true! In keeping with the original Japanese format, **One Piece** is meant to be read from right to left, starting in the upper-right corner.

Unlike English, which is read from left to right, Japanese is read from right to left, meaning that action, sound effects, and word-balloon order are completely reversed...something which can make readers unfamiliar with Japanese feel pretty backwards themselves. For this reason, manga or Japanese comics published in the U.S. in English have sometimes been published "flopped"— that is, printed in exact reverse order, as though seen from the other side of a mirror.

By flopping pages, U.S. publishers can avoid confusing readers, but the compromise is not without its downside. For one thing, a character in a flopped manga series who once wore in the original Japanese version a T-shirt emblazoned with "M A Y" (as in "the merry month of") now wears one which reads "Y A M"! Additionally, many manga creators in Japan are themselves unhappy with the process, as some feel the mirror-imaging of their art skews their original intentions.

We are proud to bring you Eiichiro Oda's **One Piece** in the original unflopped format. For now, though, turn to the other side of the book and let the journey begin...!

—Editor

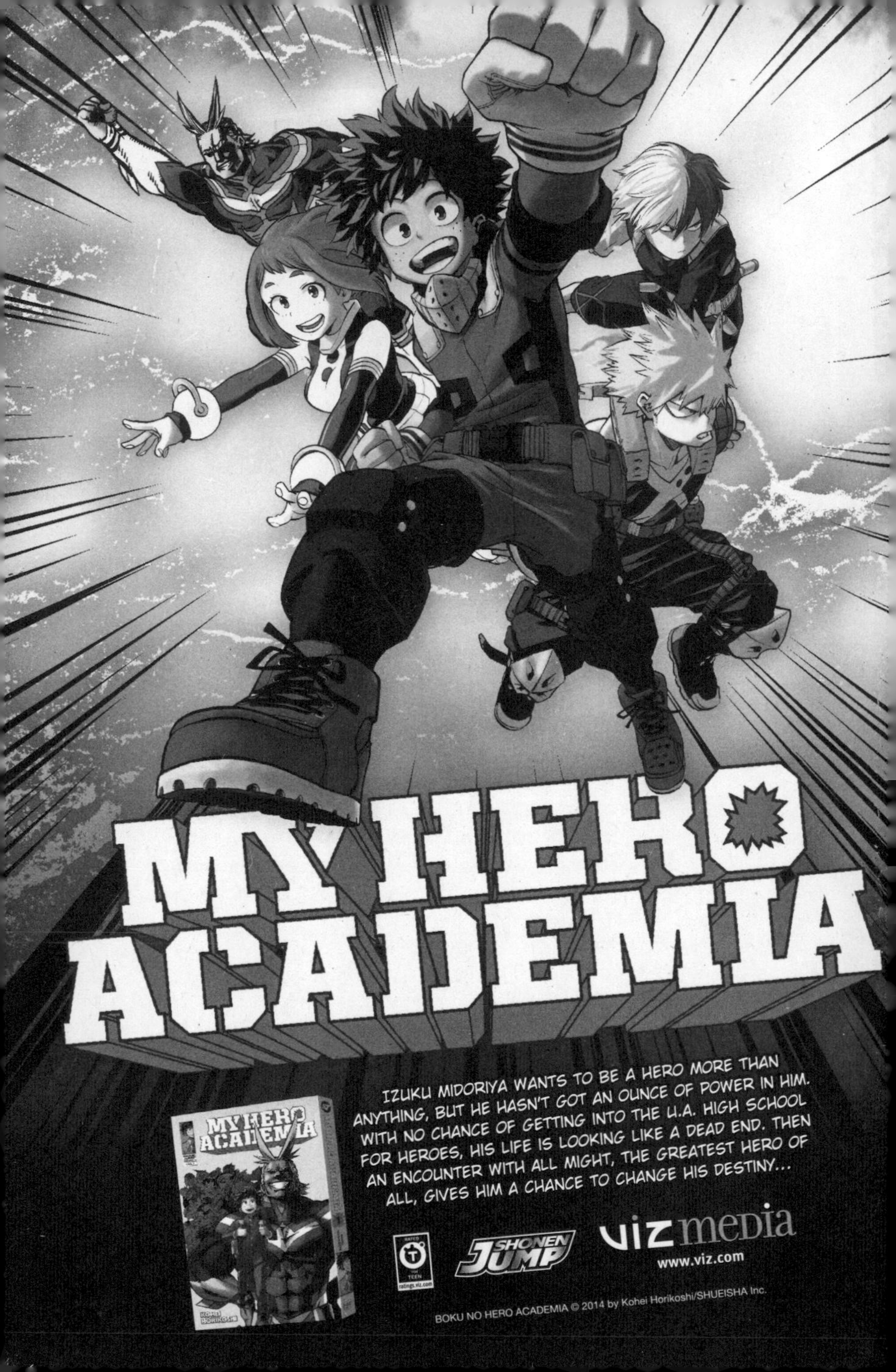
MY HERO ACADEMIA
IZUKU MIDORIYA WANTS TO BE A HERO MORE THAN ANYTHING, BUT HE HASN'T GOT AN OUNCE OF POWER IN HIM. WITH NO CHANCE OF GETTING INTO THE U.A. HIGH SCHOOL FOR HEROES, HIS LIFE IS LOOKING LIKE A DEAD END. THEN AN ENCOUNTER WITH ALL MIGHT, THE GREATEST HERO OF ALL, GIVES HIM A CHANCE TO CHANGE HIS DESTINY...
MY HERO ACADEMIA
KOHEI HORIKOSHI
RATED T FOR TEEN
ratings.viz.com
SHONEN JUMP
VIZ MEDIA
www.viz.com
BOKU NO HERO ACADEMIA © 2014 by Kohei Horikoshi/SHUEISHA Inc.

SHONEN JUMP MANGA

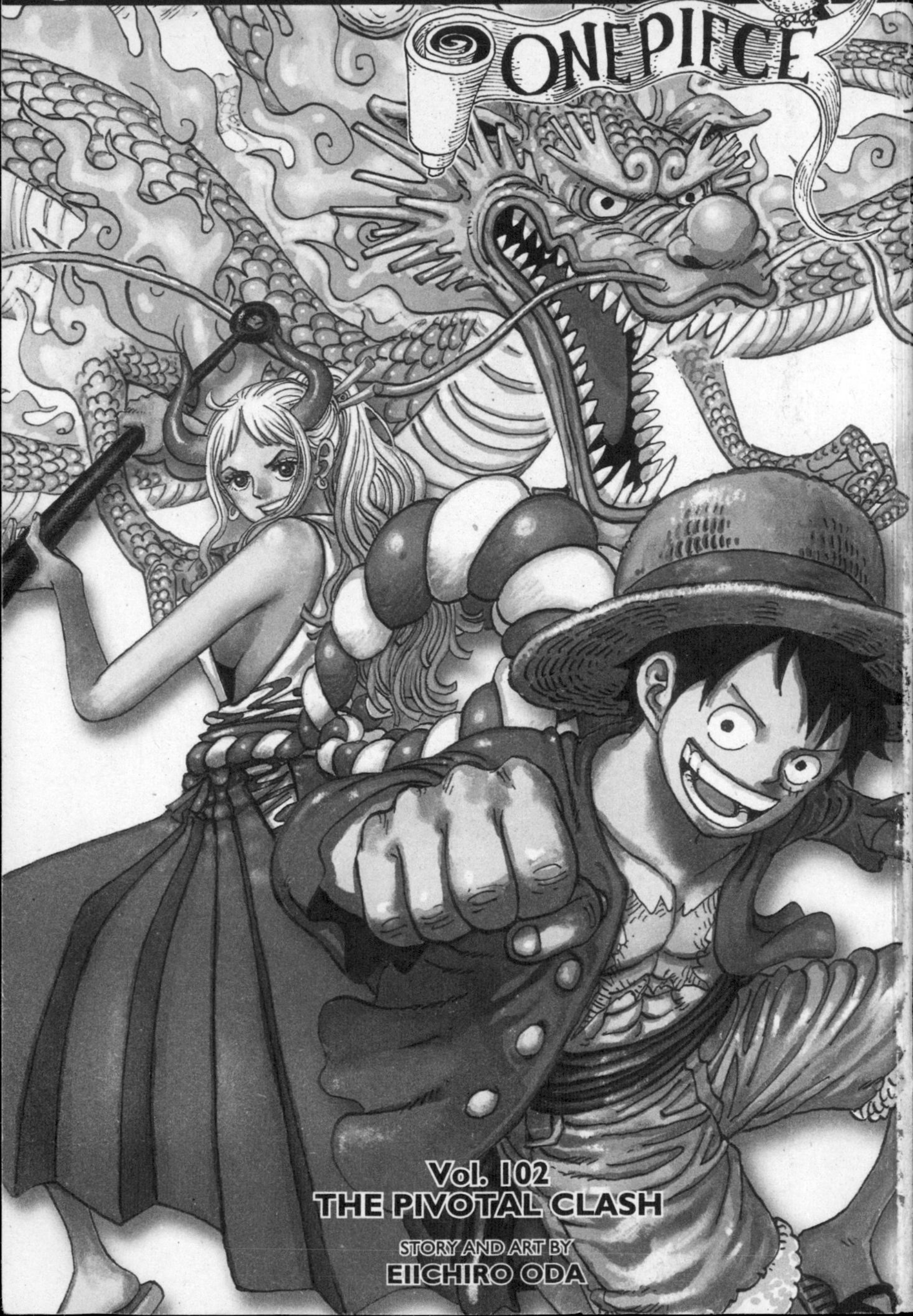
ONE PIECE

Vol. 102
THE PIVOTAL CLASH

STORY AND ART BY
EIICHIRO ODA

The Straw Hat Crew

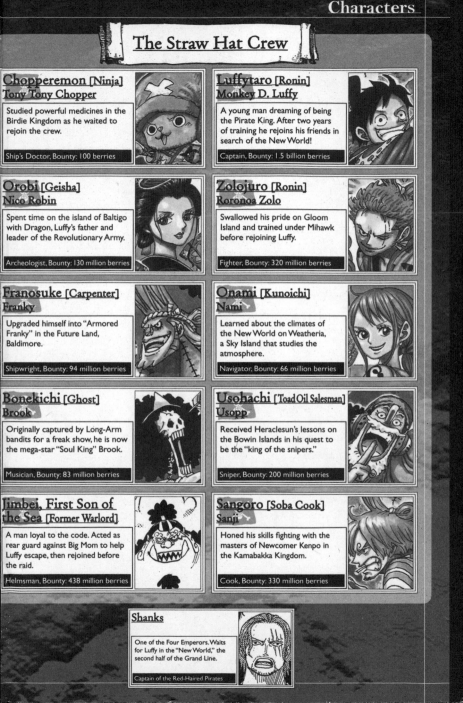

Chopperemon [Ninja]
Tony Tony Chopper

Studied powerful medicines in the Birdie Kingdom as he waited to rejoin the crew.

Ship's Doctor, Bounty: 100 berries

Luffytaro [Ronin]
Monkey D. Luffy

A young man dreaming of being the Pirate King. After two years of training he rejoins his friends in search of the New World!

Captain, Bounty: 1.5 billion berries

Orobi [Geisha]
Nico Robin

Spent time on the island of Baltigo with Dragon, Luffy's father, and leader of the Revolutionary Army.

Archeologist, Bounty: 130 million berries

Zolojuro [Ronin]
Roronoa Zolo

Swallowed his pride on Gloom Island and trained under Mihawk before rejoining Luffy.

Fighter, Bounty: 320 million berries

Franosuke [Carpenter]
Franky

Upgraded himself into "Armored Franky" in the Future Land, Baldimore.

Shipwright, Bounty: 94 million berries

Onami [Kunoichi]
Nami

Learned about the climates of the New World on Weatheria, a Sky Island that studies the atmosphere.

Navigator, Bounty: 66 million berries

Bonekichi [Ghost]
Brook

Originally captured by Long-Arm bandits for a freak show, he is now the mega-star "Soul King" Brook.

Musician, Bounty: 83 million berries

Usohachi [Toad Oil Salesman]
Usopp

Received Heraclesun's lessons on the Bowin Islands in his quest to be the "king of the snipers."

Sniper, Bounty: 200 million berries

Jimbei, First Son of the Sea [Former Warlord]

A man loyal to the code. Acted as rear guard against Big Mom to help Luffy escape, then rejoined before the raid.

Helmsman, Bounty: 438 million berries

Sangoro [Soba Cook]
Sanji

Honed his skills fighting with the masters of Newcomer Kenpo in the Kamabakka Kingdom.

Cook, Bounty: 330 million berries

Shanks

One of the Four Emperors. Waits for Luffy in the "New World," the second half of the Grand Line.

Captain of the Red-Haired Pirates

The story of ONE PIECE 1»102

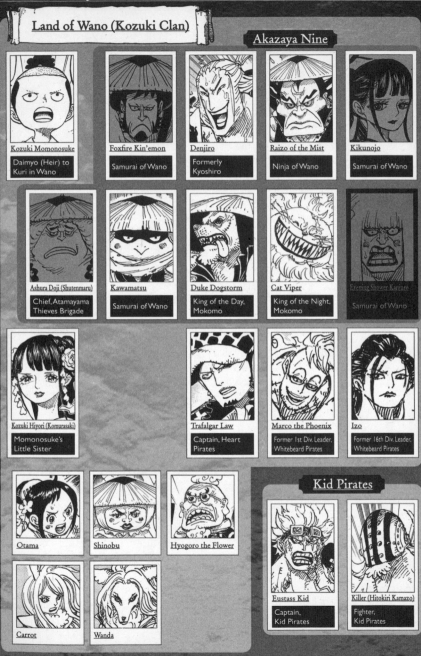

Land of Wano (Kozuki Clan)

Akazaya Nine

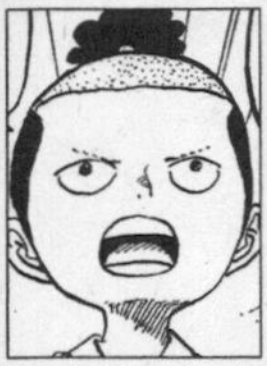

Kozuki Momonosuke

Daimyo (Heir) to Kuri in Wano

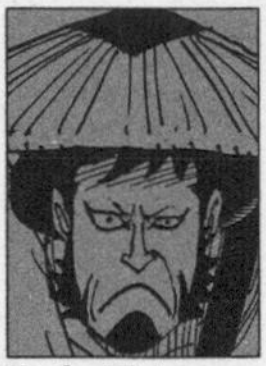

Foxfire Kin'emon

Samurai of Wano

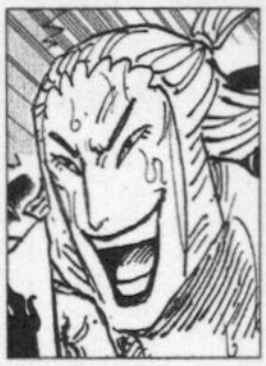

Denjiro

Formerly Kyoshiro

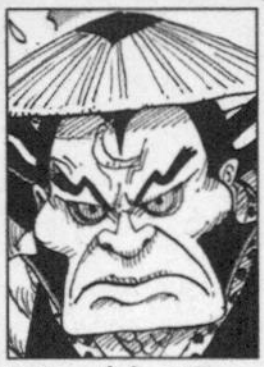

Raizo of the Mist

Ninja of Wano

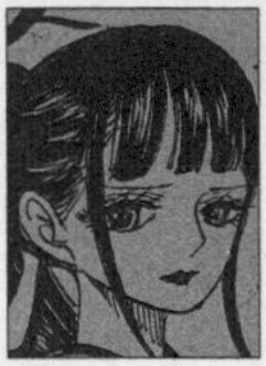

Kikunojo

Samurai of Wano

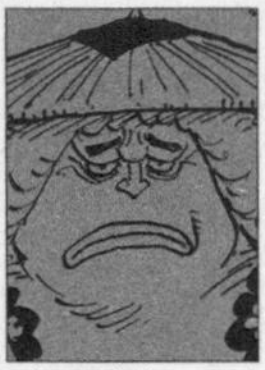

Ashura Doji (Shutenmaru)

Chief, Atamayama Thieves Brigade

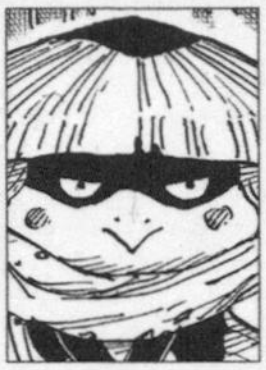

Kawamatsu

Samurai of Wano

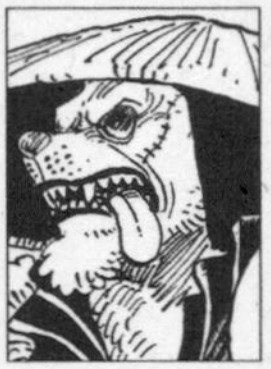

Duke Dogstorm

King of the Day, Mokomo

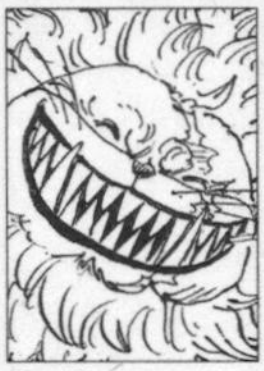

Cat Viper

King of the Night, Mokomo

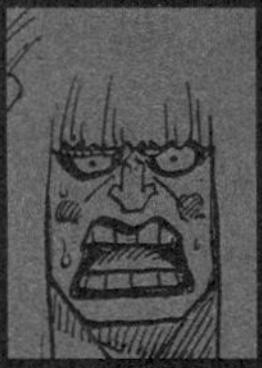

Evening Shower Kanjuro

Samurai of Wano

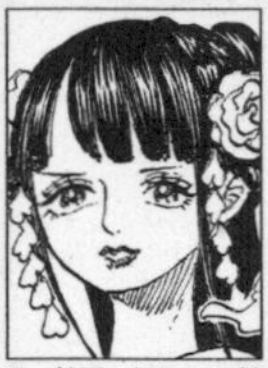

Kozuki Hiyori (Komurasaki)

Momonosuke's Little Sister

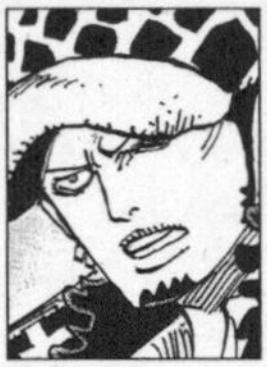

Trafalgar Law

Captain, Heart Pirates

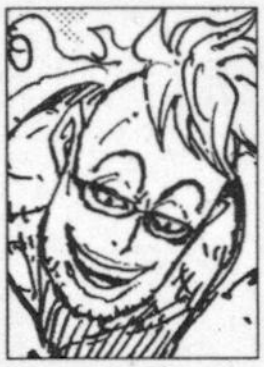

Marco the Phoenix

Former 1st Div. Leader, Whitebeard Pirates

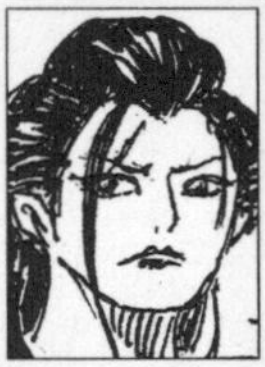

Izo

Former 16th Div. Leader, Whitebeard Pirates

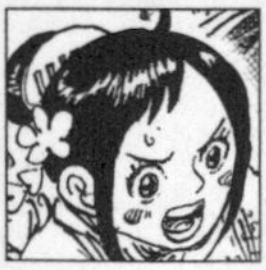

Otama

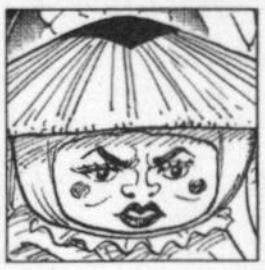

Shinobu

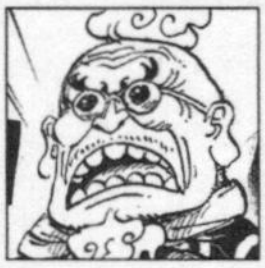

Hyogoro the Flower

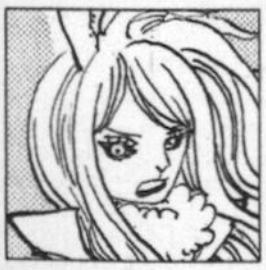

Carrot

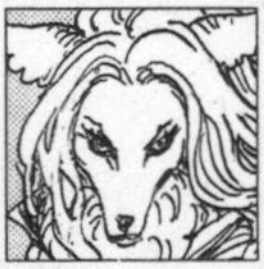

Wanda

Kid Pirates

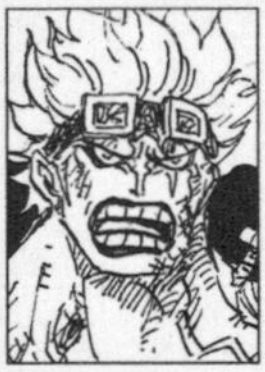

Eustass Kid

Captain, Kid Pirates

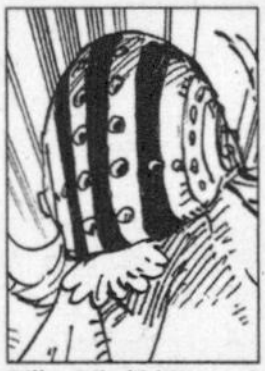

Killer (Hitokiri Kamazo)

Fighter, Kid Pirates

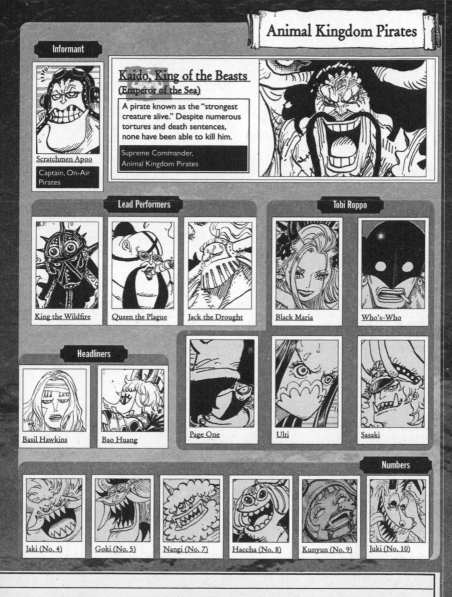

Animal Kingdom Pirates

Informant

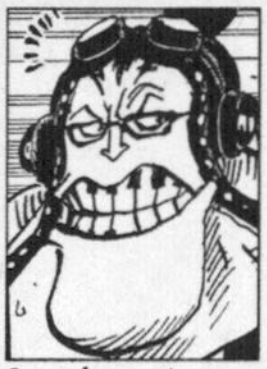

Scratchmen Apoo

Captain, On-Air Pirates

Kaido, King of the Beasts
(Emperor of the Sea)

A pirate known as the "strongest creature alive." Despite numerous tortures and death sentences, none have been able to kill him.

Supreme Commander, Animal Kingdom Pirates

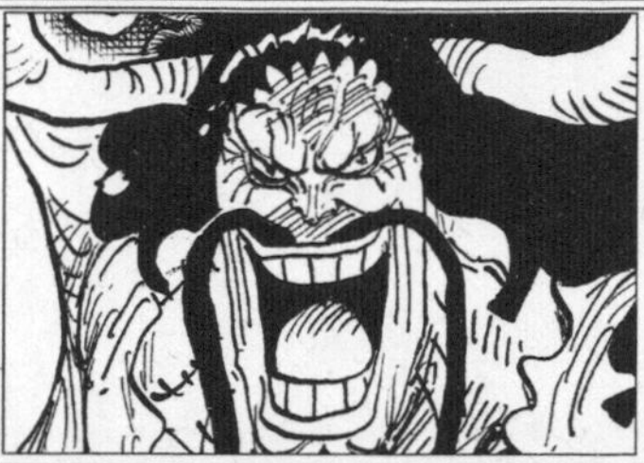

Lead Performers

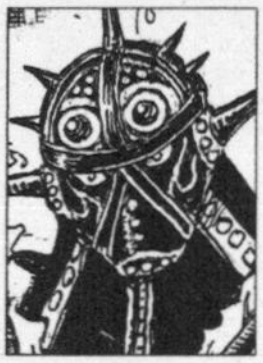

King the Wildfire

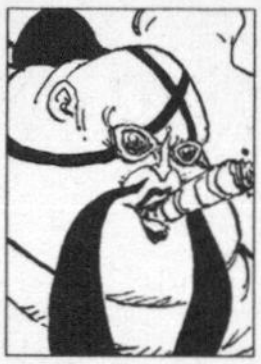

Queen the Plague

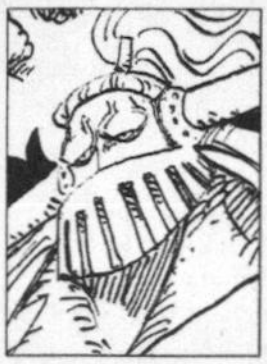

Jack the Drought

Tobi Roppo

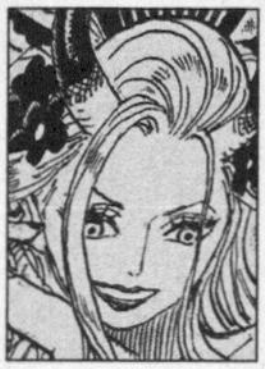

Black Maria

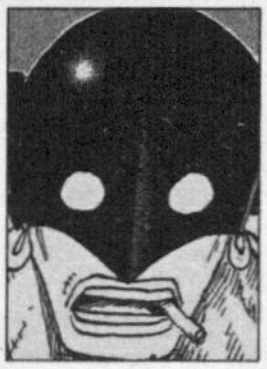

Who's-Who

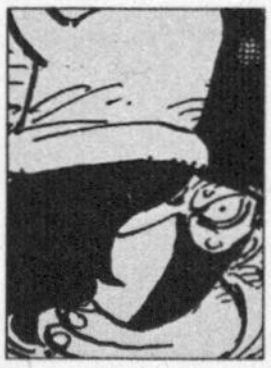

Page One

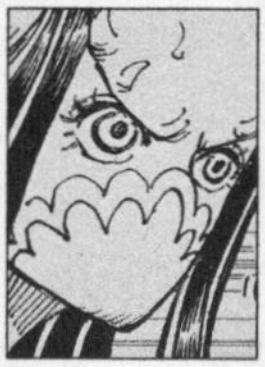

Ulti

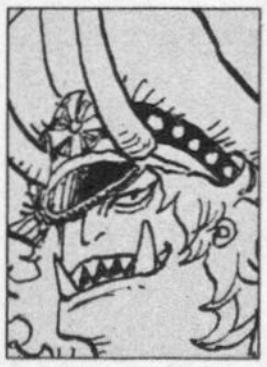

Sasaki

Headliners

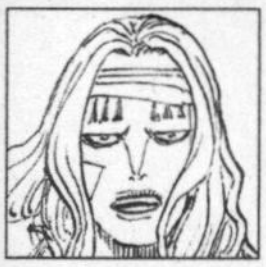

Basil Hawkins

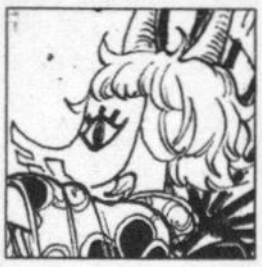

Bao Huang

Numbers

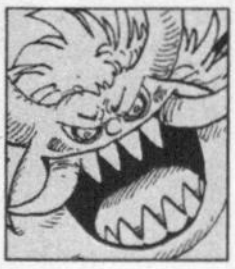

Jaki (No. 4)

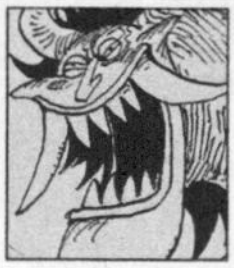

Goki (No. 5)

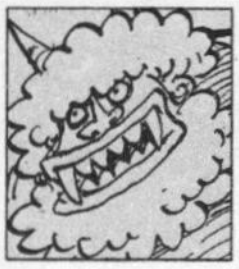

Nangi (No. 7)

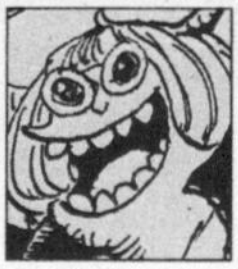

Haccha (No. 8)

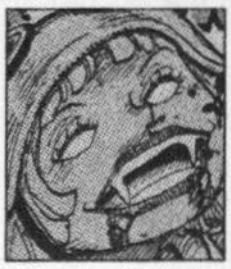

Kunyun (No. 9)

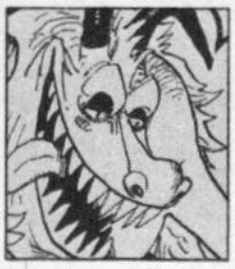

Juki (No. 10)

to fight on Luffy's side. On the roof of the castle, Luffy squares off with Kaido!! But the wall of the Emperor's strength is too high to scale, and Luffy falls in battle. His friends and companions, believing in his return, fight and defeat the Tobi Roppo! Luffy reappears at last, along with Momonosuke in dragon form, and heads for the roof to fight Kaido again. Kaido and Yamato are in the midst of a family duel, and just as Yamato is being overpowered, Luffy arrives!!

The story of ONE PIECE 1»102

Big Mom Pirates

Big Mom
(Emperor of the Sea)

One of the Four Emperors. Uses the Soul-Soul Fruit that extracts life span from others.

Captain, Big Mom Pirates

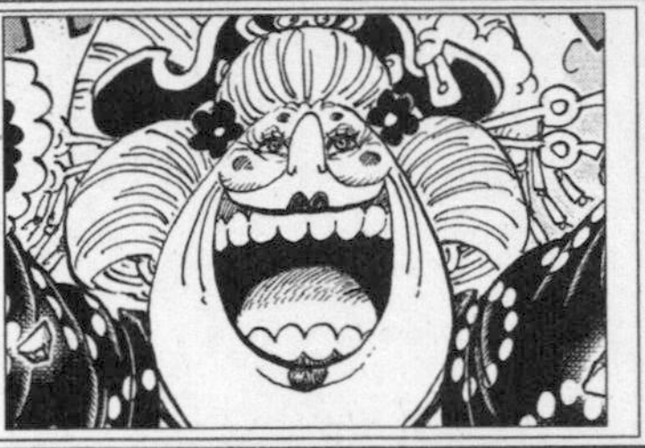

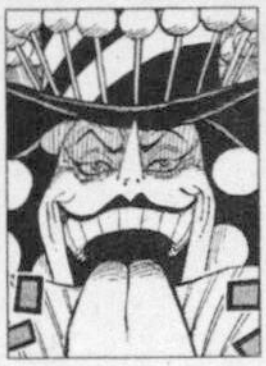

C. Perospero

1st Son of Charlotte

Land of Wano (Kurozumi Clan)

Kurozumi Orochi

The ruler of Wano, using Kaido's help. He cunningly schemed to overthrow his archenemy, the Kozuki Clan.

Shogun of Wano

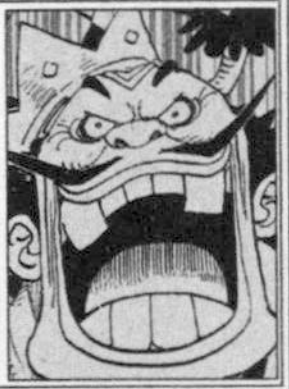

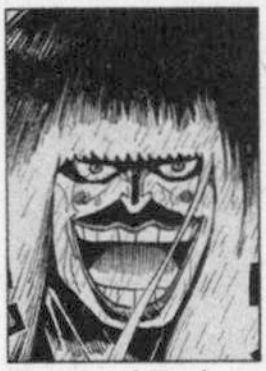

Kurozumi Kanjuro

Orochi's Spy

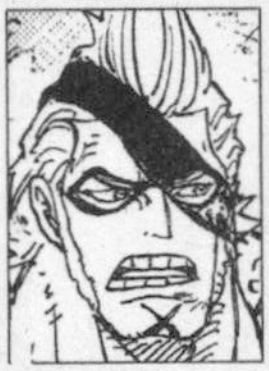

X. (Diez) Drake

Former Tobi Roppo

Left Kaido's Pirates to fight on Luffy's side!

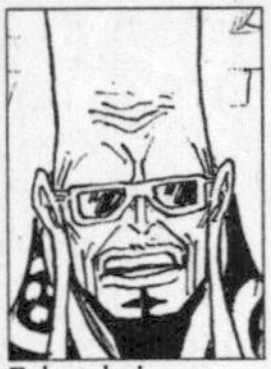

Fukurokuju

Former Leader, Orochi Oniwabanshu

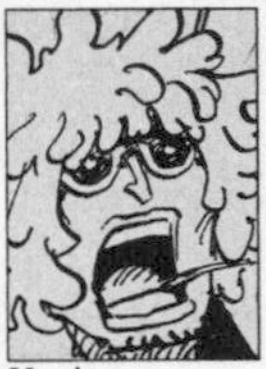

Hotei

Former Leader, Mimawari-gumi

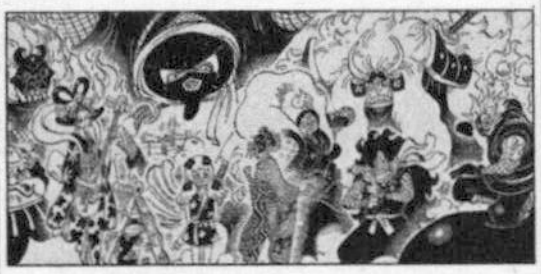

Orochi Oniwabanshu

Former Private Ninja Squad of the Shogun

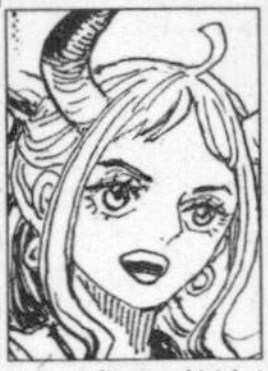

Yamato (Alias: Kozuki Oden)

Kaido's Daughter

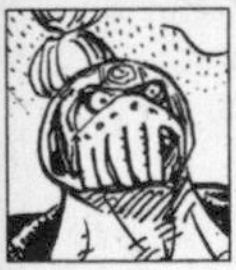

Daifugo

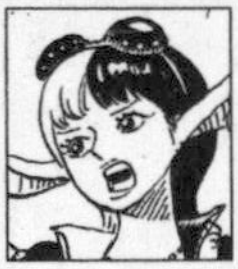

Speed

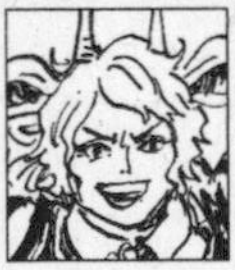

Hamlet

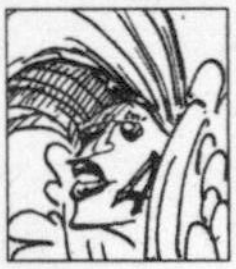

Fourtricks

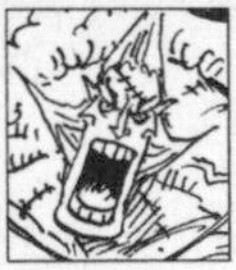

Briscola

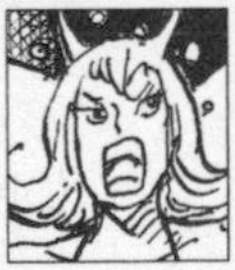

Mizerka

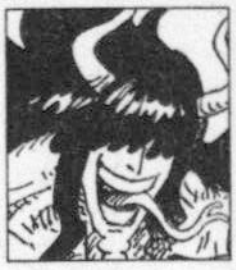

Poker

Turned coat on the Animal Kingdom Pirates thanks to Otama's power!

Story

After two years of hard training, the Straw Hat pirates are back together, first at the Sabaody Archipelago and then through Fish-Man Island to their next stage: the New World!!

Luffy and crew join with Momonosuke's faction in order to defeat Kaido, one of the Four Emperors. With all the allies in place, the raid on Onigashima begins!! As battles break out across the island, Kaido's daughter Yamato shows up and swears

WANO ONE PIECE

Vol. 102
THE PIVOTAL CLASH

CONTENTS

Chapter 1026:

THE PIVOTAL CLASH

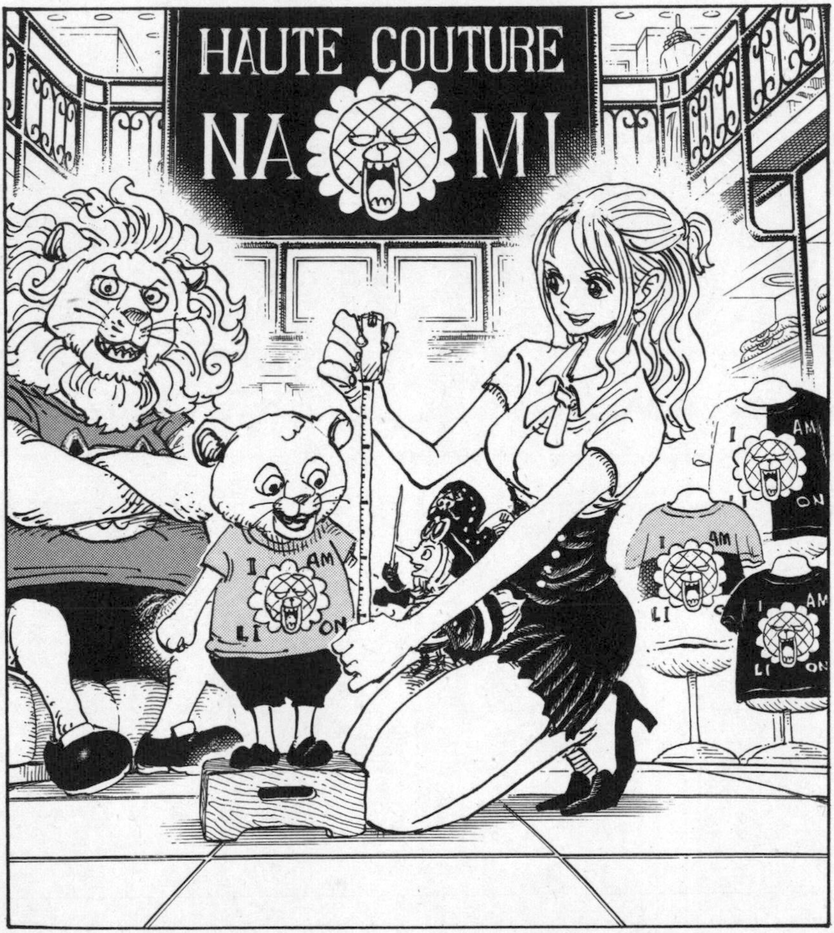
HAUTE COUTURE
NA MI
I AM LI ON

READER REQUEST: "NAMI AND LEO FASHIONING CUTE CLOTHES FOR A LION CUB" BY EBI

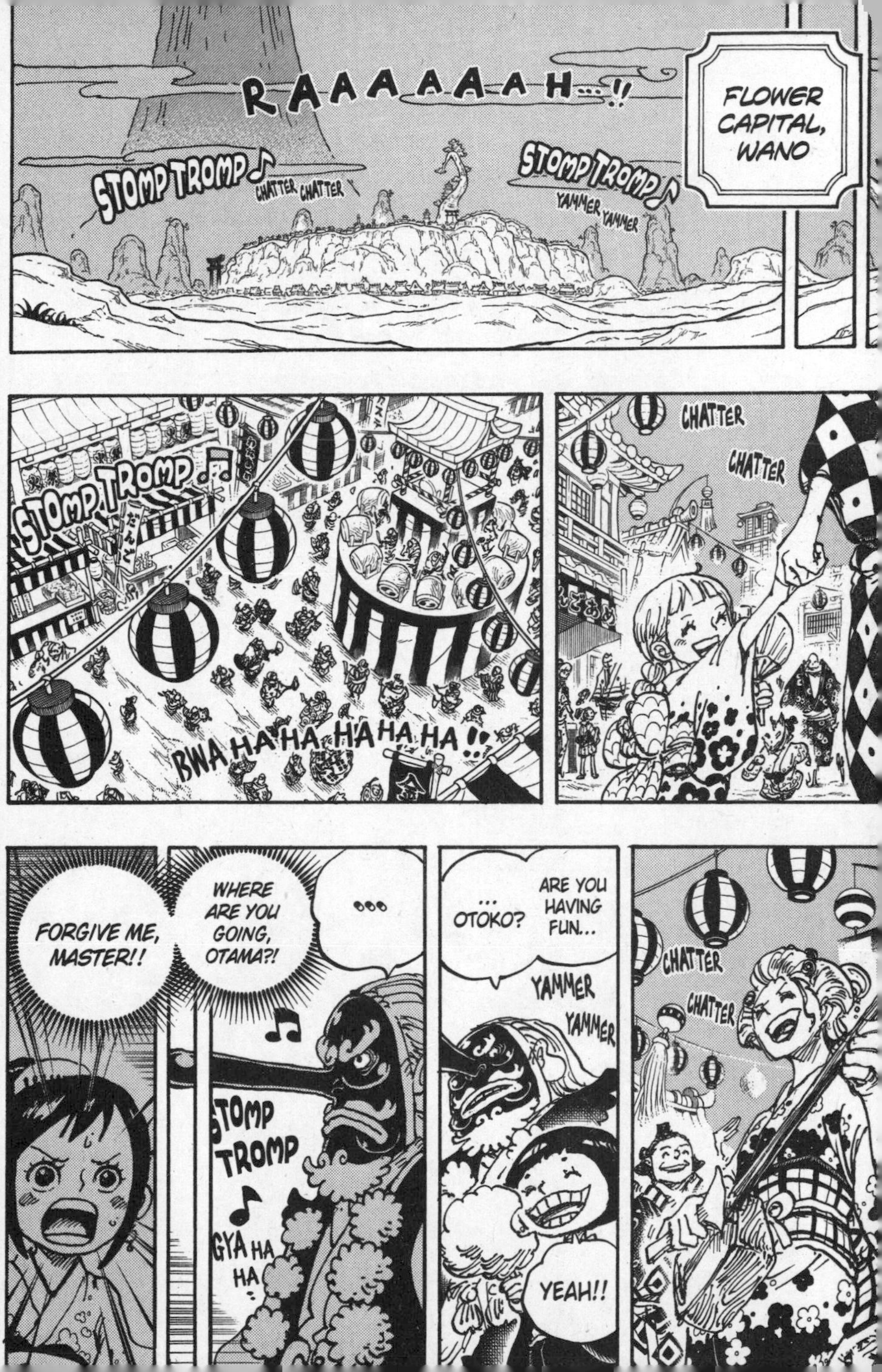
FLOWER CAPITAL, WANO
STOMP TROMP♪
YAMMER YAMMER
RAAAAAAAH...!!
STOMP TROMP♪
CHATTER CHATTER
CHATTER
CHATTER
STOMP TROMP♫
BWAHAHAHAHAHA!!
CHATTER
CHATTER
ARE YOU HAVING FUN...
...OTOKO?
YAMMER
YAMMER
YEAH!!
•••
STOMP TROMP
GYA HA HA
WHERE ARE YOU GOING, OTAMA?!
FORGIVE ME, MASTER!!

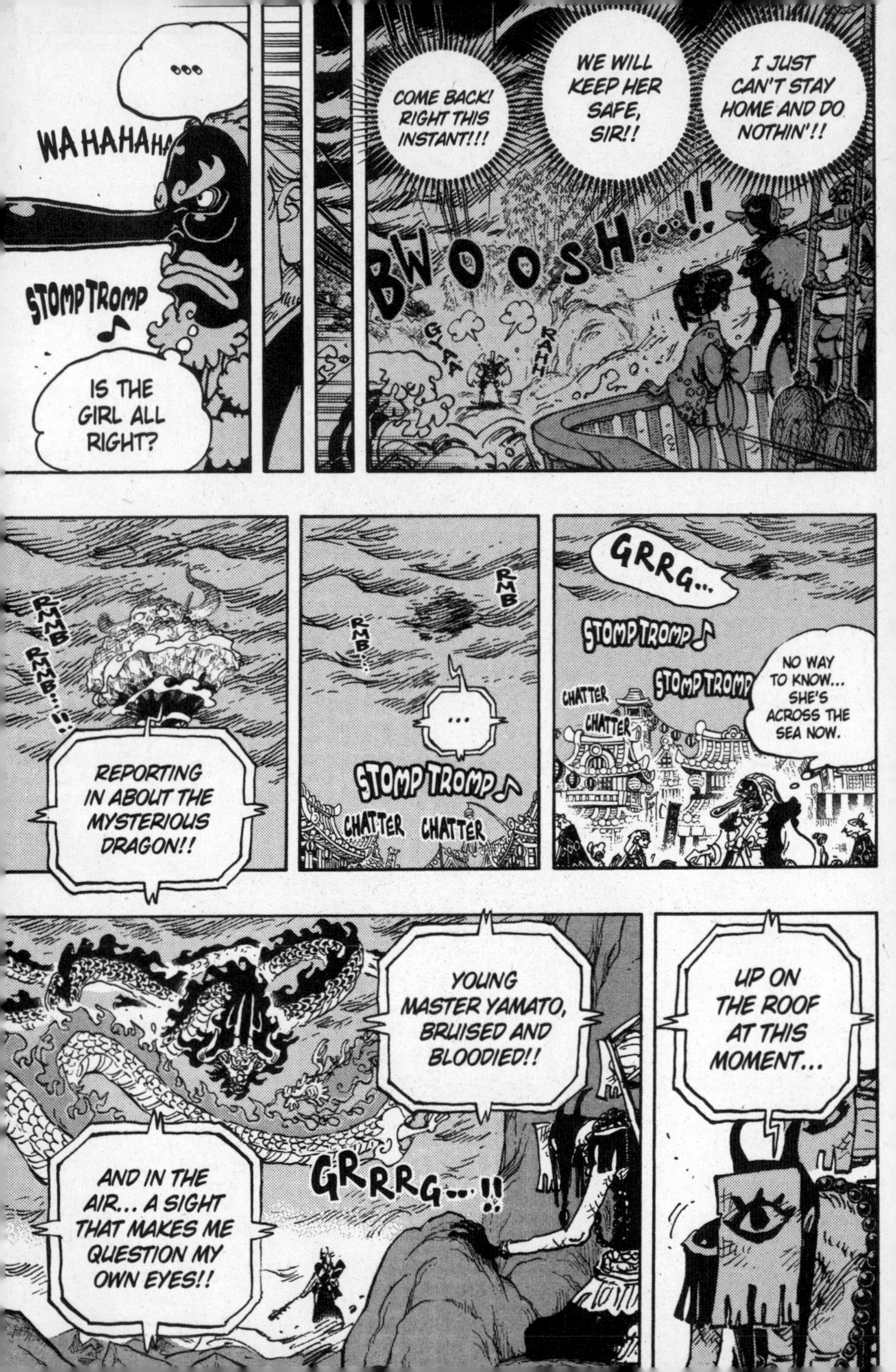
I JUST CAN'T STAY HOME AND DO NOTHIN'!!
WE WILL KEEP HER SAFE, SIR!!
COME BACK! RIGHT THIS INSTANT!!!
BWOOSH...!!
RAHH
GYAA
...
WA HAHAHA
STOMP TROMP ♪
IS THE GIRL ALL RIGHT?
GRRG...
STOMP TROMP ♪
STOMP TROMP
CHATTER
CHATTER
NO WAY TO KNOW... SHE'S ACROSS THE SEA NOW.
RMB
RMB...
...
STOMP TROMP ♪
CHATTER CHATTER
RMMB
RMMB...!!
REPORTING IN ABOUT THE MYSTERIOUS DRAGON!!
UP ON THE ROOF AT THIS MOMENT...
YOUNG MASTER YAMATO, BRUISED AND BLOODIED!!
GRRRG...!!
AND IN THE AIR... A SIGHT THAT MAKES ME QUESTION MY OWN EYES!!

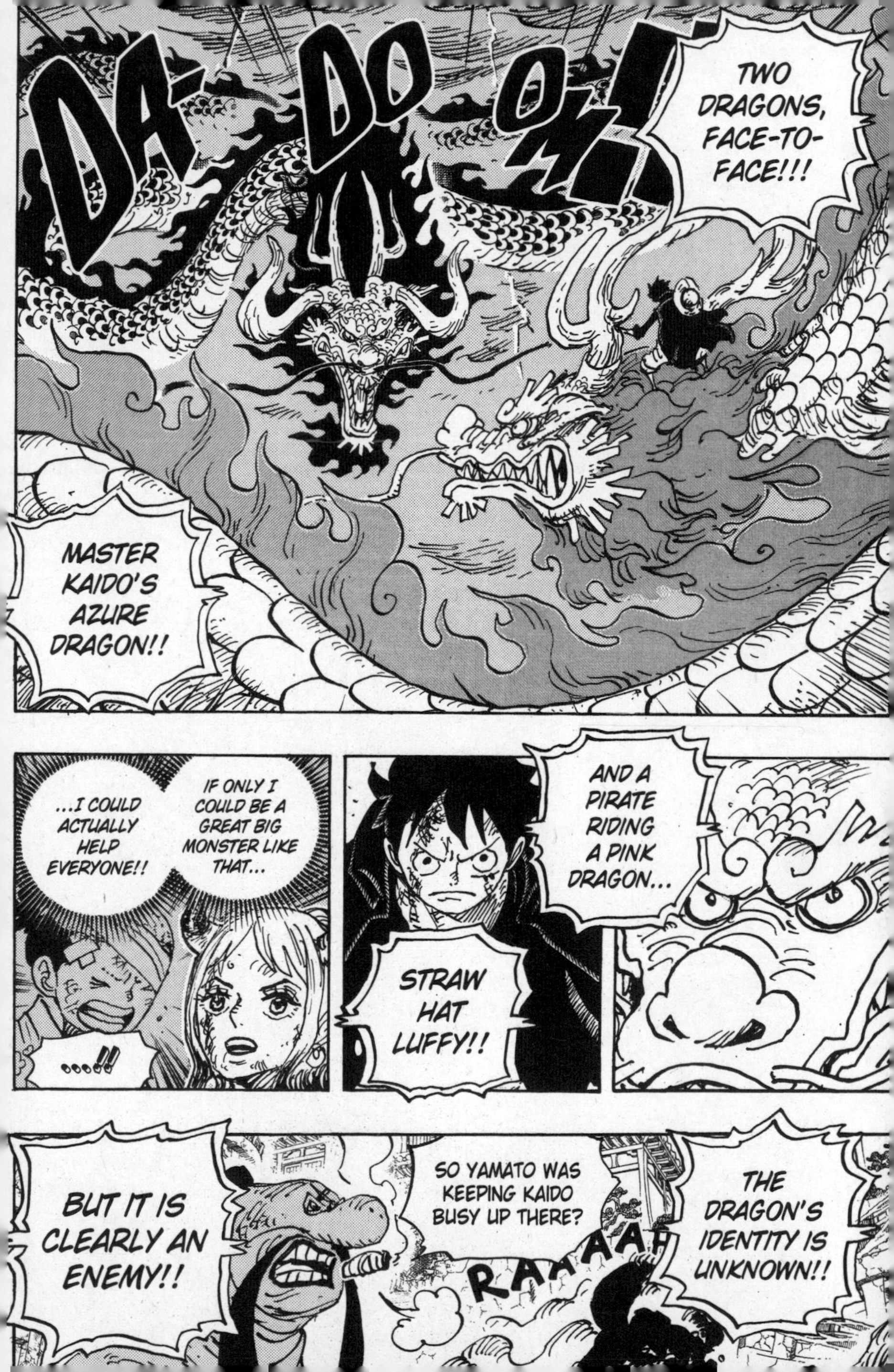
TWO DRAGONS, FACE-TO-FACE!!!
DA-DO-OM!!
MASTER KAIDO'S AZURE DRAGON!!
AND A PIRATE RIDING A PINK DRAGON...
STRAW HAT LUFFY!!
IF ONLY I COULD BE A GREAT BIG MONSTER LIKE THAT...
...I COULD ACTUALLY HELP EVERYONE!!
....!!
THE DRAGON'S IDENTITY IS UNKNOWN!!
SO YAMATO WAS KEEPING KAIDO BUSY UP THERE?
RAAAAH
BUT IT IS CLEARLY AN ENEMY!!

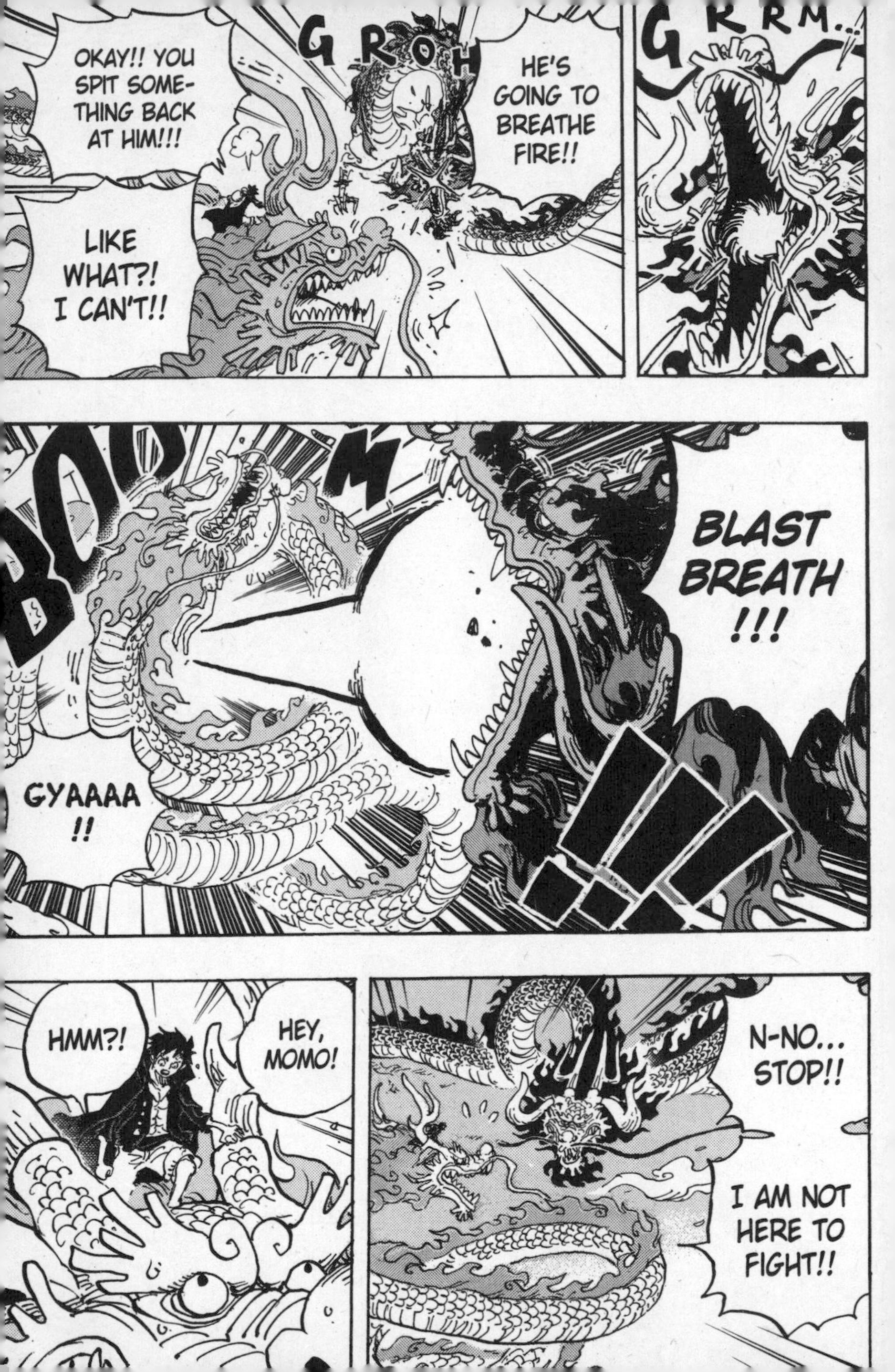
GRRM...
GROH
HE'S GOING TO BREATHE FIRE!!
OKAY!! YOU SPIT SOME-THING BACK AT HIM!!!
LIKE WHAT?! I CAN'T!!
BLAST BREATH !!!
BOOM
GYAAAA !!
N-NO... STOP!!
I AM NOT HERE TO FIGHT!!
HEY, MOMO!
HMM?!

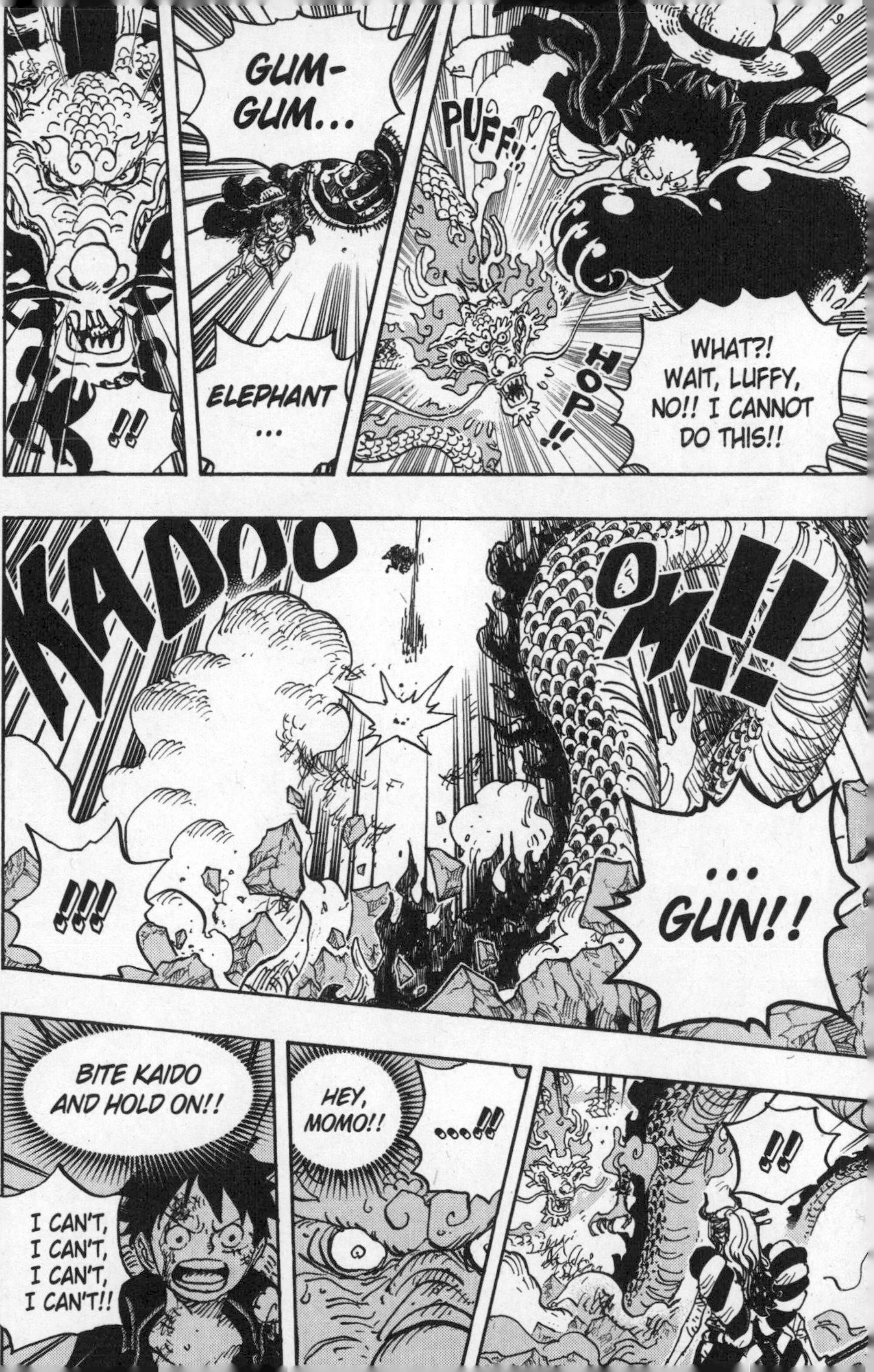
PUFF!!
WHAT?! WAIT, LUFFY, NO!! I CANNOT DO THIS!!
HOP!!
GUM-GUM...
ELEPHANT ...
!!
KADOOOM!!
...GUN!!
!!!
!!
HEY, MOMO!!
...!!
BITE KAIDO AND HOLD ON!!
I CAN'T, I CAN'T, I CAN'T, I CAN'T!!

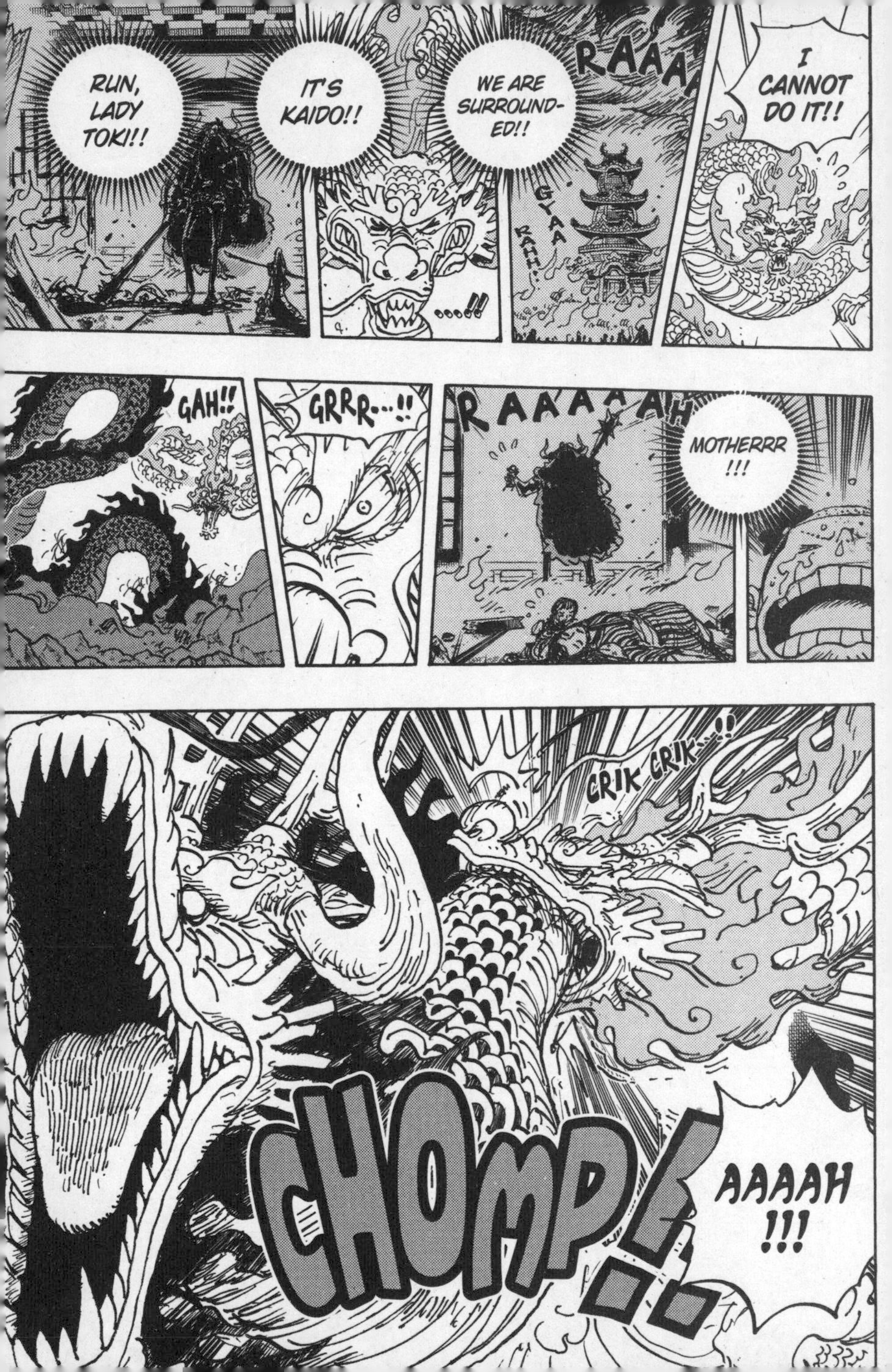
I CANNOT DO IT!!
RAAAA
WE ARE SURROUND-ED!!
GYAA
RAHH...
IT'S KAIDO!!
....!!
RUN, LADY TOKI!!
MOTHERRR!!!
RAAAAAH
GRRR...!!
GAH!!
CRIK CRIK...!!
AAAAH!!!
CHOMP!!

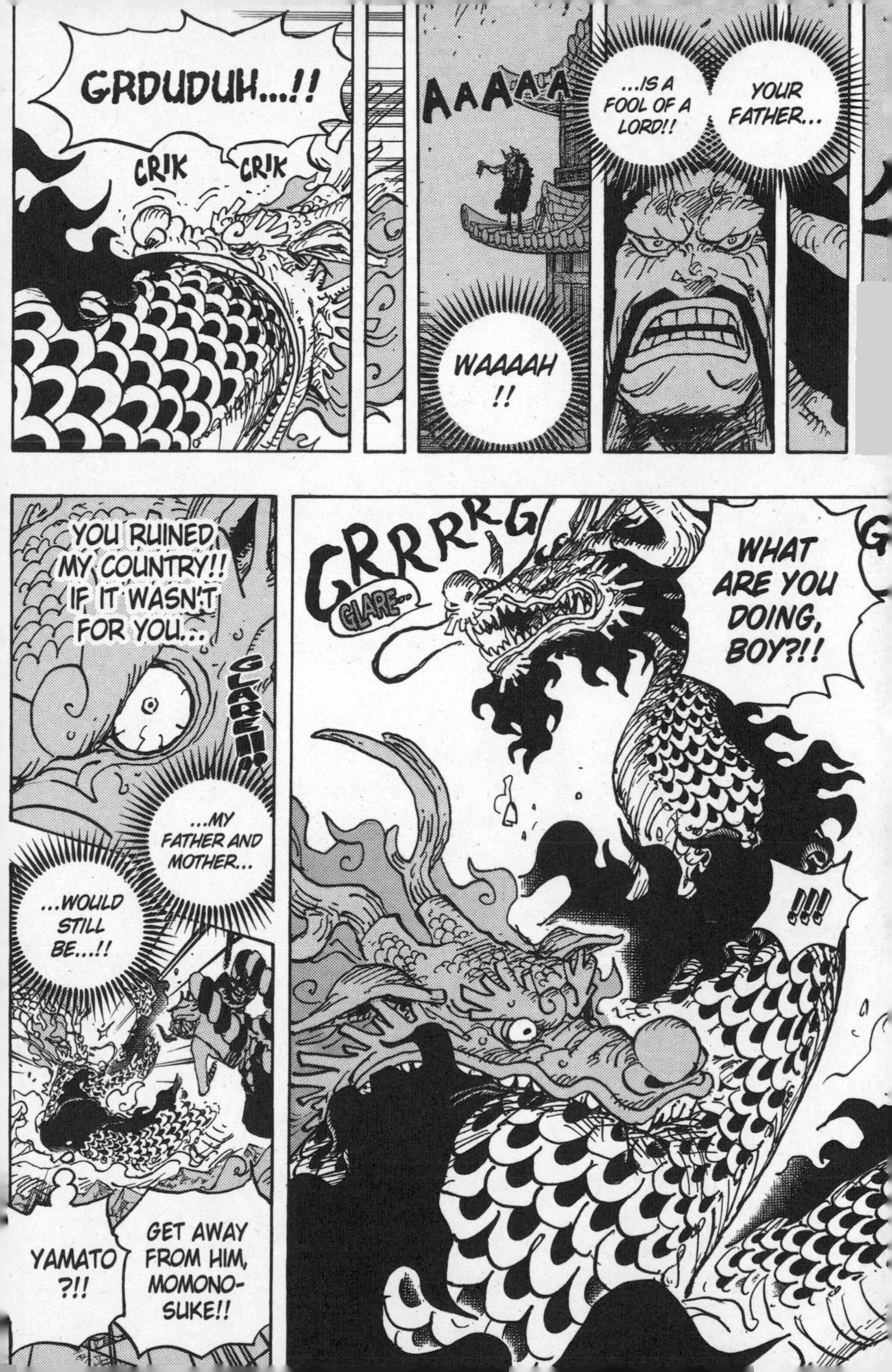

YOUR FATHER...
...IS A FOOL OF A LORD!!
AAAAA
WAAAAH !!
GRDUDUH...!!
CRIK
CRIK
WHAT ARE YOU DOING, BOY?!!
GRRRRG
GLARE...
!!!
YOU RUINED MY COUNTRY!! IF IT WASN'T FOR YOU...
GLARE!!
...MY FATHER AND MOTHER...
...WOULD STILL BE...!!
GET AWAY FROM HIM, MOMONOSUKE!!
YAMATO ?!!

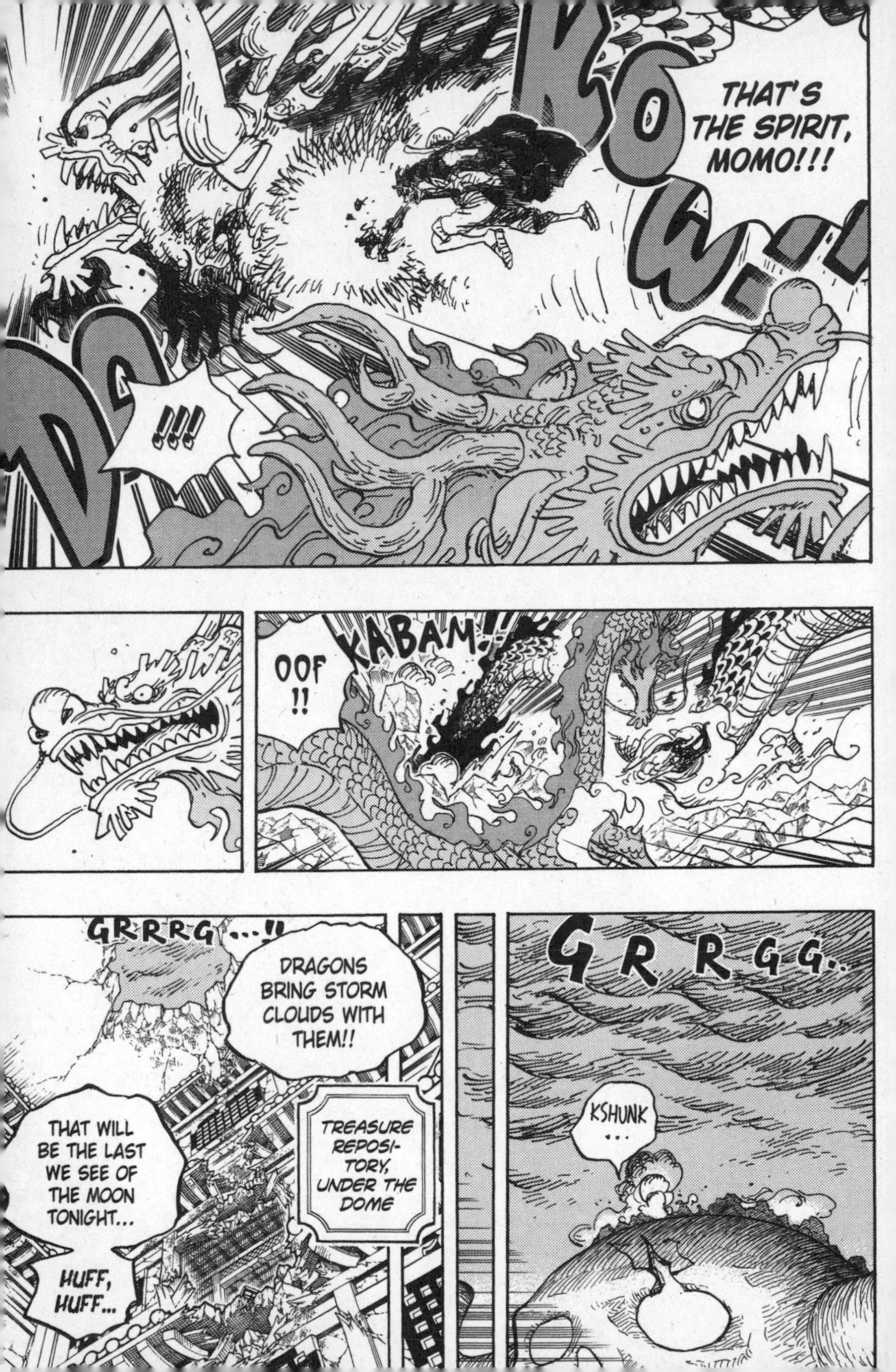

THAT'S THE SPIRIT, MOMO!!!
KABAM!!
OOF !!
GRRGG..
KSHUNK ...
GRRRG...!!
DRAGONS BRING STORM CLOUDS WITH THEM!!
TREASURE REPOSITORY, UNDER THE DOME
THAT WILL BE THE LAST WE SEE OF THE MOON TONIGHT...
HUFF, HUFF...

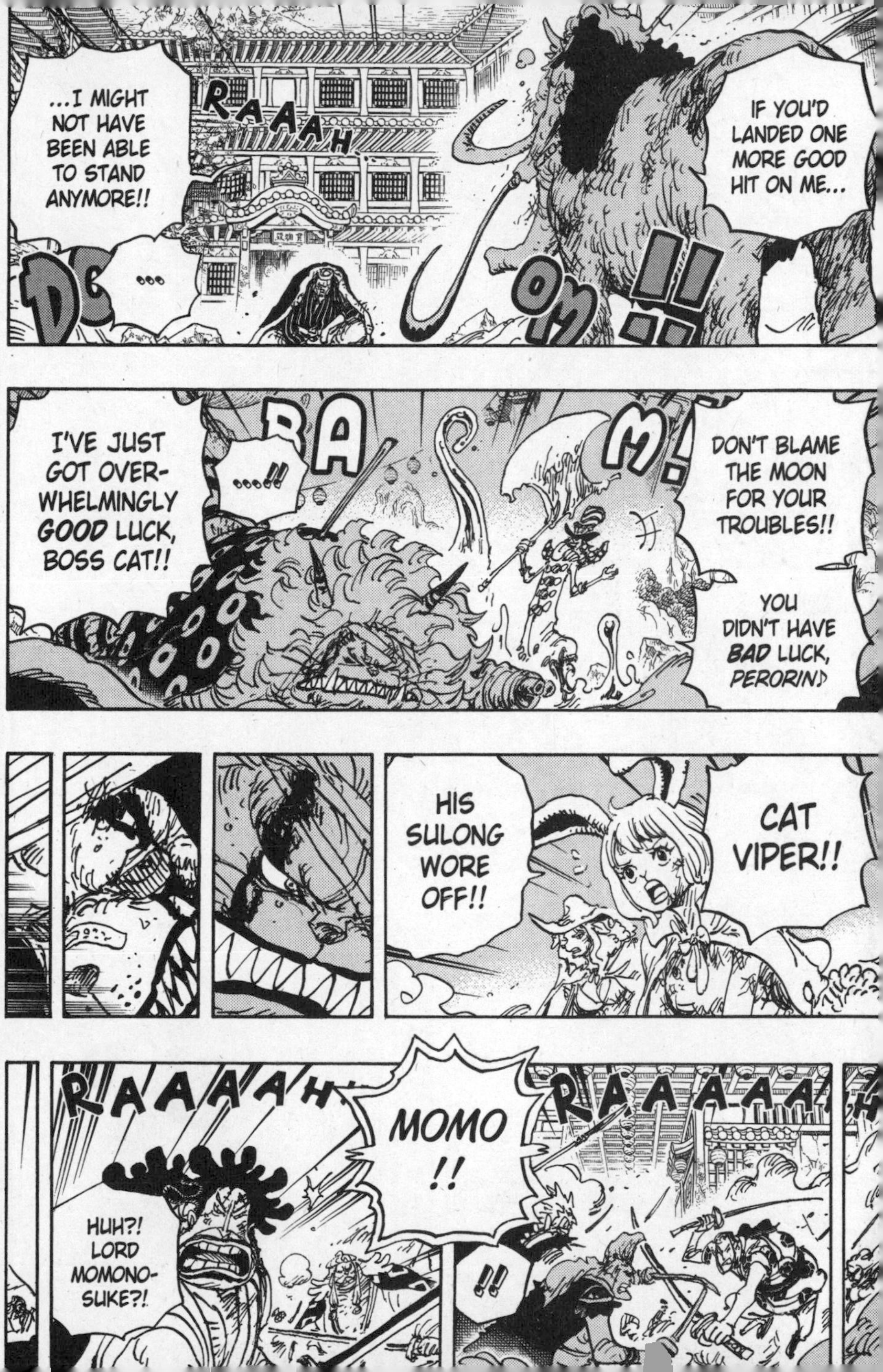
IF YOU'D LANDED ONE MORE GOOD HIT ON ME...
OM!!
RAAAH
...I MIGHT NOT HAVE BEEN ABLE TO STAND ANYMORE!!
DO
...
DON'T BLAME THE MOON FOR YOUR TROUBLES!!
YOU DIDN'T HAVE BAD LUCK, PERORIN♪
M!
BA
...!!
I'VE JUST GOT OVER-WHELMINGLY GOOD LUCK, BOSS CAT!!
CAT VIPER!!
HIS SULONG WORE OFF!!
RAAAAAH
MOMO !!
!!
RAAAAH
HUH?! LORD MOMONO-SUKE?!

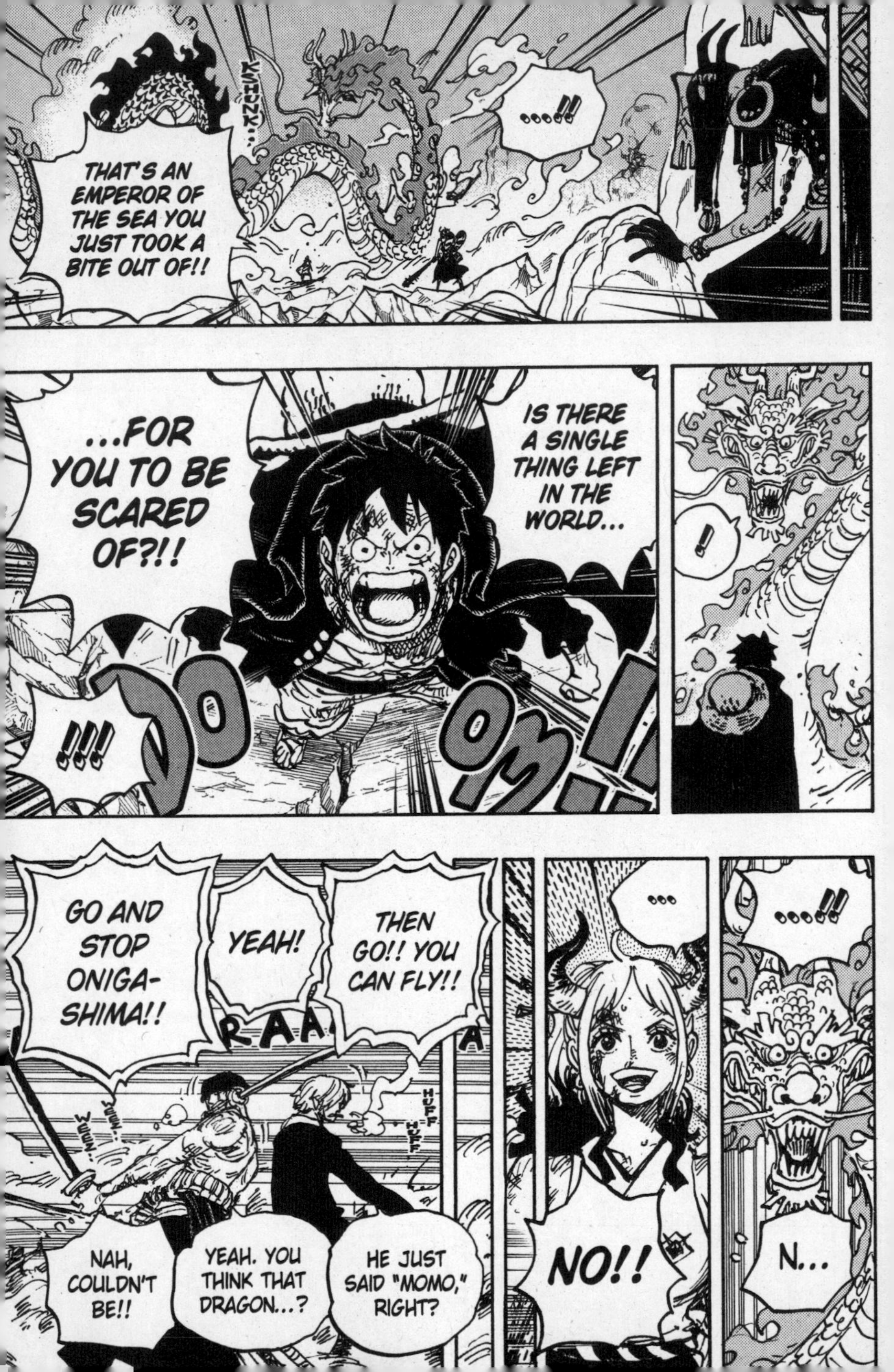
....!!
KSHUNK...
THAT'S AN EMPEROR OF THE SEA YOU JUST TOOK A BITE OUT OF!!
!
IS THERE A SINGLE THING LEFT IN THE WORLD...
...FOR YOU TO BE SCARED OF?!!
!!!
DOOM!!
....!!
N...
...
NO!!
THEN GO!! YOU CAN FLY!!
YEAH!
GO AND STOP ONIGA-SHIMA!!
RAA
A
HUFF
HUFF
WEEZ..
WEEZ..
HE JUST SAID "MOMO," RIGHT?
YEAH. YOU THINK THAT DRAGON...?
NAH, COULDN'T BE!!

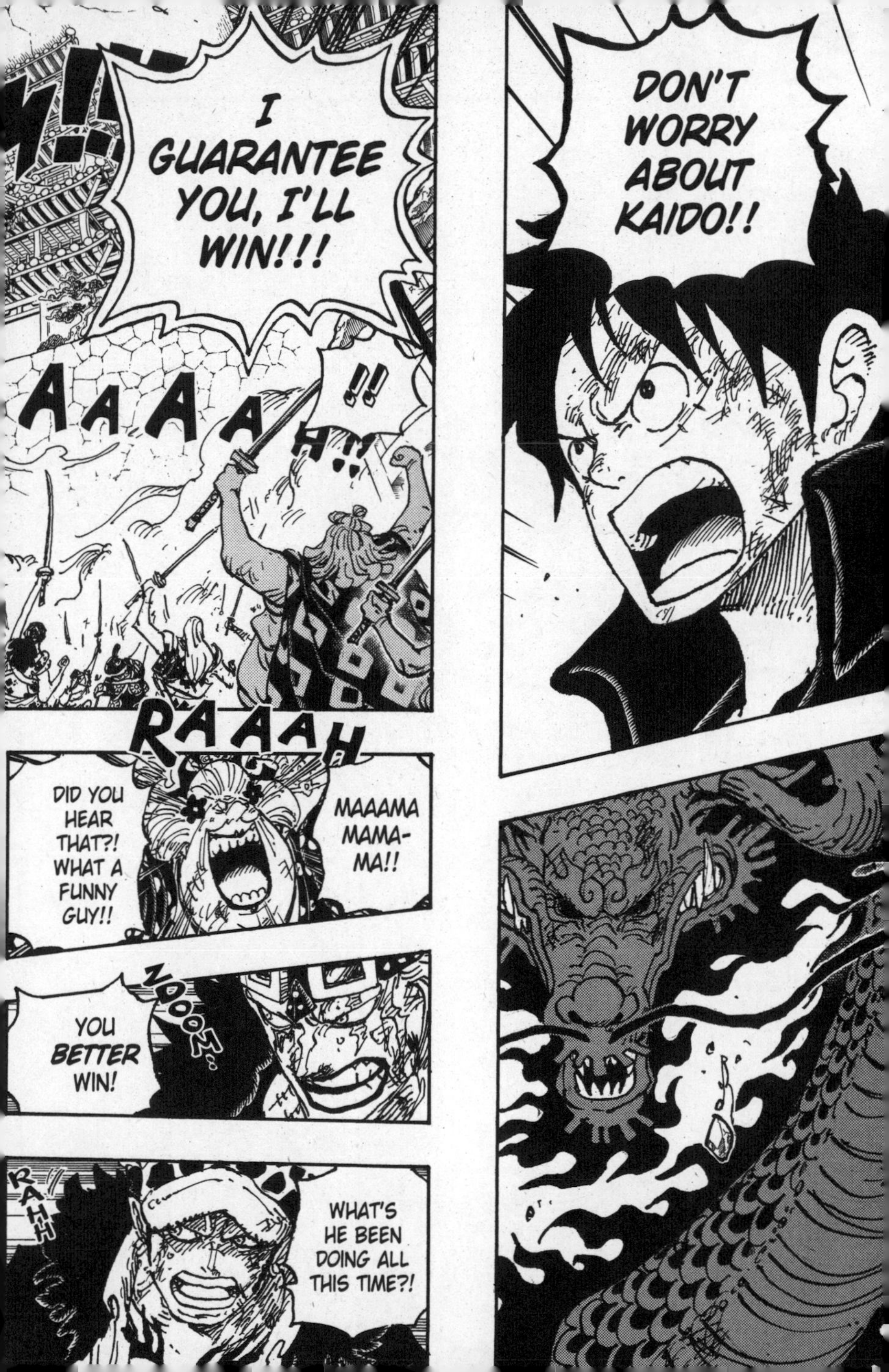
DON'T WORRY ABOUT KAIDO!!
I GUARANTEE YOU, I'LL WIN!!!
AAAAH!!
RAAAH
MAAAMA MAMAMA!!
DID YOU HEAR THAT?! WHAT A FUNNY GUY!!
DOOM..
YOU BETTER WIN!
WHAT'S HE BEEN DOING ALL THIS TIME?!
RAHH

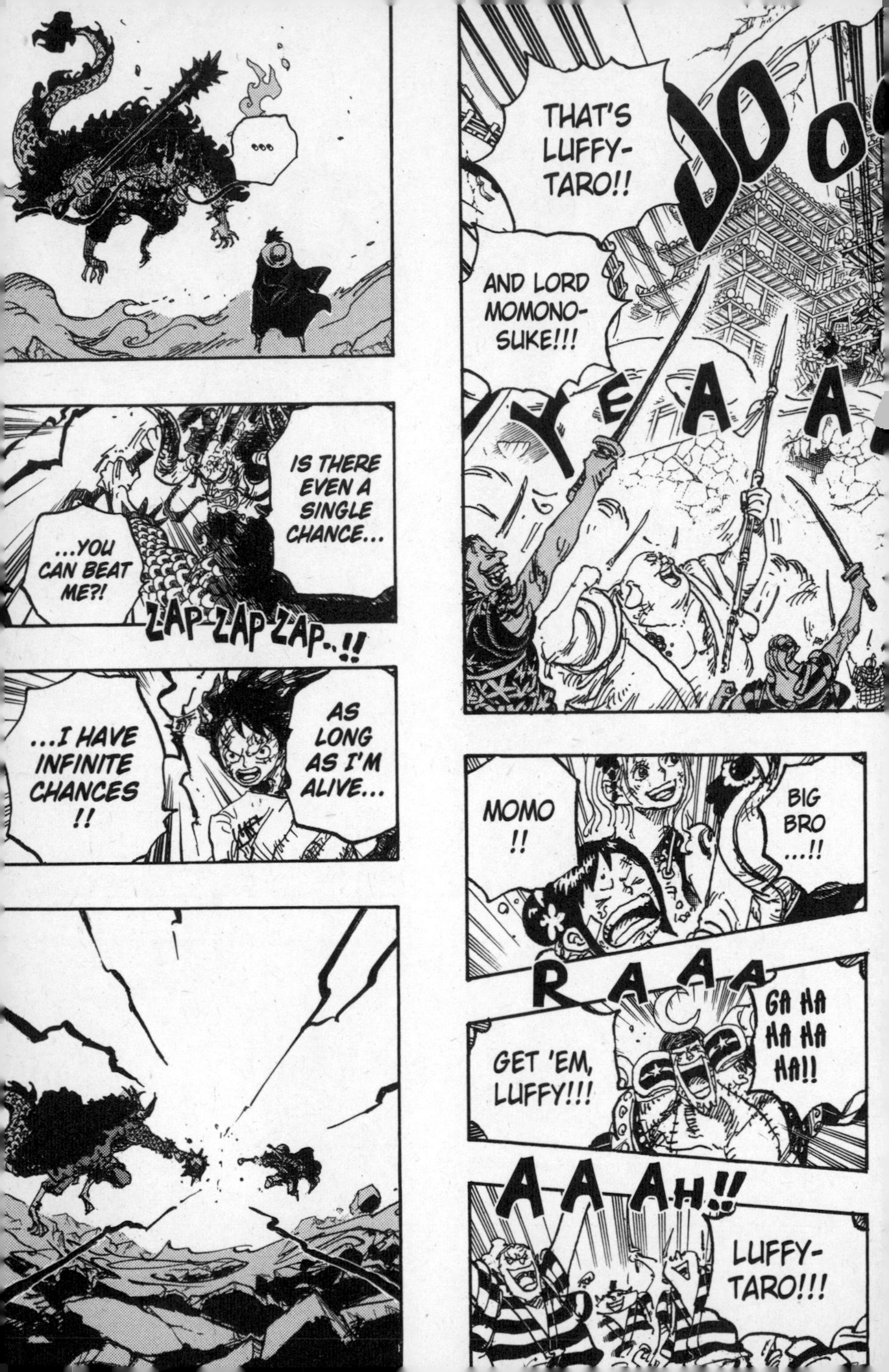

DOO
THAT'S LUFFY-TARO!!
AND LORD MOMONO-SUKE!!!
YEAA
BIG BRO ...!!
MOMO !!
RAAAA
GA HA HA HA HA!!
GET 'EM, LUFFY!!!
AAAH!!
LUFFY-TARO!!!
...
IS THERE EVEN A SINGLE CHANCE...
...YOU CAN BEAT ME?!
ZAP ZAP ZAP..!!
AS LONG AS I'M ALIVE...
...I HAVE INFINITE CHANCES !!

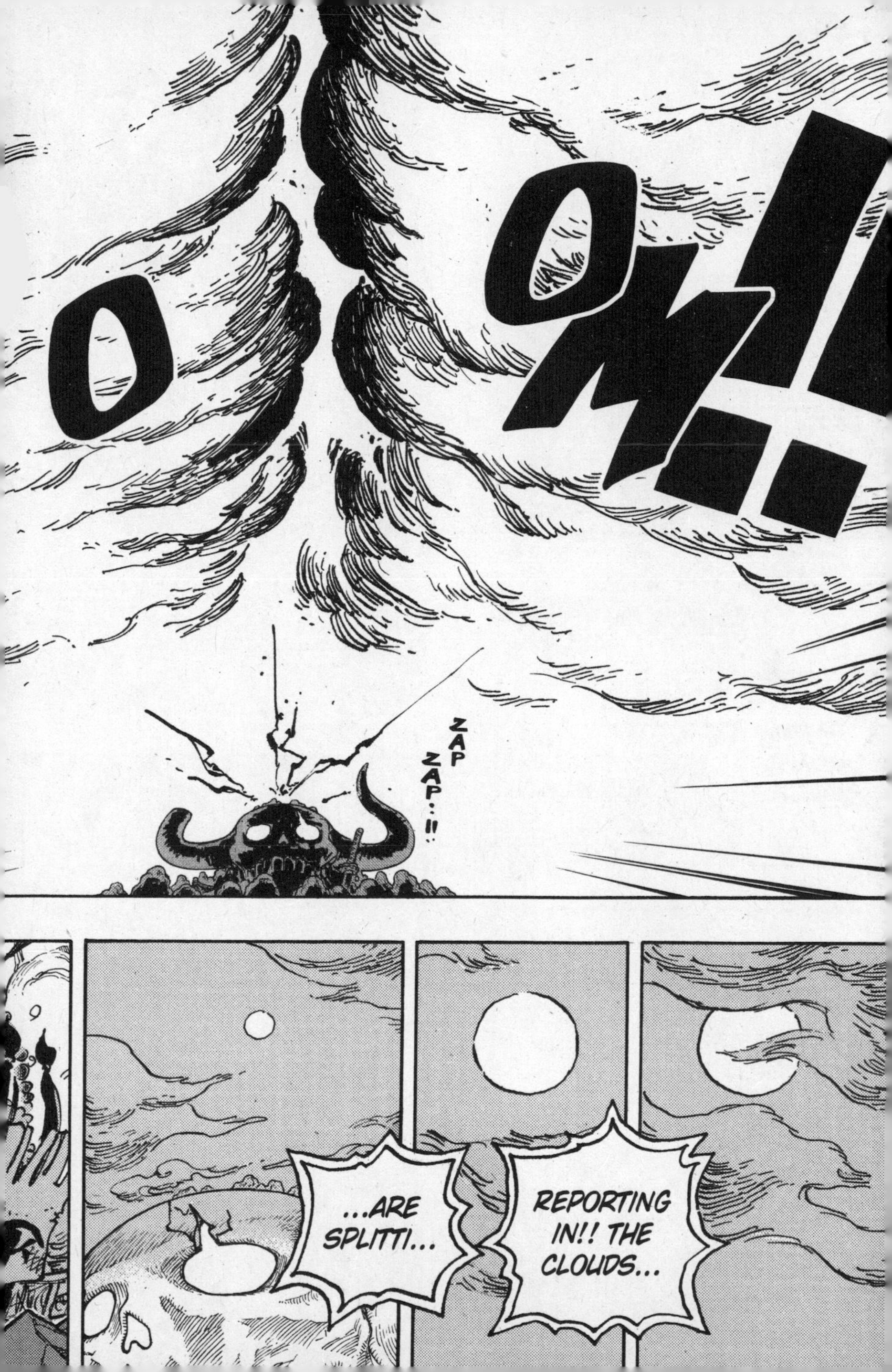
O
OM!!
ZAP ZAP..!!
REPORTING IN!! THE CLOUDS...
...ARE SPLITTI...

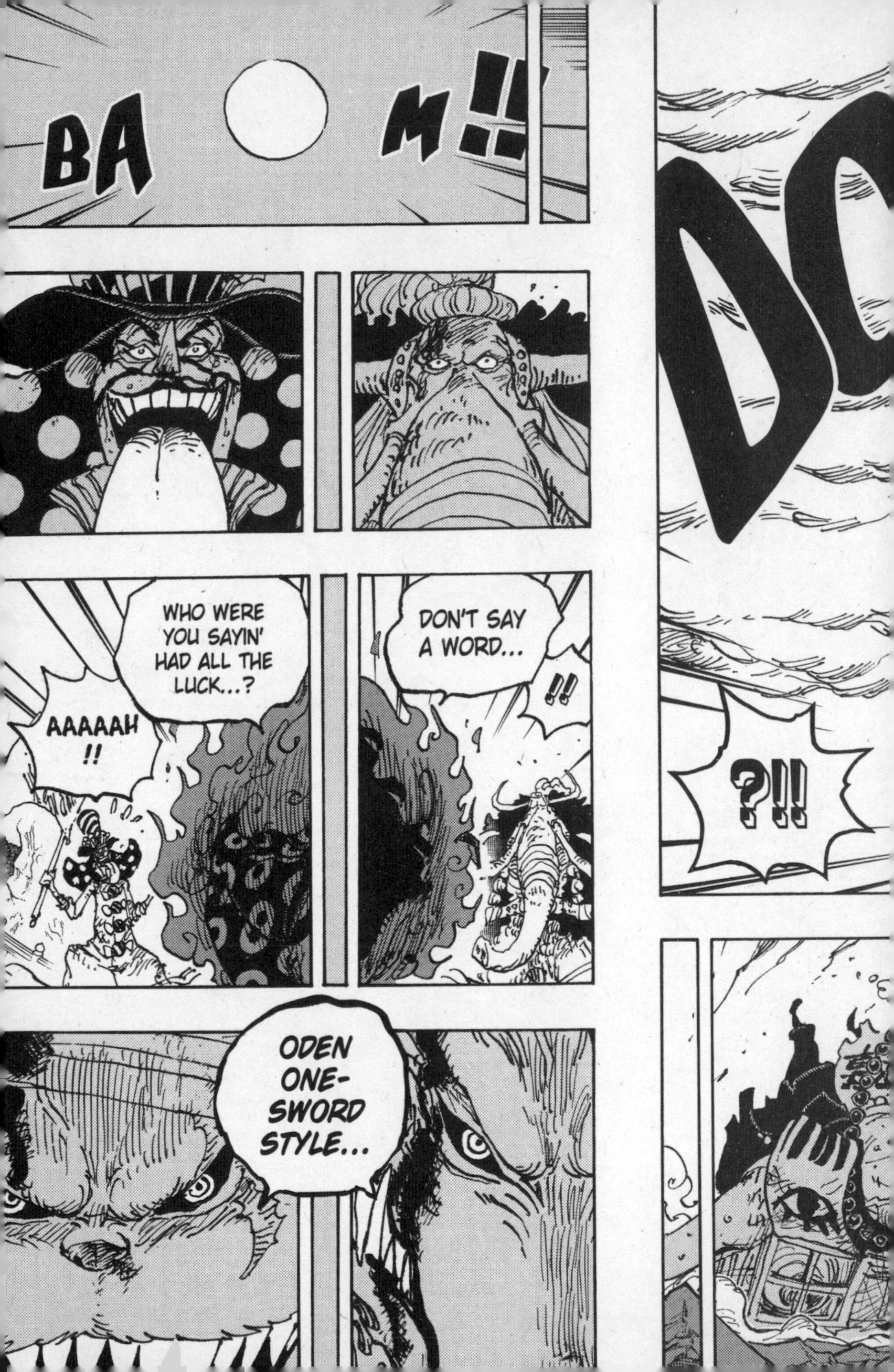

DO
?!!
BA M!!
DON'T SAY A WORD...
!!
WHO WERE YOU SAYIN' HAD ALL THE LUCK...?
AAAAAH !!
ODEN ONE-SWORD STYLE...

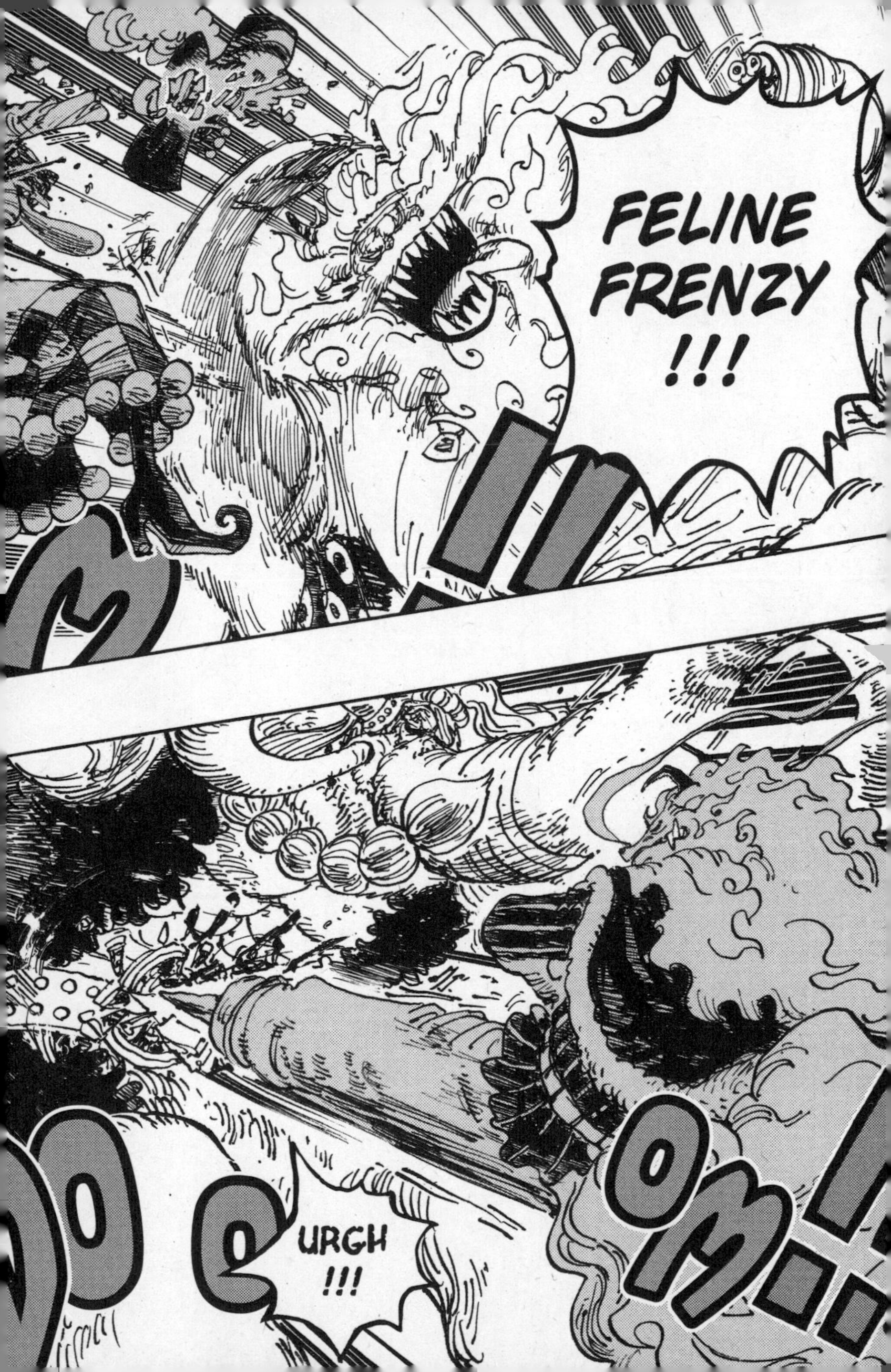
FELINE FRENZY !!!
URGH !!!

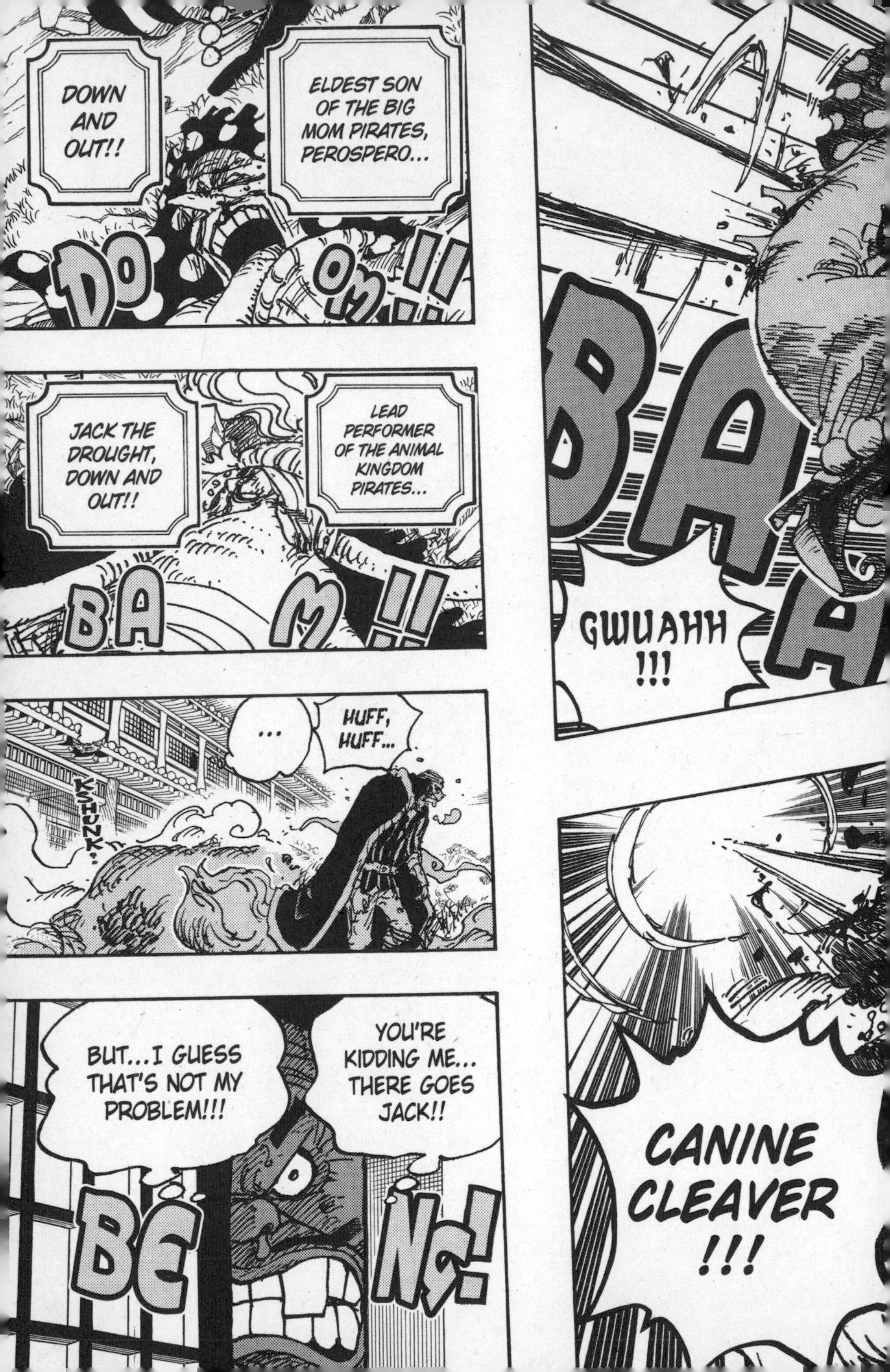
BA
GWUAHH!!!
CANINE CLEAVER!!!
ELDEST SON OF THE BIG MOM PIRATES, PEROSPERO...
DOWN AND OUT!!
DO
OM!!
LEAD PERFORMER OF THE ANIMAL KINGDOM PIRATES...
JACK THE DROUGHT, DOWN AND OUT!!
BA
M!!
HUFF, HUFF...
...
KSHUNK
YOU'RE KIDDING ME... THERE GOES JACK!!
BUT...I GUESS THAT'S NOT MY PROBLEM!!!
BE
NG!

SBS Question Corner

CORNER

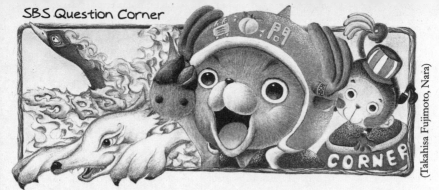

(Takahisa Fujimoto, Nara)

Q: C'mon, guys! We have to let Odacchi say "Start the SBS" every now and then! Go on, Odacchi!

(0.1 seconds later) Well, you heard him! The SBS has started already!!

--SumitaroYato

A: S...!! It's already started!!
I can't do this in just 0.1 seconds!!

Q: I want a Happiness Punch figure.

--Captain Nobuo

A: You shut up!!
What kind of leadoff question is this?! That one's off-limits, because you can turn figures around 360 degrees!!

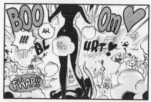

BOO
Om
AH.
!!!
BL
URT!
FHAP!!

Q:

ルフィとキッドとロ
ーがじゃんけんした
らだれがかちま
すかみらいを
みえるからルフィ
ですか

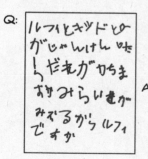

(If Luffy and Kid and Law played rock-paper-scissors who would win? Would Luffy win because he can see the future?)

--Taisei (Age 6, the oldest)

A: Wow. This is a great question! Yes, Luffy might win, because he can see the future! But Luffy doesn't like cheating, so I don't think he'll look into the future. And those three are always arguing, so whoever wins, they're going to fight about it!

Q: Oda Sensei, heso! If Eneru became a pirate down on the Blue Sea, what sort of Jolly Roger would he fly? I'm so curious. Like this? ➡

--Shiba

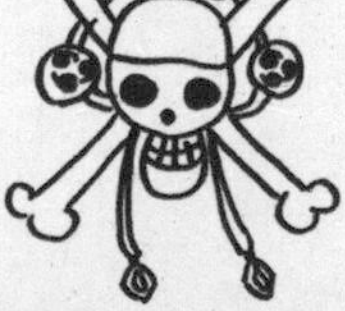

A: Oh, sure. Let's go with that.

Chapter 1027:

DANGER BEYOND IMAGINING

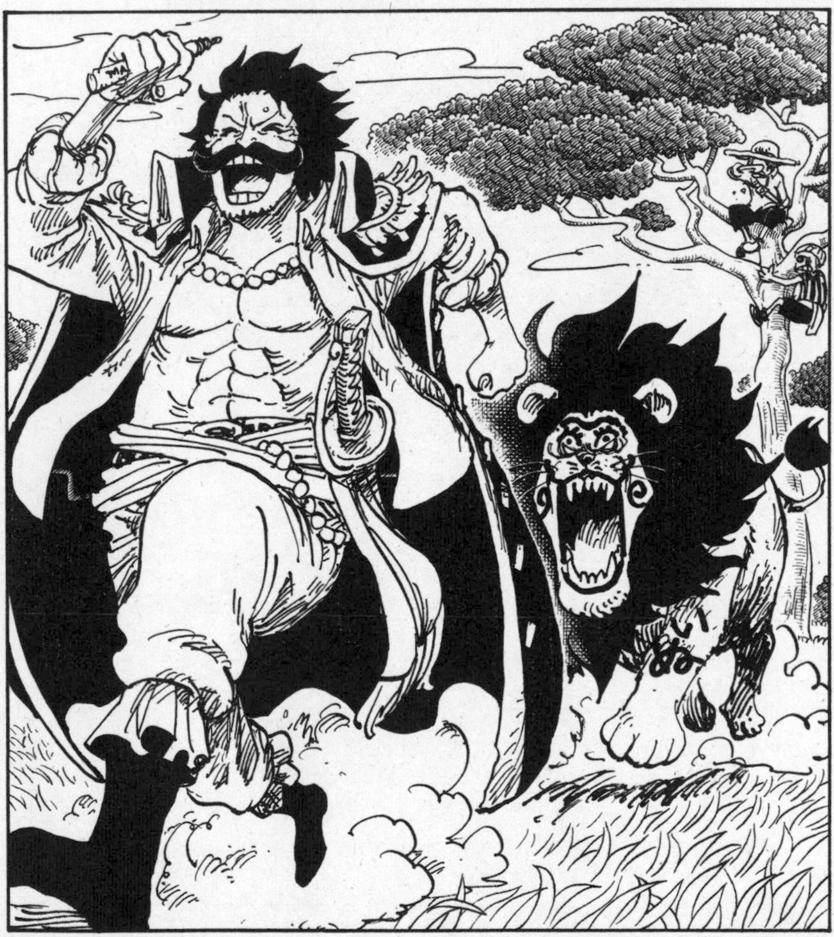

READER REQUEST: "ROGER GLEEFULLY RUNNING FROM A LION WHOSE FACE HE SCRIBBLED ON" BY TOSHIKIYA

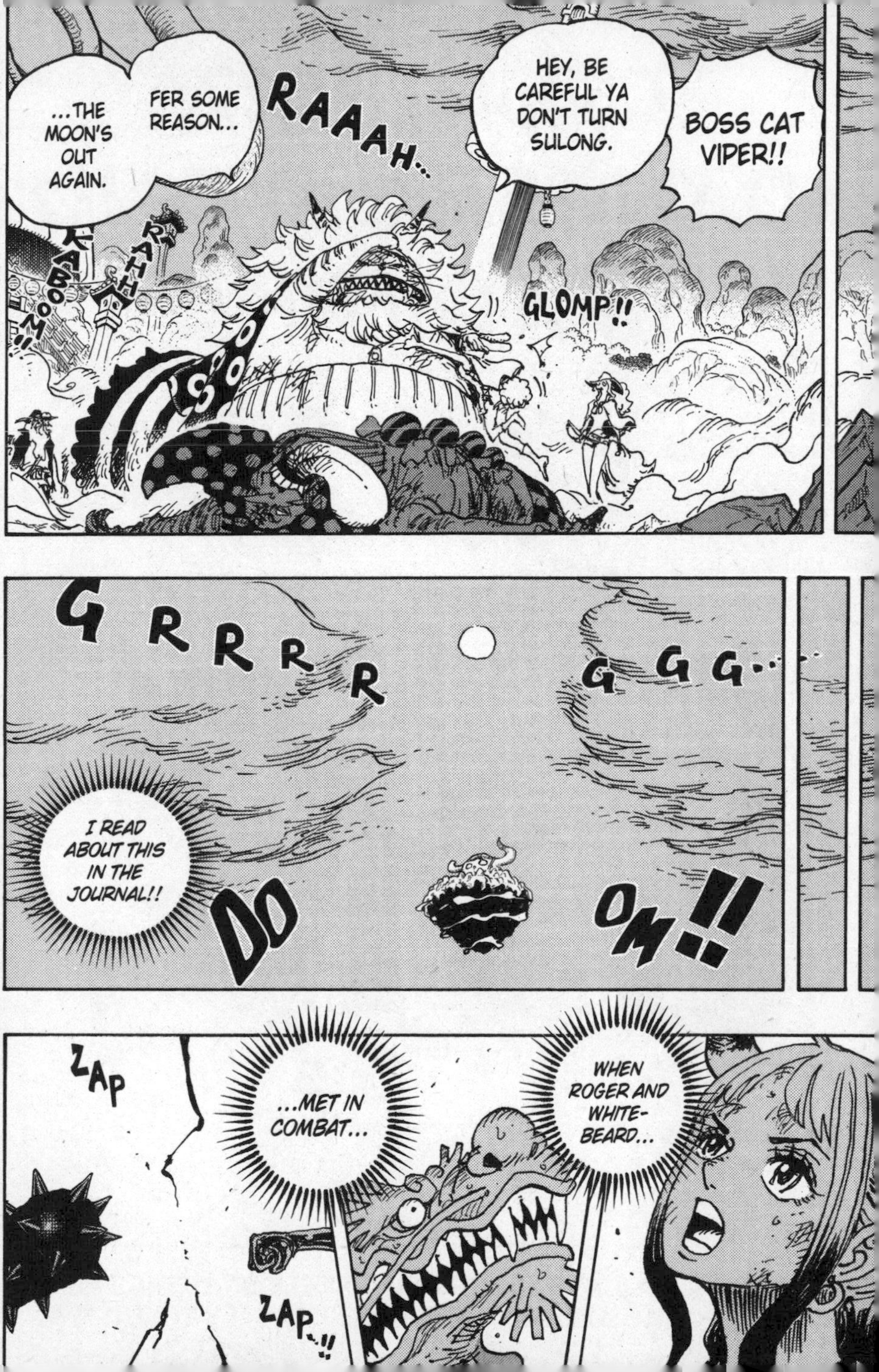
BOSS CAT VIPER!!
HEY, BE CAREFUL YA DON'T TURN SULONG.
RAAAAH...
FER SOME REASON...
...THE MOON'S OUT AGAIN.
GLOMP!!
KRAHH
KABOOM!!
G G G...
GRRRRR
DO OM!!
I READ ABOUT THIS IN THE JOURNAL!!
WHEN ROGER AND WHITE-BEARD...
...MET IN COMBAT...
ZAP
ZAP..!!

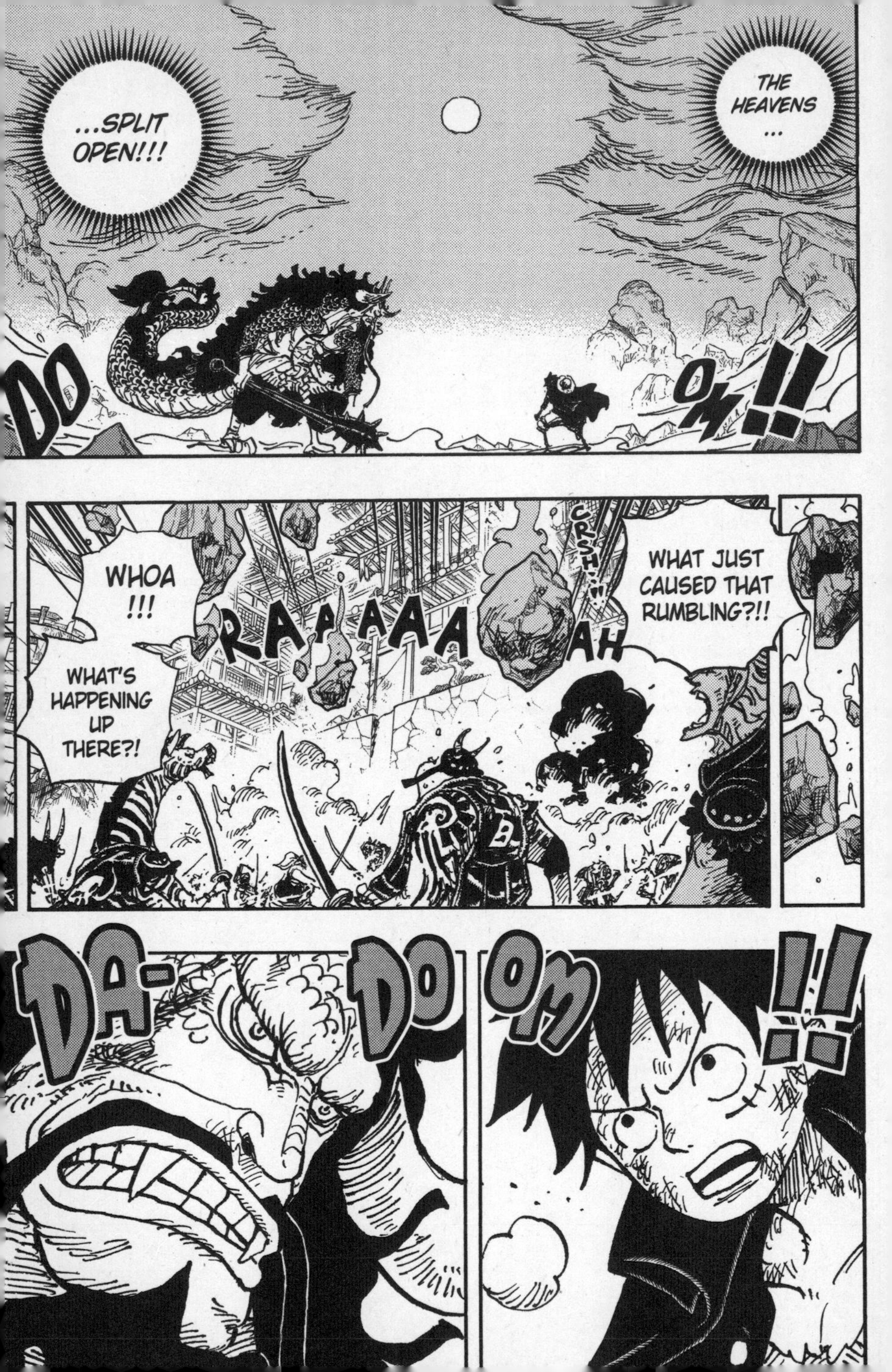
THE HEAVENS ...
...SPLIT OPEN!!!
DOOM!!
WHAT JUST CAUSED THAT RUMBLING?!!
CRSH...
RAAAAAAH
WHOA !!!
WHAT'S HAPPENING UP THERE?!
DA-DOOM!!

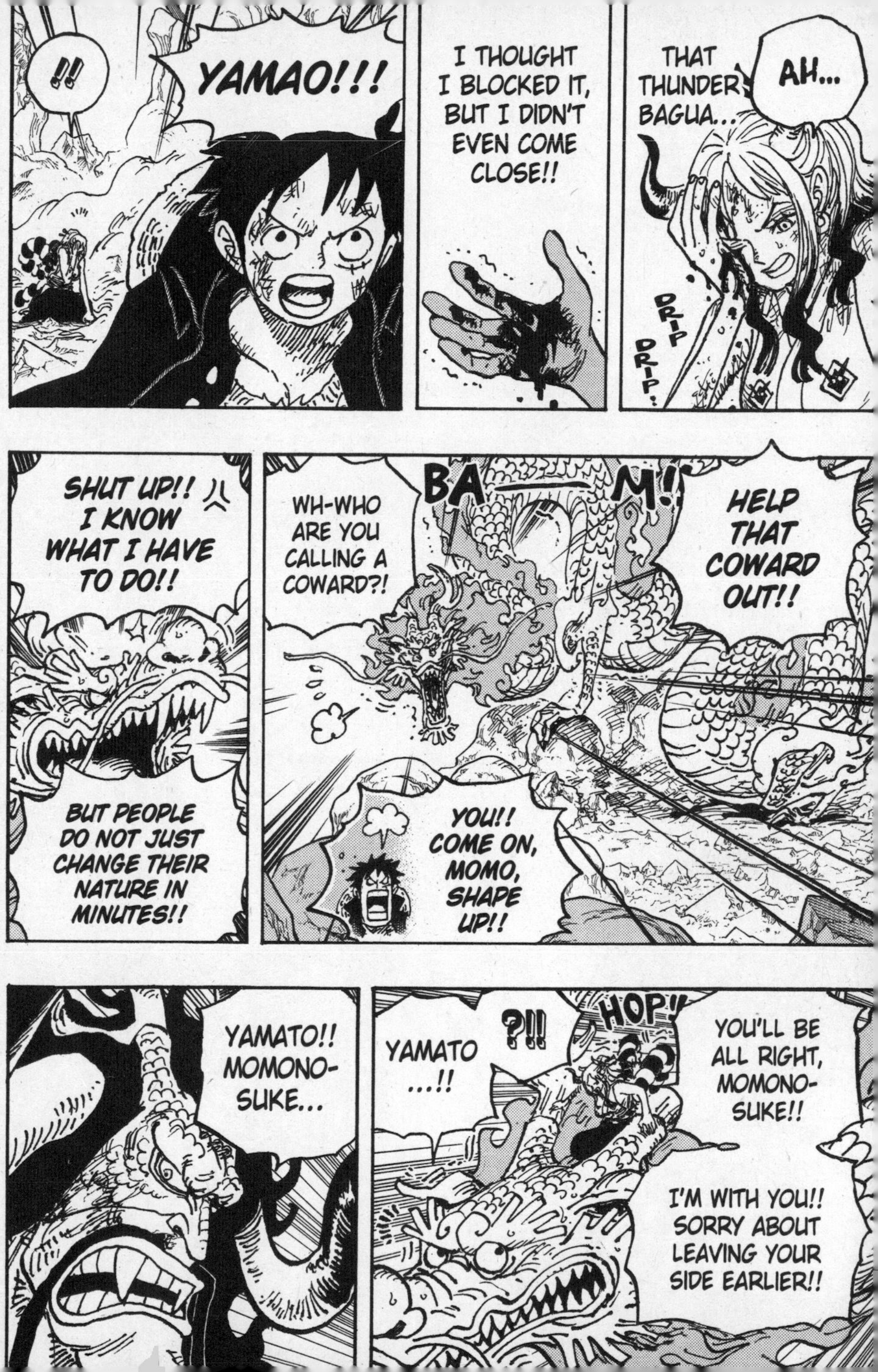
AH...
THAT THUNDER BAGUA...
DRIP DRIP
I THOUGHT I BLOCKED IT, BUT I DIDN'T EVEN COME CLOSE!!
YAMAO!!!
!!
BA—M!
HELP THAT COWARD OUT!!
WH-WHO ARE YOU CALLING A COWARD?!
YOU!! COME ON, MOMO, SHAPE UP!!
SHUT UP!! I KNOW WHAT I HAVE TO DO!!
BUT PEOPLE DO NOT JUST CHANGE THEIR NATURE IN MINUTES!!
HOP!!
YOU'LL BE ALL RIGHT, MOMONO-SUKE!!
?!!
YAMATO ...!!
I'M WITH YOU!! SORRY ABOUT LEAVING YOUR SIDE EARLIER!!
YAMATO!! MOMONO-SUKE...

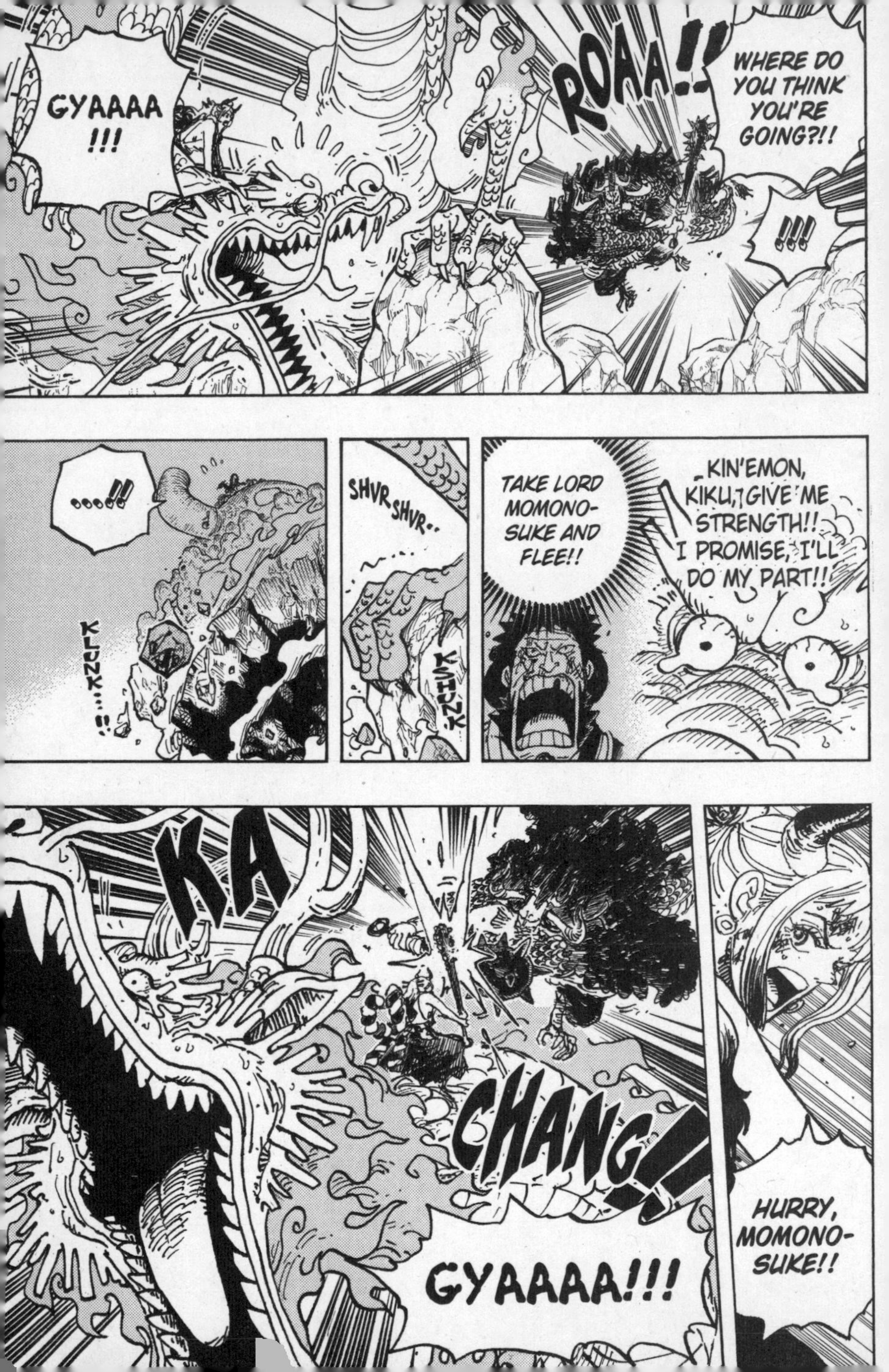
WHERE DO YOU THINK YOU'RE GOING?!!
ROAA!!
!!!
GYAAAA !!!
KIN'EMON, KIKU, GIVE ME STRENGTH!! I PROMISE, I'LL DO MY PART!!
TAKE LORD MOMONO-SUKE AND FLEE!!
SHVR SHVR..
KSHUNK
.....!!
KLUNK...!!
HURRY, MOMONO-SUKE!!
KA
CHANG!!
GYAAAA!!!

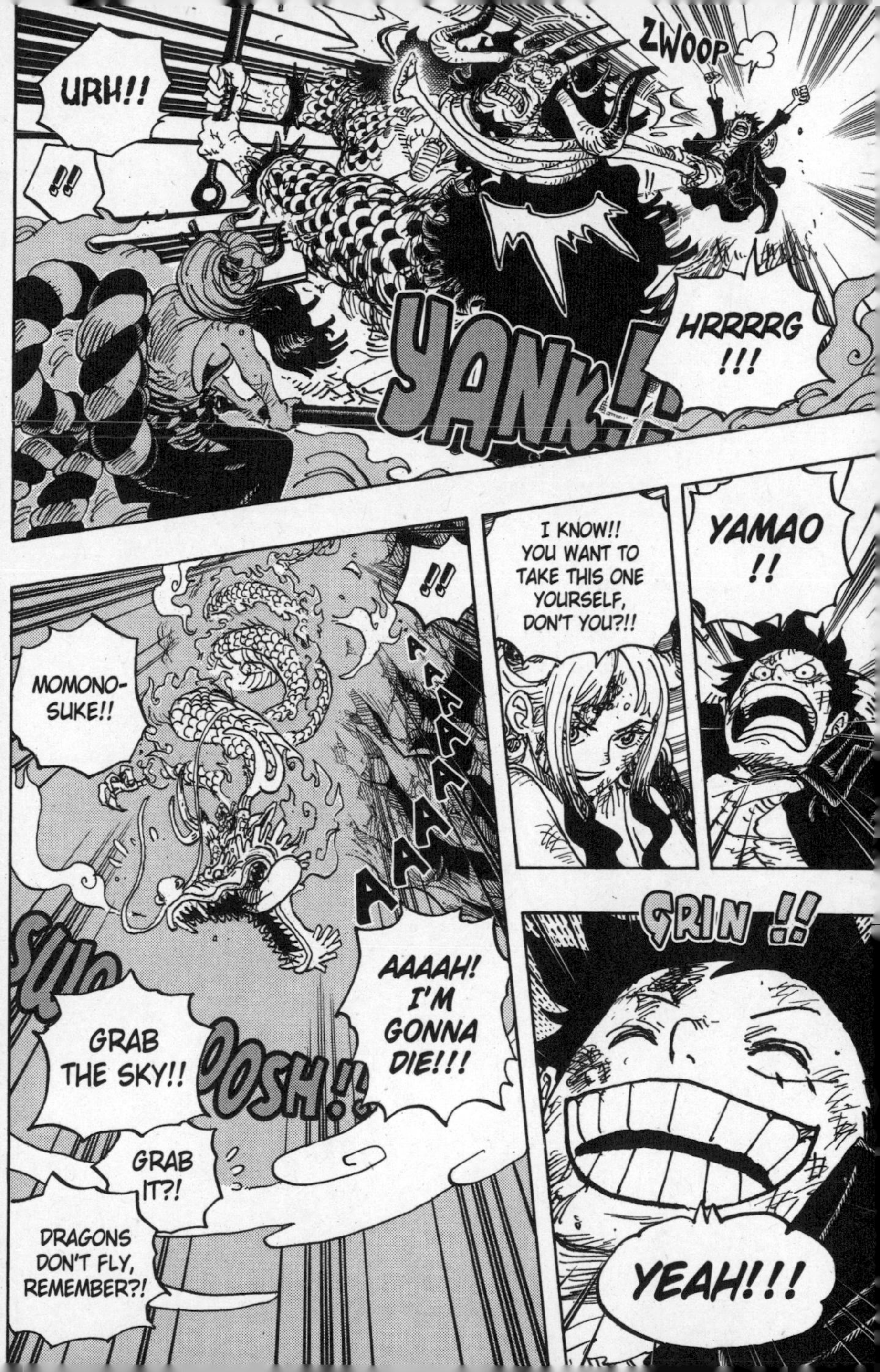
ZWOOP
HRRRRG!!!
YANK!!
URH!!
!!
YAMAO!!
I KNOW!! YOU WANT TO TAKE THIS ONE YOURSELF, DON'T YOU?!!
GRIN!!
YEAH!!!
!!
AAAAAAA
MOMONO-SUKE!!
AAAAH! I'M GONNA DIE!!!
SUO
OOSH!!
GRAB THE SKY!!
GRAB IT?!
DRAGONS DON'T FLY, REMEMBER?!

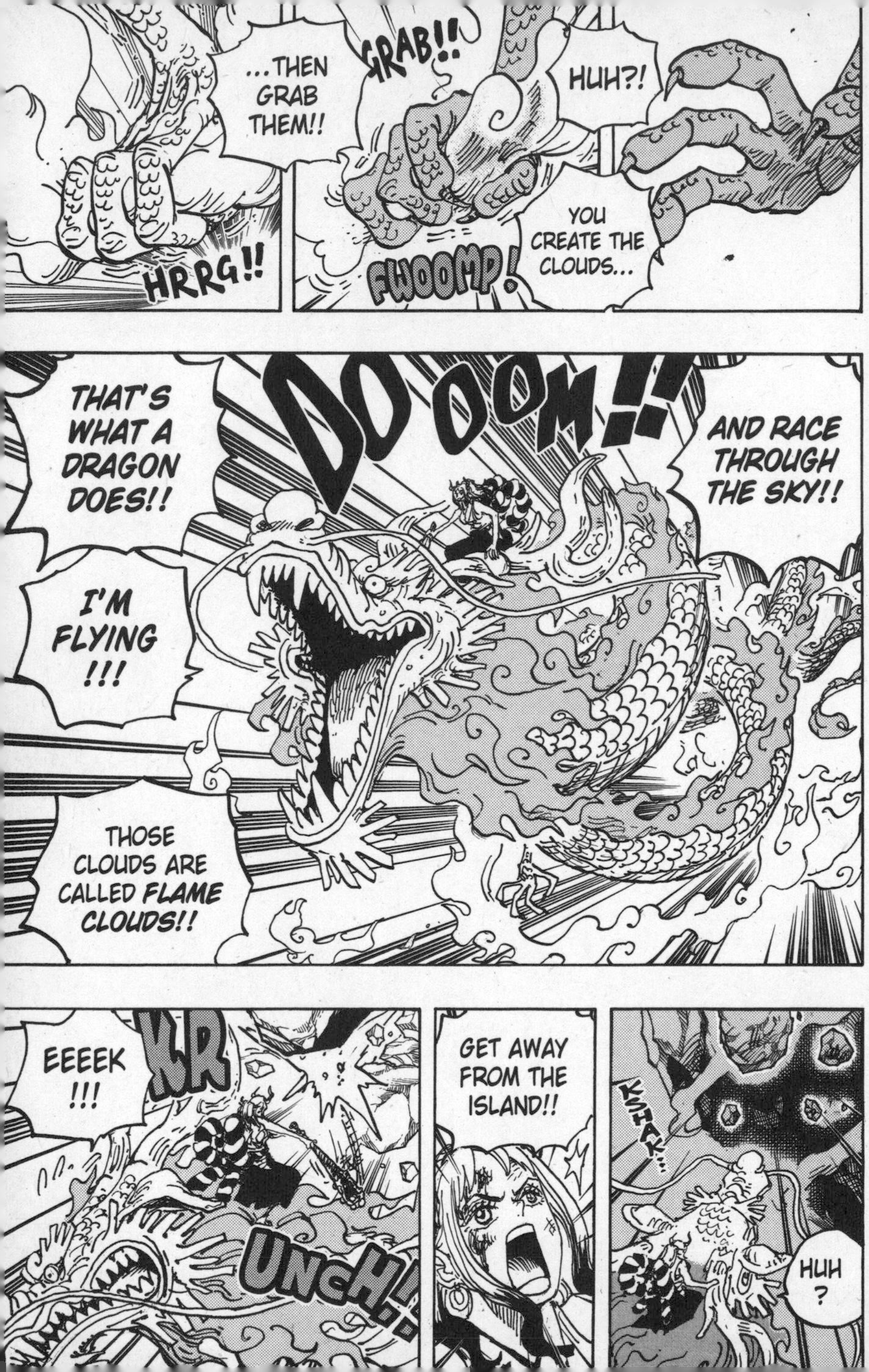
HUH?!
GRAB!!
YOU CREATE THE CLOUDS...
FWOOMP!
...THEN GRAB THEM!!
HRRG!!
AND RACE THROUGH THE SKY!!
DOOM!!
THAT'S WHAT A DRAGON DOES!!
I'M FLYING!!!
THOSE CLOUDS ARE CALLED *FLAME CLOUDS*!!
KSHAK...
HUH?
GET AWAY FROM THE ISLAND!!
EEEEK!!!
KR
UNCH!!

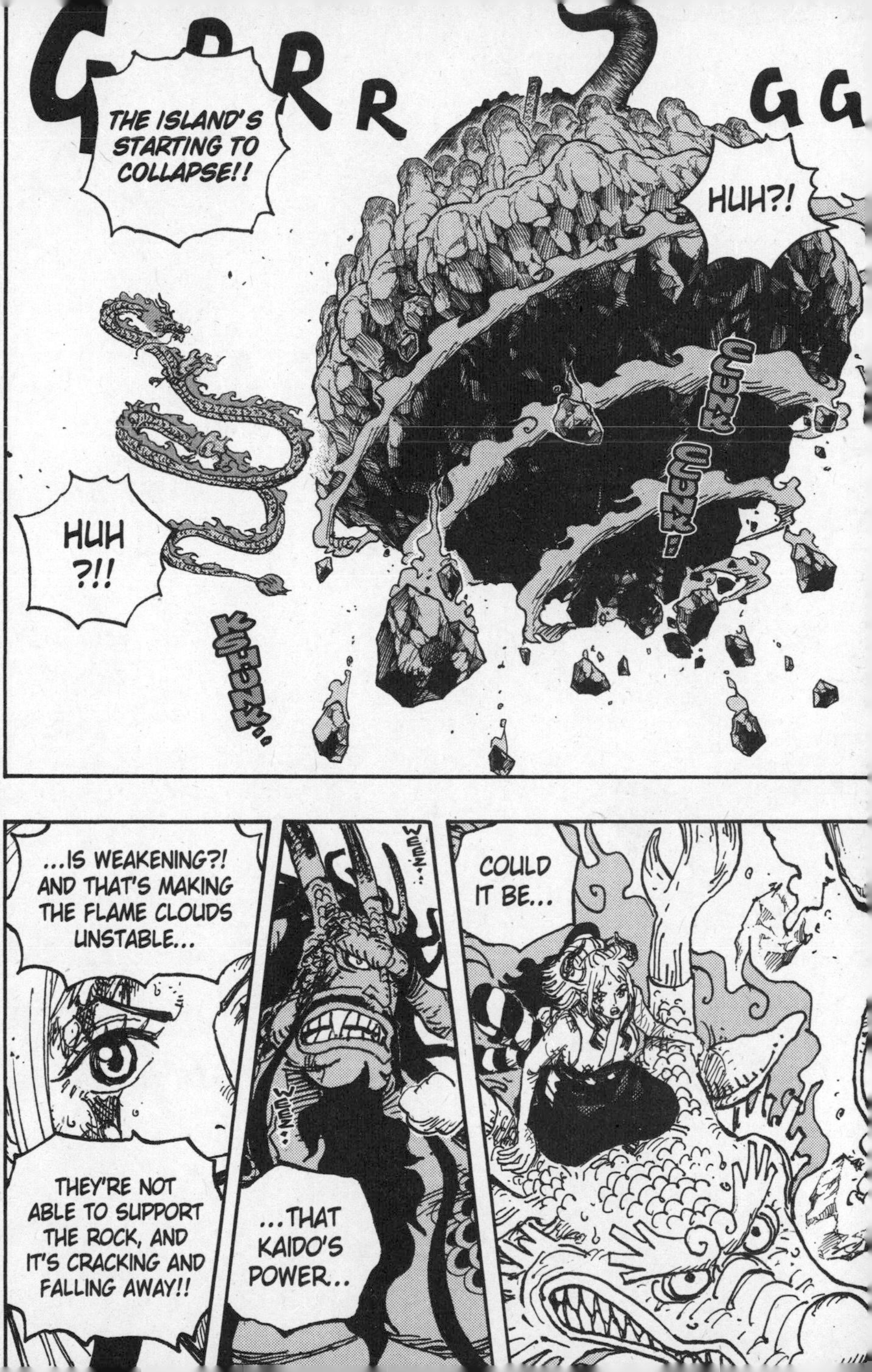
GG
HUH?!
THE ISLAND'S STARTING TO COLLAPSE!!
CLUNK
CLUNK!
HUH ?!!
KSHUNK...
COULD IT BE...
WEEN...
...THAT KAIDO'S POWER...
...IS WEAKENING?! AND THAT'S MAKING THE FLAME CLOUDS UNSTABLE...
THEY'RE NOT ABLE TO SUPPORT THE ROCK, AND IT'S CRACKING AND FALLING AWAY!!

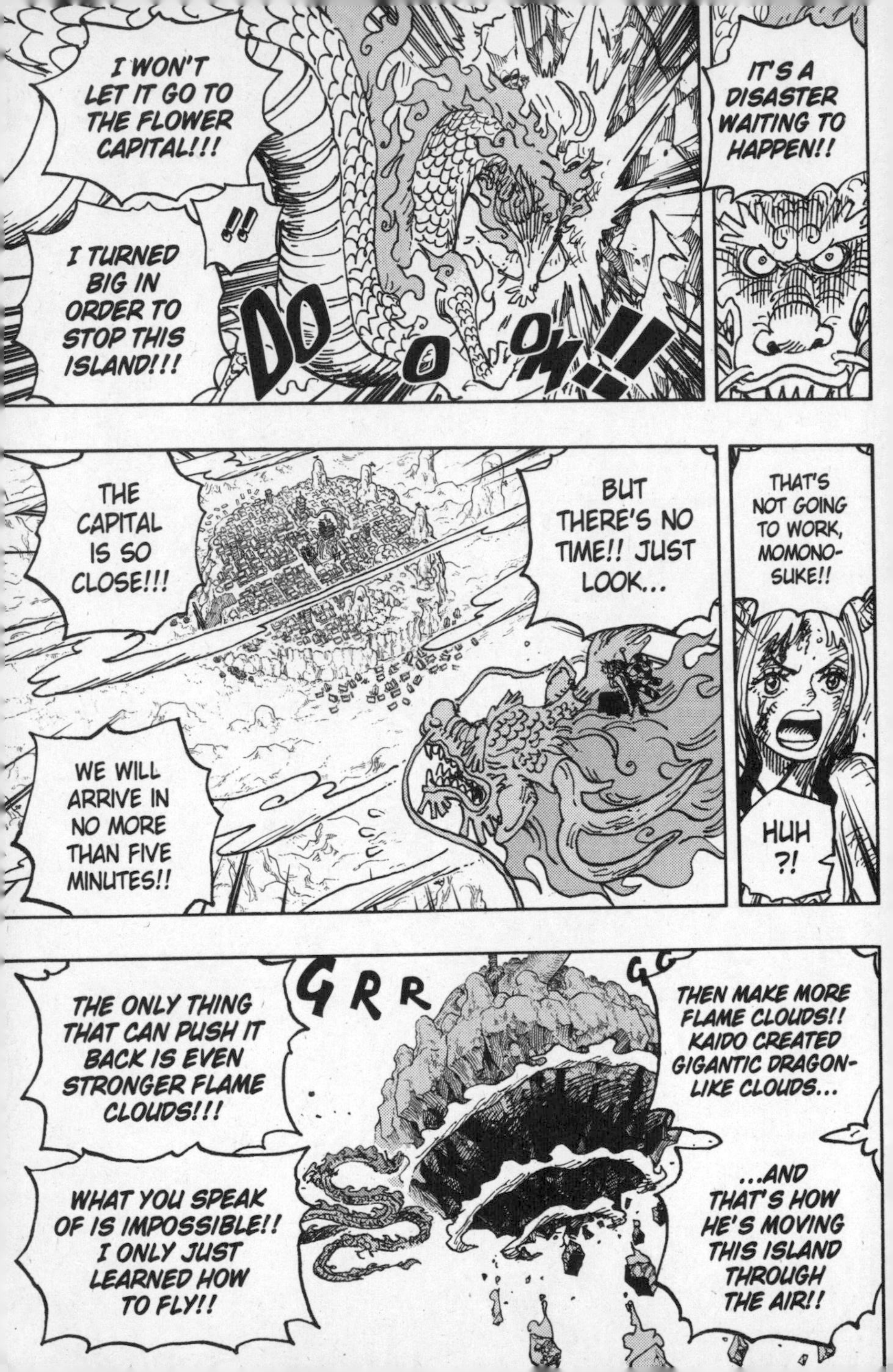
IT'S A DISASTER WAITING TO HAPPEN!!
I WON'T LET IT GO TO THE FLOWER CAPITAL!!!
!!
I TURNED BIG IN ORDER TO STOP THIS ISLAND!!!
DOoOM!!
THAT'S NOT GOING TO WORK, MOMONOSUKE!!
HUH?!
BUT THERE'S NO TIME!! JUST LOOK...
THE CAPITAL IS SO CLOSE!!!
WE WILL ARRIVE IN NO MORE THAN FIVE MINUTES!!
GG
THEN MAKE MORE FLAME CLOUDS!! KAIDO CREATED GIGANTIC DRAGON-LIKE CLOUDS...
...AND THAT'S HOW HE'S MOVING THIS ISLAND THROUGH THE AIR!!
GRR
THE ONLY THING THAT CAN PUSH IT BACK IS EVEN STRONGER FLAME CLOUDS!!!
WHAT YOU SPEAK OF IS IMPOSSIBLE!! I ONLY JUST LEARNED HOW TO FLY!!

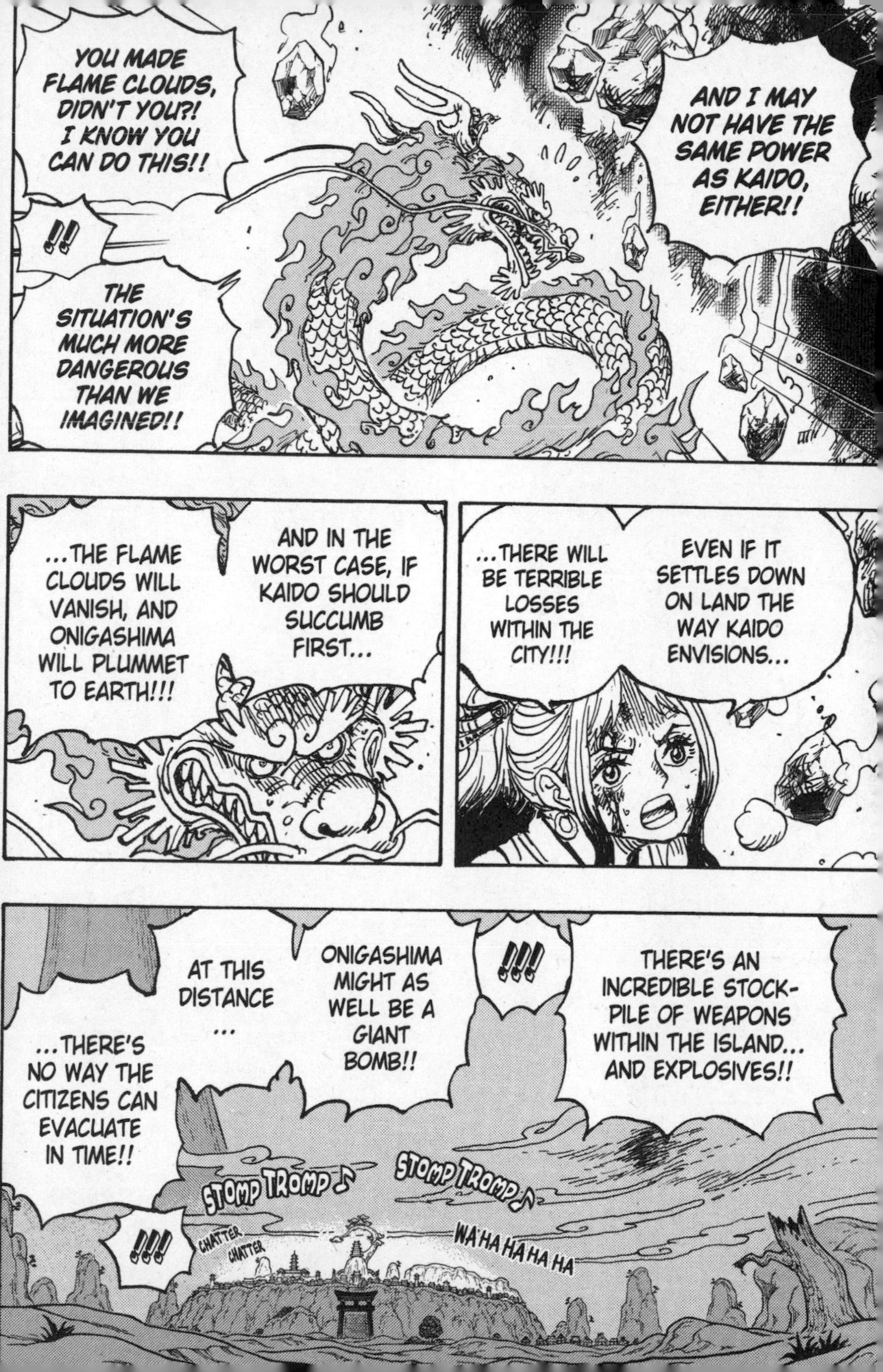

AND I MAY NOT HAVE THE SAME POWER AS KAIDO, EITHER!!
YOU MADE FLAME CLOUDS, DIDN'T YOU?! I KNOW YOU CAN DO THIS!!
!!
THE SITUATION'S MUCH MORE DANGEROUS THAN WE IMAGINED!!
EVEN IF IT SETTLES DOWN ON LAND THE WAY KAIDO ENVISIONS...
...THERE WILL BE TERRIBLE LOSSES WITHIN THE CITY!!!
AND IN THE WORST CASE, IF KAIDO SHOULD SUCCUMB FIRST...
...THE FLAME CLOUDS WILL VANISH, AND ONIGASHIMA WILL PLUMMET TO EARTH!!!
THERE'S AN INCREDIBLE STOCK-PILE OF WEAPONS WITHIN THE ISLAND... AND EXPLOSIVES!!
!!!
ONIGASHIMA MIGHT AS WELL BE A GIANT BOMB!!
AT THIS DISTANCE ...
...THERE'S NO WAY THE CITIZENS CAN EVACUATE IN TIME!!
STOMP TROMP ♪
STOMP TROMP ♪
WA HA HA HA HA HA
CHATTER CHATTER
!!!

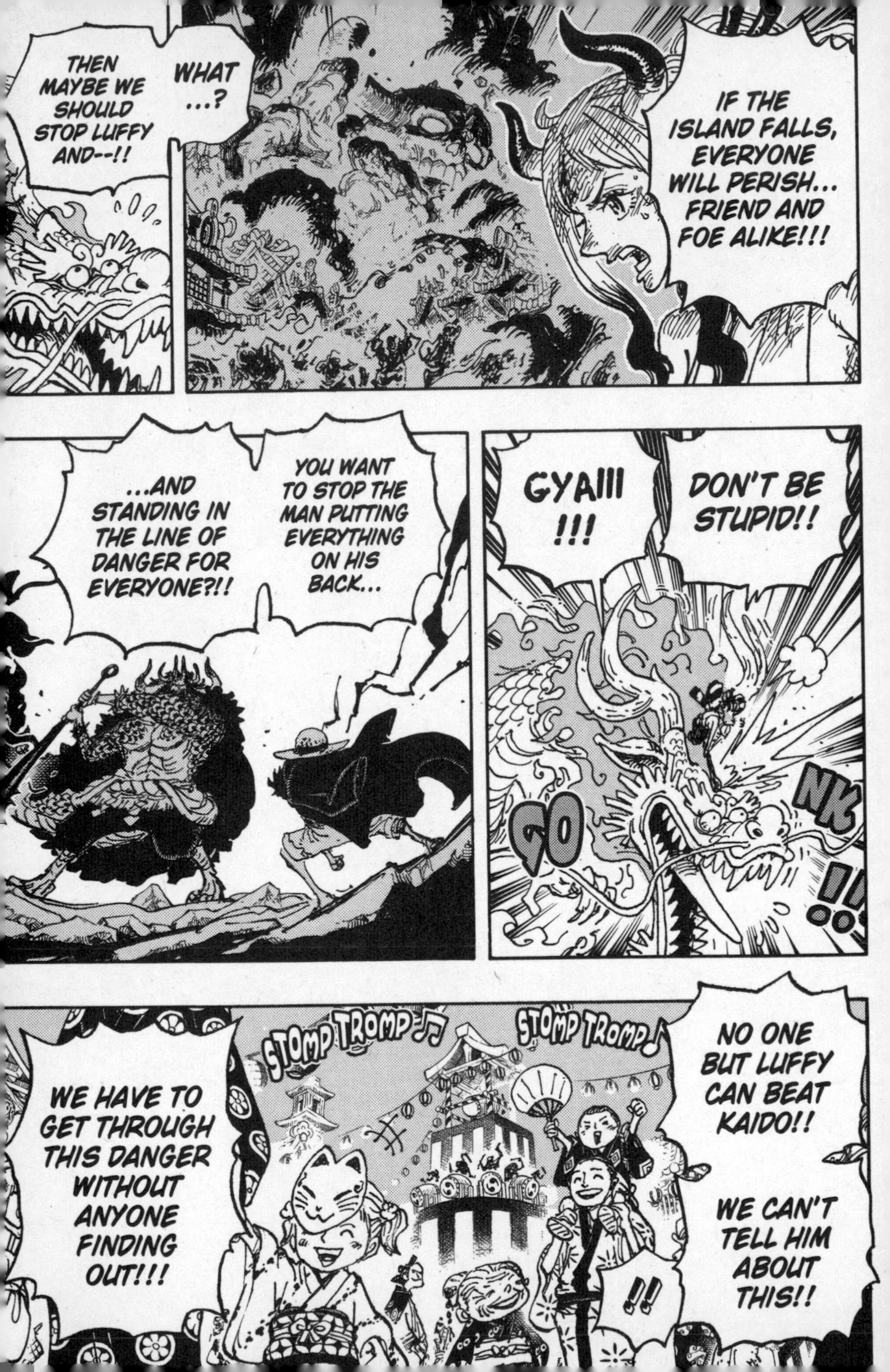
IF THE ISLAND FALLS, EVERYONE WILL PERISH... FRIEND AND FOE ALIKE!!!
WHAT ...?
THEN MAYBE WE SHOULD STOP LUFFY AND--!!
DON'T BE STUPID!!
GYAIII !!!
NK
GO
!!
YOU WANT TO STOP THE MAN PUTTING EVERYTHING ON HIS BACK...
...AND STANDING IN THE LINE OF DANGER FOR EVERYONE?!!
NO ONE BUT LUFFY CAN BEAT KAIDO!!
WE CAN'T TELL HIM ABOUT THIS!!
STOMP TROMP
STOMP TROMP
!!
WE HAVE TO GET THROUGH THIS DANGER WITHOUT ANYONE FINDING OUT!!!

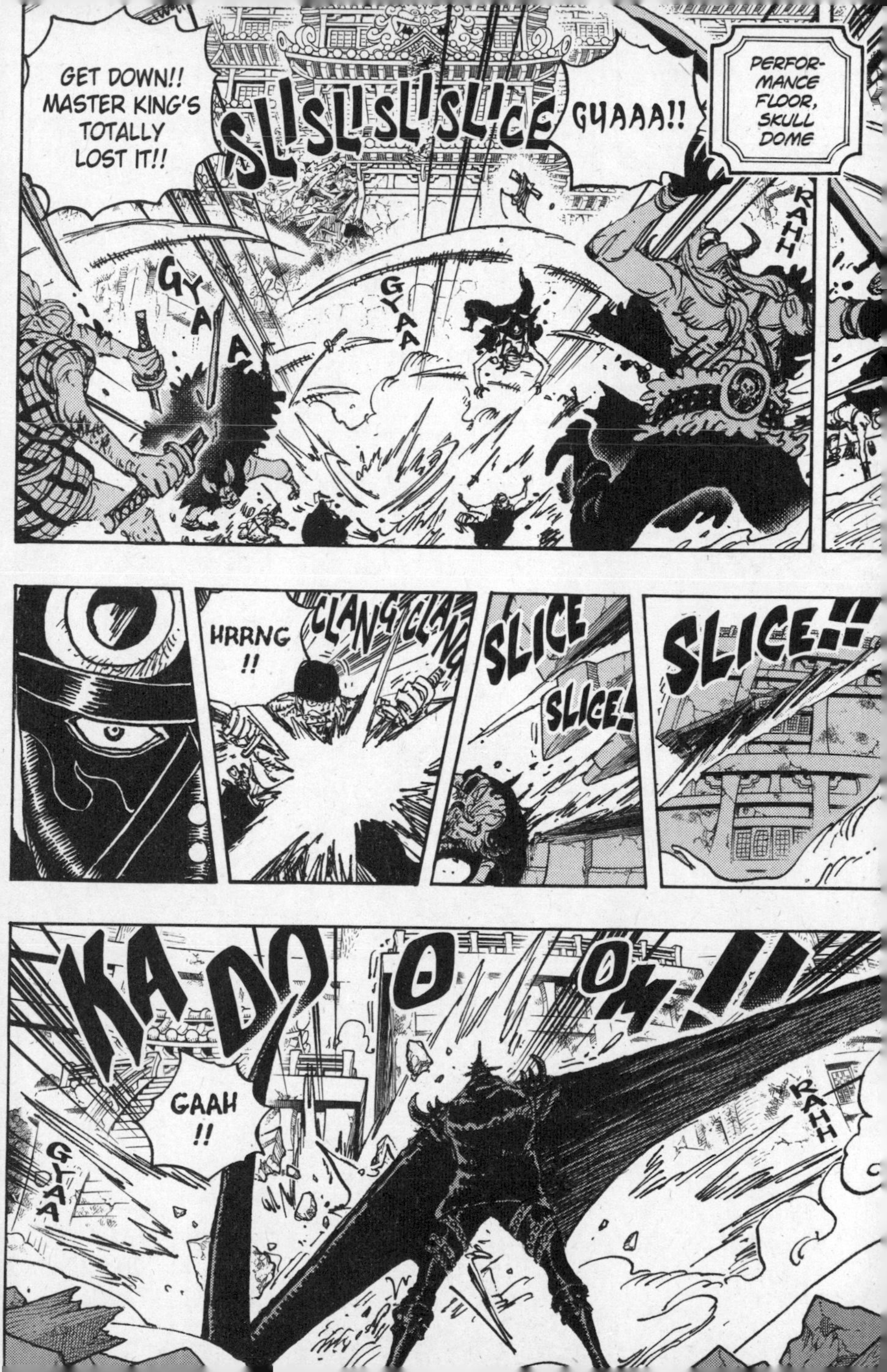
PERFORMANCE FLOOR, SKULL DOME
RAHH
GYAAA!!
SLISLISLISLICE
GET DOWN!! MASTER KING'S TOTALLY LOST IT!!
GYAA
GYAAA
SLICE!!
SLICE
SLICE!
CLANG CLANG
HRRNG!!
KADOOOM!!
RAHH
GAAH!!
GYAA

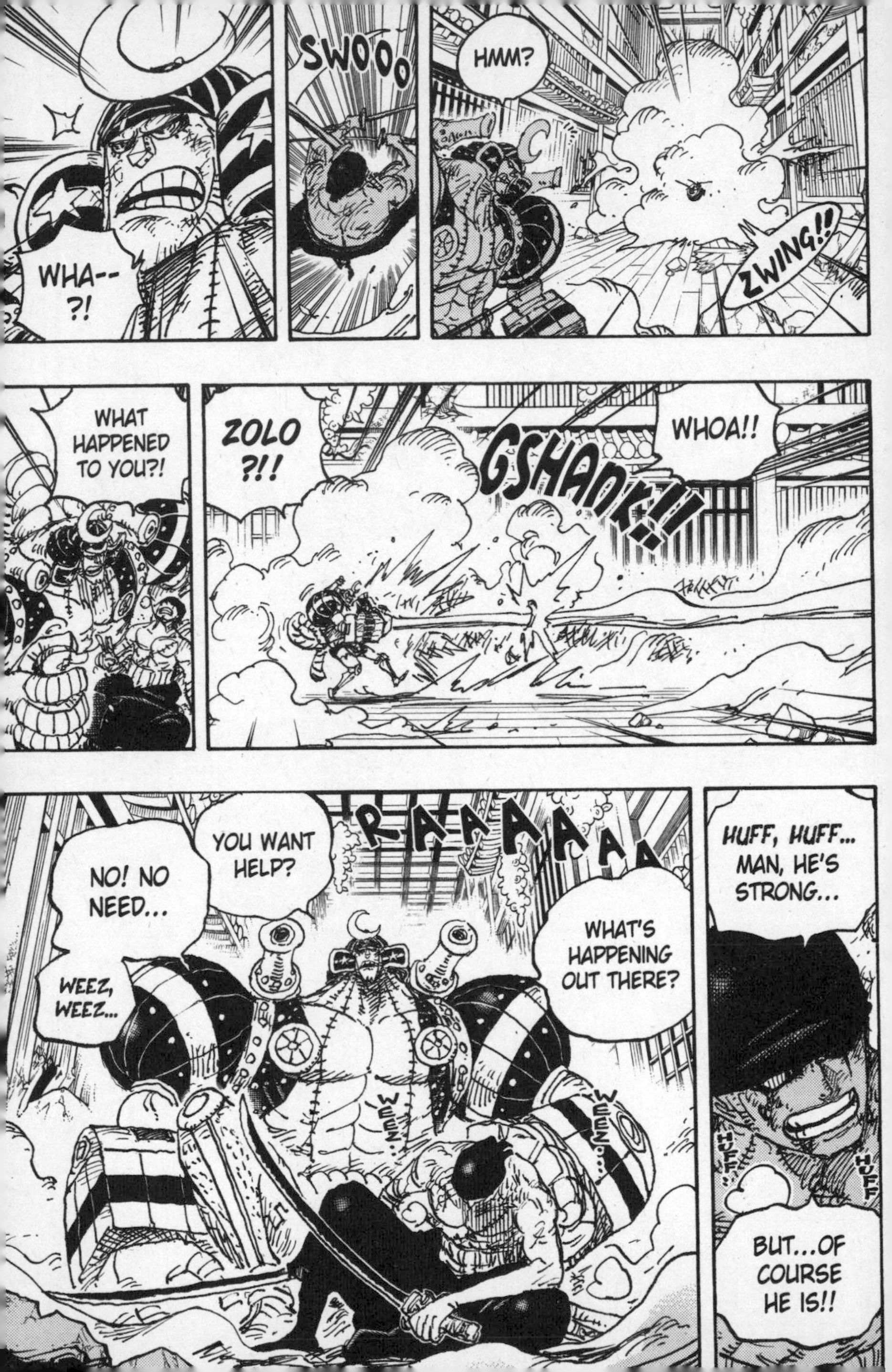
HMM?
ZWING!!
SWOOO
WHA-- ?!
WHOA!!
GSHANK!!
ZOLO ?!!
WHAT HAPPENED TO YOU?!
HUFF, HUFF... MAN, HE'S STRONG...
HUFF
HUFF
BUT...OF COURSE HE IS!!
RAAAAAA
WHAT'S HAPPENING OUT THERE?
YOU WANT HELP?
NO! NO NEED...
WEEZ, WEEZ...
WEEZ...
WEEZ...

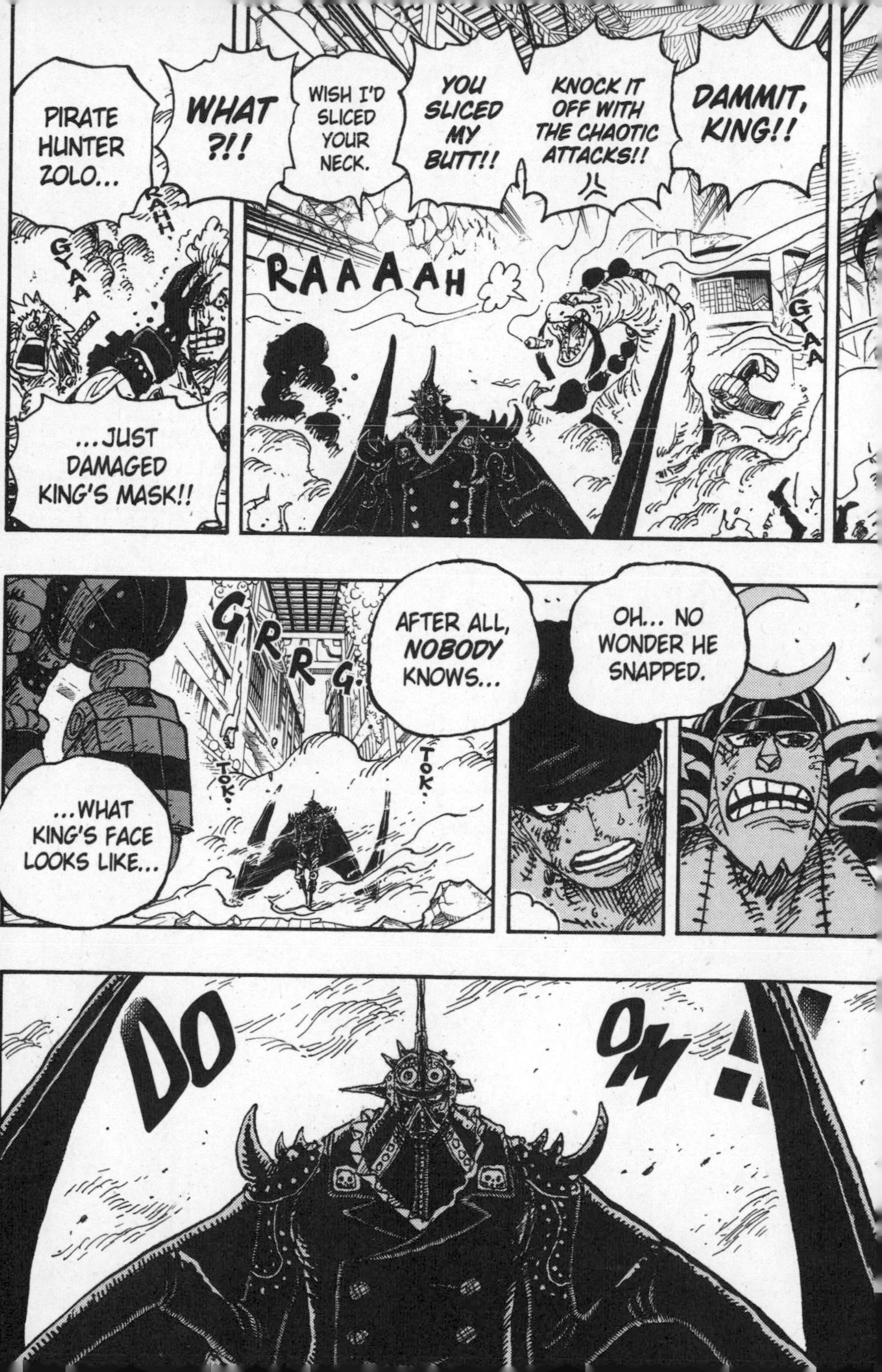

DAMMIT, KING!!
KNOCK IT OFF WITH THE CHAOTIC ATTACKS!!
YOU SLICED MY BUTT!!
WISH I'D SLICED YOUR NECK.
WHAT ?!!
RAAAAH
GYAA
PIRATE HUNTER ZOLO...
RAHH
GYAA
...JUST DAMAGED KING'S MASK!!
OH... NO WONDER HE SNAPPED.
AFTER ALL, *NOBODY* KNOWS...
TOK
TOK
GRRRG.
...WHAT KING'S FACE LOOKS LIKE...
DOOM

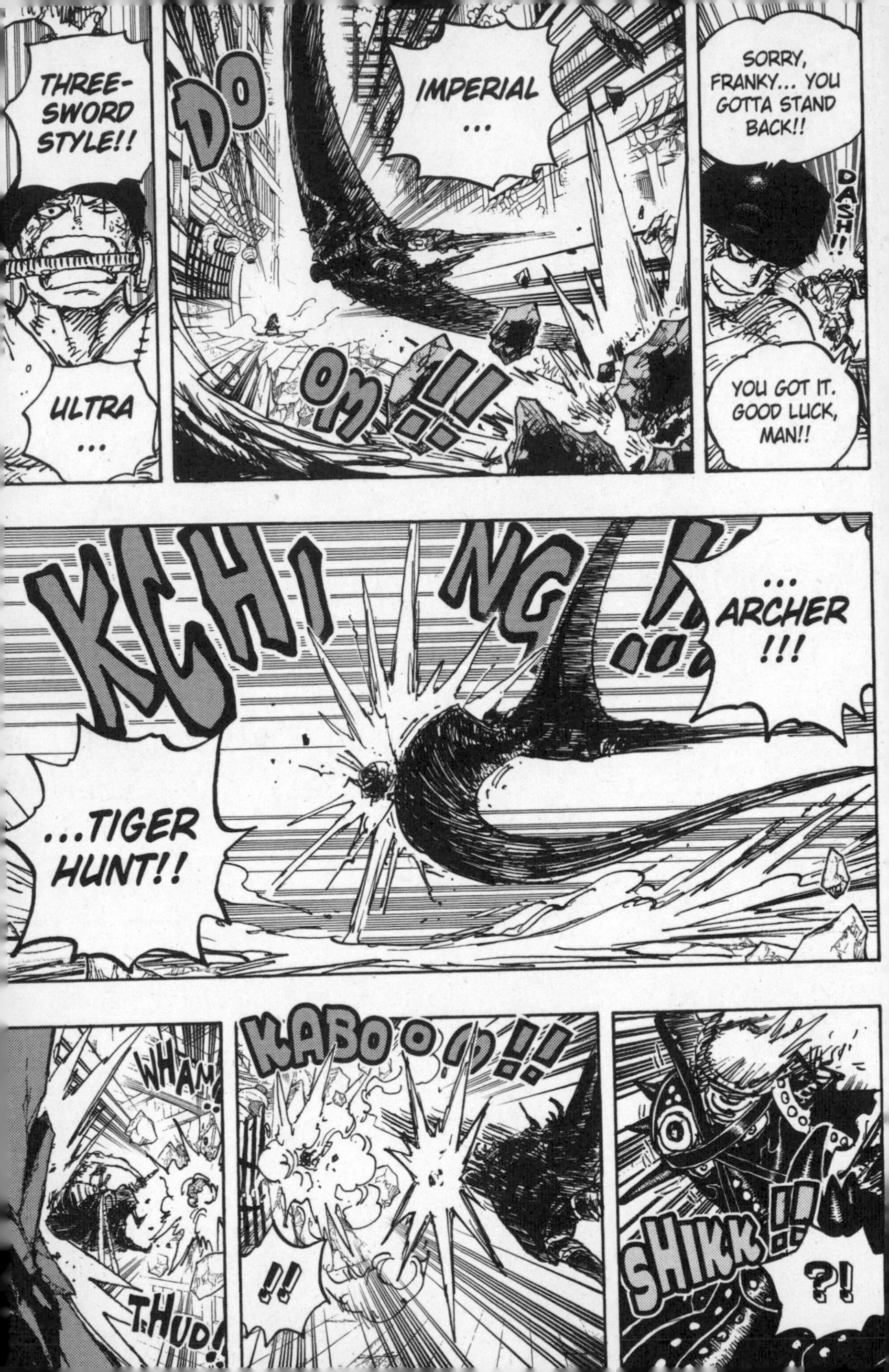
SORRY, FRANKY... YOU GOTTA STAND BACK!!
DASH!!
YOU GOT IT. GOOD LUCK, MAN!!
IMPERIAL ...
DOOM!!
THREE-SWORD STYLE!!
ULTRA ...
...ARCHER!!!
KCHIING!!
...TIGER HUNT!!
SHIKK!!
?!
KABOOM!!
!!
WHAM!!
THUD!!

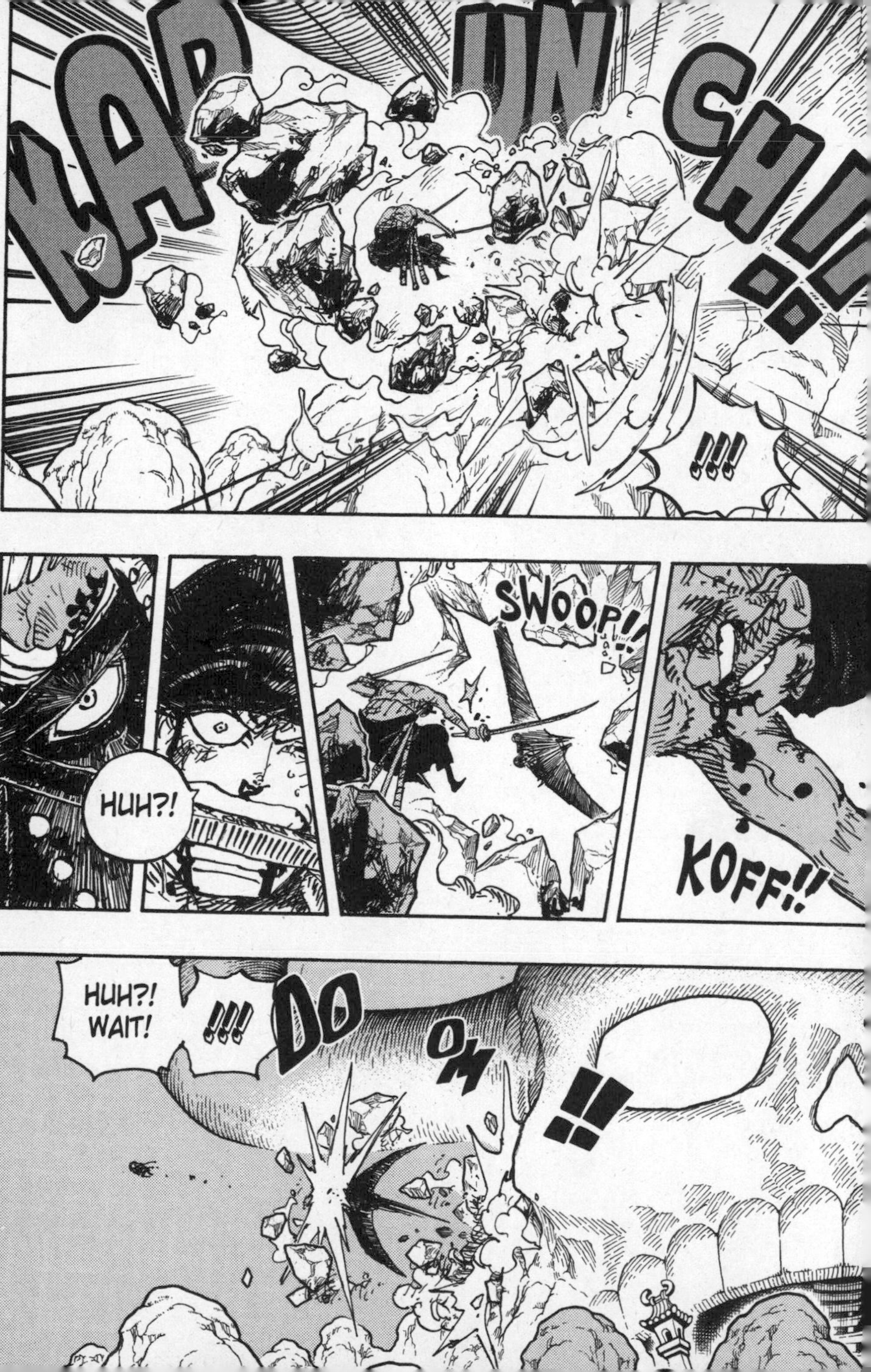

KAPUNCH!!
!!!
KOFF!!
SWOOP!!
HUH?!
HUH?! WAIT!
!!!
DOOM!!

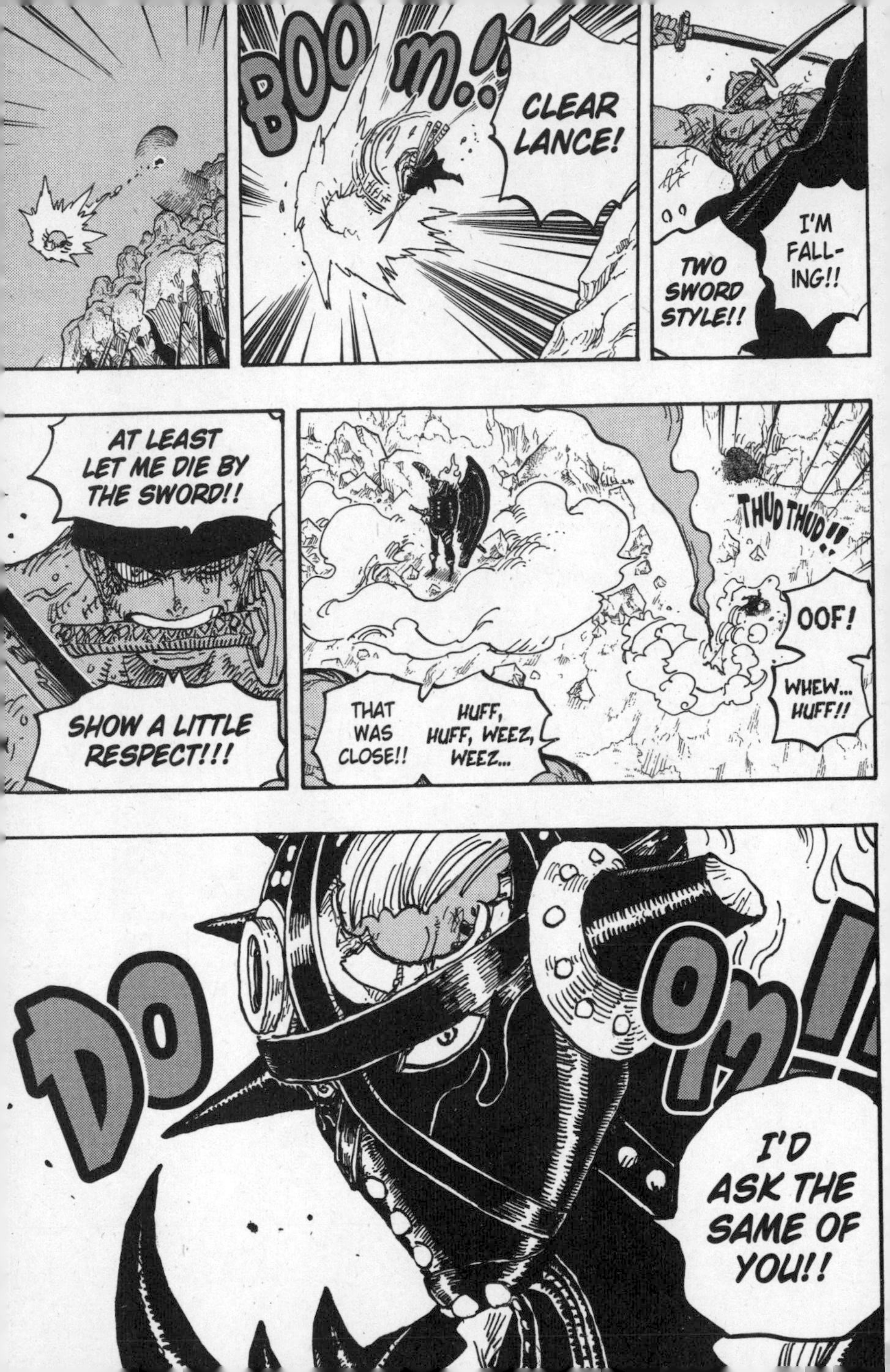
I'M FALLING!!
TWO SWORD STYLE!!
BOOM..!!
CLEAR LANCE!
THUD THUD!!
OOF!
WHEW... HUFF!!
HUFF, HUFF, WEEZ, WEEZ...
THAT WAS CLOSE!!
AT LEAST LET ME DIE BY THE SWORD!!
SHOW A LITTLE RESPECT!!!
DOOM!!
I'D ASK THE SAME OF YOU!!

Chapter 1028: BRACHIOSNAKEUS

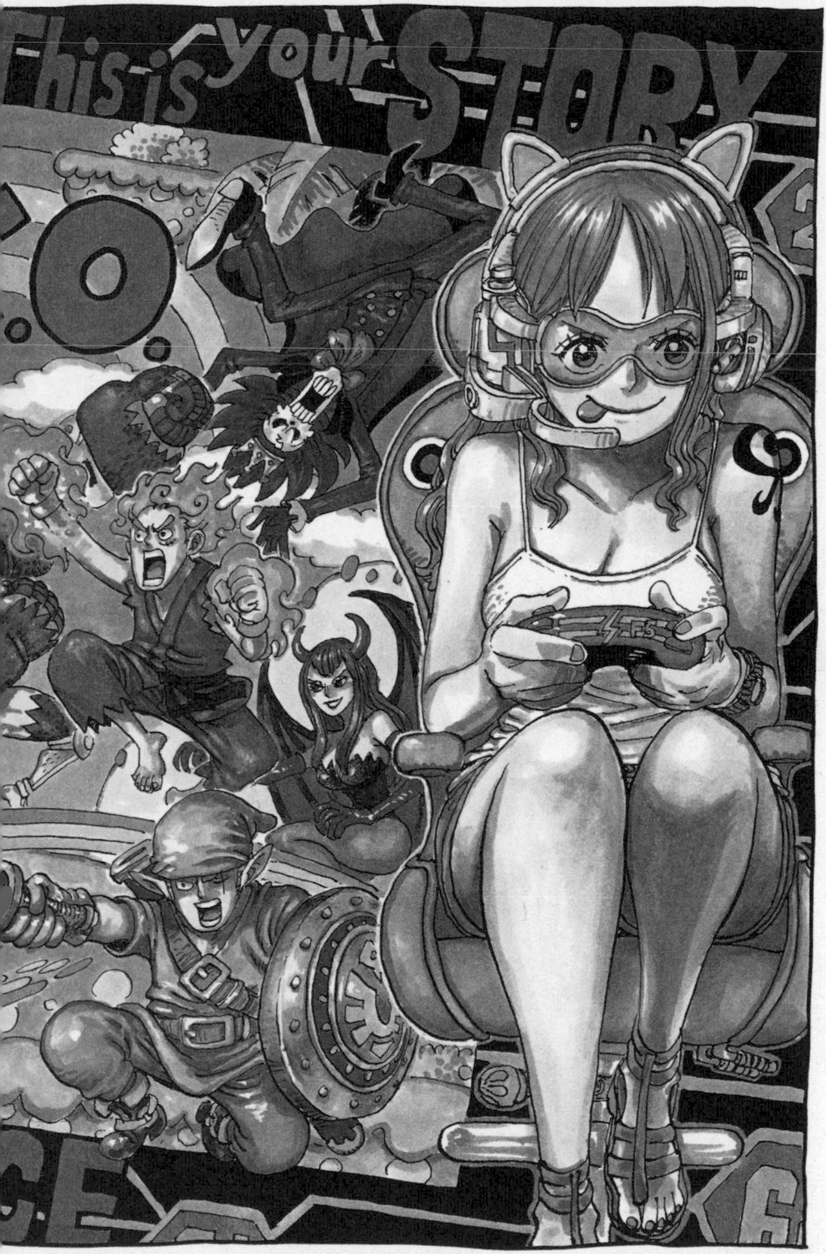
This is your STORY

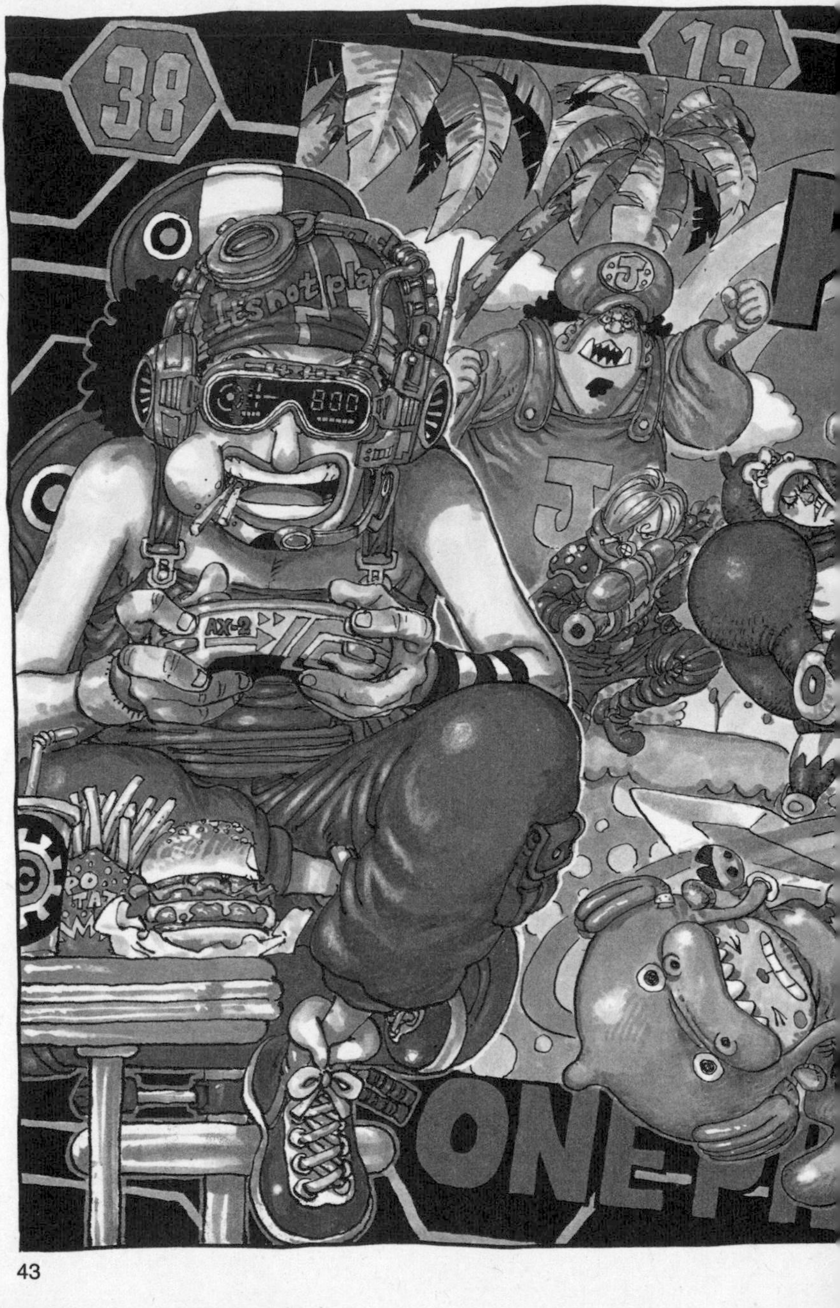
38
19
AX-2
ONE

vol.102

ONE PIECE

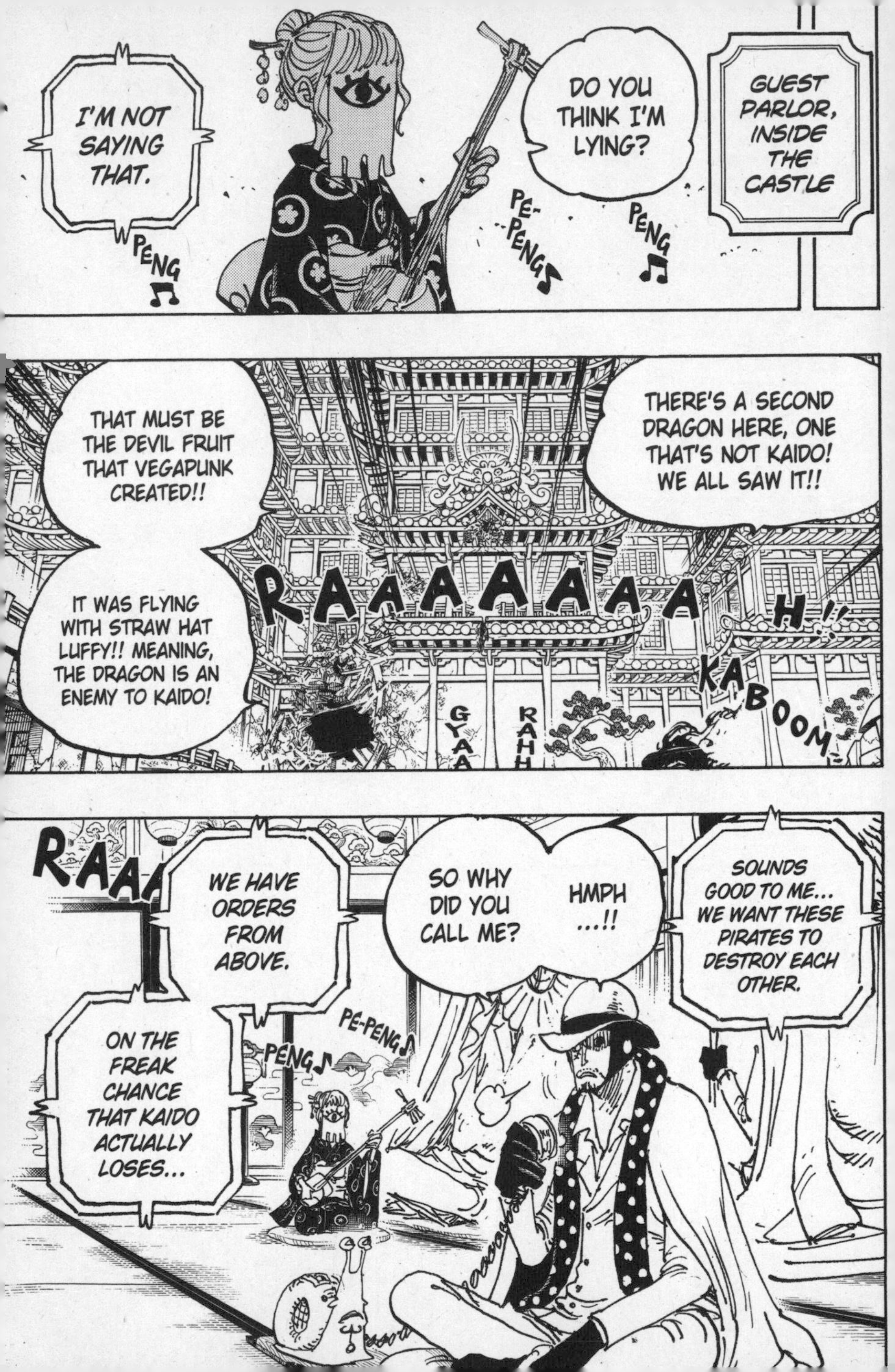
GUEST PARLOR, INSIDE THE CASTLE
DO YOU THINK I'M LYING?
PENG
PE-PENGS
I'M NOT SAYING THAT.
PENG
THERE'S A SECOND DRAGON HERE, ONE THAT'S NOT KAIDO! WE ALL SAW IT!!
THAT MUST BE THE DEVIL FRUIT THAT VEGAPUNK CREATED!!
IT WAS FLYING WITH STRAW HAT LUFFY!! MEANING, THE DRAGON IS AN ENEMY TO KAIDO!
RAAAAAAAH!!
KABOOM
RAHH
GYAA
SOUNDS GOOD TO ME... WE WANT THESE PIRATES TO DESTROY EACH OTHER.
HMPH ...!!
SO WHY DID YOU CALL ME?
WE HAVE ORDERS FROM ABOVE.
ON THE FREAK CHANCE THAT KAIDO ACTUALLY LOSES...
PE-PENG
PENG
RAA

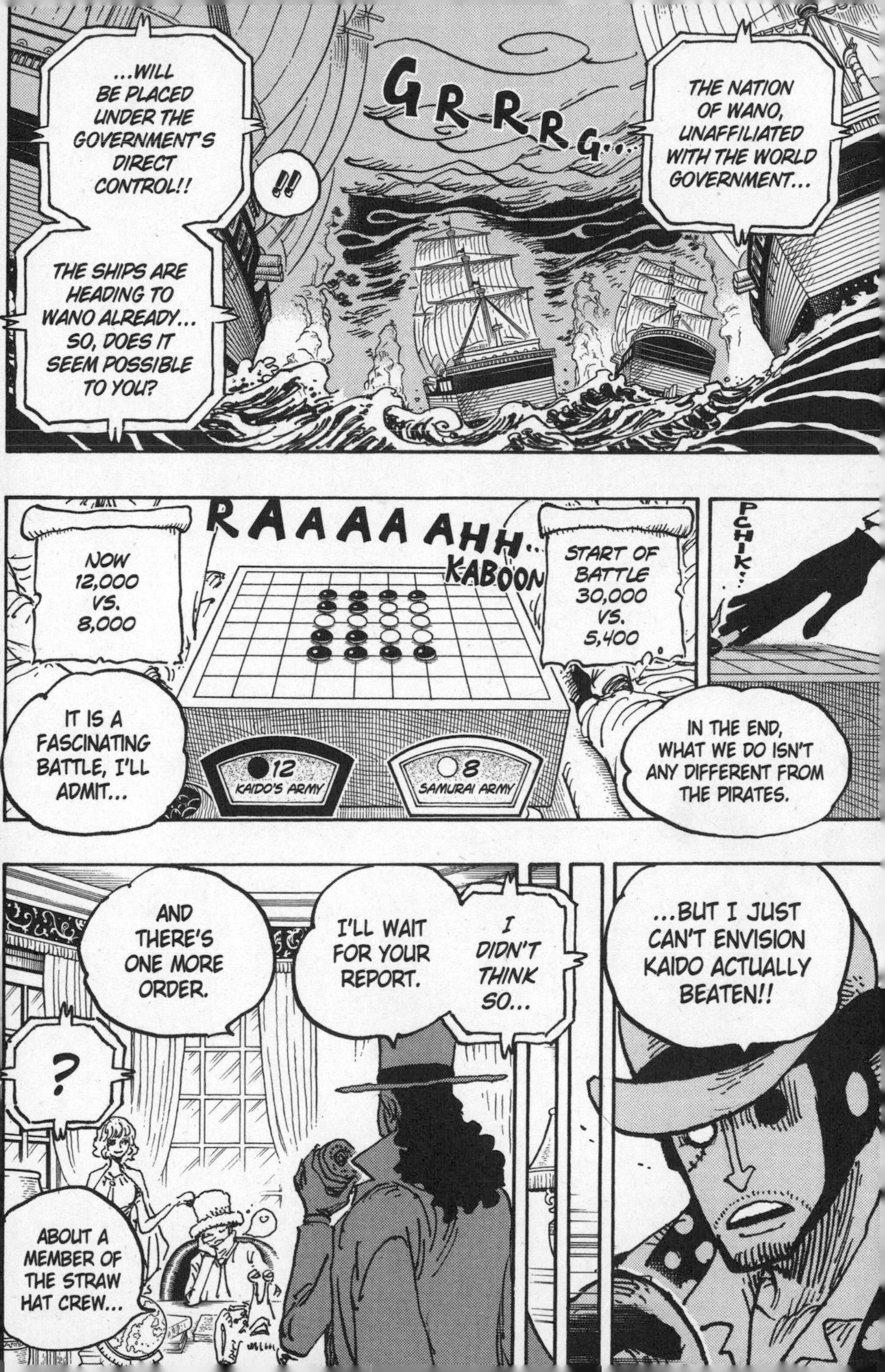
THE NATION OF WANO, UNAFFILIATED WITH THE WORLD GOVERNMENT...
GRRRRG...
...WILL BE PLACED UNDER THE GOVERNMENT'S DIRECT CONTROL!!
!!
THE SHIPS ARE HEADING TO WANO ALREADY... SO, DOES IT SEEM POSSIBLE TO YOU?
PCHIK...
START OF BATTLE 30,000 VS. 5,400
RAAAAAHH...
KABOON
NOW 12,000 VS. 8,000
12 KAIDO'S ARMY
8 SAMURAI ARMY
IN THE END, WHAT WE DO ISN'T ANY DIFFERENT FROM THE PIRATES.
IT IS A FASCINATING BATTLE, I'LL ADMIT...
...BUT I JUST CAN'T ENVISION KAIDO ACTUALLY BEATEN!!
I DIDN'T THINK SO...
I'LL WAIT FOR YOUR REPORT.
AND THERE'S ONE MORE ORDER.
?
ABOUT A MEMBER OF THE STRAW HAT CREW...

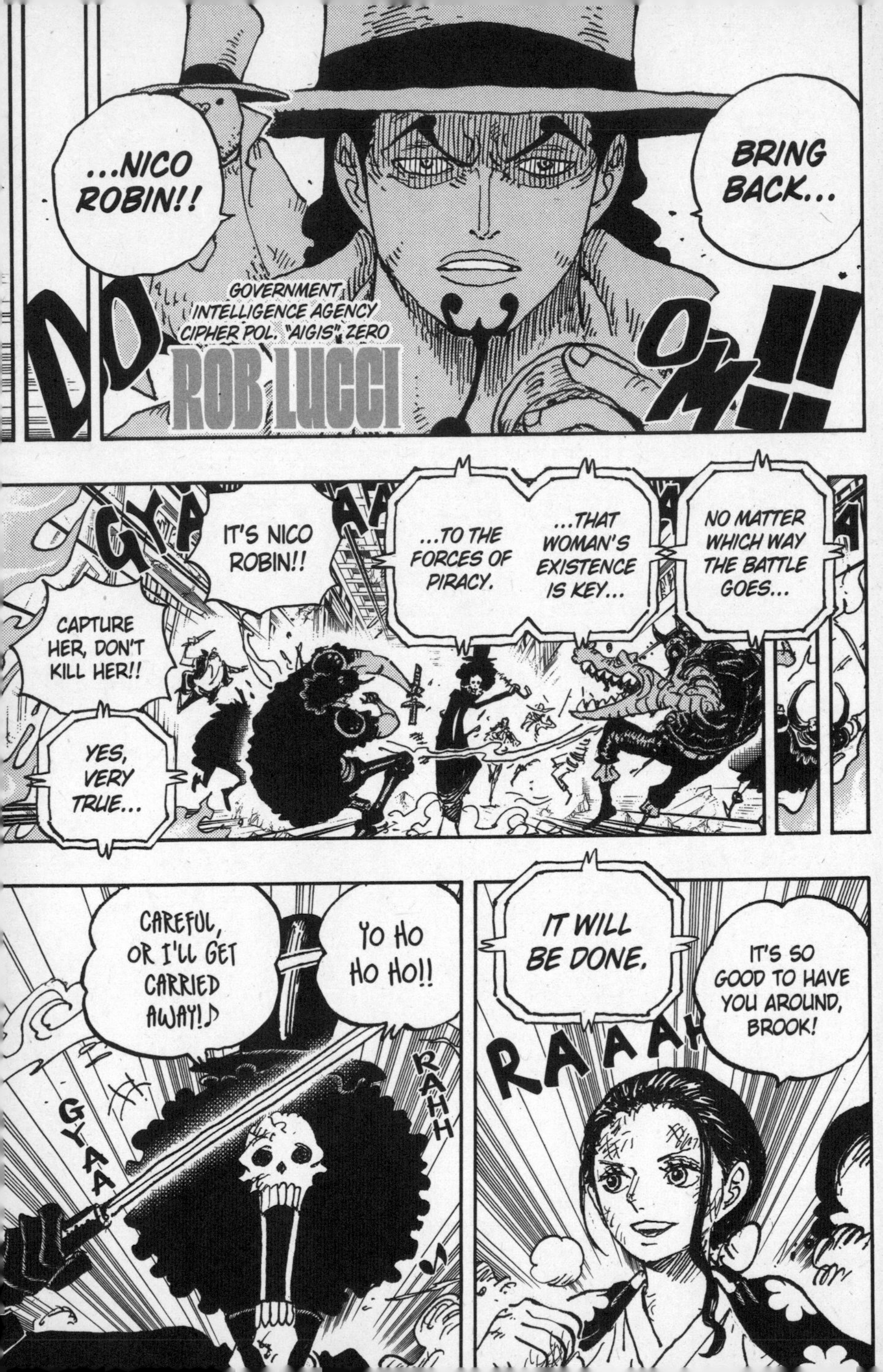

BRING BACK...
...NICO ROBIN!!
DOOM!!
GOVERNMENT INTELLIGENCE AGENCY CIPHER POL. "AIGIS" ZERO
ROB LUCCI
NO MATTER WHICH WAY THE BATTLE GOES...
...THAT WOMAN'S EXISTENCE IS KEY...
...TO THE FORCES OF PIRACY.
IT'S NICO ROBIN!!
GYA
CAPTURE HER, DON'T KILL HER!!
YES, VERY TRUE...
IT WILL BE DONE.
IT'S SO GOOD TO HAVE YOU AROUND, BROOK!
RAAAA
YO HO HO HO!!
CAREFUL, OR I'LL GET CARRIED AWAY!♪
RAHH
GYAA

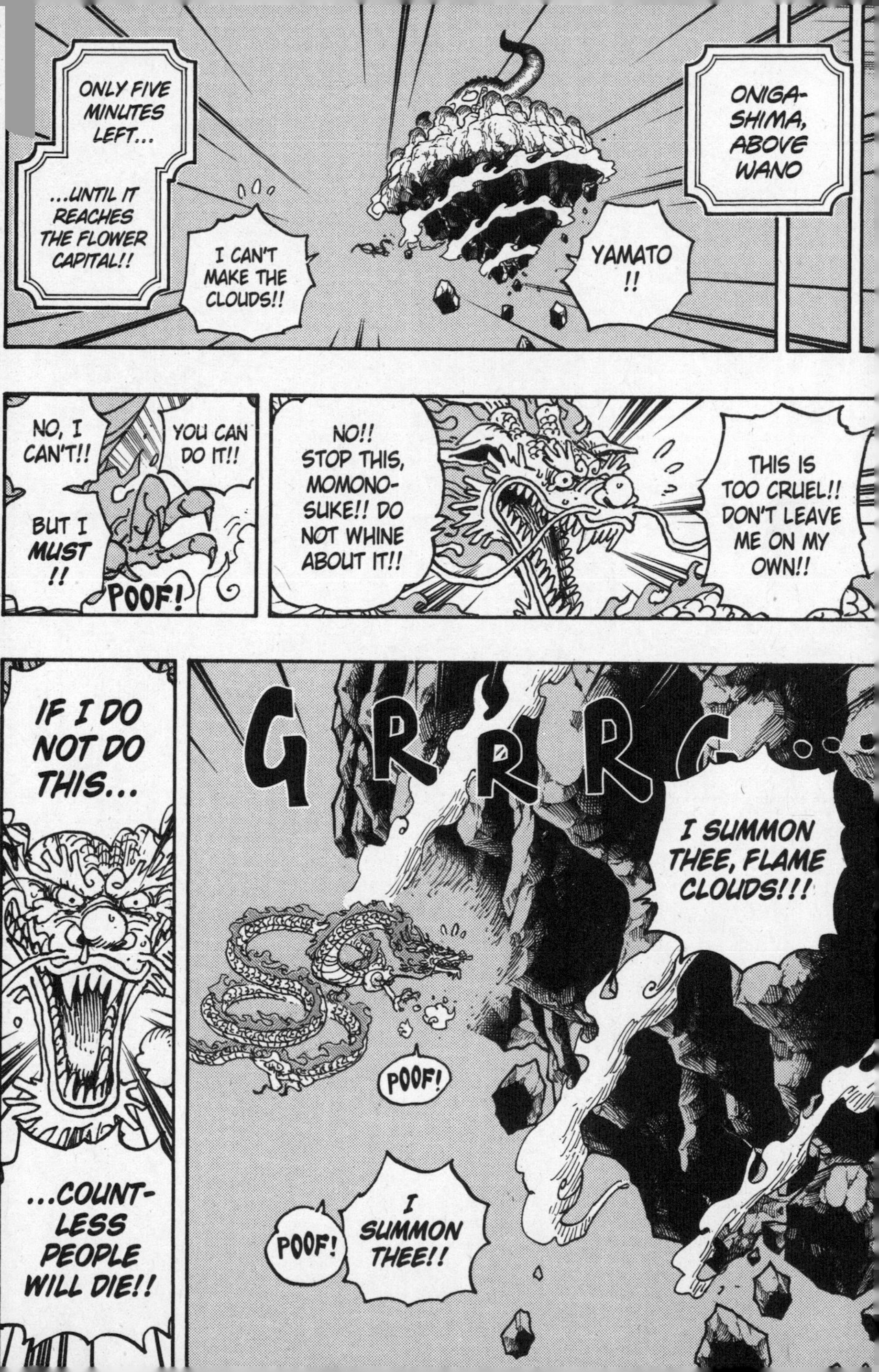
ONIGA-SHIMA, ABOVE WANO
YAMATO!!
I CAN'T MAKE THE CLOUDS!!
ONLY FIVE MINUTES LEFT...
...UNTIL IT REACHES THE FLOWER CAPITAL!!
THIS IS TOO CRUEL!! DON'T LEAVE ME ON MY OWN!!
NO!! STOP THIS, MOMONO-SUKE!! DO NOT WHINE ABOUT IT!!
YOU CAN DO IT!!
NO, I CAN'T!!
BUT I MUST!!
POOF!
GRRRG...
I SUMMON THEE, FLAME CLOUDS!!!
POOF!
I SUMMON THEE!!
POOF!
IF I DO NOT DO THIS...
...COUNT-LESS PEOPLE WILL DIE!!

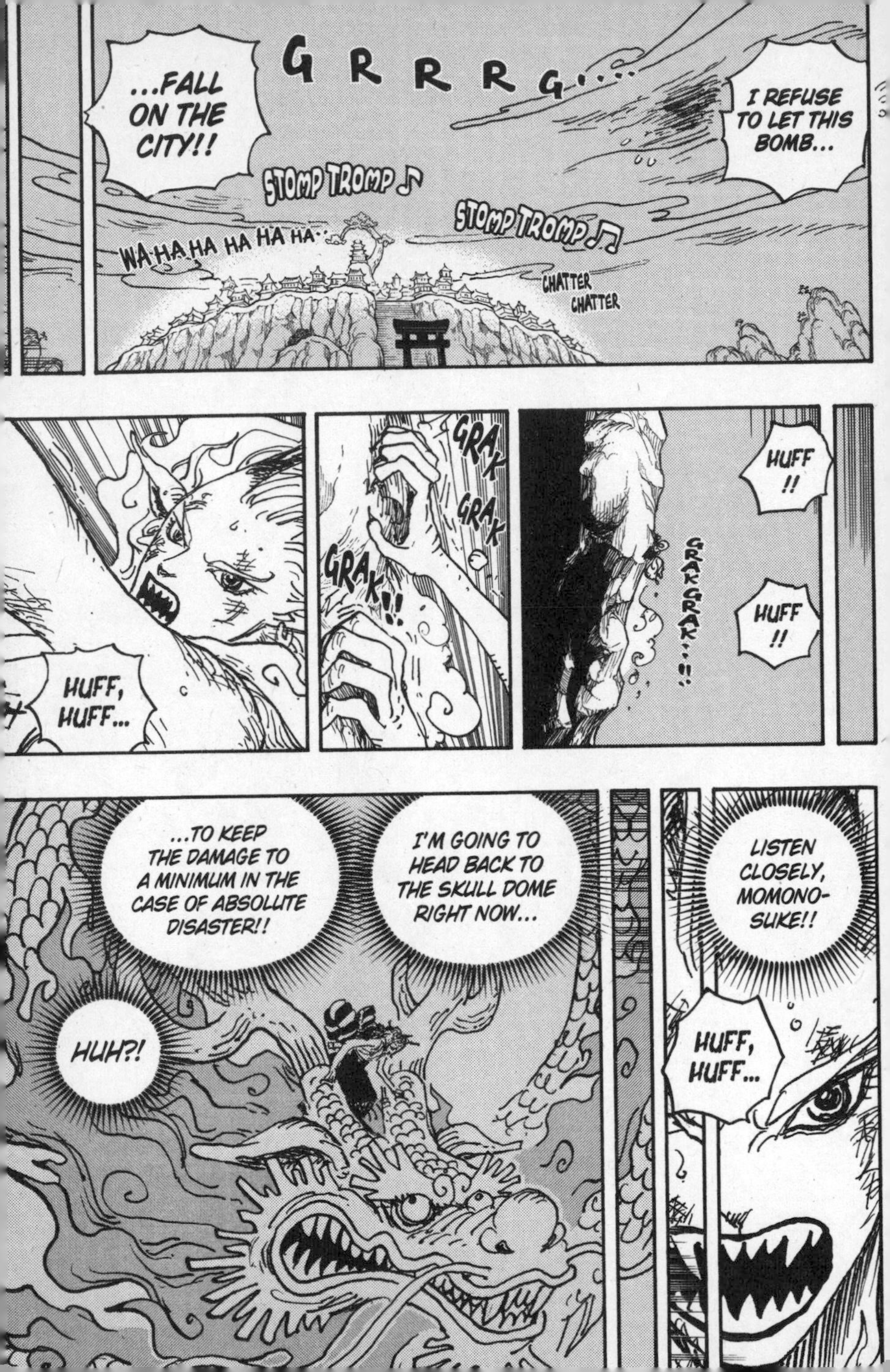
I REFUSE TO LET THIS BOMB...
GRRRRG...
...FALL ON THE CITY!!
STOMP TROMP
STOMP TROMP
WA HA HA HA HA HA...
CHATTER CHATTER
HUFF!!
HUFF!!
GRAKGRAK...!!
GRAK GRAK
GRAK!!
HUFF, HUFF...
LISTEN CLOSELY, MOMONOSUKE!!
HUFF, HUFF...
I'M GOING TO HEAD BACK TO THE SKULL DOME RIGHT NOW...
...TO KEEP THE DAMAGE TO A MINIMUM IN THE CASE OF ABSOLUTE DISASTER!!
HUH?!

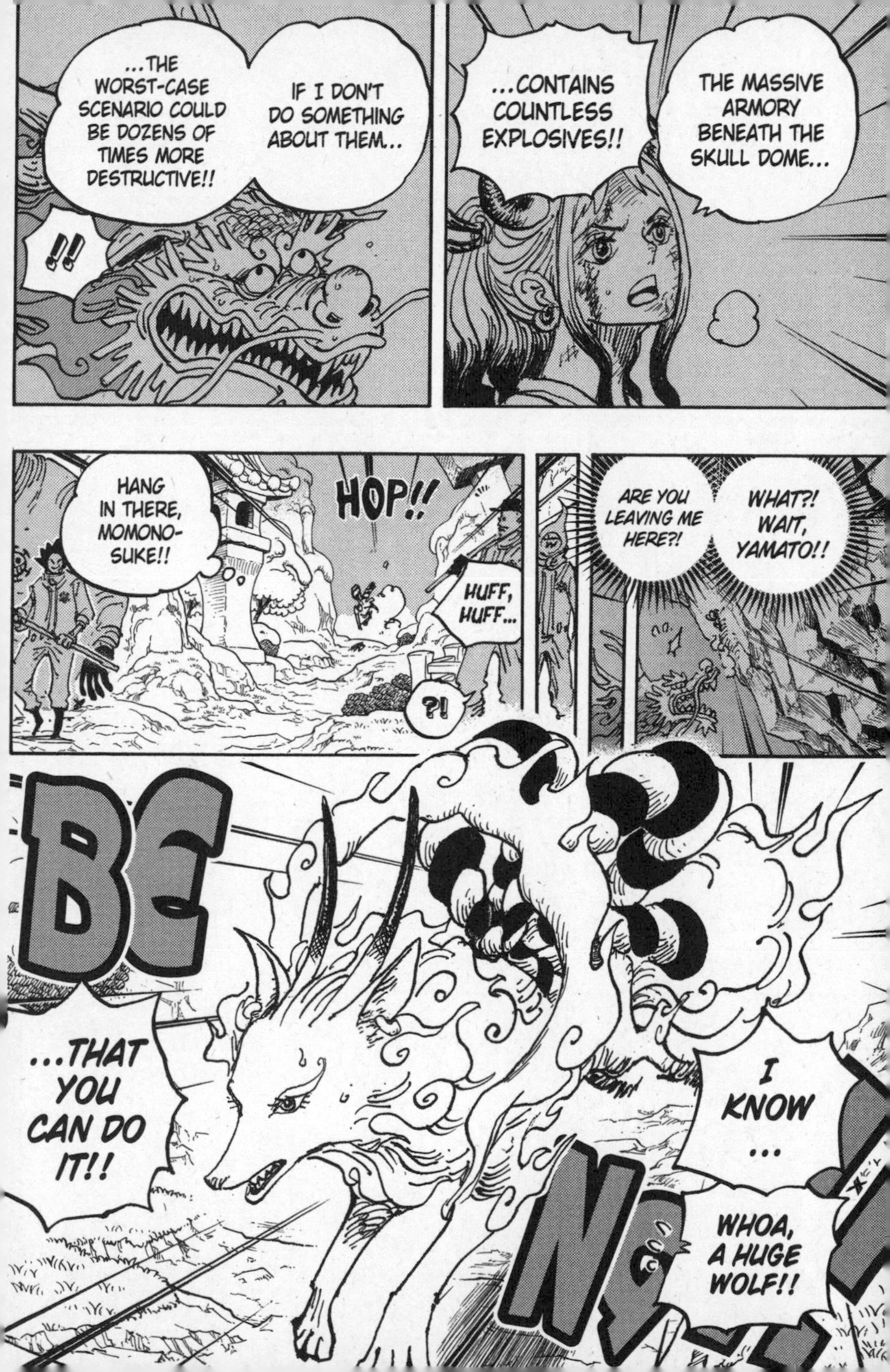
THE MASSIVE ARMORY BENEATH THE SKULL DOME...
...CONTAINS COUNTLESS EXPLOSIVES!!
IF I DON'T DO SOMETHING ABOUT THEM...
...THE WORST-CASE SCENARIO COULD BE DOZENS OF TIMES MORE DESTRUCTIVE!!
!!
WHAT?! WAIT, YAMATO!!
ARE YOU LEAVING ME HERE?!
HOP!!
HUFF, HUFF...
HANG IN THERE, MOMONOSUKE!!
?!
I KNOW...
WHOA, A HUGE WOLF!!
N
BE
...THAT YOU CAN DO IT!!

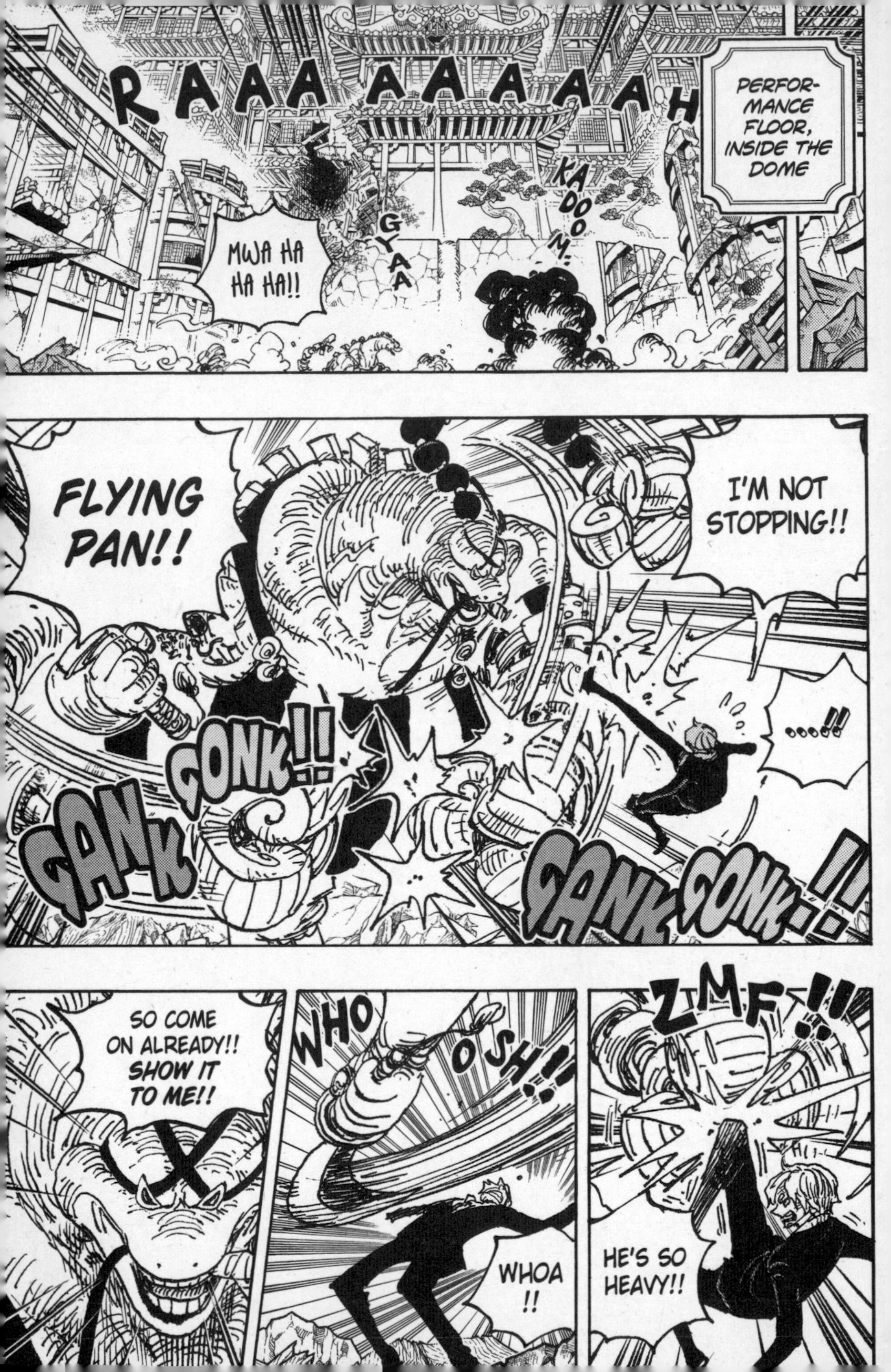
PERFORMANCE FLOOR, INSIDE THE DOME
RAAAAAAAAH
KADOOM
GYAA
MWA HA HA HA!!
I'M NOT STOPPING!!
....!!
GANK GONK!!
FLYING PAN!!
GONK!!
GANK
ZMF!!!
HE'S SO HEAVY!!
WHOOSH!!
WHOA!!
SO COME ON ALREADY!! SHOW IT TO ME!!

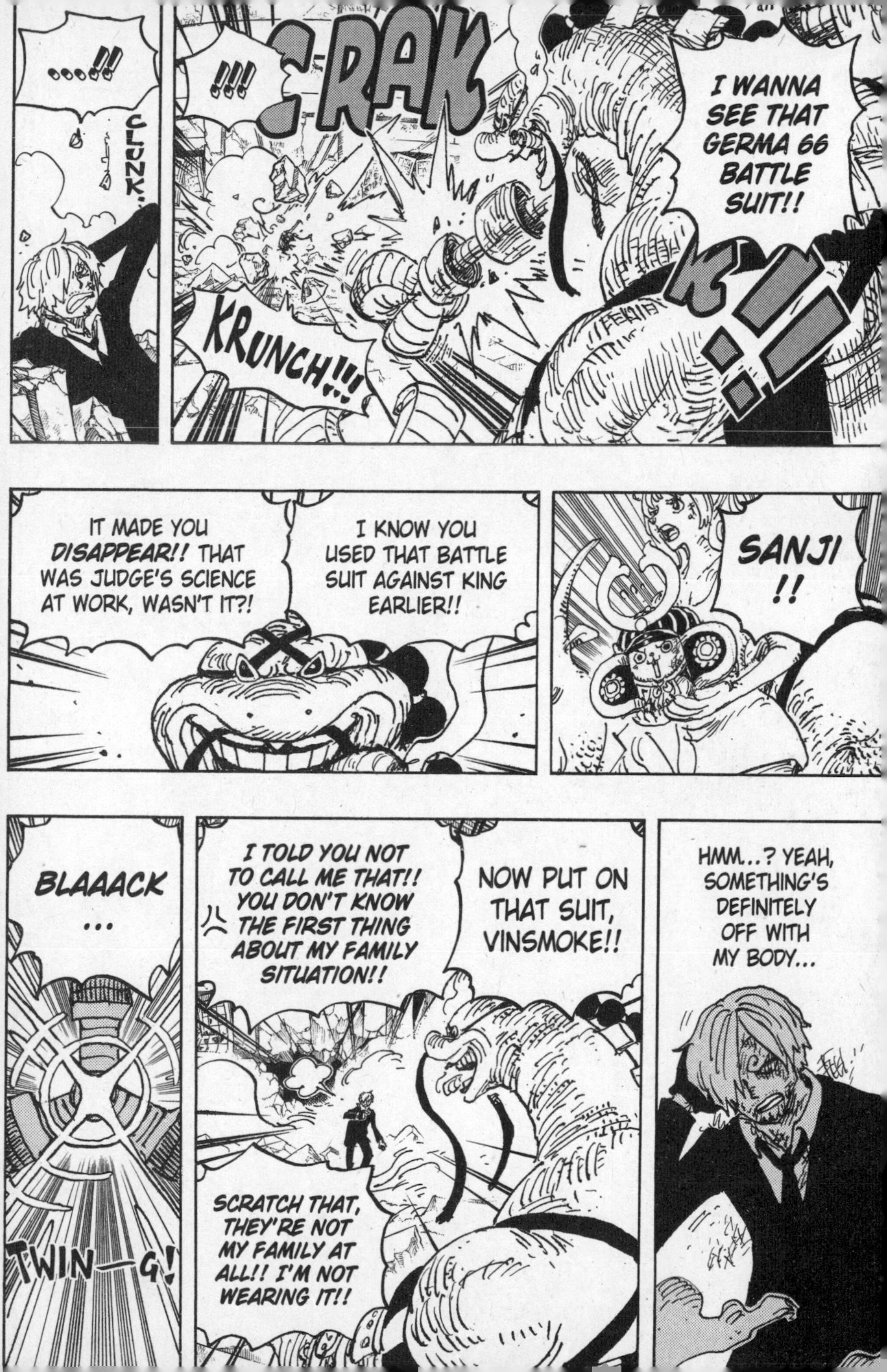
I WANNA SEE THAT GERMA 66 BATTLE SUIT!!
K!!
C-RAK
!!!
KRUNCH!!!
...!!
CLUNK..
SANJI !!
I KNOW YOU USED THAT BATTLE SUIT AGAINST KING EARLIER!!
IT MADE YOU DISAPPEAR!! THAT WAS JUDGE'S SCIENCE AT WORK, WASN'T IT?!
HMM...? YEAH, SOMETHING'S DEFINITELY OFF WITH MY BODY...
NOW PUT ON THAT SUIT, VINSMOKE!!
I TOLD YOU NOT TO CALL ME THAT!! YOU DON'T KNOW THE FIRST THING ABOUT MY FAMILY SITUATION!!
SCRATCH THAT, THEY'RE NOT MY FAMILY AT ALL!! I'M NOT WEARING IT!!
BLAAACK ...
TWIN—G!

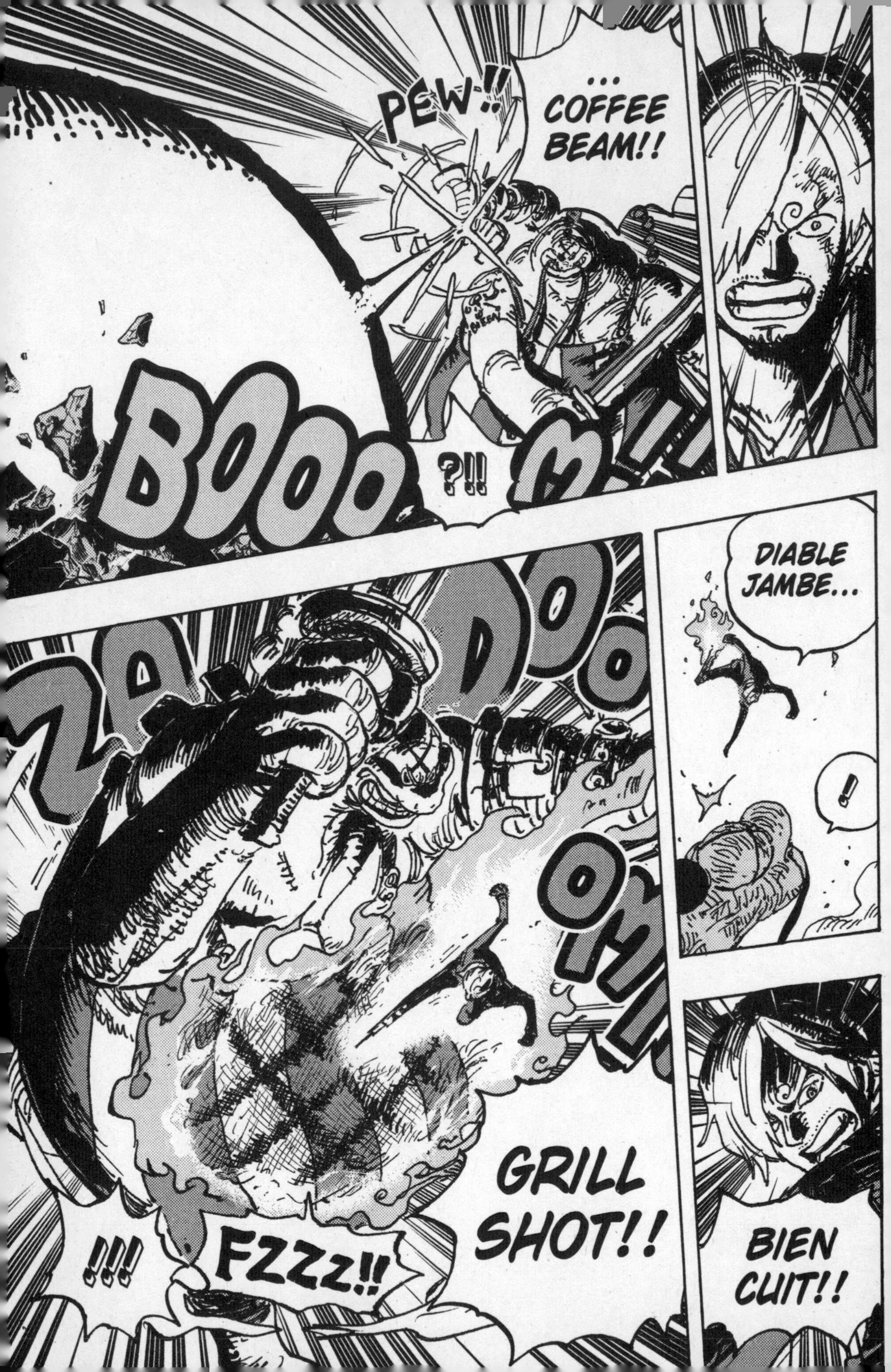
... COFFEE BEAM!!
PEW!!
?!!
BOOOM!!
DIABLE JAMBE...
!
BIEN CUIT!!
ZADOOOOM
GRILL SHOT!!
FZZZ!!
!!!

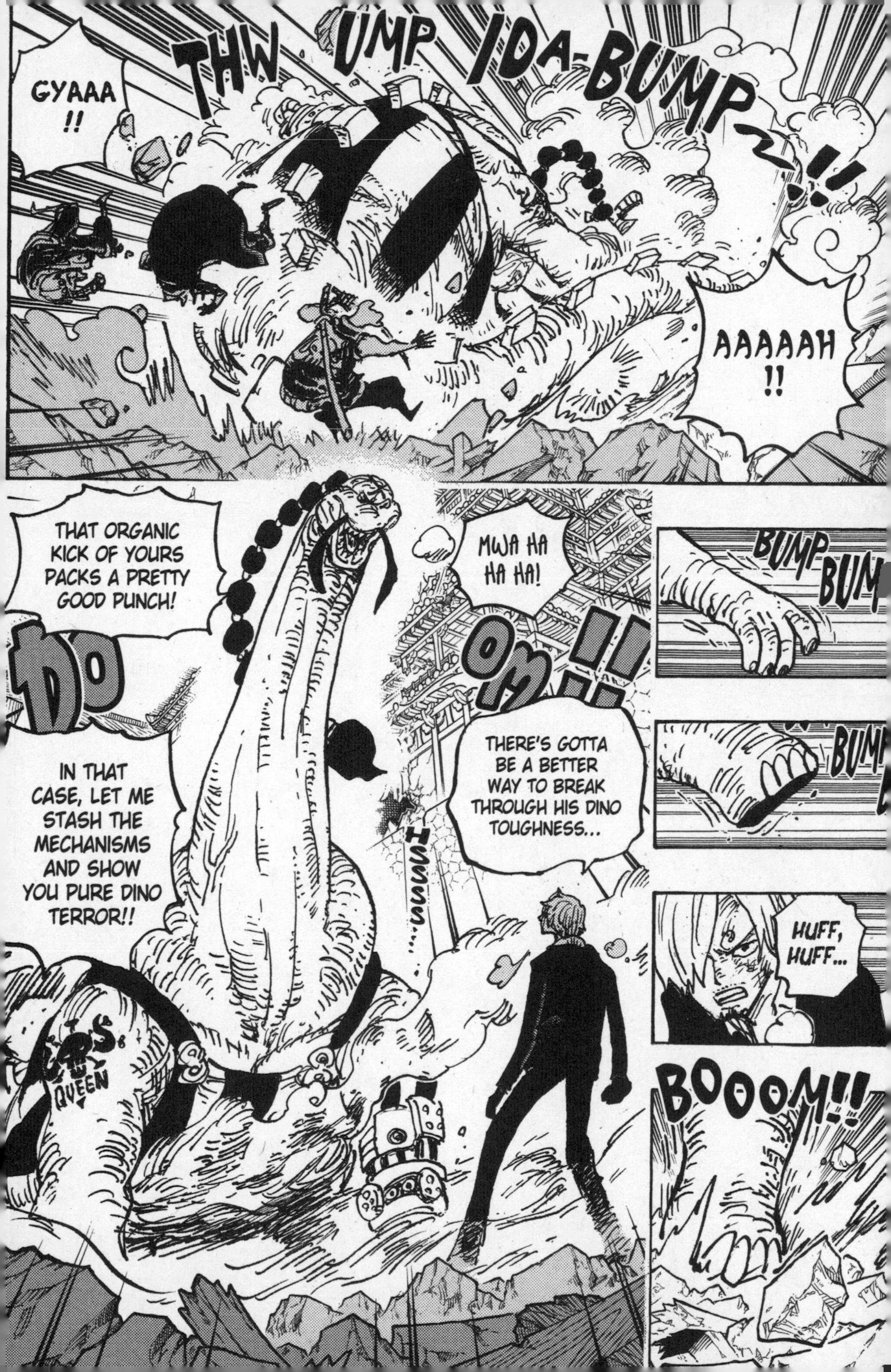
THWUMP IDA-BUMP!!
AAAAAH!!
GYAAA!!
BUMP BUM
BUM
HUFF, HUFF...
BOOOM!!
MWA HA HA HA!
THAT ORGANIC KICK OF YOURS PACKS A PRETTY GOOD PUNCH!
DOOM!!
THERE'S GOTTA BE A BETTER WAY TO BREAK THROUGH HIS DINO TOUGHNESS...
IN THAT CASE, LET ME STASH THE MECHANISMS AND SHOW YOU PURE DINO TERROR!!
HSSSS...
QUEEN

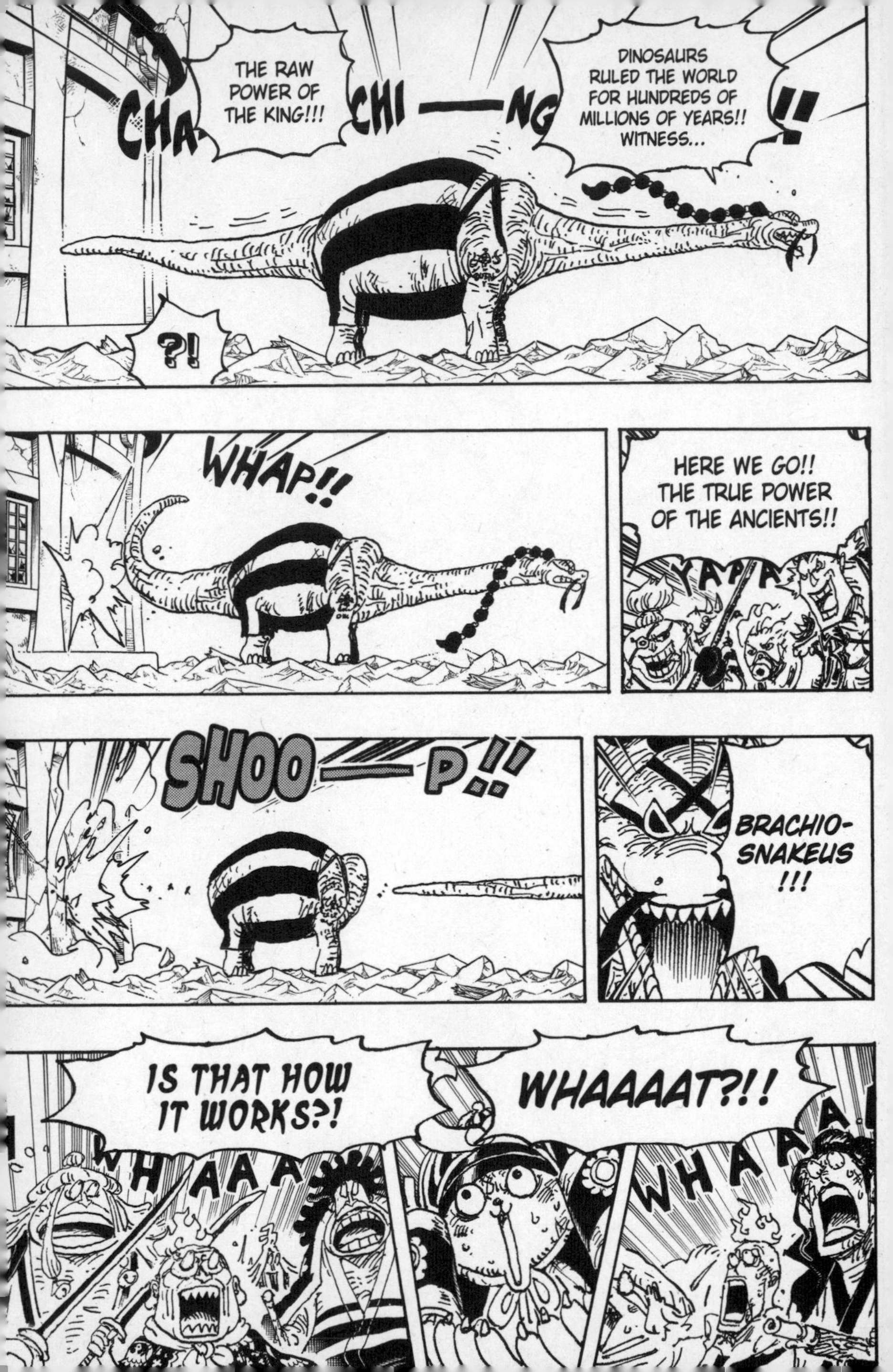

DINOSAURS RULED THE WORLD FOR HUNDREDS OF MILLIONS OF YEARS!! WITNESS...
THE RAW POWER OF THE KING!!!
CHA CHI—NG!!
?!
HERE WE GO!! THE TRUE POWER OF THE ANCIENTS!!
WHAP!!
BRACHIO-SNAKEUS !!!
SHOO—P!!
WHAAAAT?!!
IS THAT HOW IT WORKS?!
WHAAAA
WHAAAA

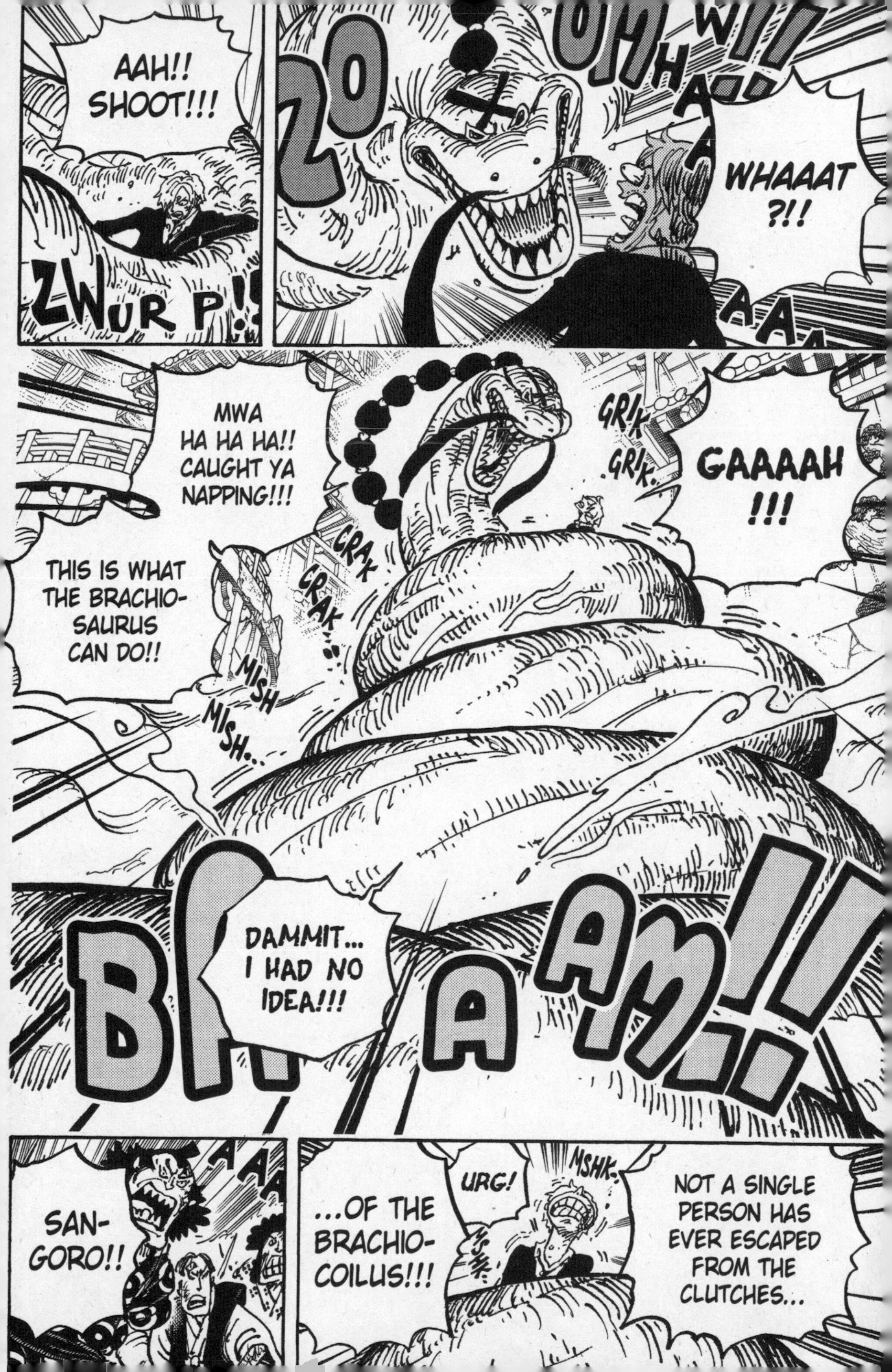
WHAAAT ?!!
AAH!! SHOOT!!!
ZWURP!!
GAAAAH !!!
GRIK GRIK
MWA HA HA HA!! CAUGHT YA NAPPING!!!
THIS IS WHAT THE BRACHIO-SAURUS CAN DO!!
CRAK CRAK
MISH MISH...
BAAAM!!
DAMMIT... I HAD NO IDEA!!!
NOT A SINGLE PERSON HAS EVER ESCAPED FROM THE CLUTCHES...
MSHK
URG!
MSHK
...OF THE BRACHIO-COILUS!!!
SAN-GORO!!

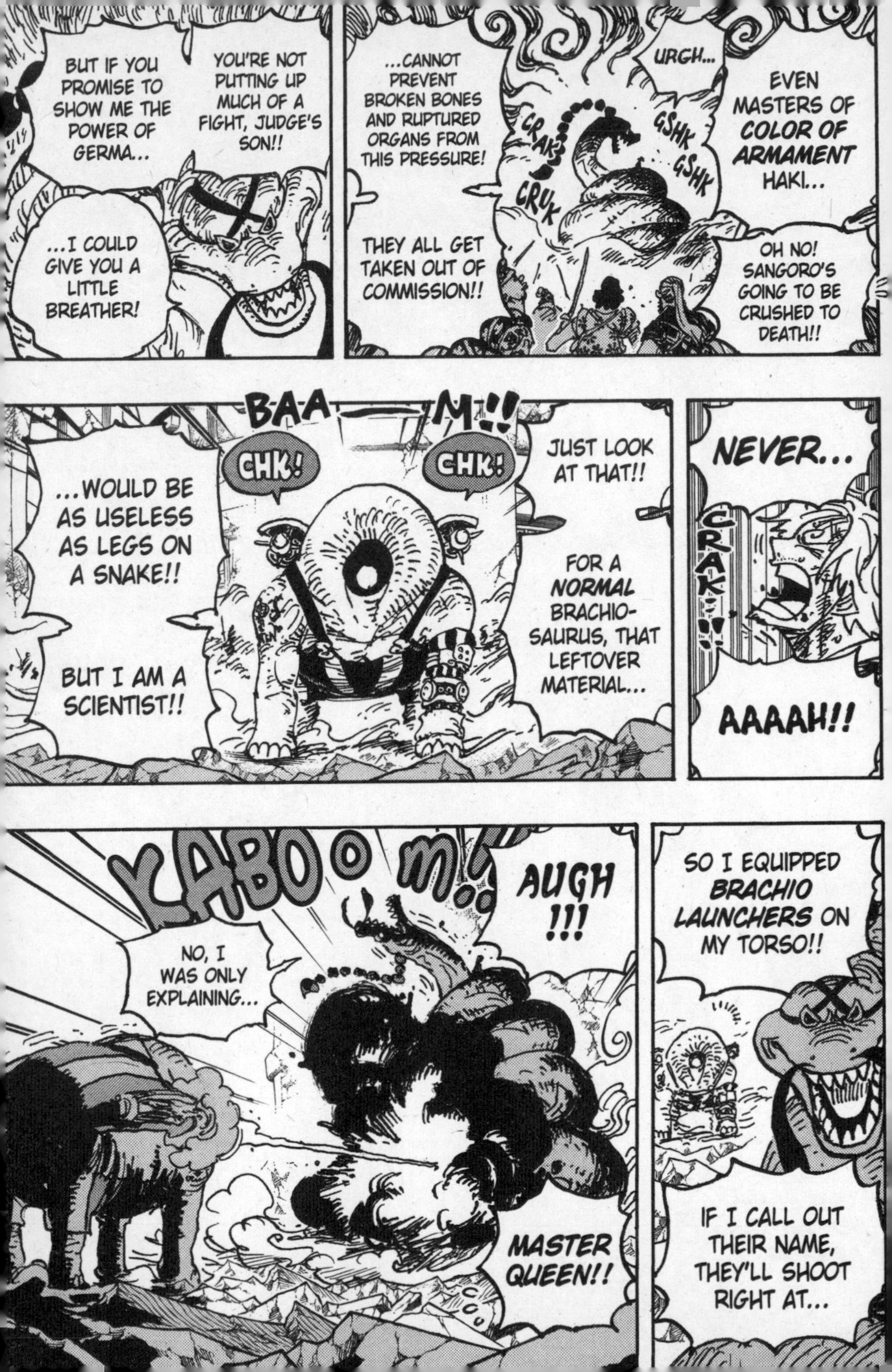
URGH...
EVEN MASTERS OF COLOR OF ARMAMENT HAKI...
GSHK
GSHK
CRAK
CRUK
...CANNOT PREVENT BROKEN BONES AND RUPTURED ORGANS FROM THIS PRESSURE!
OH NO! SANGORO'S GOING TO BE CRUSHED TO DEATH!!
THEY ALL GET TAKEN OUT OF COMMISSION!!
YOU'RE NOT PUTTING UP MUCH OF A FIGHT, JUDGE'S SON!!
BUT IF YOU PROMISE TO SHOW ME THE POWER OF GERMA...
...I COULD GIVE YOU A LITTLE BREATHER!
NEVER...
CRAK!!
AAAAH!!
BAA—M!!
CHK!
CHK!
JUST LOOK AT THAT!!
FOR A NORMAL BRACHIO-SAURUS, THAT LEFTOVER MATERIAL...
...WOULD BE AS USELESS AS LEGS ON A SNAKE!!
BUT I AM A SCIENTIST!!
SO I EQUIPPED BRACHIO LAUNCHERS ON MY TORSO!!
IF I CALL OUT THEIR NAME, THEY'LL SHOOT RIGHT AT...
KABOOM!!
AUGH!!!
MASTER QUEEN!!
NO, I WAS ONLY EXPLAINING...

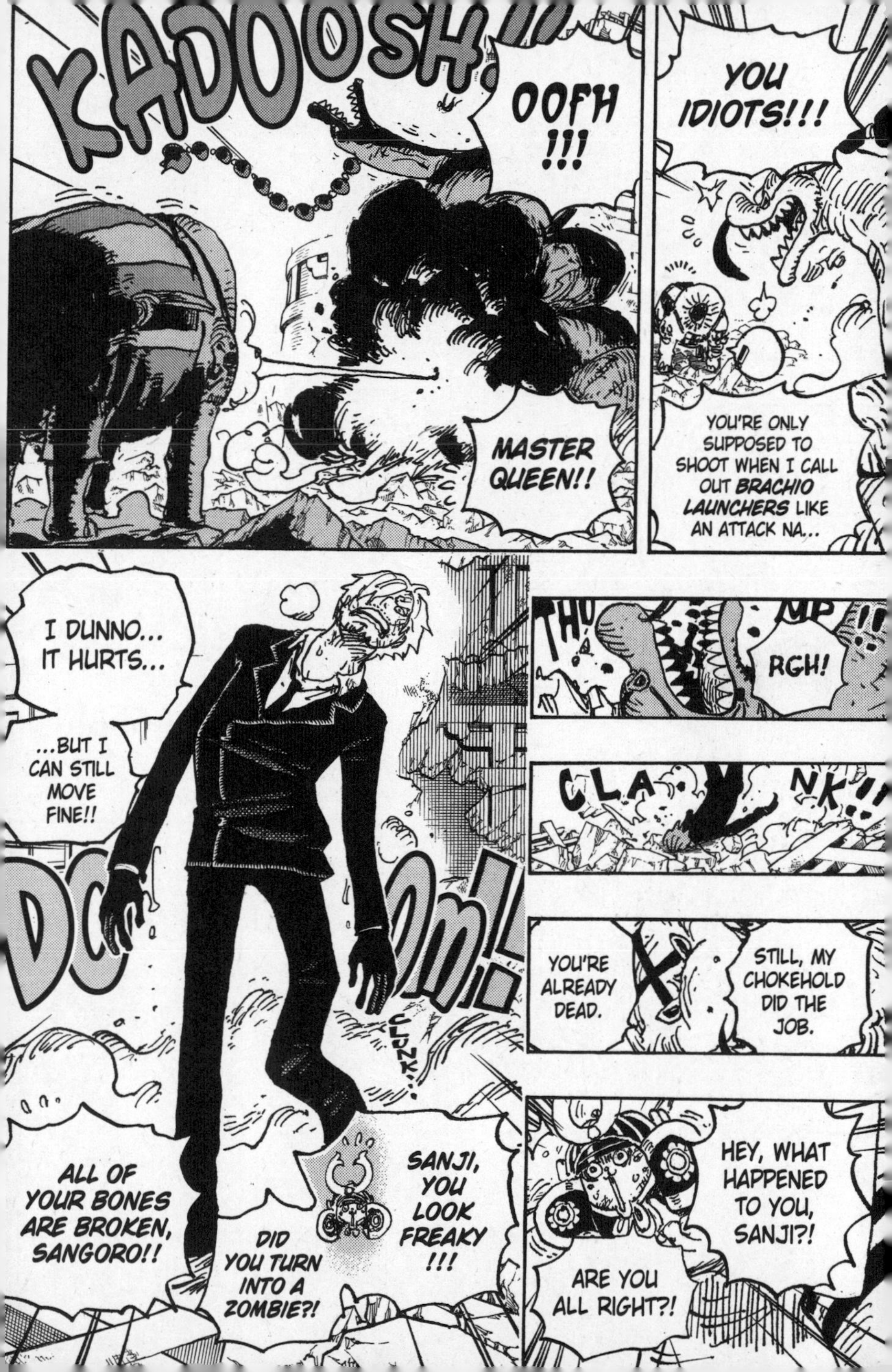
YOU IDIOTS!!!
YOU'RE ONLY SUPPOSED TO SHOOT WHEN I CALL OUT BRACHIO LAUNCHERS LIKE AN ATTACK NA...
OOFH!!!
KADOOSH!!
MASTER QUEEN!!
THU MP!!
RGH!
CLA NK!!
STILL, MY CHOKEHOLD DID THE JOB.
YOU'RE ALREADY DEAD.
HEY, WHAT HAPPENED TO YOU, SANJI?!
ARE YOU ALL RIGHT?!
I DUNNO... IT HURTS...
...BUT I CAN STILL MOVE FINE!!
DOOM!!
CLUNK
SANJI, YOU LOOK FREAKY!!!
DID YOU TURN INTO A ZOMBIE?!
ALL OF YOUR BONES ARE BROKEN, SANGORO!!

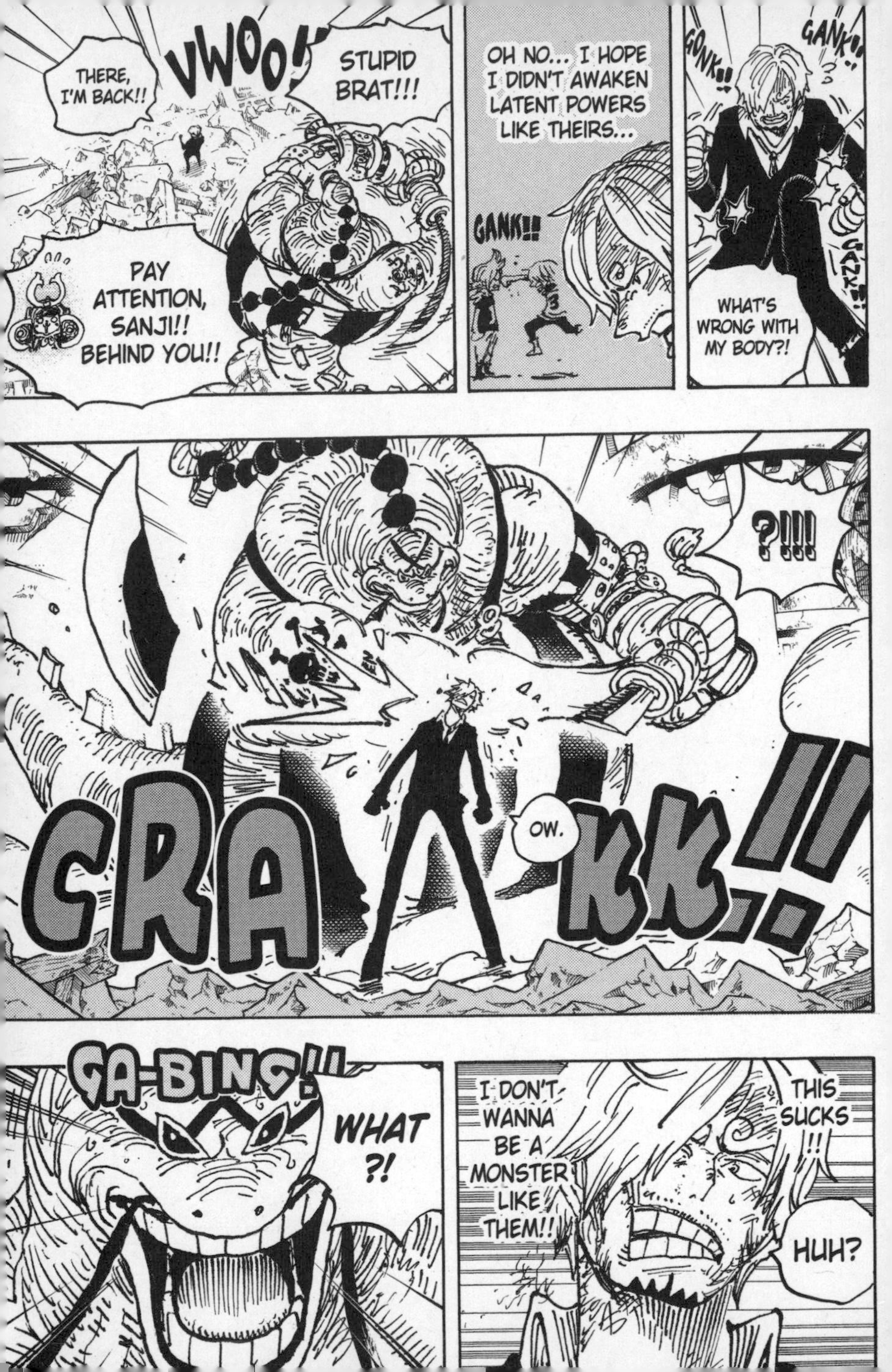
GANK!!
GONK!!
GANK!!
WHAT'S WRONG WITH MY BODY?!
OH NO... I HOPE I DIDN'T AWAKEN LATENT POWERS LIKE THEIRS...
GANK!!
STUPID BRAT!!!
VWOO!
THERE, I'M BACK!!
PAY ATTENTION, SANJI!! BEHIND YOU!!
?!!!
CRAKK!!
OW.
THIS SUCKS!!!
I DON'T WANNA BE A MONSTER LIKE THEM!!
HUH?
GA-BING!!
WHAT?!

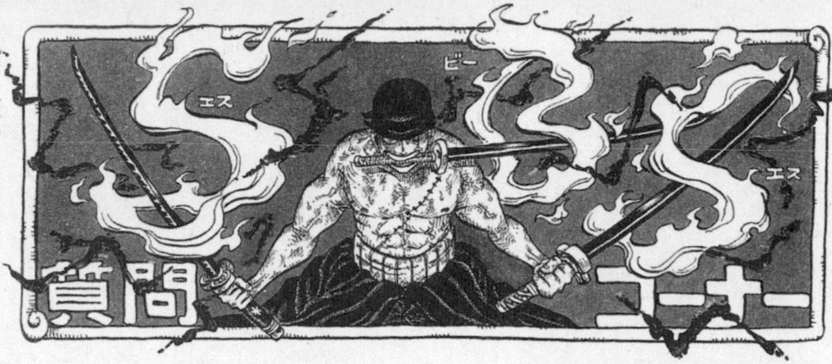

(Kentaro Ito, Gifu)

Q: The scene where Dragon Momo faces off against Dragon Kaido was so stunning and exhilarating!!! Was it based on the painting of twin dragons featured at Kennin-ji Temple, which you mentioned visiting for reference before?

--Tsubocchi

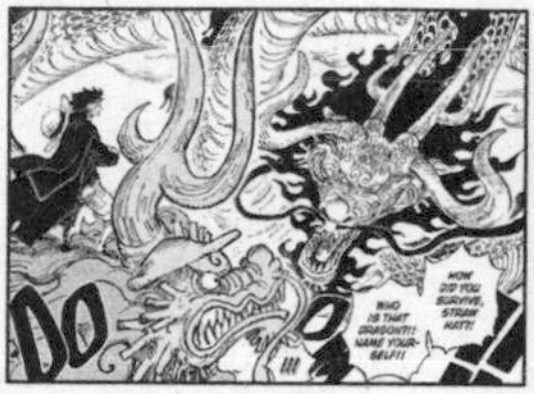
DO

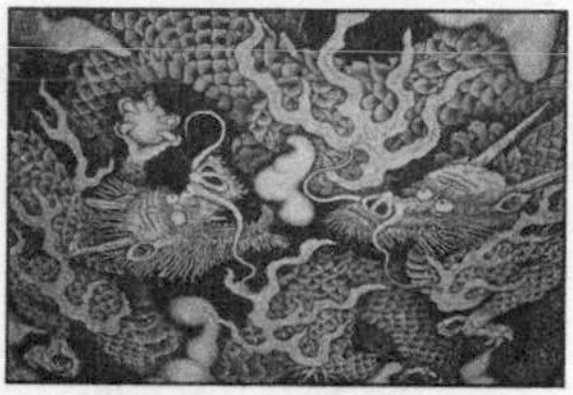

A: That's right. I went to Kyoto before we started the Wano story. I got to see this painting in person. It's a huge thing right on the ceiling, with two gigantic dragons. It totally blew me away. I knew right then and there that I had to draw it!

Q: How does Franky sleep?

--Born on New Year's

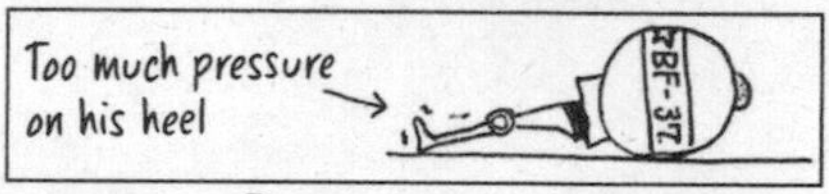
Too much pressure on his heel
BF-37

A: Thank you for the diagram, LOL. No, Franky's just fine. He deploys a cushion called the "Franky Air Bag" from the back of his head and waist, so he can sleep in comfort wherever he wants.

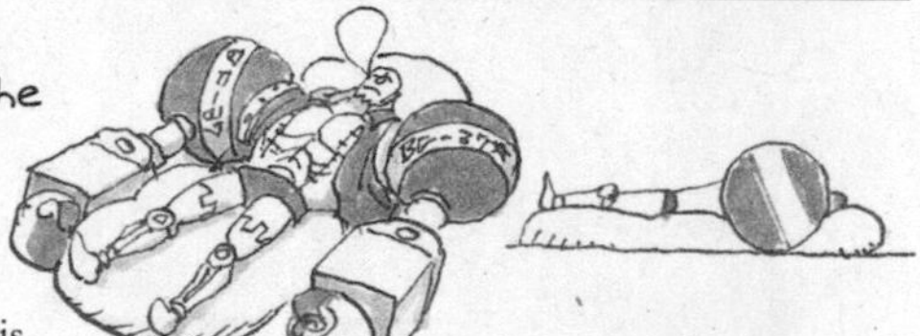

Q: Are those lines on Franky's arms his arm hair?

--Takataka

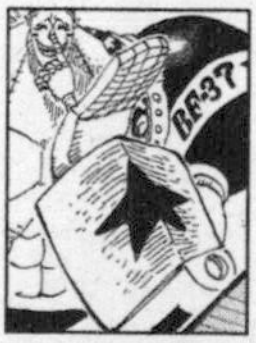
BF-37

A: It's arm hair.

Q: In chapter 1010, Zolo uses the technique "Nine-Sword Style, Asura Blades Drawn, Dead Man's Game." Did that come from the Rakugo story called "Eight Views of Hell, Dead Man's Game"?

--Keima

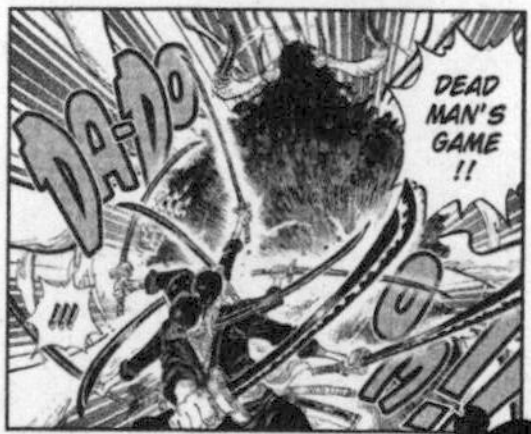
DEAD MAN'S GAME !!

A: That's right! It's another Rakugo reference. Yeah, I know you guys don't usually listen to them! But the title is cool, right?! This story is a famous specialty of Master Beicho Katsura, and it's about going on a sightseeing tourist trip in Hell. It's quite funny.

Chapter 1029:
THE TOWER

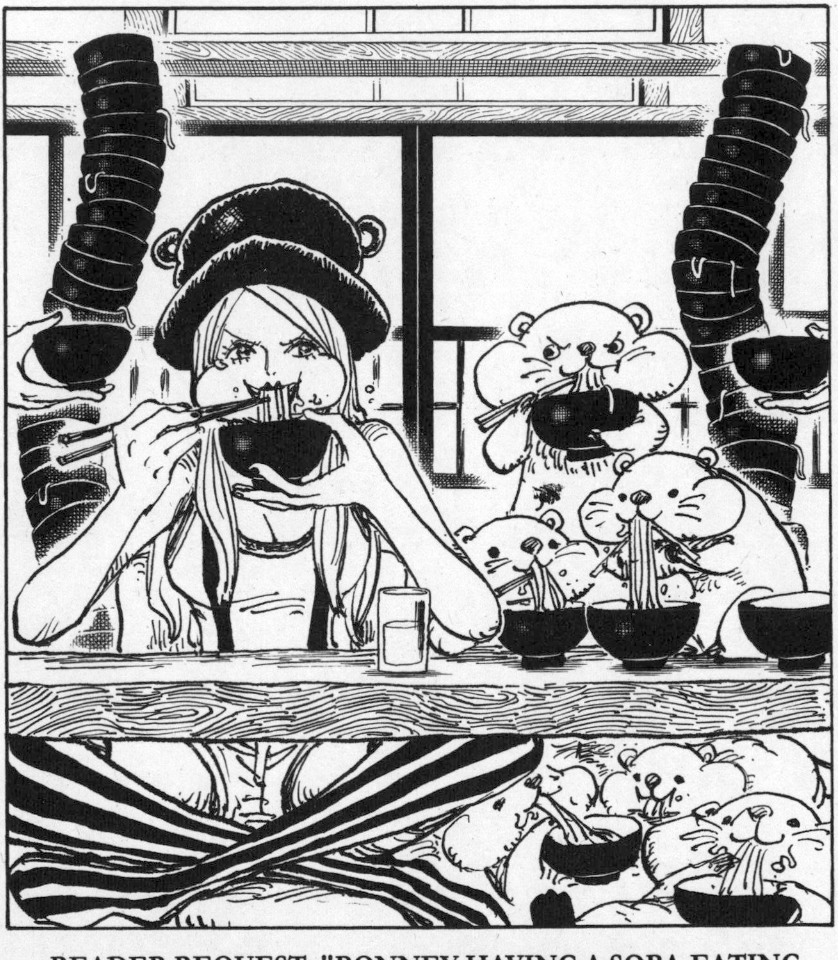

READER REQUEST: "BONNEY HAVING A SOBA-EATING CONTEST WITH SOME OTTERS" BY ARINKO

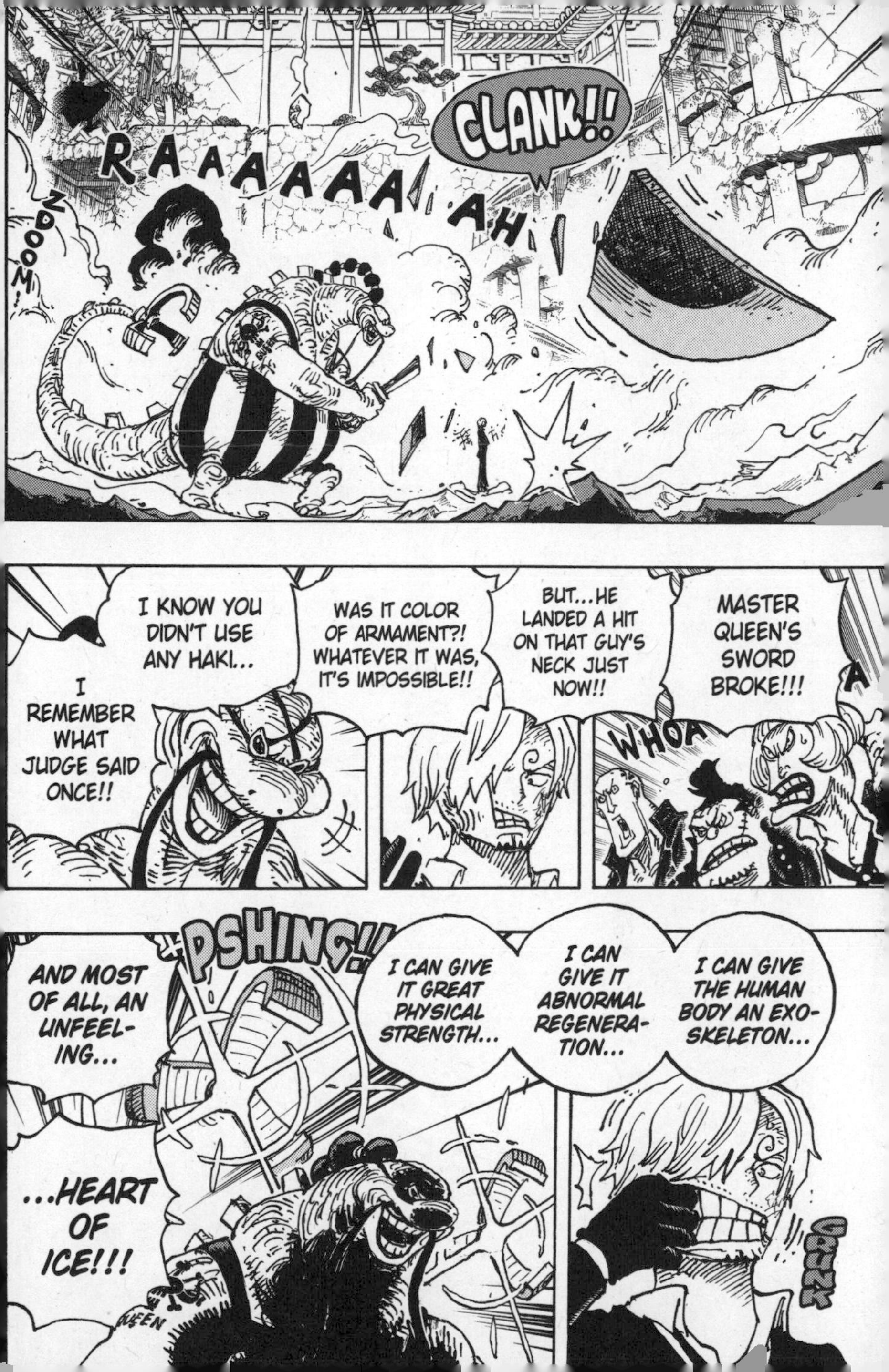
CLANK!!
RAAAAAAAH
ZDOOOM
MASTER QUEEN'S SWORD BROKE!!!
A
WHOA
BUT...HE LANDED A HIT ON THAT GUY'S NECK JUST NOW!!
WAS IT COLOR OF ARMAMENT?! WHATEVER IT WAS, IT'S IMPOSSIBLE!!
I KNOW YOU DIDN'T USE ANY HAKI...
I REMEMBER WHAT JUDGE SAID ONCE!!
I CAN GIVE THE HUMAN BODY AN EXO-SKELETON...
GRINK
I CAN GIVE IT ABNORMAL REGENERA-TION...
I CAN GIVE IT GREAT PHYSICAL STRENGTH...
PSHING!!
AND MOST OF ALL, AN UNFEEL-ING...
...HEART OF ICE!!!

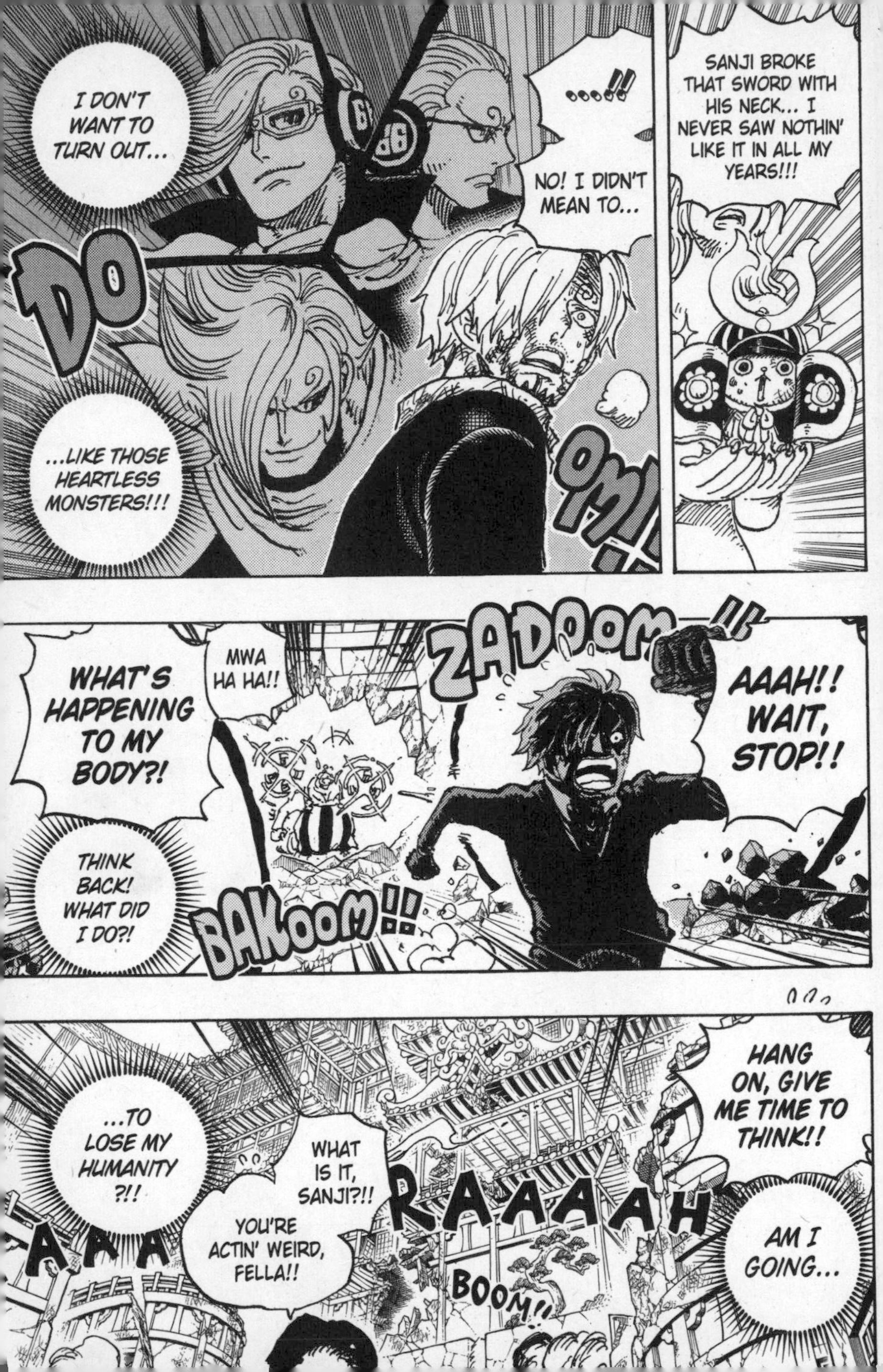
SANJI BROKE THAT SWORD WITH HIS NECK... I NEVER SAW NOTHIN' LIKE IT IN ALL MY YEARS!!!
....!!
NO! I DIDN'T MEAN TO...
I DON'T WANT TO TURN OUT...
DO
OM!!
...LIKE THOSE HEARTLESS MONSTERS!!!
ZADOOM!!
AAAH!! WAIT, STOP!!
MWA HA HA!!
WHAT'S HAPPENING TO MY BODY?!
BAKOOM!!
THINK BACK! WHAT DID I DO?!
HANG ON, GIVE ME TIME TO THINK!!
AM I GOING...
RAAAAH
BOOM!!
WHAT IS IT, SANJI?!!
YOU'RE ACTIN' WEIRD, FELLA!!
...TO LOSE MY HUMANITY ?!!
AAA

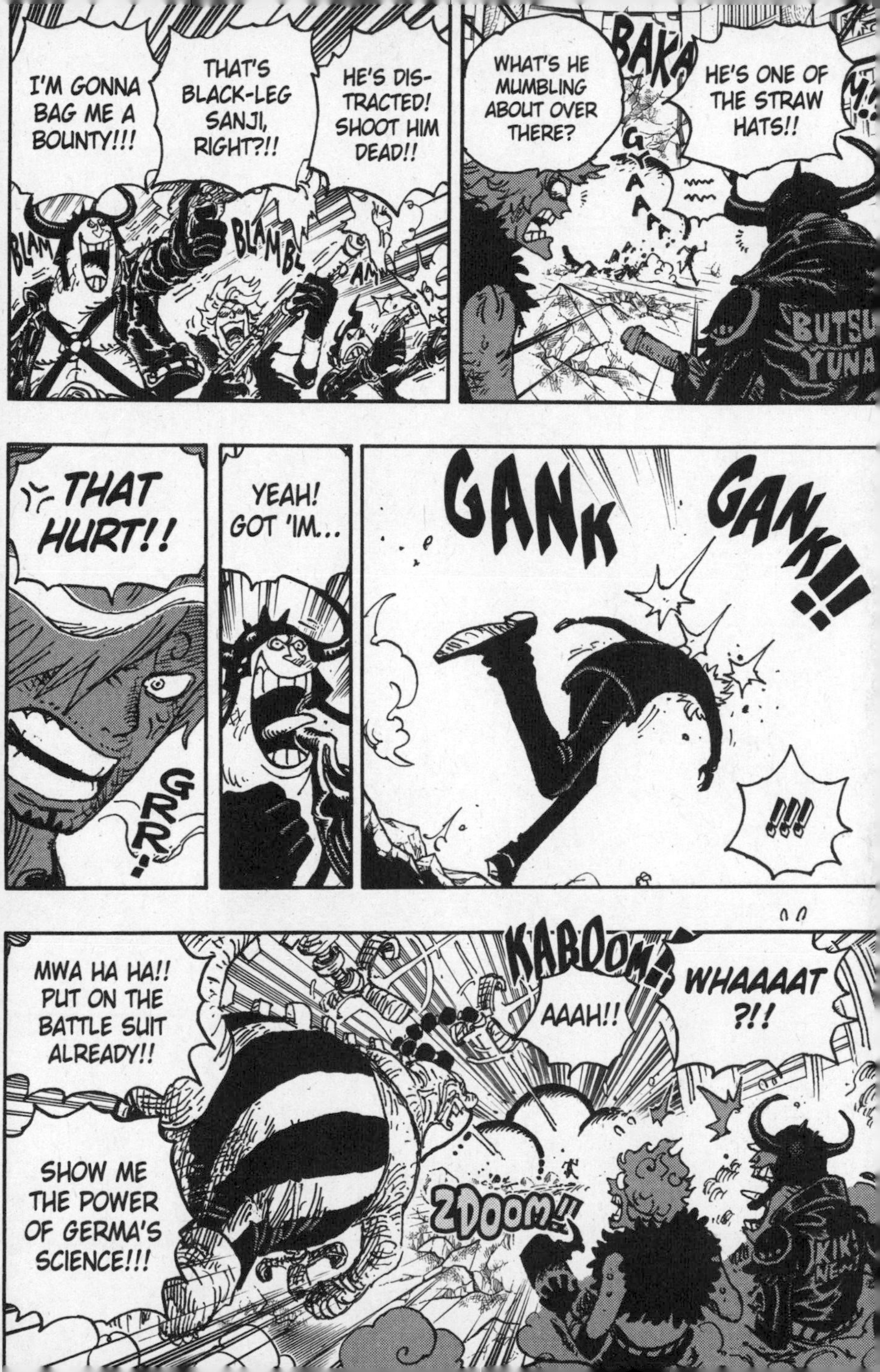
HE'S ONE OF THE STRAW HATS!!
BAKA
WHAT'S HE MUMBLING ABOUT OVER THERE?
GYAAA
BUTSU YUNA
HE'S DIS-TRACTED! SHOOT HIM DEAD!!
THAT'S BLACK-LEG SANJI, RIGHT?!!
I'M GONNA BAG ME A BOUNTY!!!
BLAMBL
BLAM
GANK GANK!!
!!!
YEAH! GOT 'IM...
THAT HURT!!
GRR!
WHAAAAT ?!!
AAAH!!
KABOOM!!
MWA HA HA!! PUT ON THE BATTLE SUIT ALREADY!!
SHOW ME THE POWER OF GERMA'S SCIENCE!!!
ZDOOM!!

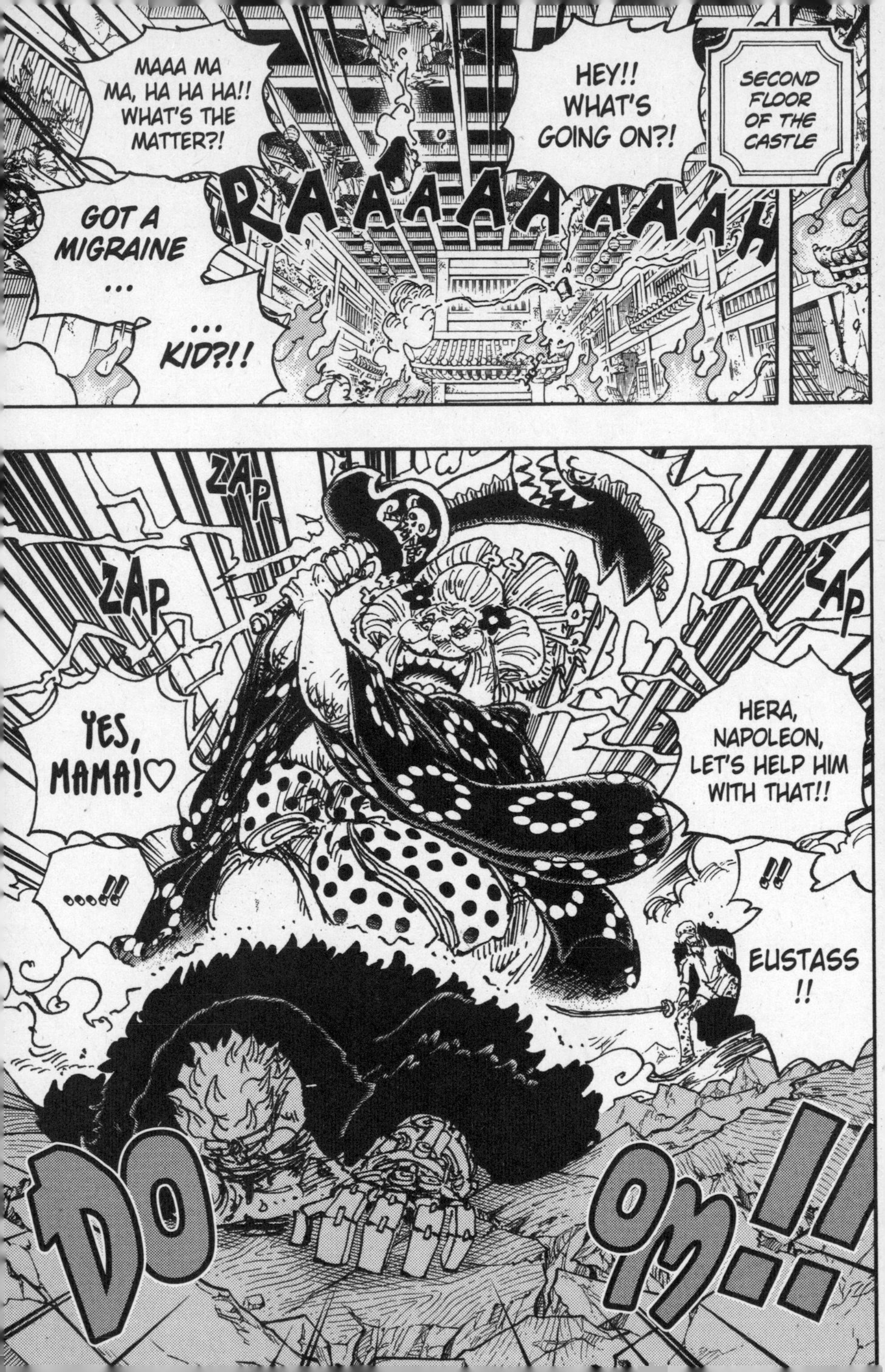
SECOND FLOOR OF THE CASTLE
HEY!! WHAT'S GOING ON?!
RAAAAAAAAH
MAAA MA MA, HA HA HA!! WHAT'S THE MATTER?!
GOT A MIGRAINE ...
... KID?!!
ZAP
HERA, NAPOLEON, LET'S HELP HIM WITH THAT!!
ZAP
ZAP
YES, MAMA!♡
!!
...!!
EUSTASS !!
DOOM..!!

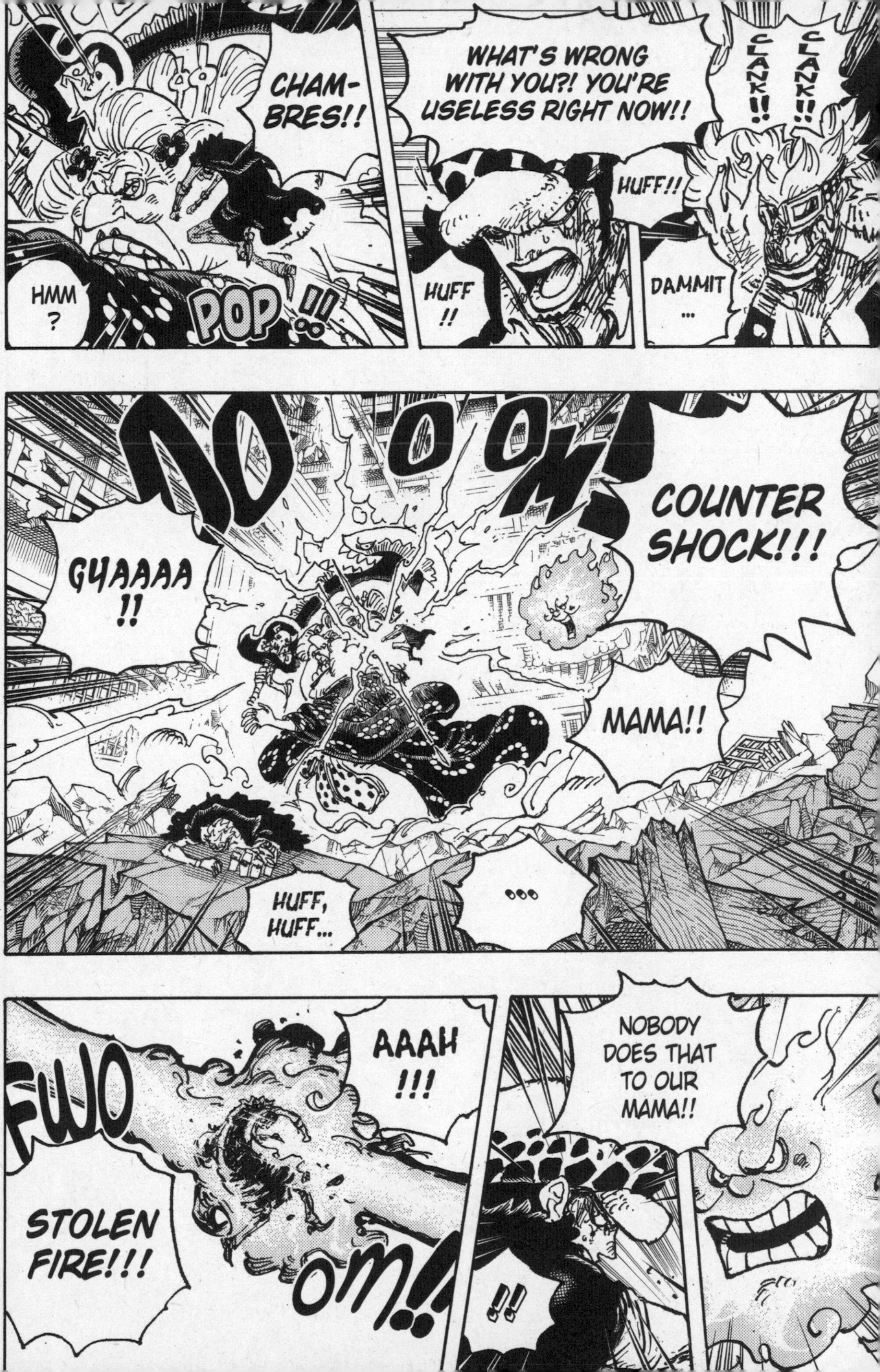
CLANK!!
CLANK!!
DAMMIT...
WHAT'S WRONG WITH YOU?! YOU'RE USELESS RIGHT NOW!!
HUFF!!
HUFF!!
CHAM-BRES!!
HMM?
POP!!
COUNTER SHOCK!!!
GYAAAA!!
MAMA!!
...
HUFF, HUFF...
NOBODY DOES THAT TO OUR MAMA!!
!!
AAAH!!!
FWO
STOLEN FIRE!!!
OM!!

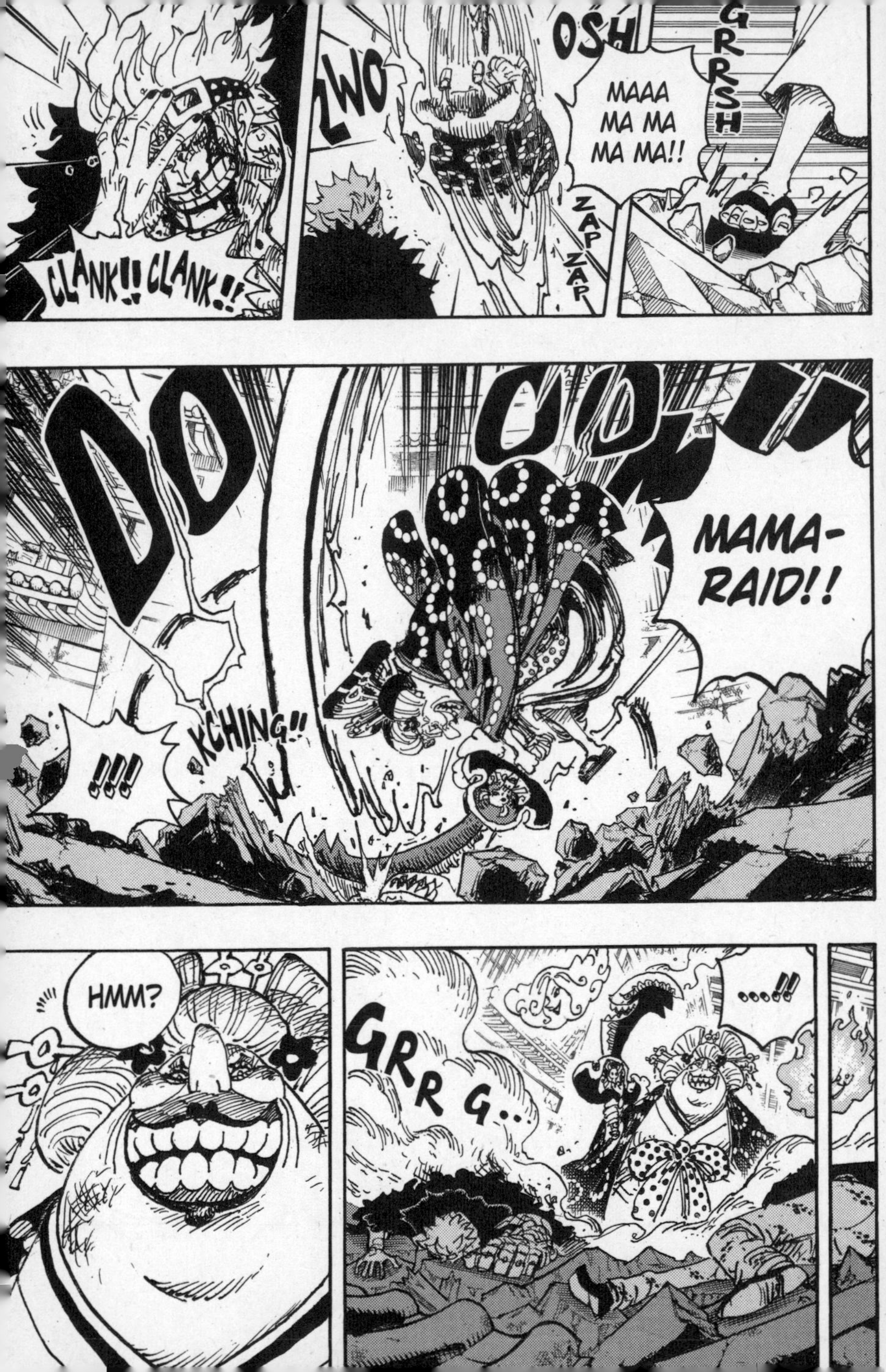

GRRSH
MAAA MA MA MA MA!!
ZWO OSH
ZAP ZAP
CLANK!! CLANK!!
MAMA-RAID!!
DOOO
KCHING!!
!!!
...!!
GRRRG...
HMM?

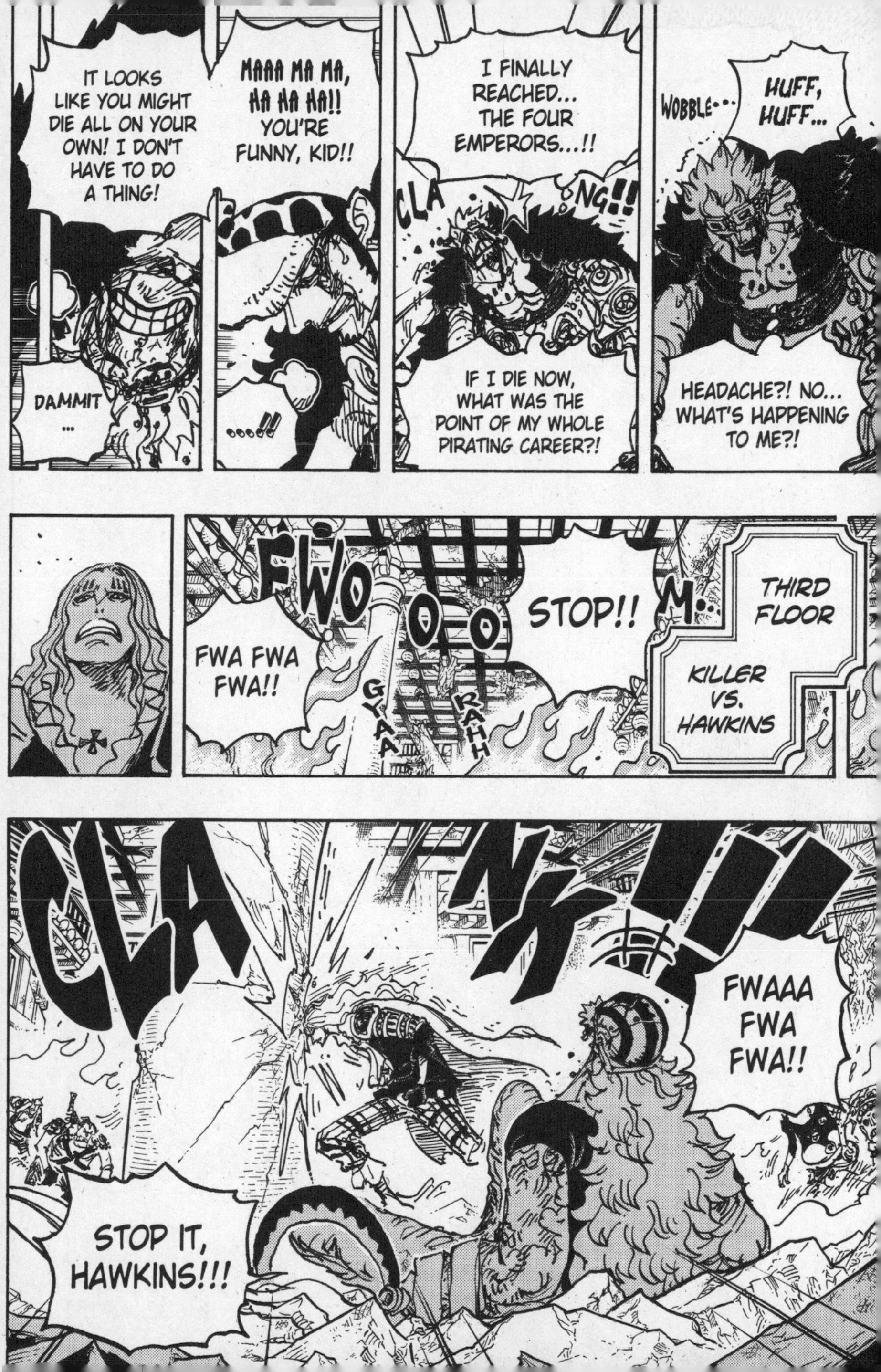
WOBBLE...
HUFF, HUFF...
HEADACHE?! NO... WHAT'S HAPPENING TO ME?!
I FINALLY REACHED... THE FOUR EMPERORS...!!
CLANG!!
IF I DIE NOW, WHAT WAS THE POINT OF MY WHOLE PIRATING CAREER?!
MAAAA MA MA, HA HA HA!! YOU'RE FUNNY, KID!!
....!!
IT LOOKS LIKE YOU MIGHT DIE ALL ON YOUR OWN! I DON'T HAVE TO DO A THING!
DAMMIT ...
THIRD FLOOR
KILLER VS. HAWKINS
FWOOOM..
STOP!!
FWA FWA FWA!!
GYAA
RAHH
CLANK!!
FWAAA FWA FWA!!
STOP IT, HAWKINS!!!

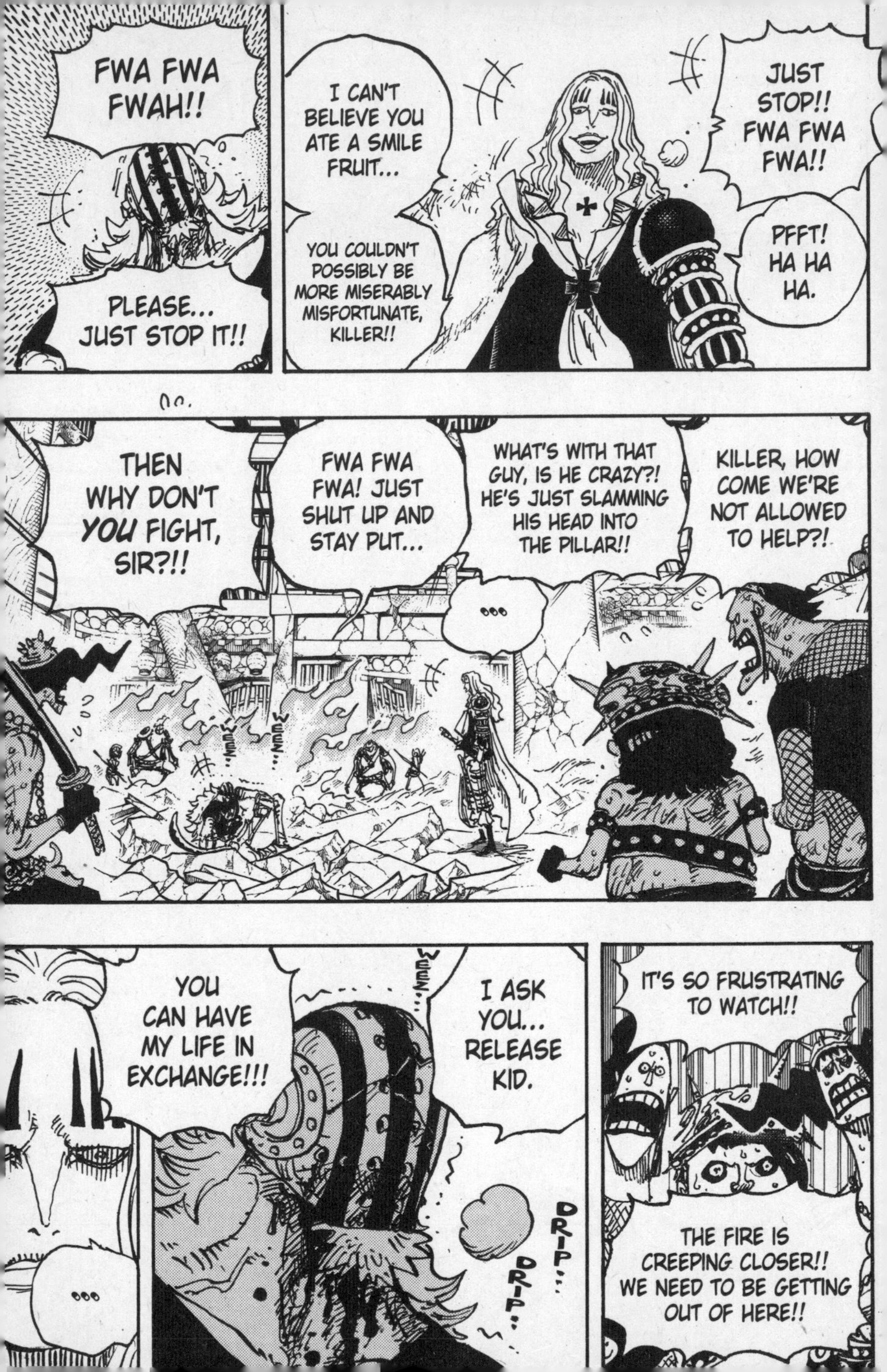
JUST STOP!! FWA FWA FWA!!
PFFT! HA HA HA.
I CAN'T BELIEVE YOU ATE A SMILE FRUIT...
YOU COULDN'T POSSIBLY BE MORE MISERABLY MISFORTUNATE, KILLER!!
FWA FWA FWAH!!
PLEASE... JUST STOP IT!!
KILLER, HOW COME WE'RE NOT ALLOWED TO HELP?!
WHAT'S WITH THAT GUY, IS HE CRAZY?! HE'S JUST SLAMMING HIS HEAD INTO THE PILLAR!!
FWA FWA FWA! JUST SHUT UP AND STAY PUT...
THEN WHY DON'T *YOU* FIGHT, SIR?!!
...
WEEZ...
WEEZ...
IT'S SO FRUSTRATING TO WATCH!!
THE FIRE IS CREEPING CLOSER!! WE NEED TO BE GETTING OUT OF HERE!!
I ASK YOU... RELEASE KID.
WEEZ...
YOU CAN HAVE MY LIFE IN EXCHANGE!!!
DRIP...
DRIP...
...

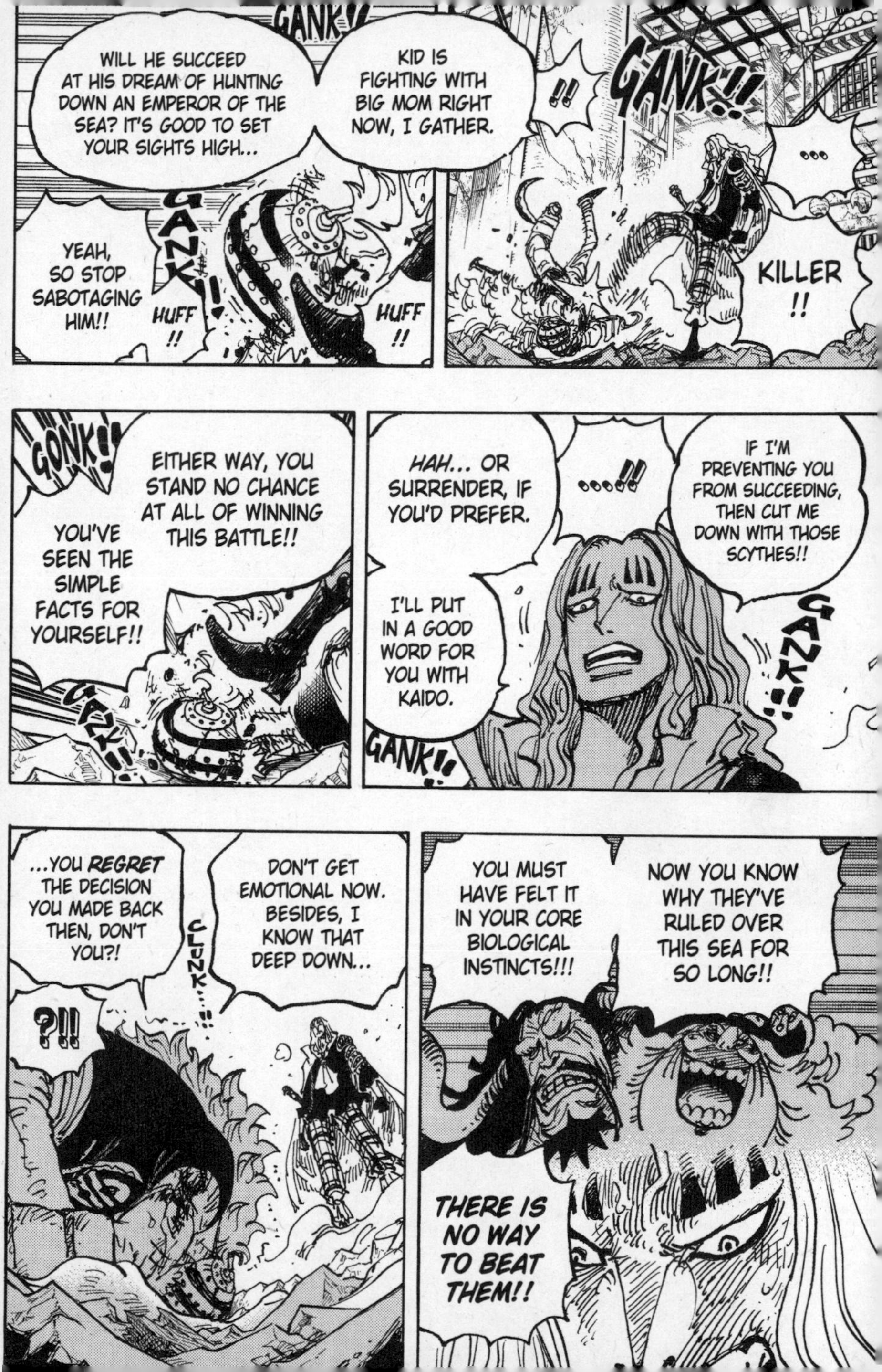
GANK!!
KID IS FIGHTING WITH BIG MOM RIGHT NOW, I GATHER.
!!
...
KILLER!!
GANK!!
WILL HE SUCCEED AT HIS DREAM OF HUNTING DOWN AN EMPEROR OF THE SEA? IT'S GOOD TO SET YOUR SIGHTS HIGH...
GANK!!
HUFF!!
HUFF!!
YEAH, SO STOP SABOTAGING HIM!!
IF I'M PREVENTING YOU FROM SUCCEEDING, THEN CUT ME DOWN WITH THOSE SCYTHES!!
...!!
HAH... OR SURRENDER, IF YOU'D PREFER.
I'LL PUT IN A GOOD WORD FOR YOU WITH KAIDO.
GANK!!
GANK!!
GONK!!
EITHER WAY, YOU STAND NO CHANCE AT ALL OF WINNING THIS BATTLE!!
YOU'VE SEEN THE SIMPLE FACTS FOR YOURSELF!!
NOW YOU KNOW WHY THEY'VE RULED OVER THIS SEA FOR SO LONG!!
YOU MUST HAVE FELT IT IN YOUR CORE BIOLOGICAL INSTINCTS!!!
THERE IS NO WAY TO BEAT THEM!!
DON'T GET EMOTIONAL NOW. BESIDES, I KNOW THAT DEEP DOWN...
...YOU ***REGRET*** THE DECISION YOU MADE BACK THEN, DON'T YOU?!
CLUNK...!!
?!!

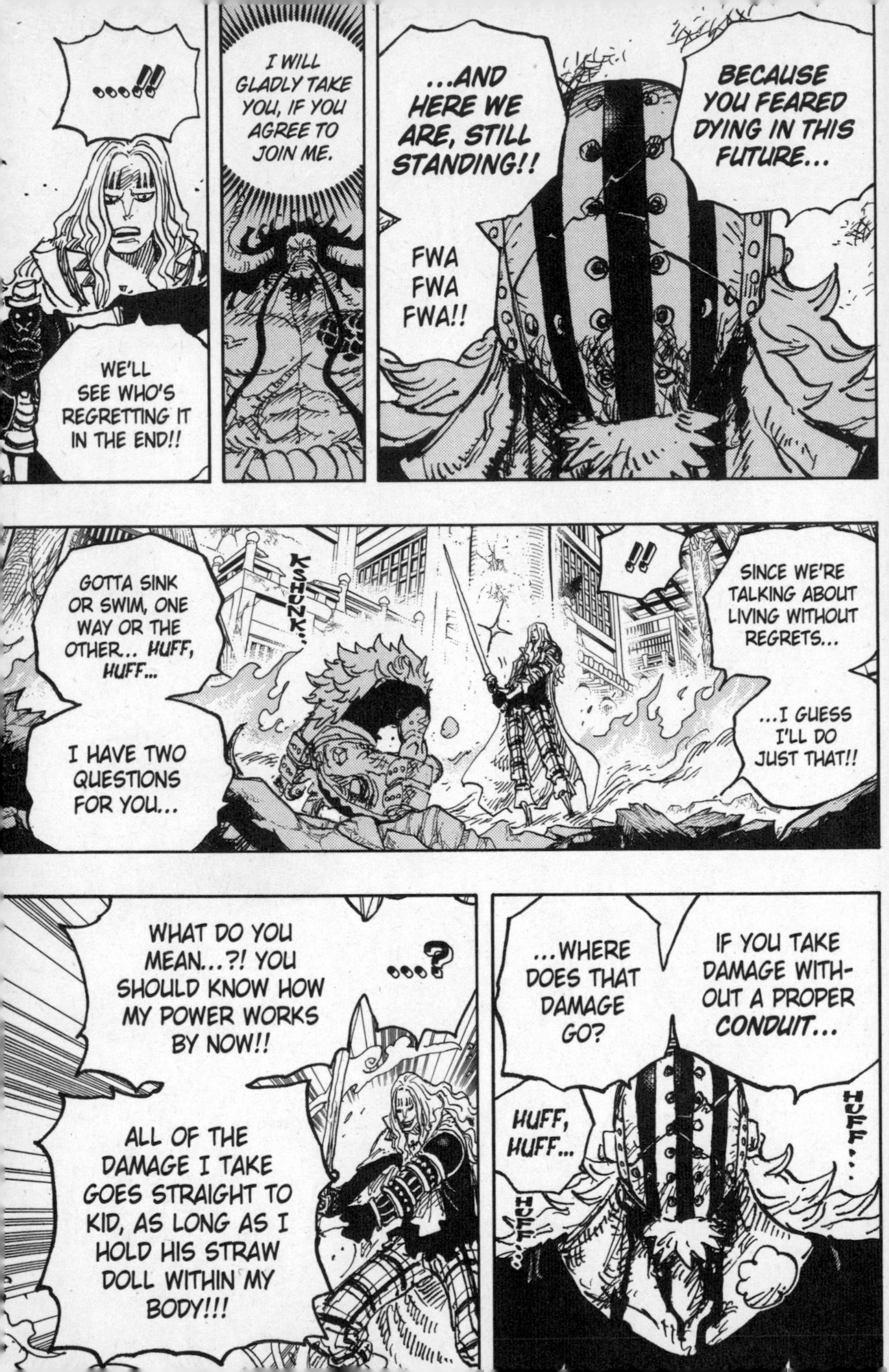
BECAUSE YOU FEARED DYING IN THIS FUTURE...
...AND HERE WE ARE, STILL STANDING!!
FWA FWA FWA!!
I WILL GLADLY TAKE YOU, IF YOU AGREE TO JOIN ME.
...!!
WE'LL SEE WHO'S REGRETTING IT IN THE END!!
!!
SINCE WE'RE TALKING ABOUT LIVING WITHOUT REGRETS...
...I GUESS I'LL DO JUST THAT!!
KSHUNK...
GOTTA SINK OR SWIM, ONE WAY OR THE OTHER... HUFF, HUFF...
I HAVE TWO QUESTIONS FOR YOU...
IF YOU TAKE DAMAGE WITH-OUT A PROPER CONDUIT...
...WHERE DOES THAT DAMAGE GO?
HUFF...
HUFF, HUFF...
HUFF...
...?
WHAT DO YOU MEAN...?! YOU SHOULD KNOW HOW MY POWER WORKS BY NOW!!
ALL OF THE DAMAGE I TAKE GOES STRAIGHT TO KID, AS LONG AS I HOLD HIS STRAW DOLL WITHIN MY BODY!!!

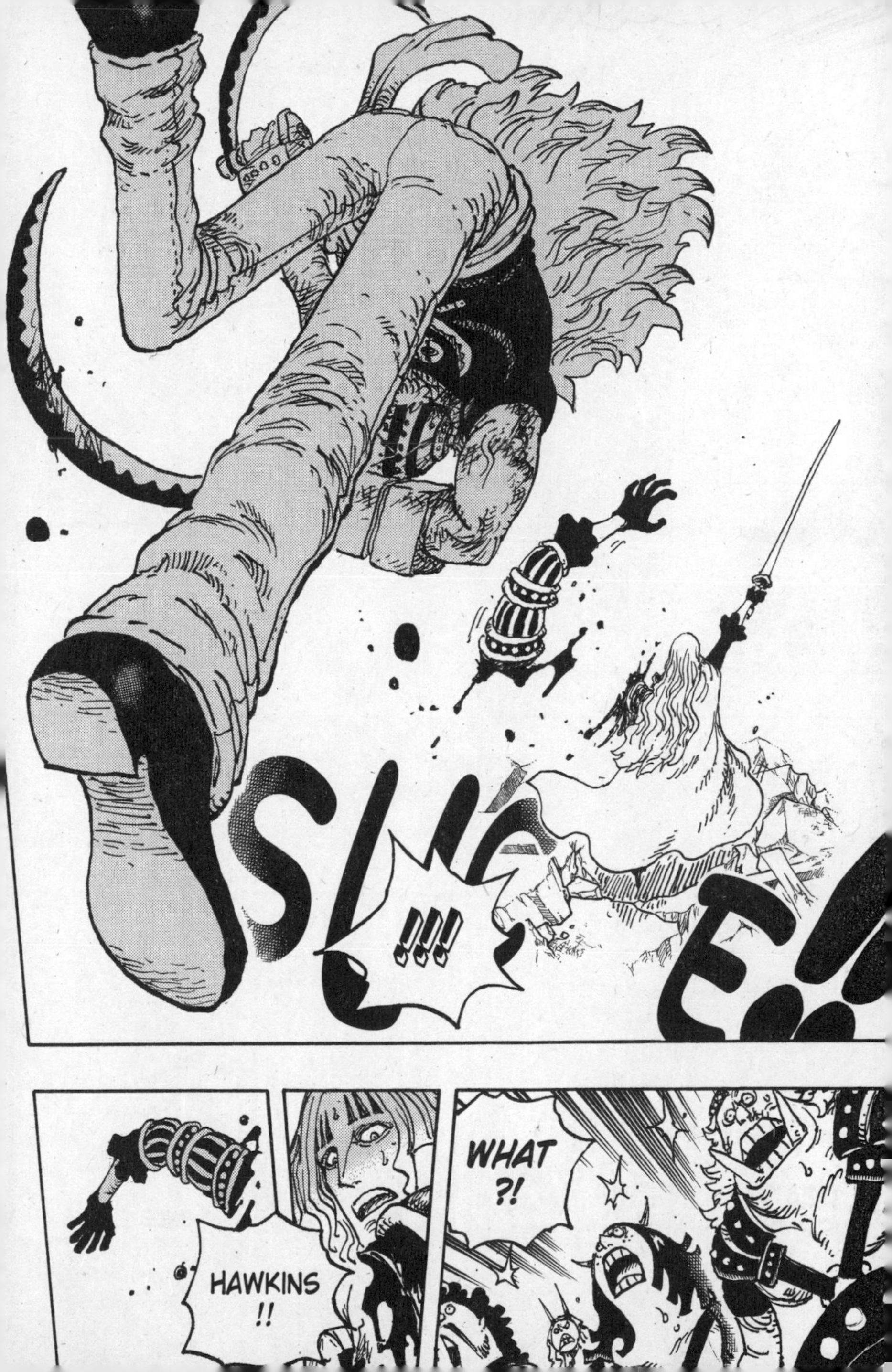
WHAT ?!
HAWKINS !!

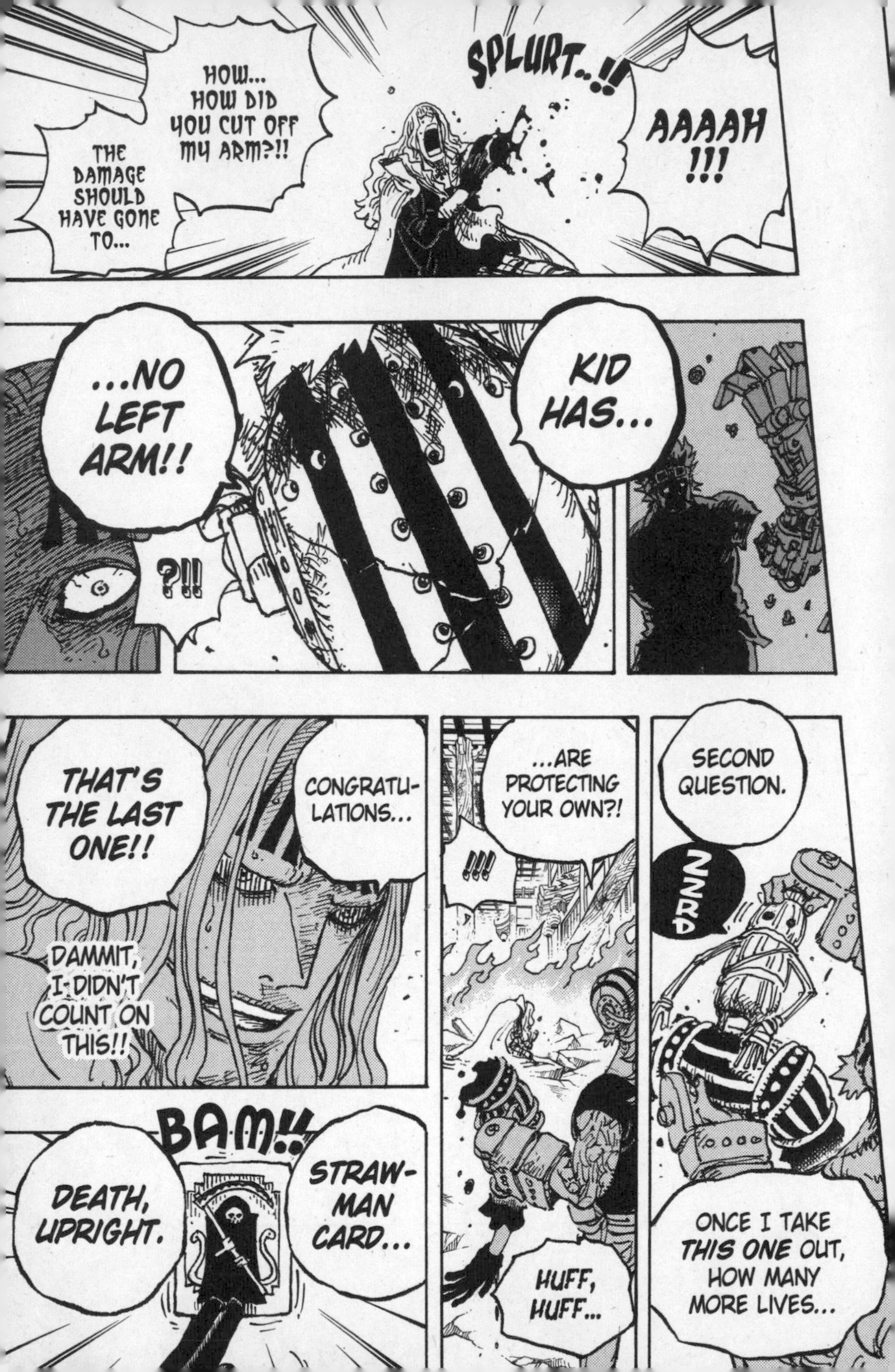
SPLURT..!!
AAAAH !!!
HOW... HOW DID YOU CUT OFF MY ARM?!!
THE DAMAGE SHOULD HAVE GONE TO...
KID HAS...
...NO LEFT ARM!!
?!!
SECOND QUESTION.
ZZRD
ONCE I TAKE THIS ONE OUT, HOW MANY MORE LIVES...
...ARE PROTECTING YOUR OWN?!
!!!
HUFF, HUFF...
CONGRATULATIONS...
THAT'S THE LAST ONE!!
DAMMIT, I DIDN'T COUNT ON THIS!!
BAM!!
STRAW-MAN CARD...
DEATH, UPRIGHT.

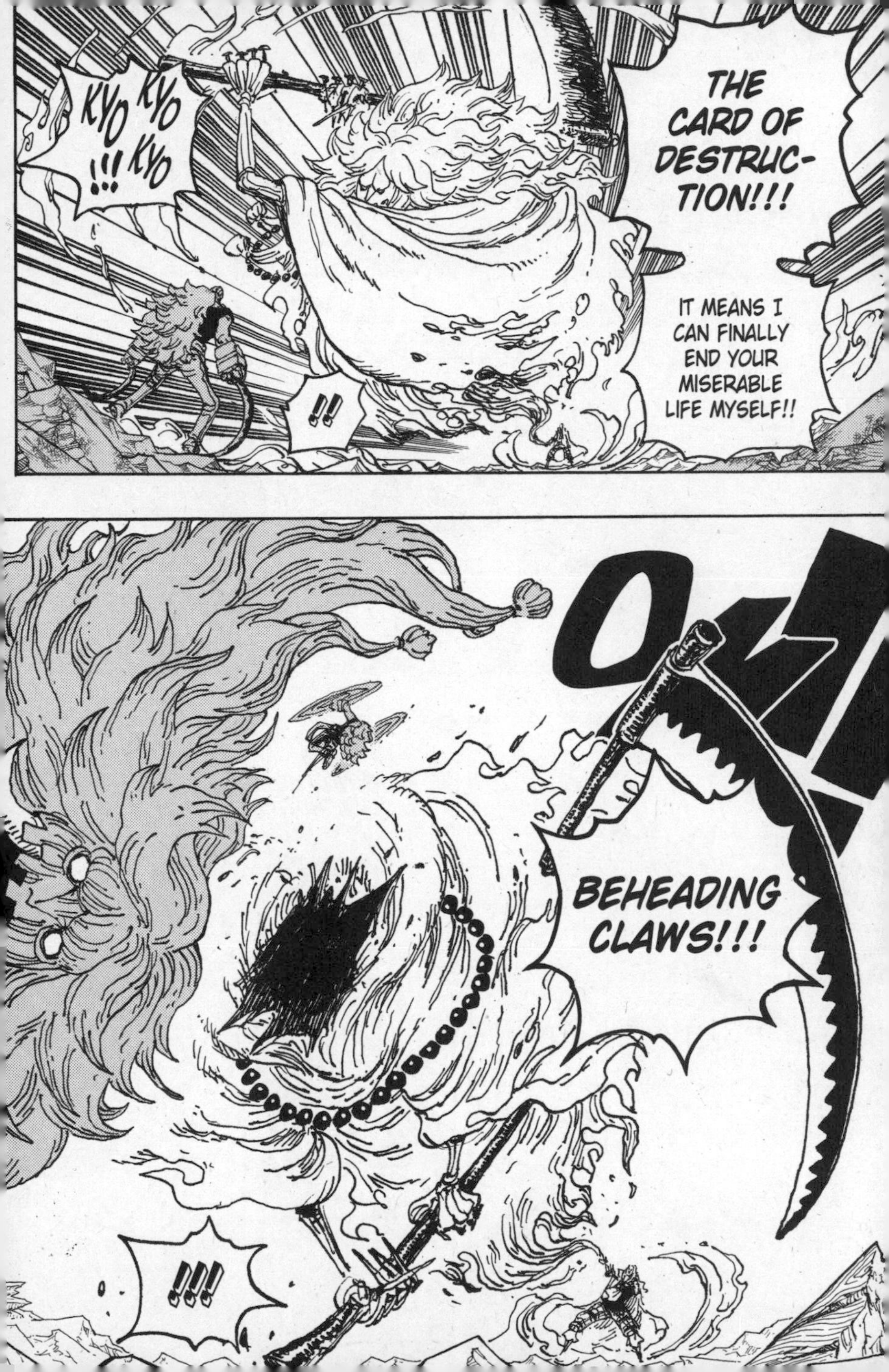
THE CARD OF DESTRUCTION!!!
IT MEANS I CAN FINALLY END YOUR MISERABLE LIFE MYSELF!!
KYO KYO KYO KYO!!!
!!
BEHEADING CLAWS!!!
!!!

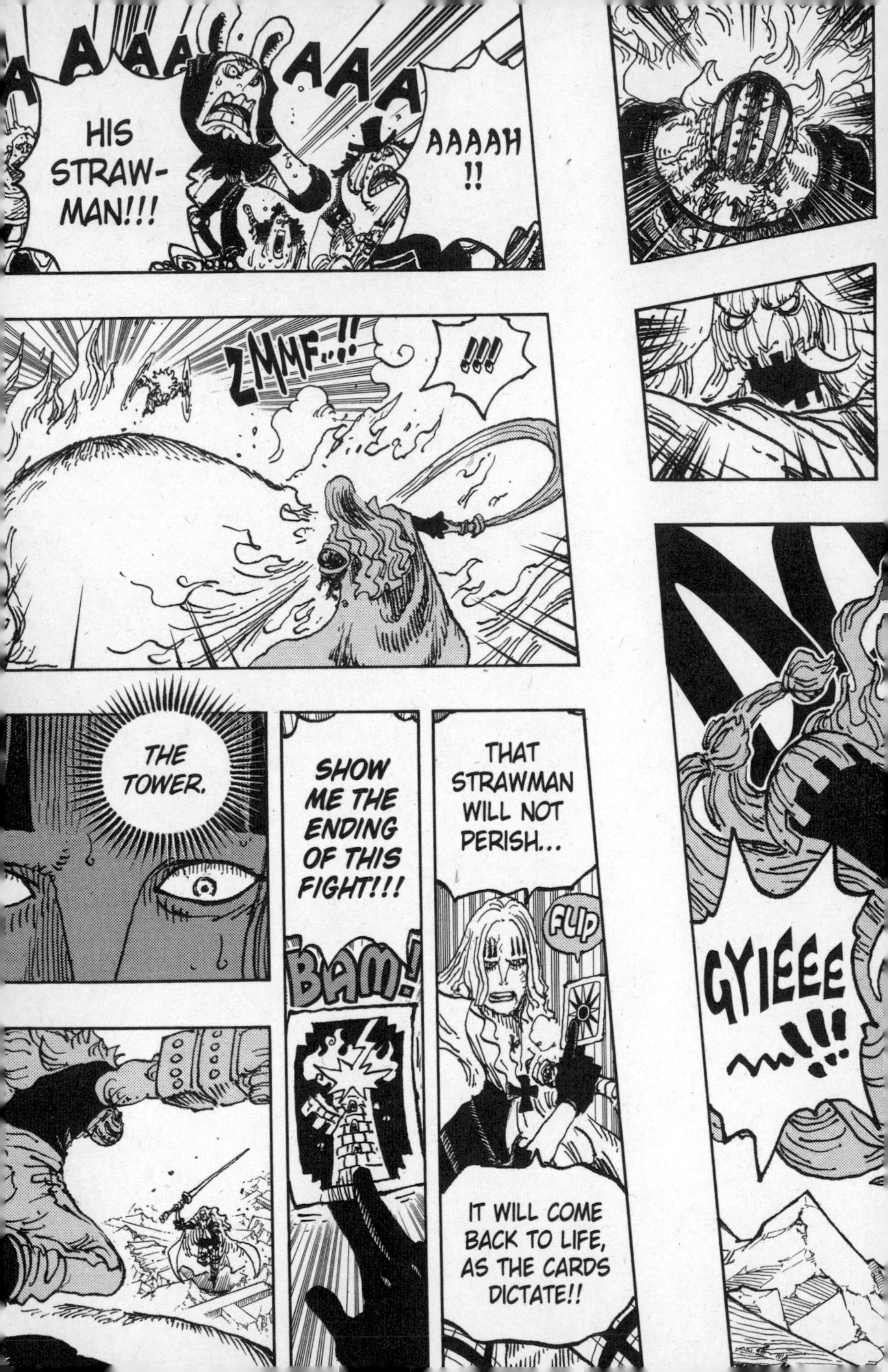

AAAAH !!
AAAAAAA
HIS STRAW-MAN!!!
!!!
ZMMF..!!
GYIEEE!!!
THAT STRAWMAN WILL NOT PERISH...
FLIP
IT WILL COME BACK TO LIFE, AS THE CARDS DICTATE!!
SHOW ME THE ENDING OF THIS FIGHT!!!
BAM!
THE TOWER.

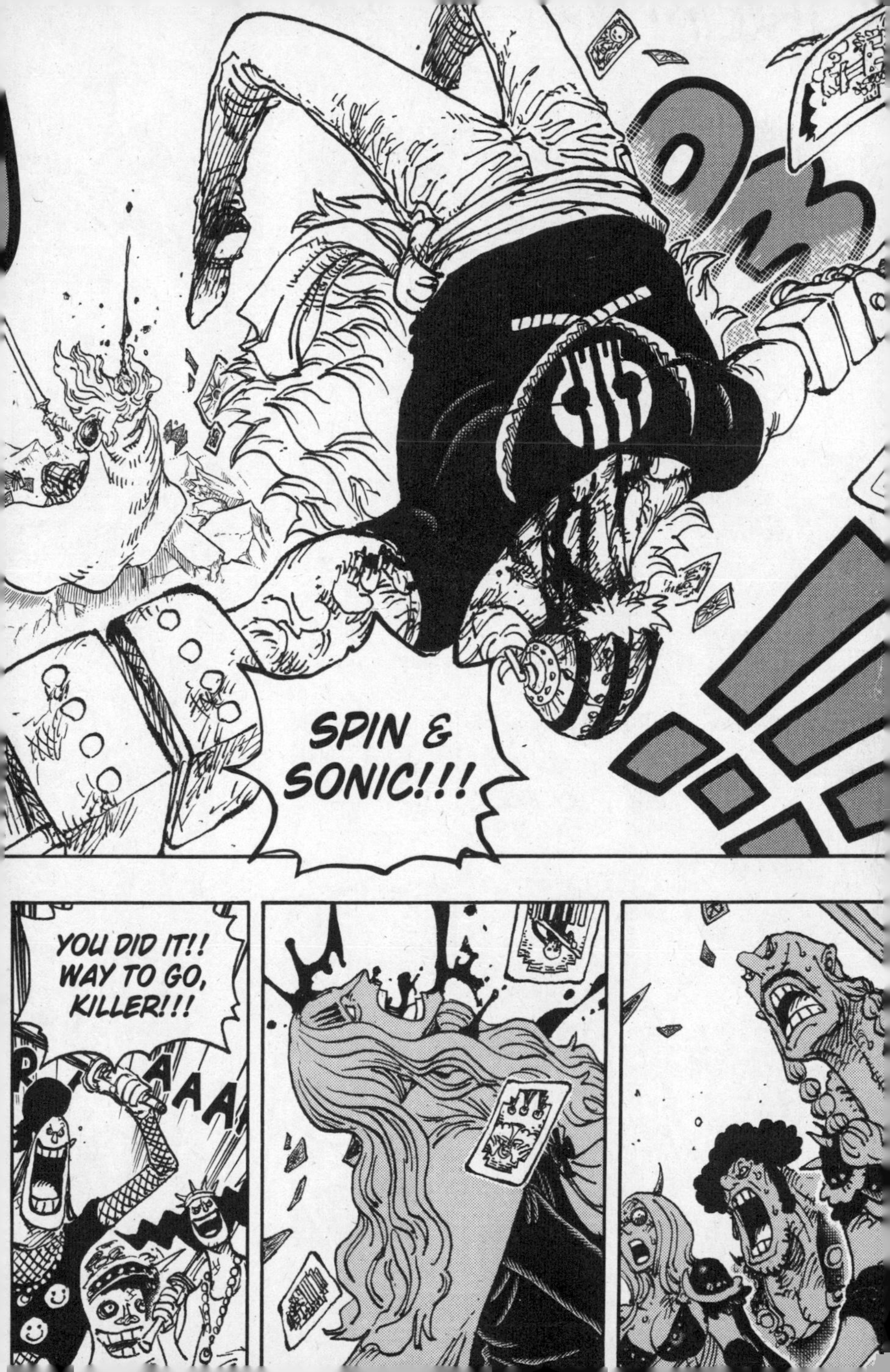
SPIN & SONIC!!!
YOU DID IT!! WAY TO GO, KILLER!!!

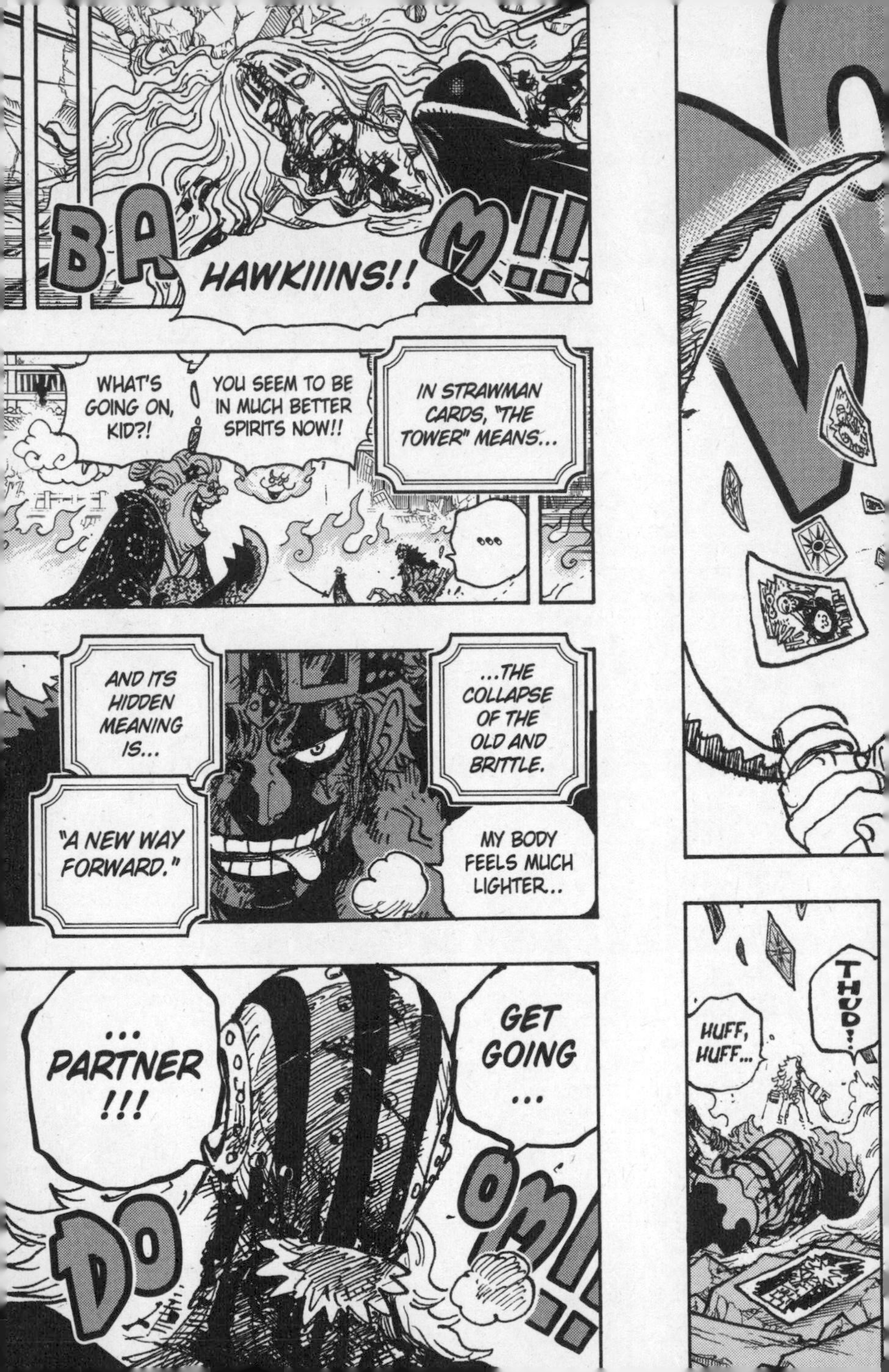
THUD!!
HUFF, HUFF...
BAM!!
HAWKIIINS!!
IN STRAWMAN CARDS, "THE TOWER" MEANS...
YOU SEEM TO BE IN MUCH BETTER SPIRITS NOW!!
WHAT'S GOING ON, KID?!
...
...THE COLLAPSE OF THE OLD AND BRITTLE.
AND ITS HIDDEN MEANING IS...
MY BODY FEELS MUCH LIGHTER...
"A NEW WAY FORWARD."
GET GOING ...
... PARTNER !!!
DOOM!!

SBS Question Corner

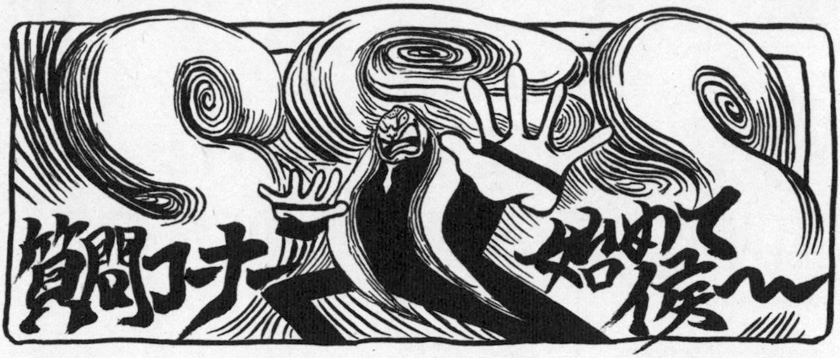
質問コーナー始めて候〜

(Hoya, Tokyo)

Q: Heso, Oda Sensei! My nose has grown every time I tell a lie for years, but I still haven't gotten it as long as Usopp's! With that said, please tell us the Top Five Longest Noses and Usopp's nose length too!!

--Toy Bakery

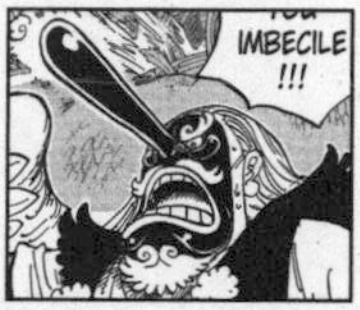
IMBECILE
!!!

A: Interesting. You gave me a list of long-nosed characters from the series, but I'm going to exclude Tenguyama Hitetsu and the giants.

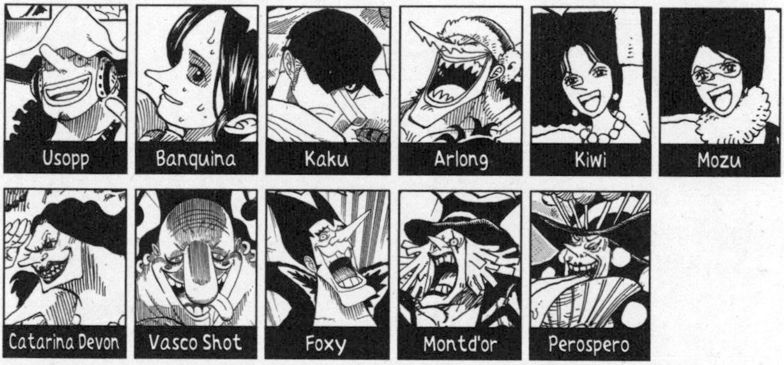
Usopp
Banquina
Kaku
Arlong
Kiwi
Mozu
Catarina Devon
Vasco Shot
Foxy
Montd'or
Perospero

Starting from number five! It's **Kaku**! Next in fourth, **Usopp**!! Hmm, too bad. He just can't make up for the gap in height and facial size with some of these others! And since you asked, Usopp's nose is 5.1 inches! In third, **Catarina Devon**! Number Two is **Arlong**! And our long-nose champion is... **Vasco Shot**!! The world is a vast place. I wonder if we'll meet someone who will set a new record!!

Q: I would like to be Onami's follower. So may I have those two large millet dumplings hanging from Onami's chest?

--Sanadacchi

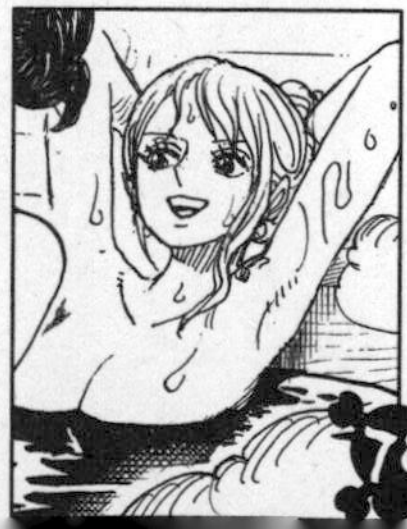

A: Oh, it's you, Sanada. What's that? You want millet dumplings? From Onami's... chest...
Get out of here!!! ゴム

Chapter 1030:
ECHOING THE IMPERMANENCE OF ALL THINGS

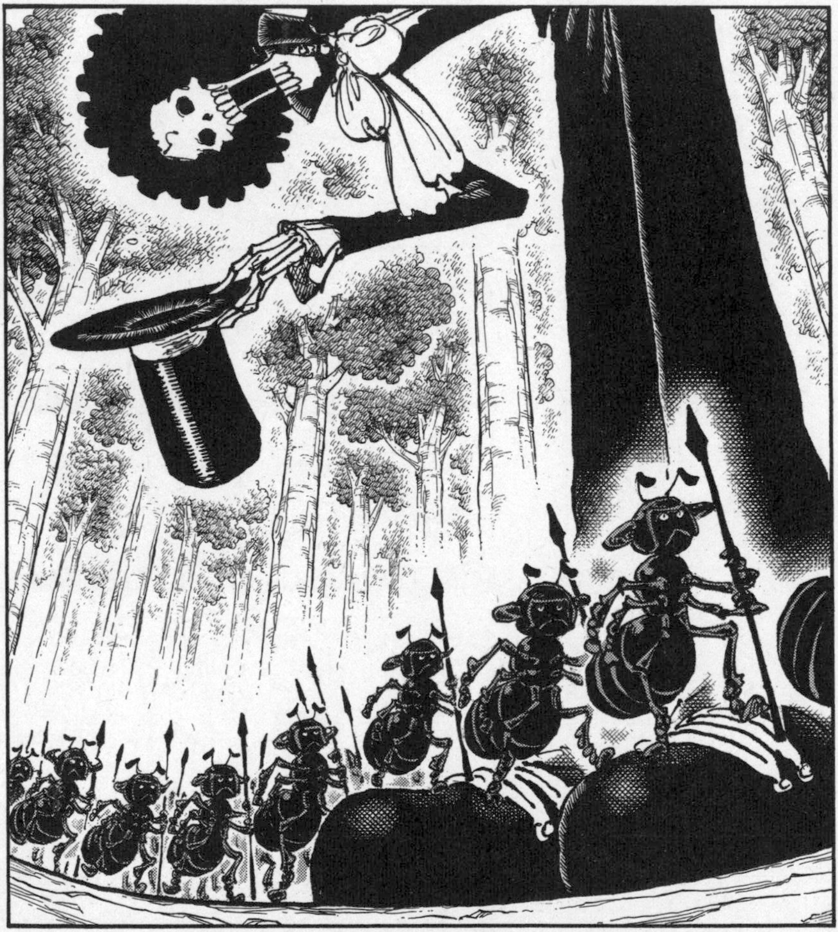

READER REQUEST: "BROOK CAREFUL NOT TO STEP ON A LINE OF ARMY ANTS" BY EBI

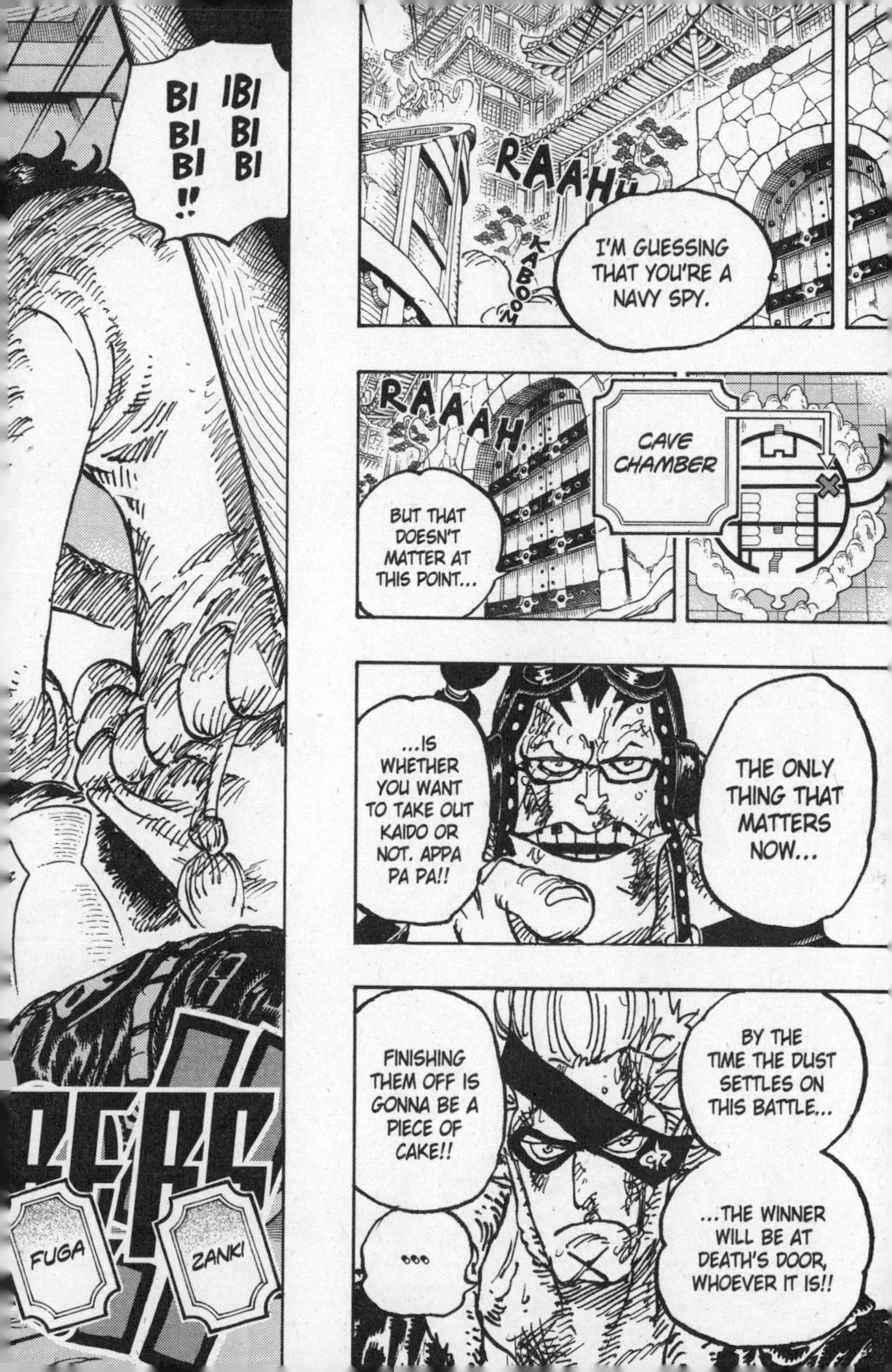
RAAHH
KABOOM
I'M GUESSING THAT YOU'RE A NAVY SPY.
CAVE CHAMBER
RAAAH
BUT THAT DOESN'T MATTER AT THIS POINT...
THE ONLY THING THAT MATTERS NOW...
...IS WHETHER YOU WANT TO TAKE OUT KAIDO OR NOT. APPA PA PA!!
BY THE TIME THE DUST SETTLES ON THIS BATTLE...
...THE WINNER WILL BE AT DEATH'S DOOR, WHOEVER IT IS!!
FINISHING THEM OFF IS GONNA BE A PIECE OF CAKE!!
...
IBI BI BI
BI BI BI!!
ZANKI
FUGA

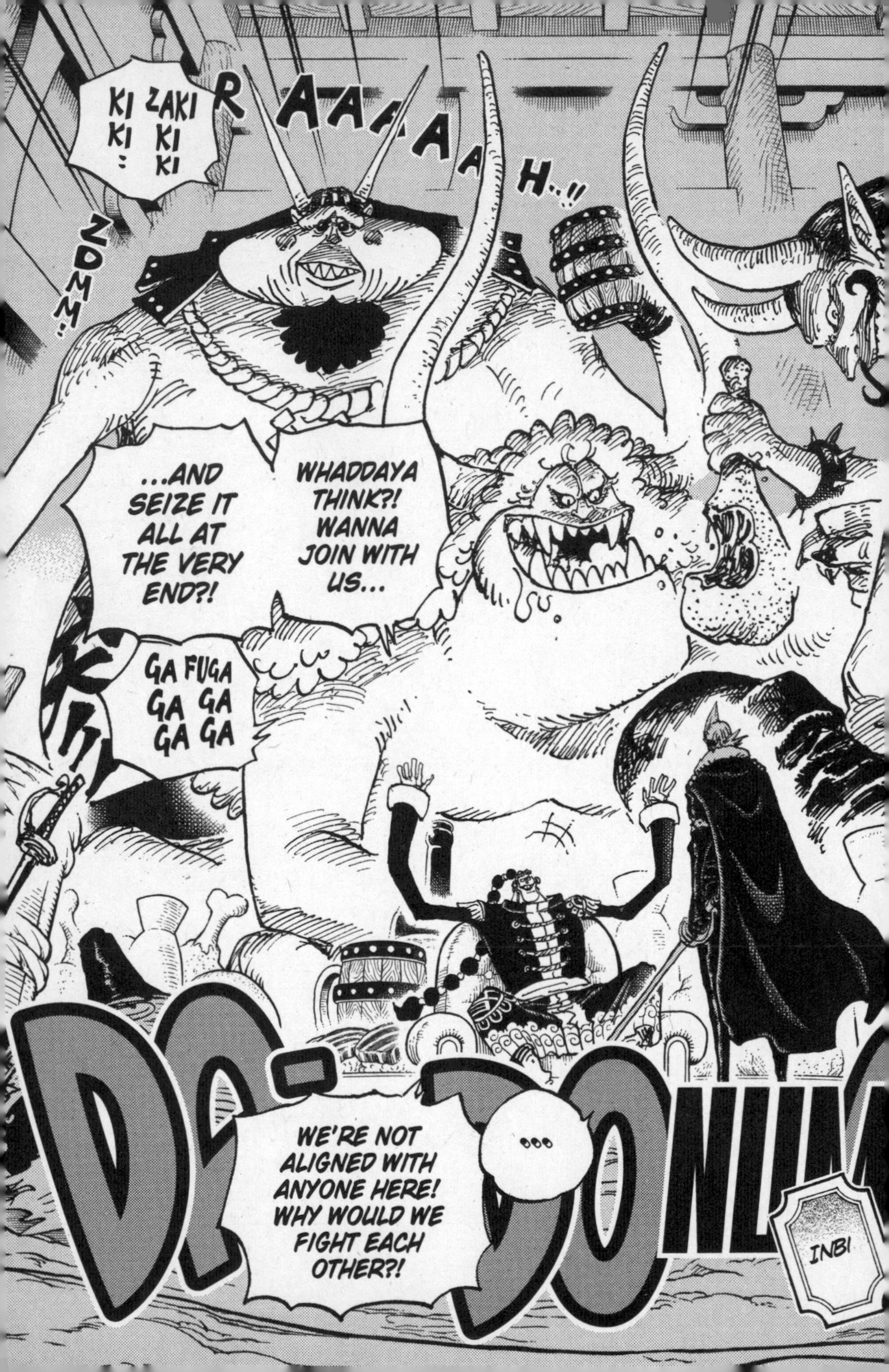
RAAAAAAH..!!
ZAKI KI KI KI KI..
ZOMM..!
WHADDAYA THINK?! WANNA JOIN WITH US...
...AND SEIZE IT ALL AT THE VERY END?!
GA FUGA GA GA GA GA
DO-DOOM
...
WE'RE NOT ALIGNED WITH ANYONE HERE! WHY WOULD WE FIGHT EACH OTHER?!
INBI

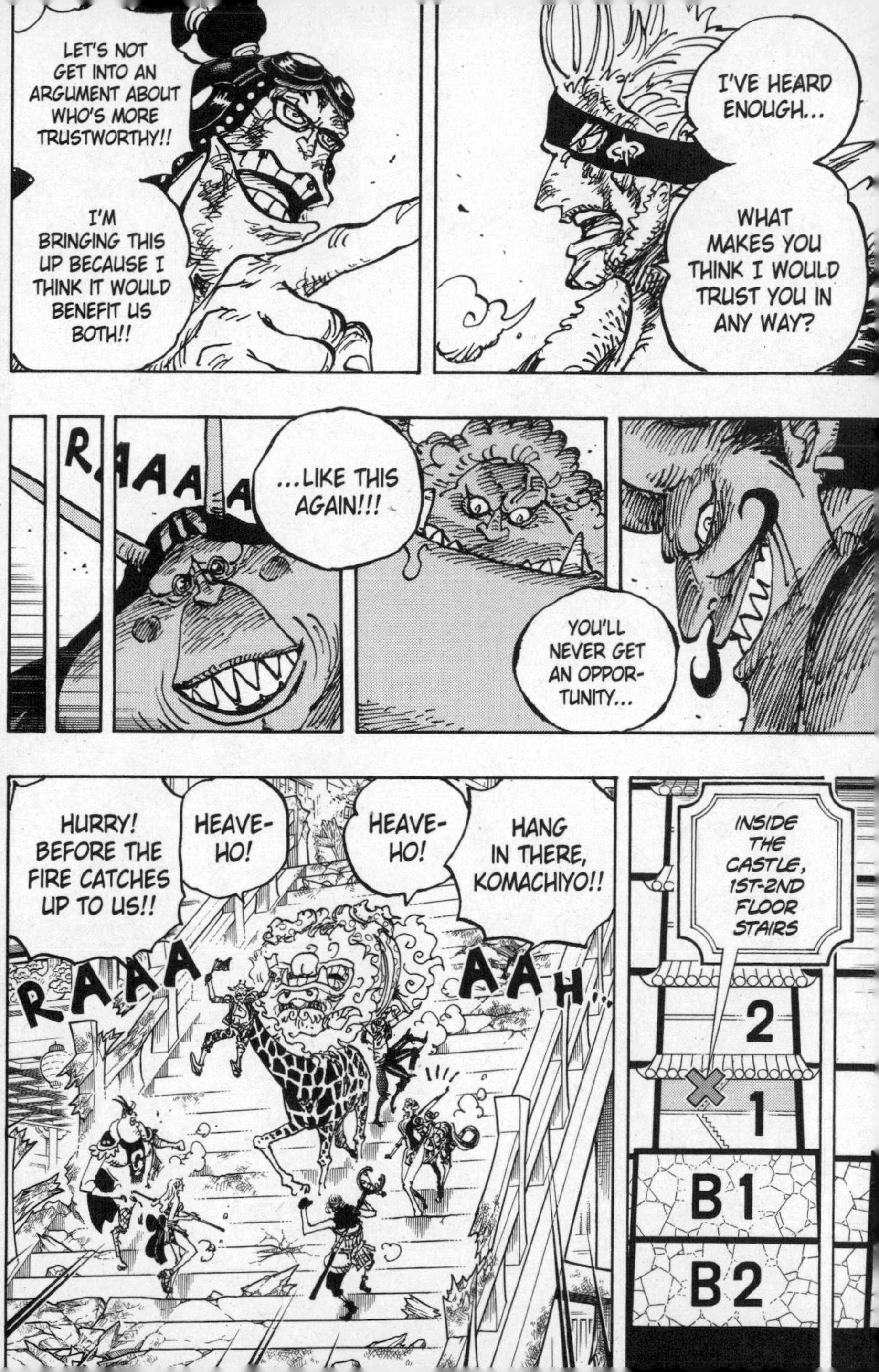
I'VE HEARD ENOUGH...
WHAT MAKES YOU THINK I WOULD TRUST YOU IN ANY WAY?
LET'S NOT GET INTO AN ARGUMENT ABOUT WHO'S MORE TRUSTWORTHY!!
I'M BRINGING THIS UP BECAUSE I THINK IT WOULD BENEFIT US BOTH!!
YOU'LL NEVER GET AN OPPOR-TUNITY...
...LIKE THIS AGAIN!!!
RAAAAA
INSIDE THE CASTLE, 1ST-2ND FLOOR STAIRS
2
1
B1
B2
HANG IN THERE, KOMACHIYO!!
HEAVE-HO!
HEAVE-HO!
HURRY! BEFORE THE FIRE CATCHES UP TO US!!
RAAAAAH...

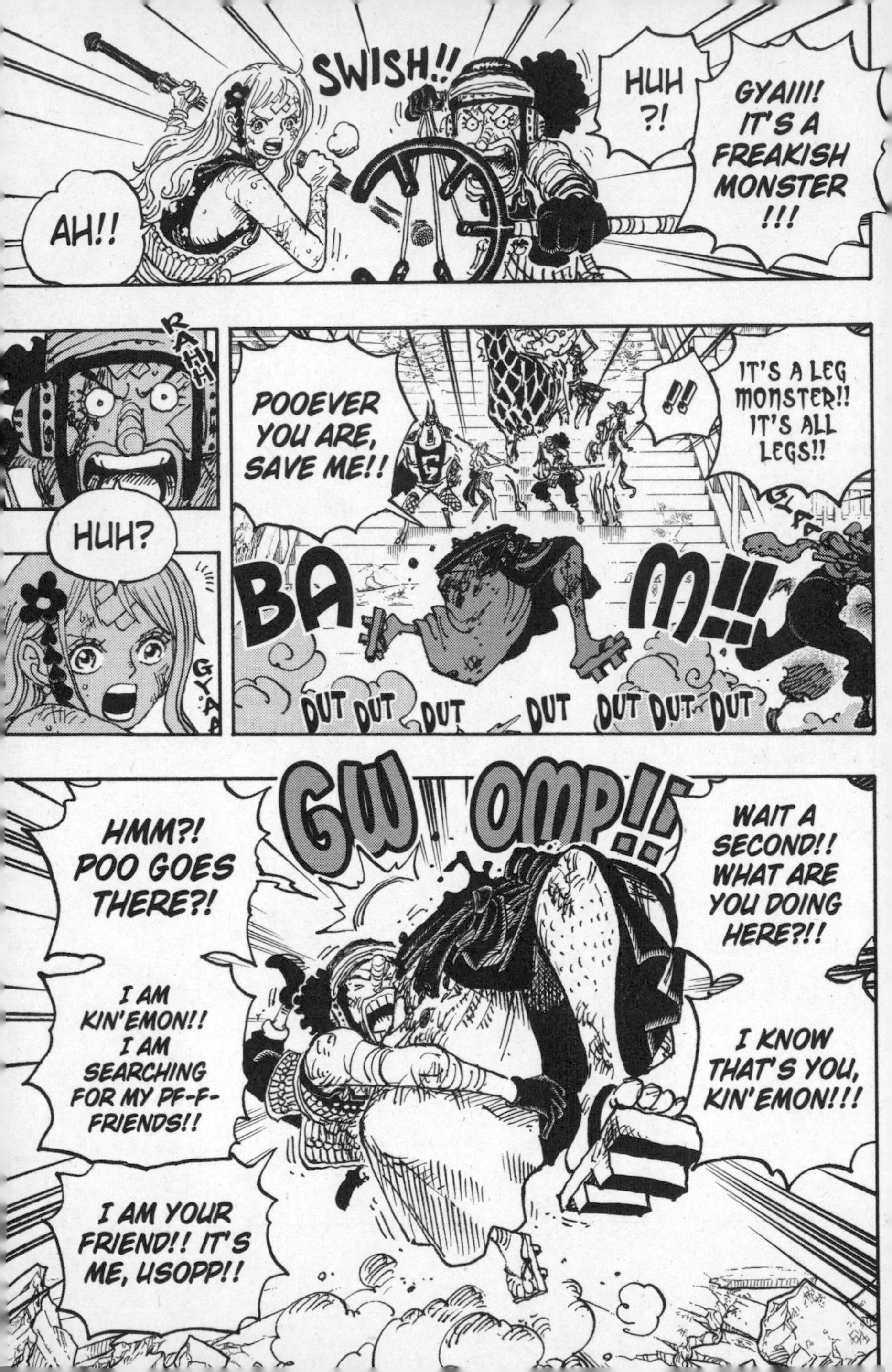
GYAIII! IT'S A FREAKISH MONSTER !!!
HUH ?!
SWISH!!
AH!!
IT'S A LEG MONSTER!! IT'S ALL LEGS!!
!!
GYAA
POOEVER YOU ARE, SAVE ME!!
BAM!!
DUT DUT DUT DUT DUT DUT DUT
RAHH
HUH?
GYAA
GWOMP!!
WAIT A SECOND!! WHAT ARE YOU DOING HERE?!!
HMM?! POO GOES THERE?!
I KNOW THAT'S YOU, KIN'EMON!!!
I AM KIN'EMON!! I AM SEARCHING FOR MY PF-F-FRIENDS!!
I AM YOUR FRIEND!! IT'S ME, USOPP!!

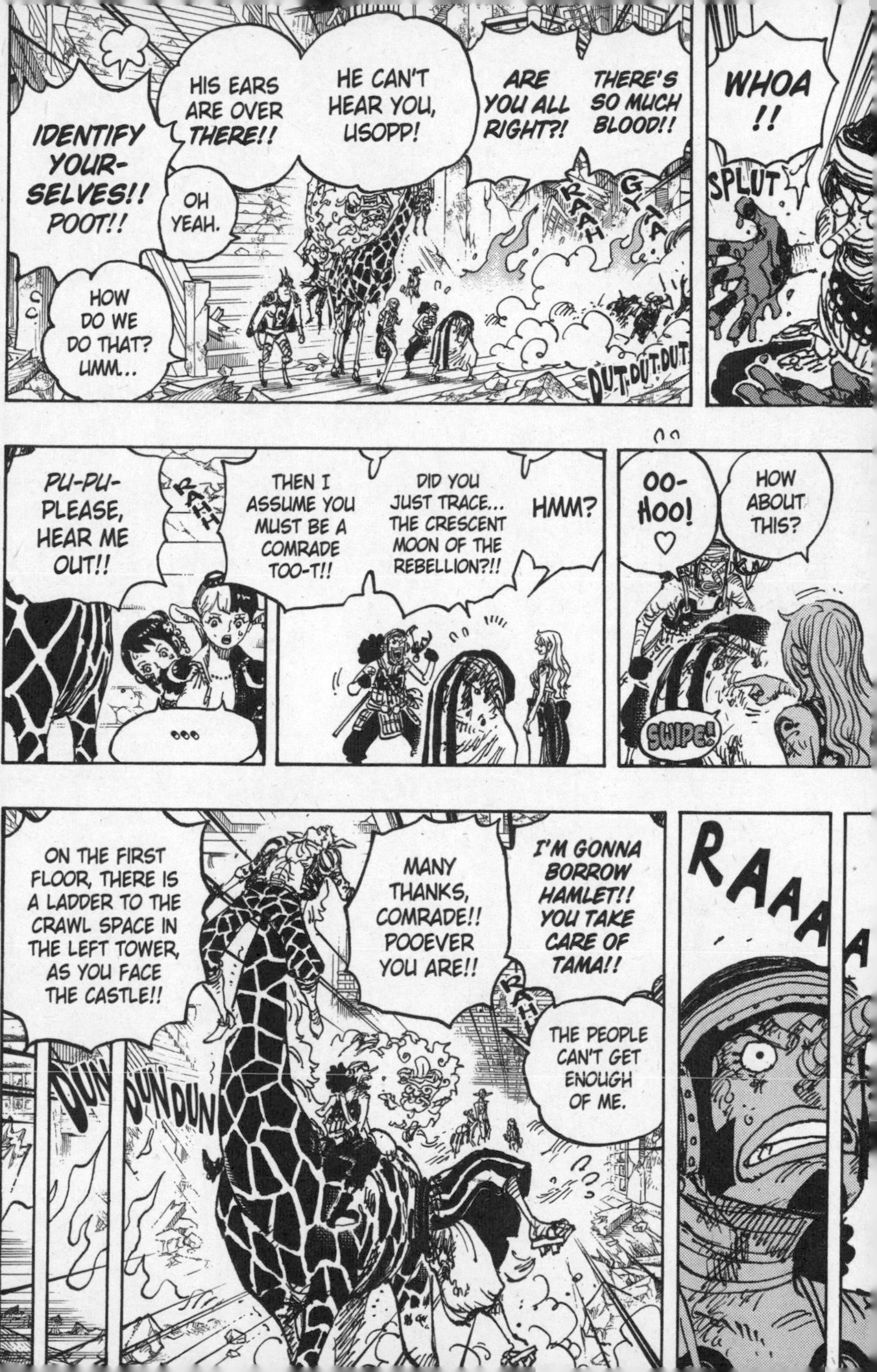
WHOA !!
SPLUT
THERE'S SO MUCH BLOOD!!
ARE YOU ALL RIGHT?!
RAAH
GYAA
HE CAN'T HEAR YOU, USOPP!
HIS EARS ARE OVER THERE!!
IDENTIFY YOUR-SELVES!! POOT!!
OH YEAH.
HOW DO WE DO THAT? UMM...
DUT DUT DUT
HOW ABOUT THIS?
OO-HOO! ♡
SWIPE!
HMM?
DID YOU JUST TRACE... THE CRESCENT MOON OF THE REBELLION?!!
THEN I ASSUME YOU MUST BE A COMRADE TOO-T!!
RAHH
PU-PU-PLEASE, HEAR ME OUT!!
...
RAAAA
I'M GONNA BORROW HAMLET!! YOU TAKE CARE OF TAMA!!
MANY THANKS, COMRADE!! POOEVER YOU ARE!!
ON THE FIRST FLOOR, THERE IS A LADDER TO THE CRAWL SPACE IN THE LEFT TOWER, AS YOU FACE THE CASTLE!!
RAAH
THE PEOPLE CAN'T GET ENOUGH OF ME.
DUN DUN DUN

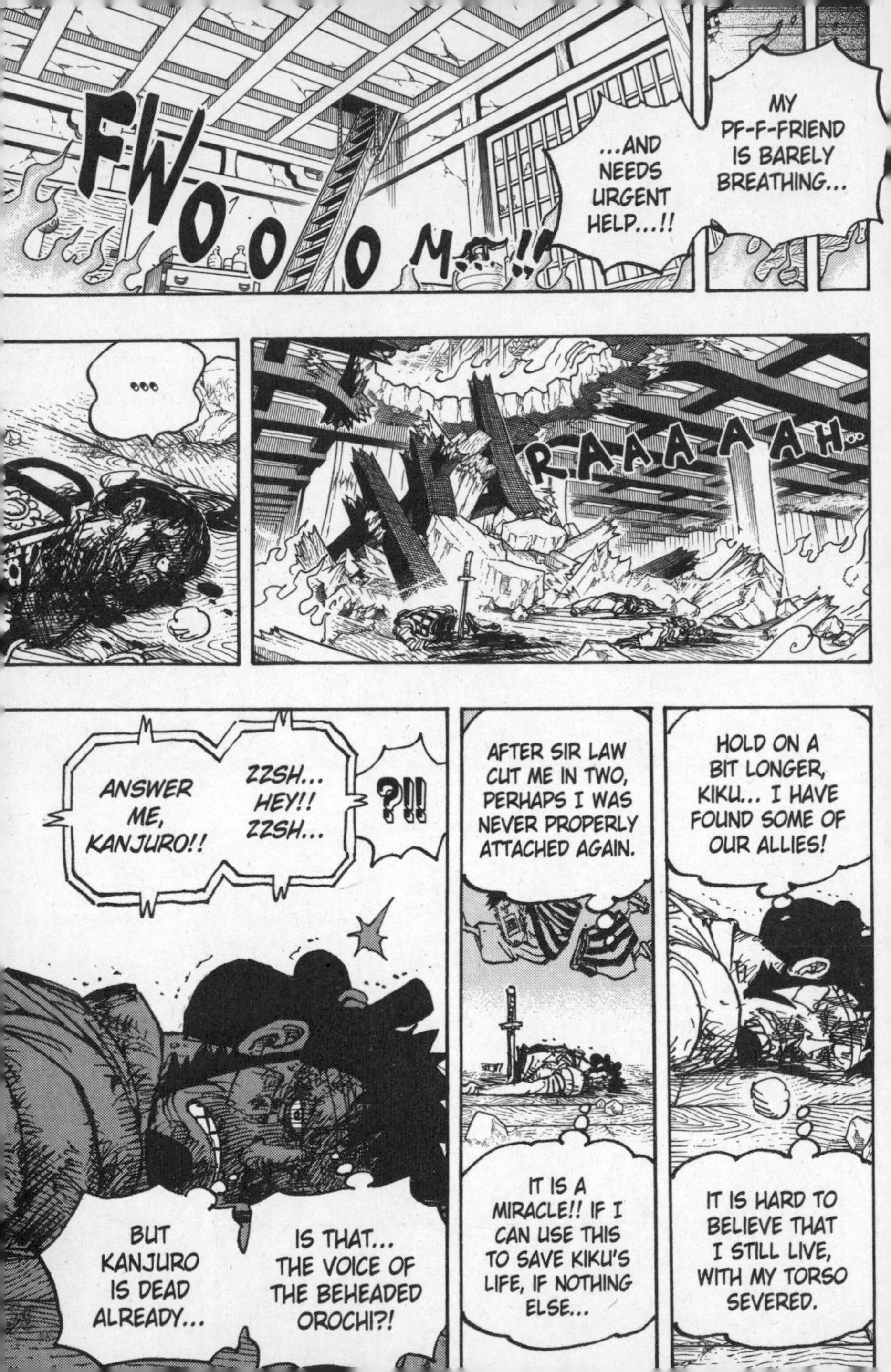
MY PF-F-FRIEND IS BARELY BREATHING...
...AND NEEDS URGENT HELP...!!
FWOOOOM!!
RAAAAAH
...
HOLD ON A BIT LONGER, KIKU... I HAVE FOUND SOME OF OUR ALLIES!
IT IS HARD TO BELIEVE THAT I STILL LIVE, WITH MY TORSO SEVERED.
AFTER SIR LAW CUT ME IN TWO, PERHAPS I WAS NEVER PROPERLY ATTACHED AGAIN.
IT IS A MIRACLE!! IF I CAN USE THIS TO SAVE KIKU'S LIFE, IF NOTHING ELSE...
?!!
ZZSH... HEY!! ZZSH...
ANSWER ME, KANJURO!!
IS THAT... THE VOICE OF THE BEHEADED OROCHI?!
BUT KANJURO IS DEAD ALREADY...

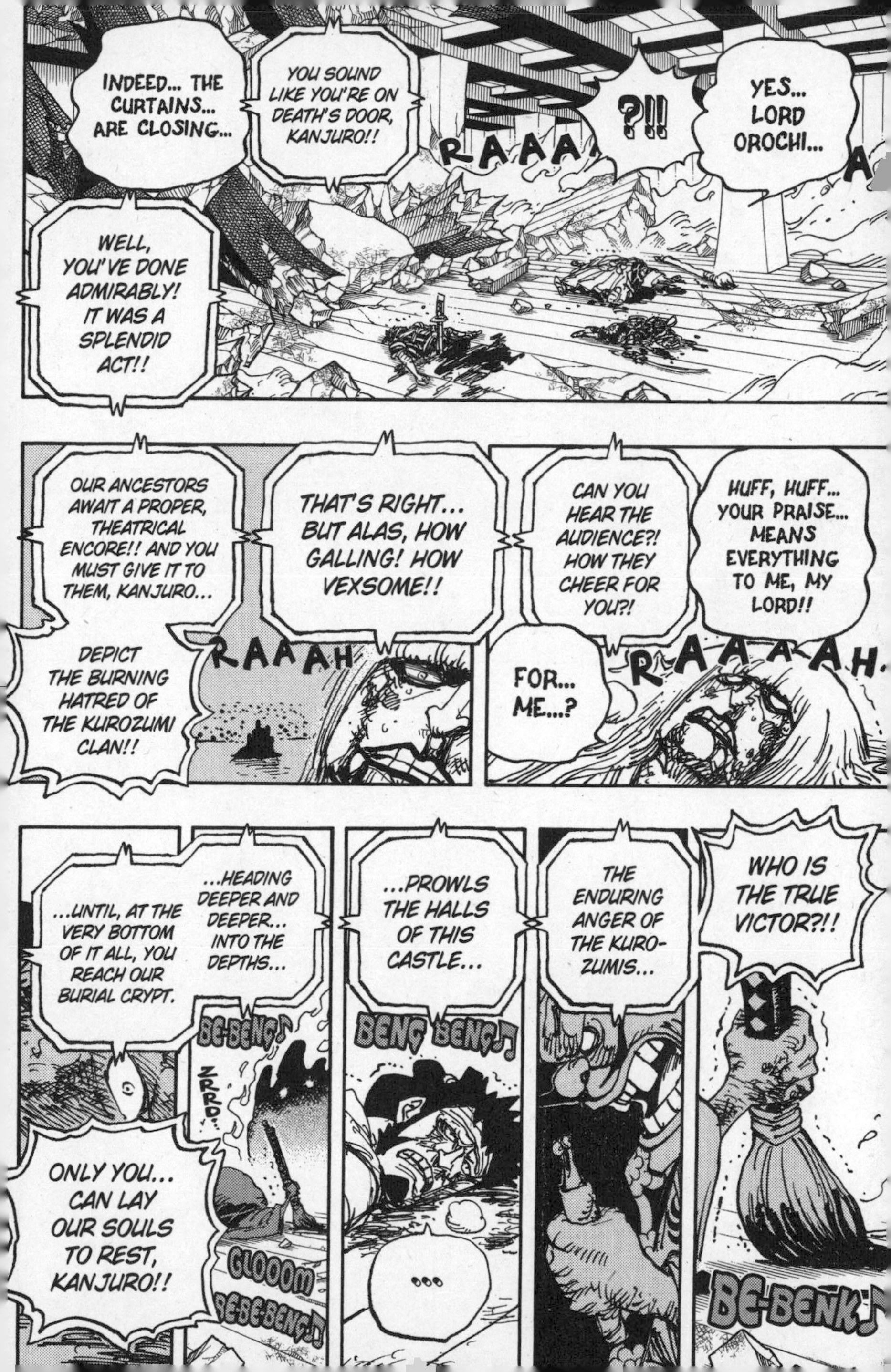
YES... LORD OROCHI...
?!!
RAAAA
YOU SOUND LIKE YOU'RE ON DEATH'S DOOR, KANJURO!!
INDEED... THE CURTAINS... ARE CLOSING...
WELL, YOU'VE DONE ADMIRABLY! IT WAS A SPLENDID ACT!!
HUFF, HUFF... YOUR PRAISE... MEANS EVERYTHING TO ME, MY LORD!!
CAN YOU HEAR THE AUDIENCE?! HOW THEY CHEER FOR YOU?!
RAAAAAH
FOR... ME...?
THAT'S RIGHT... BUT ALAS, HOW GALLING! HOW VEXSOME!!
OUR ANCESTORS AWAIT A PROPER, THEATRICAL ENCORE!! AND YOU MUST GIVE IT TO THEM, KANJURO...
RAAAH
DEPICT THE BURNING HATRED OF THE KUROZUMI CLAN!!
WHO IS THE TRUE VICTOR?!!
BE-BENK
THE ENDURING ANGER OF THE KURO-ZUMIS...
...PROWLS THE HALLS OF THIS CASTLE...
BENG BENG
...
...HEADING DEEPER AND DEEPER... INTO THE DEPTHS...
BE-BENG
ZRRRD
GLOOOM
BEBEBENG
...UNTIL, AT THE VERY BOTTOM OF IT ALL, YOU REACH OUR BURIAL CRYPT.
ONLY YOU... CAN LAY OUR SOULS TO REST, KANJURO!!

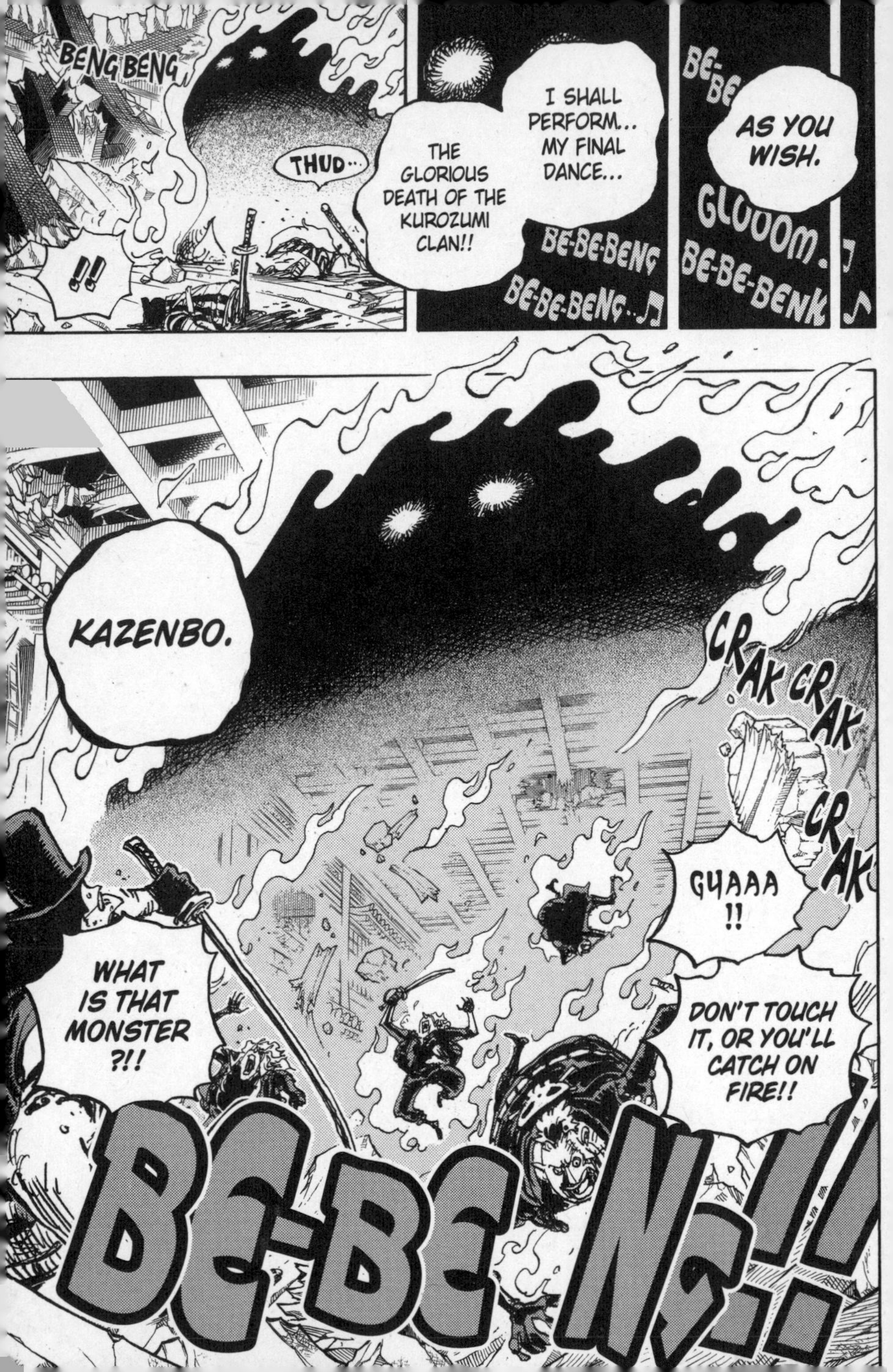
BE-BE
AS YOU WISH.
GLOOOM.
BE-BE-BENK ♪
I SHALL PERFORM... MY FINAL DANCE...
THE GLORIOUS DEATH OF THE KUROZUMI CLAN!!
BE-BE-BENG
BE-BE-BENG..♪
BENG BENG
THUD...
!!
CRAK CRAK CRAK CRAK
GUAAA !!
KAZENBO.
DON'T TOUCH IT, OR YOU'LL CATCH ON FIRE!!
WHAT IS THAT MONSTER ?!!
BE-BENG!!

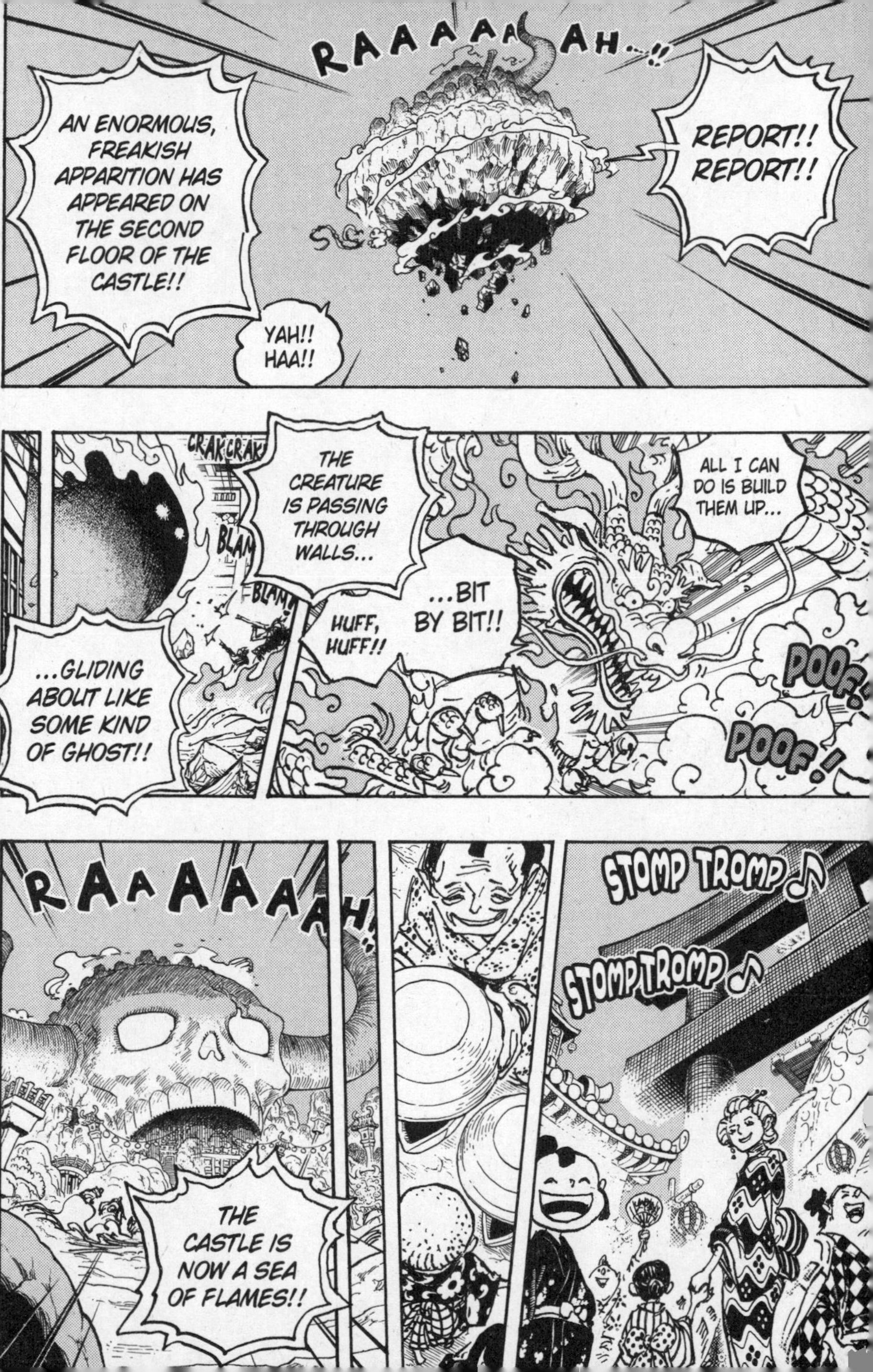
RAAAAAAH...!!
REPORT!! REPORT!!
AN ENORMOUS, FREAKISH APPARITION HAS APPEARED ON THE SECOND FLOOR OF THE CASTLE!!
YAH!! HAA!!
ALL I CAN DO IS BUILD THEM UP...
...BIT BY BIT!!
HUFF, HUFF!!
POOF!
POOF!
THE CREATURE IS PASSING THROUGH WALLS...
CRAKCRAK
BLAM
BLAM
...GLIDING ABOUT LIKE SOME KIND OF GHOST!!
STOMP TROMP ♪
STOMP TROMP ♪
RAAAAAAAH!!
THE CASTLE IS NOW A SEA OF FLAMES!!

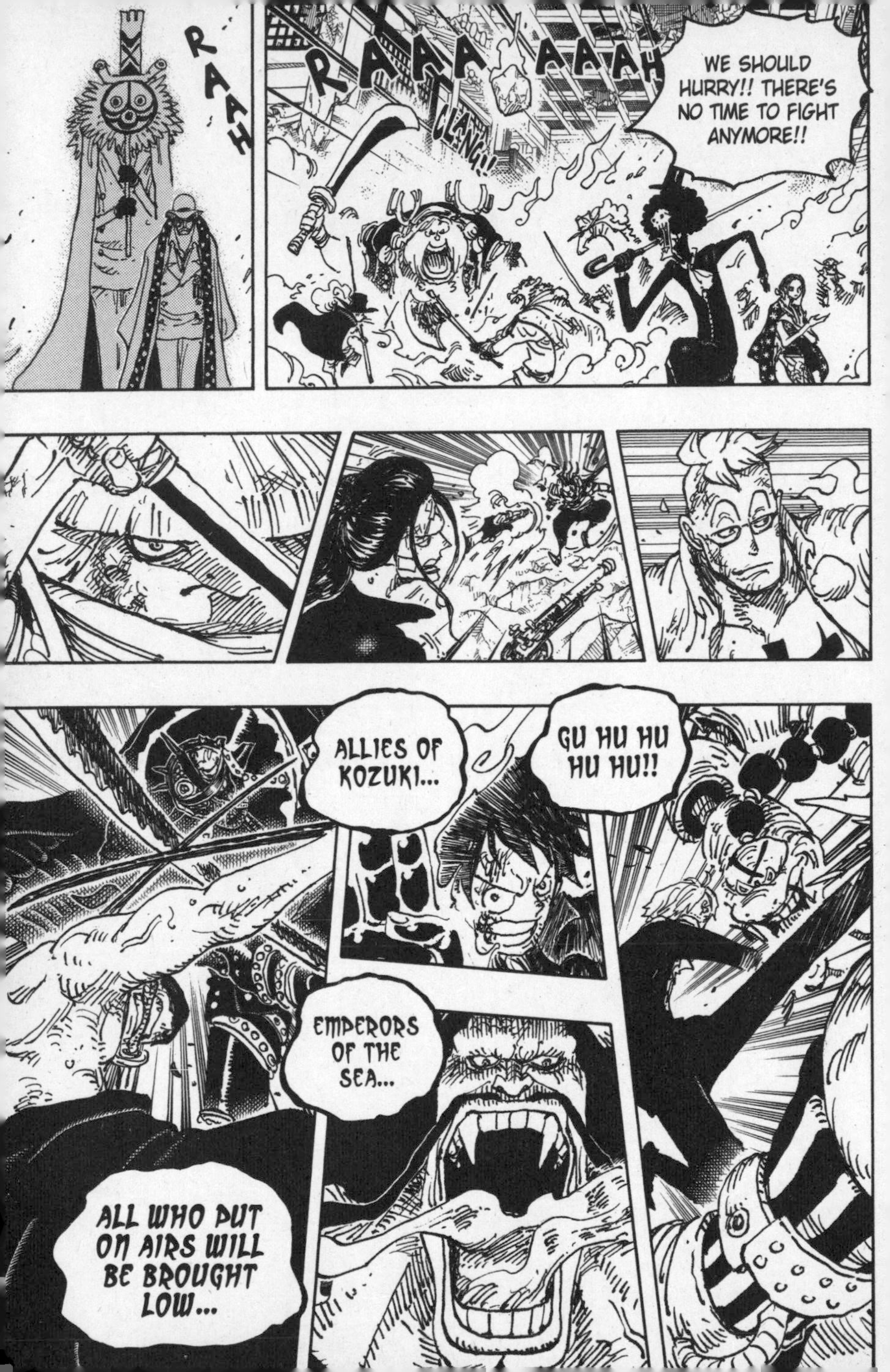

RAAAAAAH
CLANG!!
WE SHOULD HURRY!! THERE'S NO TIME TO FIGHT ANYMORE!!
RAAH
GU HU HU HU!!
ALLIES OF KOZUKI...
EMPERORS OF THE SEA...
ALL WHO PUT ON AIRS WILL BE BROUGHT LOW...

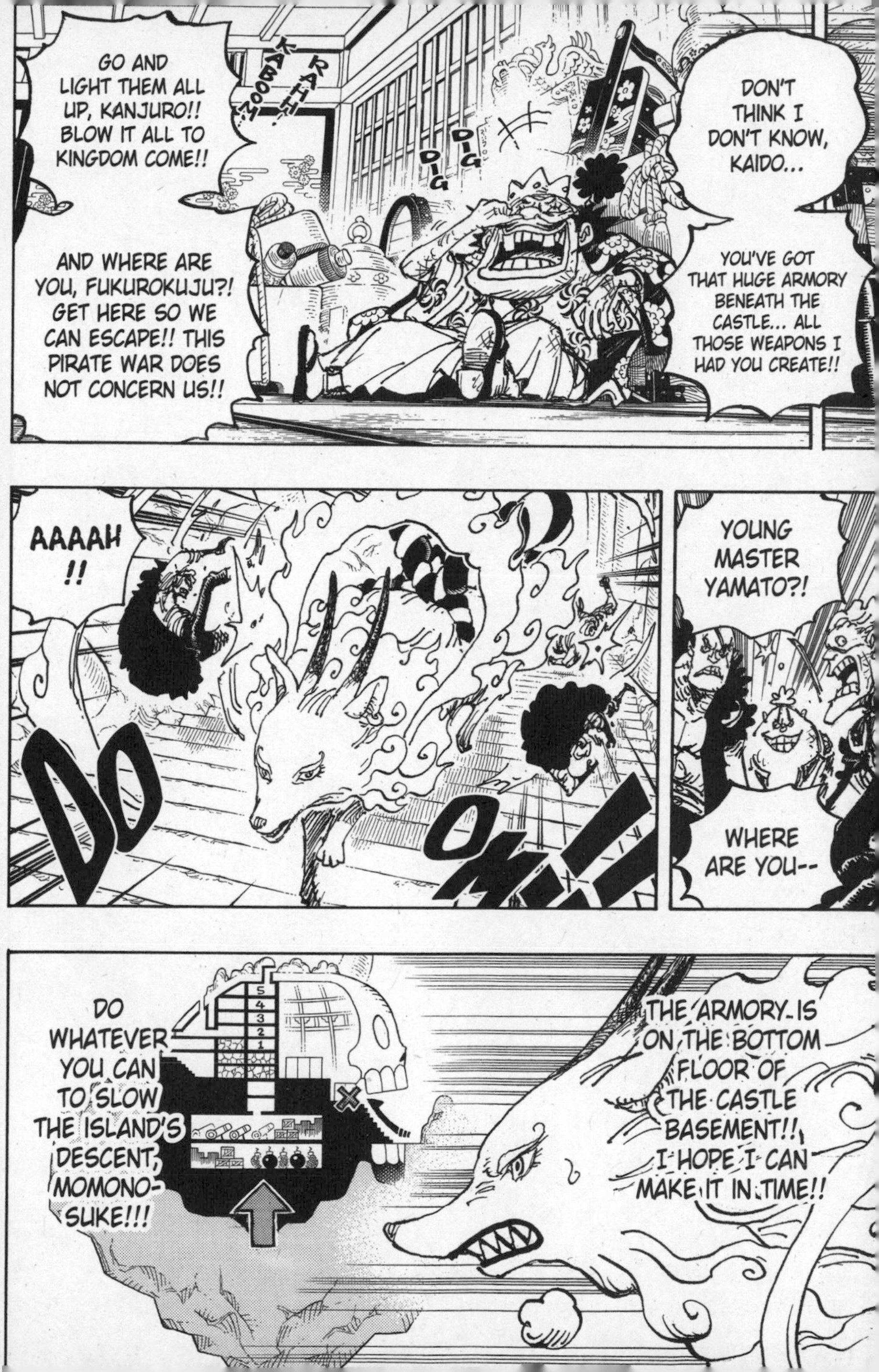
DON'T THINK I DON'T KNOW, KAIDO...
YOU'VE GOT THAT HUGE ARMORY BENEATH THE CASTLE... ALL THOSE WEAPONS I HAD YOU CREATE!!
DIG DIG
RAHH
KABOOM
GO AND LIGHT THEM ALL UP, KANJURO!! BLOW IT ALL TO KINGDOM COME!!
AND WHERE ARE YOU, FUKUROKUJU?! GET HERE SO WE CAN ESCAPE!! THIS PIRATE WAR DOES NOT CONCERN US!!
YOUNG MASTER YAMATO?!
WHERE ARE YOU--
AAAAH!!
DOOM!!
THE ARMORY IS ON THE BOTTOM FLOOR OF THE CASTLE BASEMENT!! I HOPE I CAN MAKE IT IN TIME!!
5 4 3 2 1
DO WHATEVER YOU CAN TO SLOW THE ISLAND'S DESCENT, MOMONOSUKE!!!

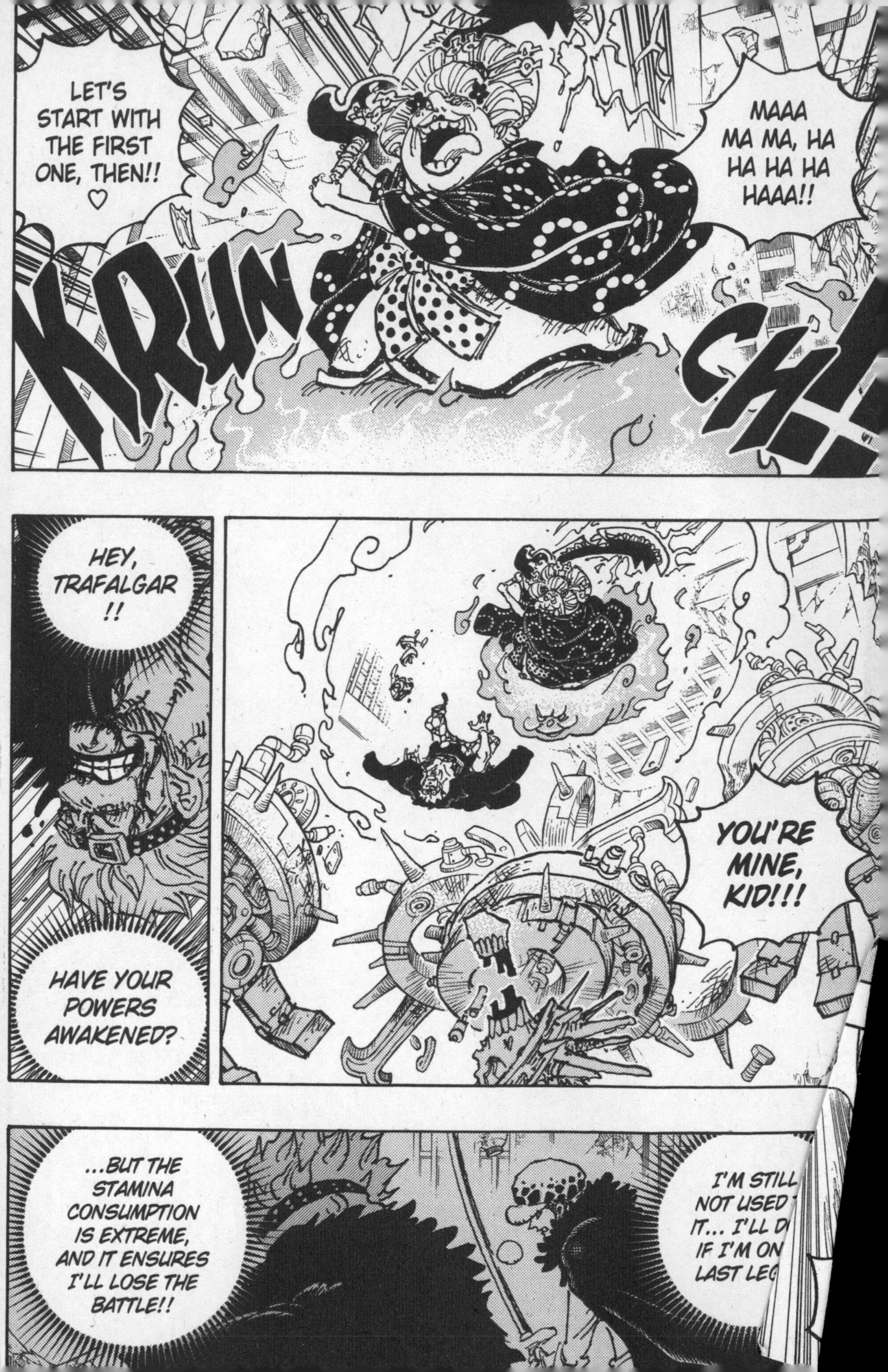
MAAA MA MA, HA HA HA HA HAAA!!
LET'S START WITH THE FIRST ONE, THEN!! ♡
CH
KRUN
YOU'RE MINE, KID!!!
HEY, TRAFALGAR!!
HAVE YOUR POWERS AWAKENED?
I'M STILL NOT USED T IT... I'LL D IF I'M ON LAST LEG
...BUT THE STAMINA CONSUMPTION IS EXTREME, AND IT ENSURES I'LL LOSE THE BATTLE!!

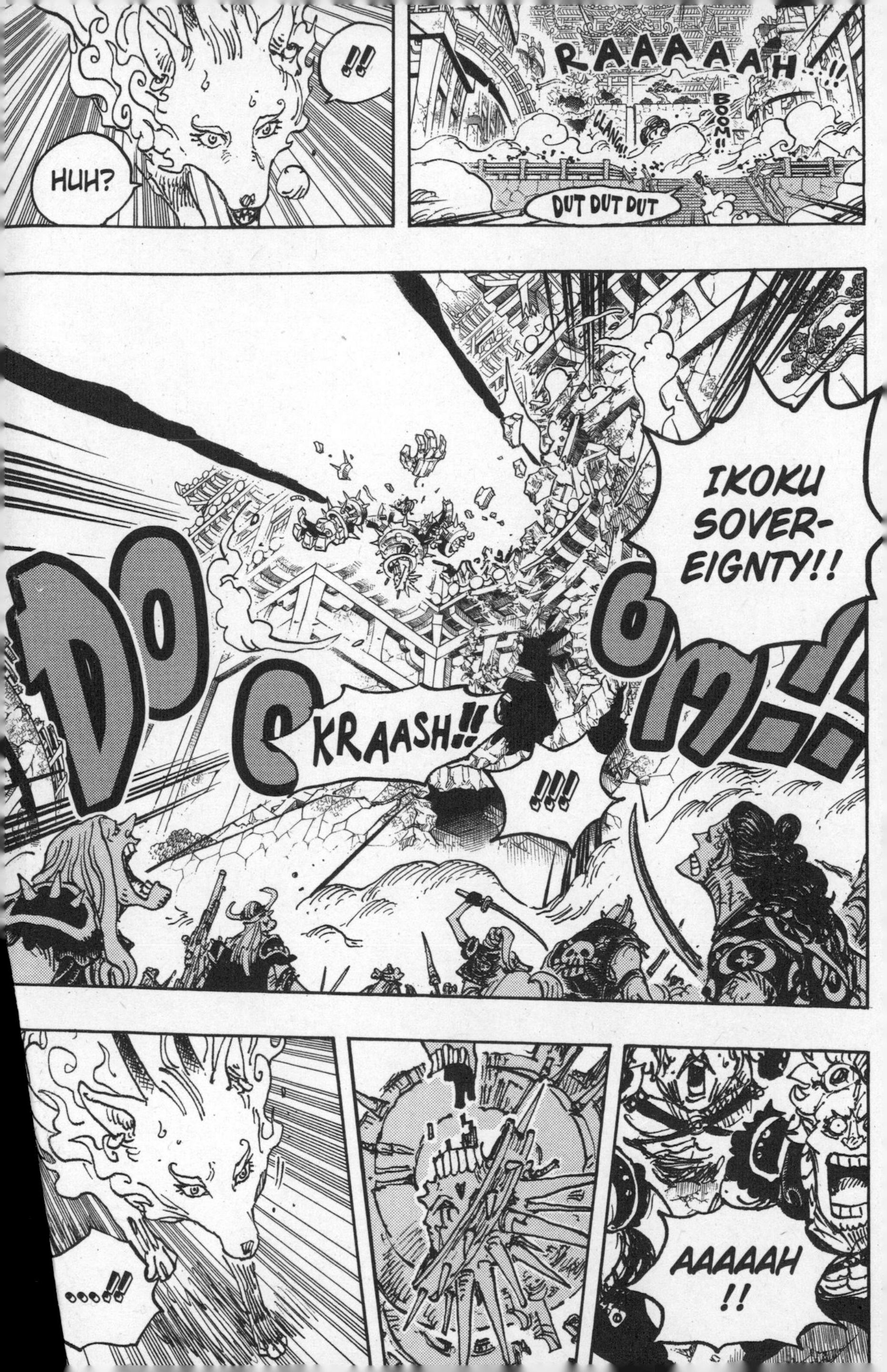
RAAAAAH!!!
BOOM!!
CLANG!!
DUT DUT DUT
!!
HUH?
IKOKU SOVEREIGNTY!!
DOGON!!
KRAASH!!
!!!
AAAAAH!!
...!!

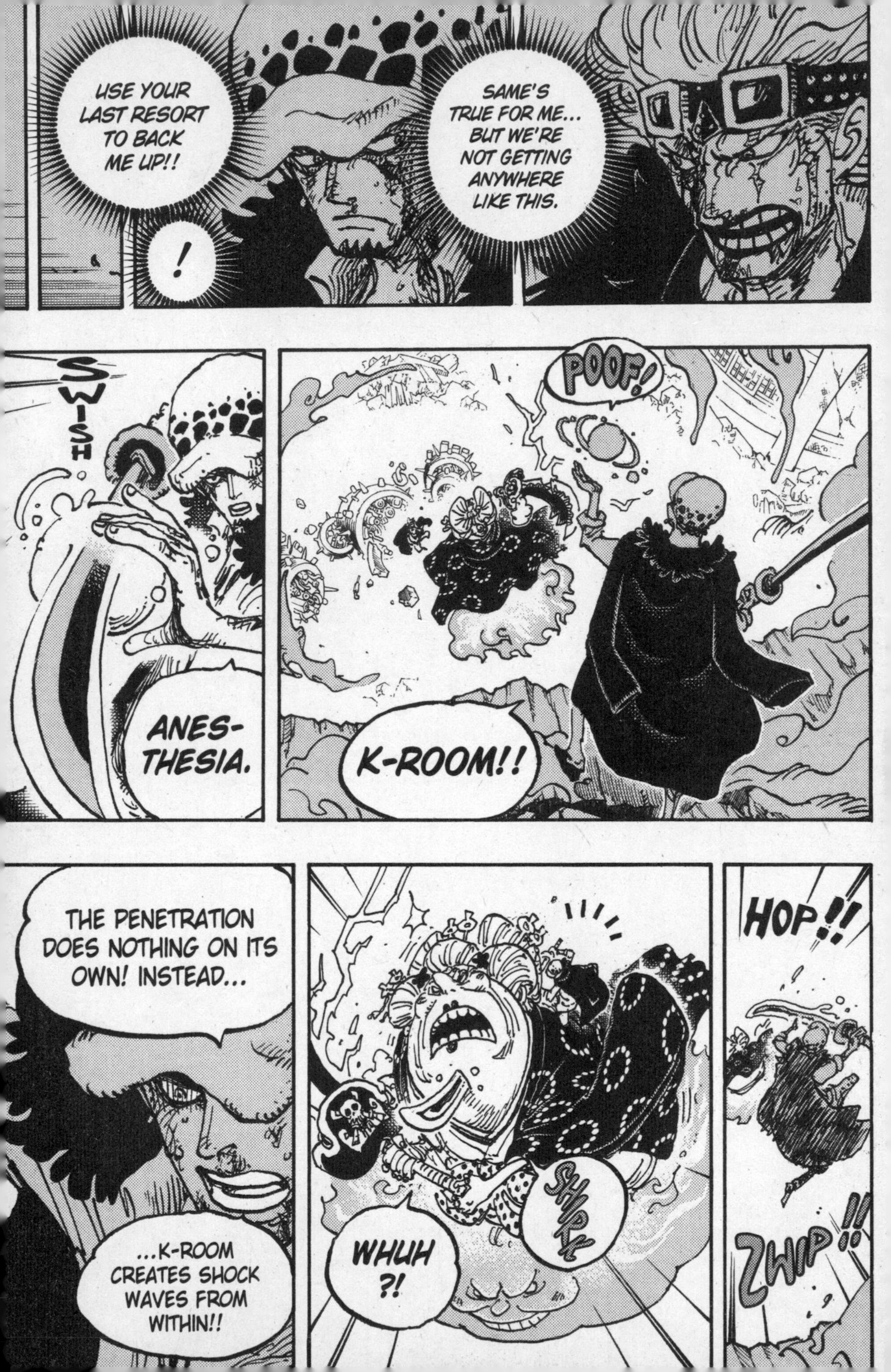

USE YOUR LAST RESORT TO BACK ME UP!!
!
SAME'S TRUE FOR ME... BUT WE'RE NOT GETTING ANYWHERE LIKE THIS.
SWISH
ANES-THESIA.
POOF!!
K-ROOM!!
THE PENETRATION DOES NOTHING ON ITS OWN! INSTEAD...
...K-ROOM CREATES SHOCK WAVES FROM WITHIN!!
SHNK
WHUH ?!
HOP!!
ZWIP!!

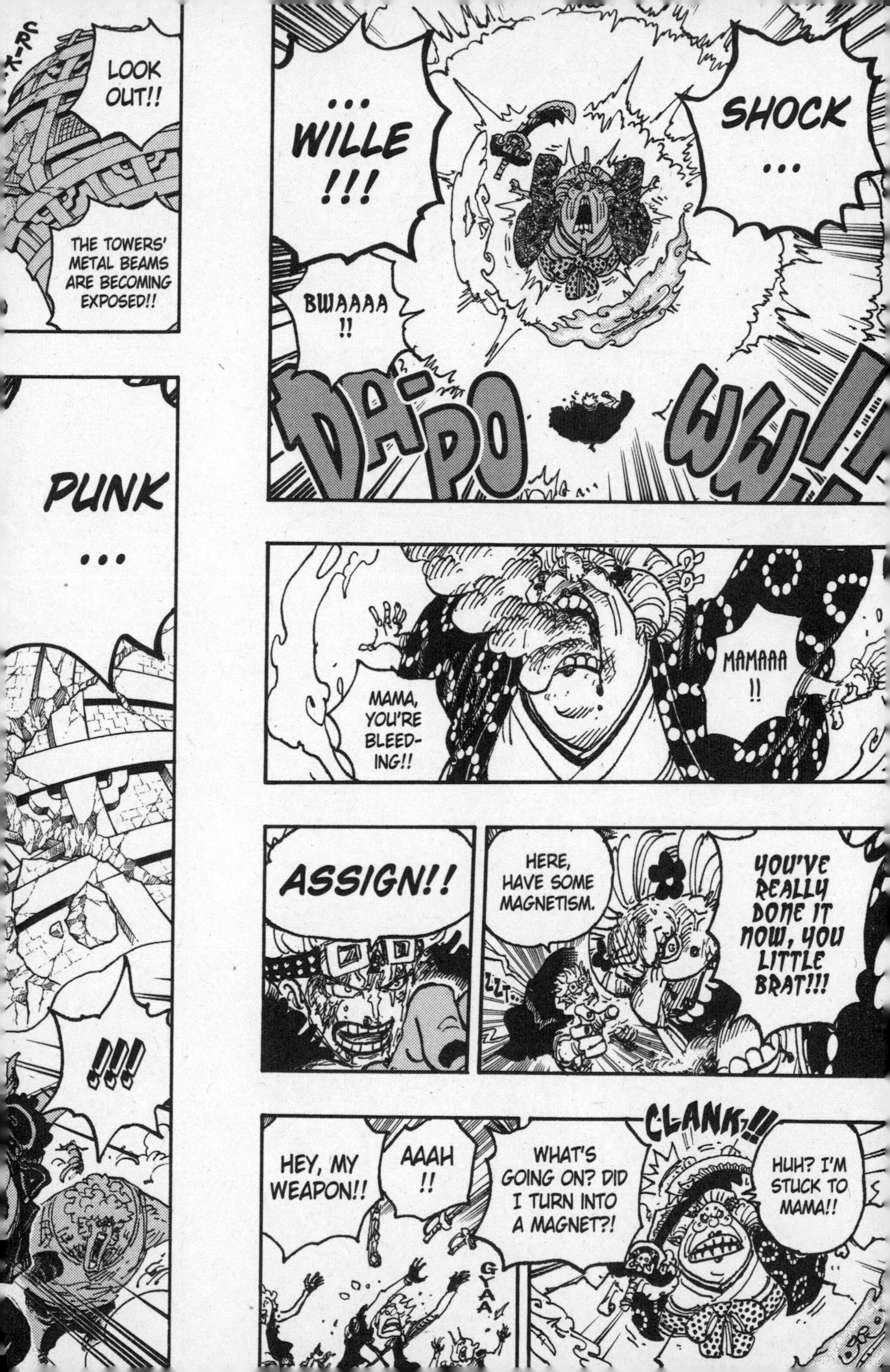
SHOCK ...
... WILLE !!!
BWAAAA !!
DA-PO-WW!!
MAMAAA !!
MAMA, YOU'RE BLEEDING!!
YOU'VE REALLY DONE IT NOW, YOU LITTLE BRAT!!!
HERE, HAVE SOME MAGNETISM.
ZZZT...
ASSIGN!!
CLANK!!!
HUH? I'M STUCK TO MAMA!!
WHAT'S GOING ON? DID I TURN INTO A MAGNET?!
AAAH !!
HEY, MY WEAPON!!
GYAA
LOOK OUT!!
THE TOWERS' METAL BEAMS ARE BECOMING EXPOSED!!
PUNK ...
!!!

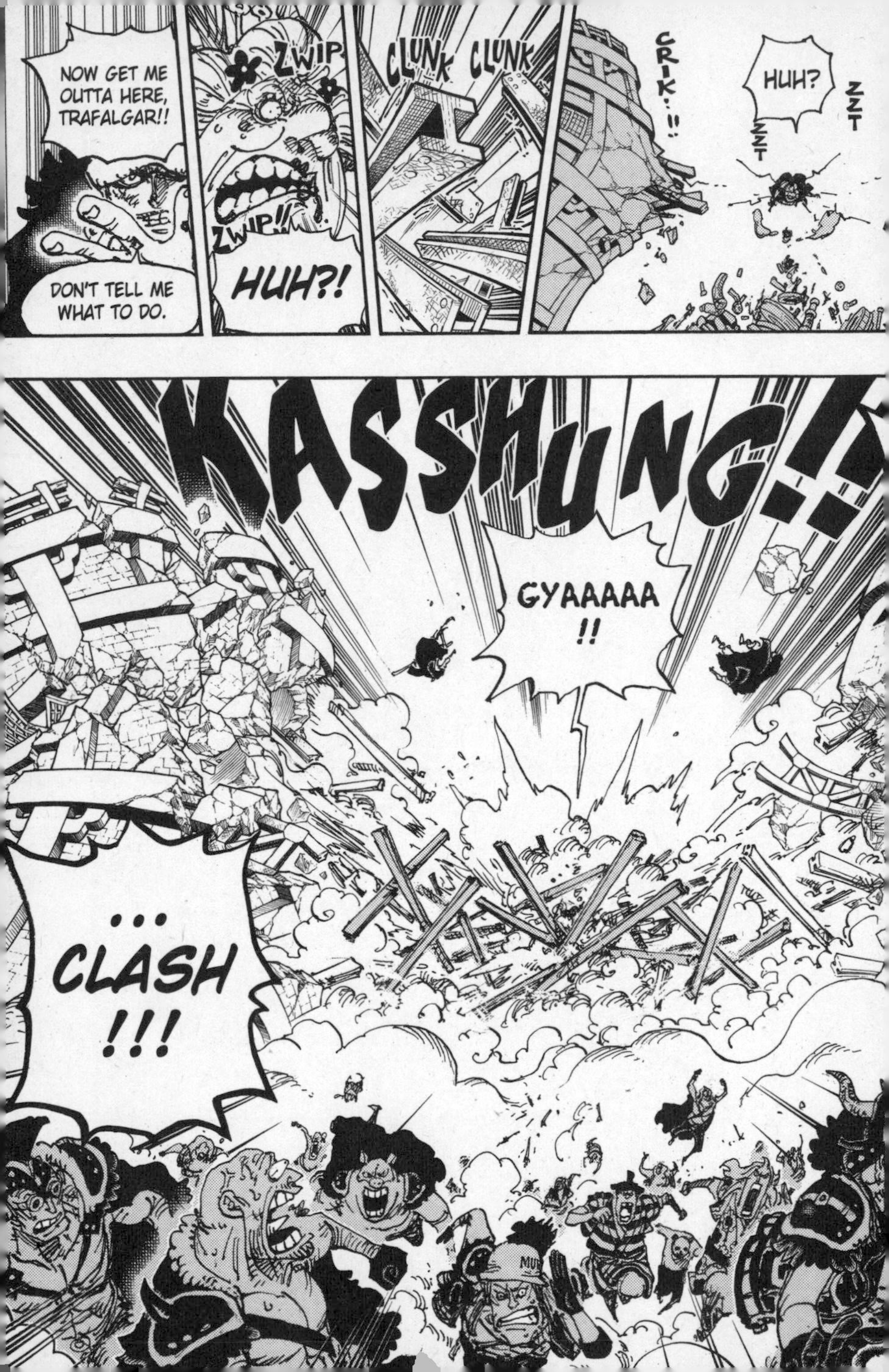

HUH?
ZZT
ZZT
CRIK..!!
CLUNK CLUNK
ZWIP
ZWIP!!
HUH?!
NOW GET ME OUTTA HERE, TRAFALGAR!!
DON'T TELL ME WHAT TO DO.
KASSHUNG!!
GYAAAAA!!
...CLASH!!!
MU

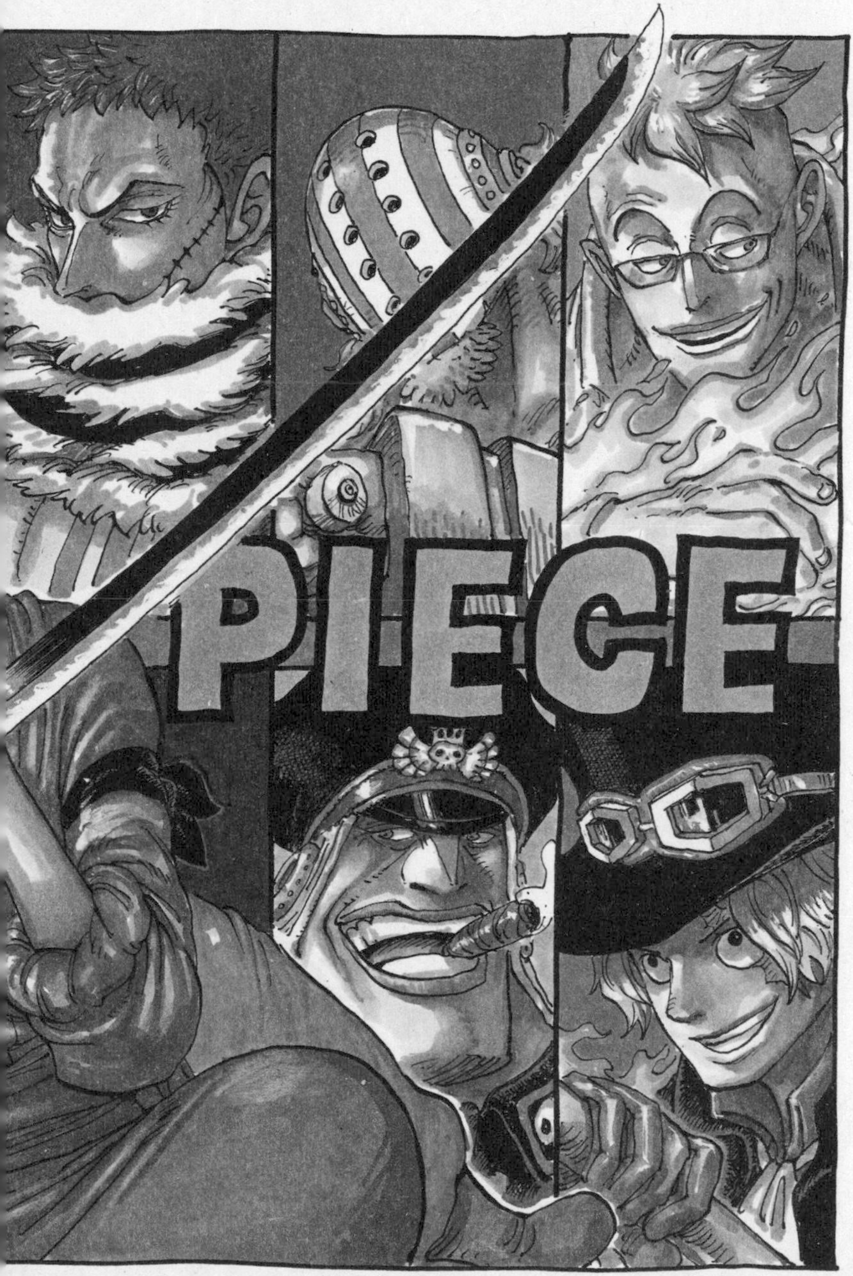
·P·I·E·C·E·

Chapter 1031: WARRIOR OF SCIENCE

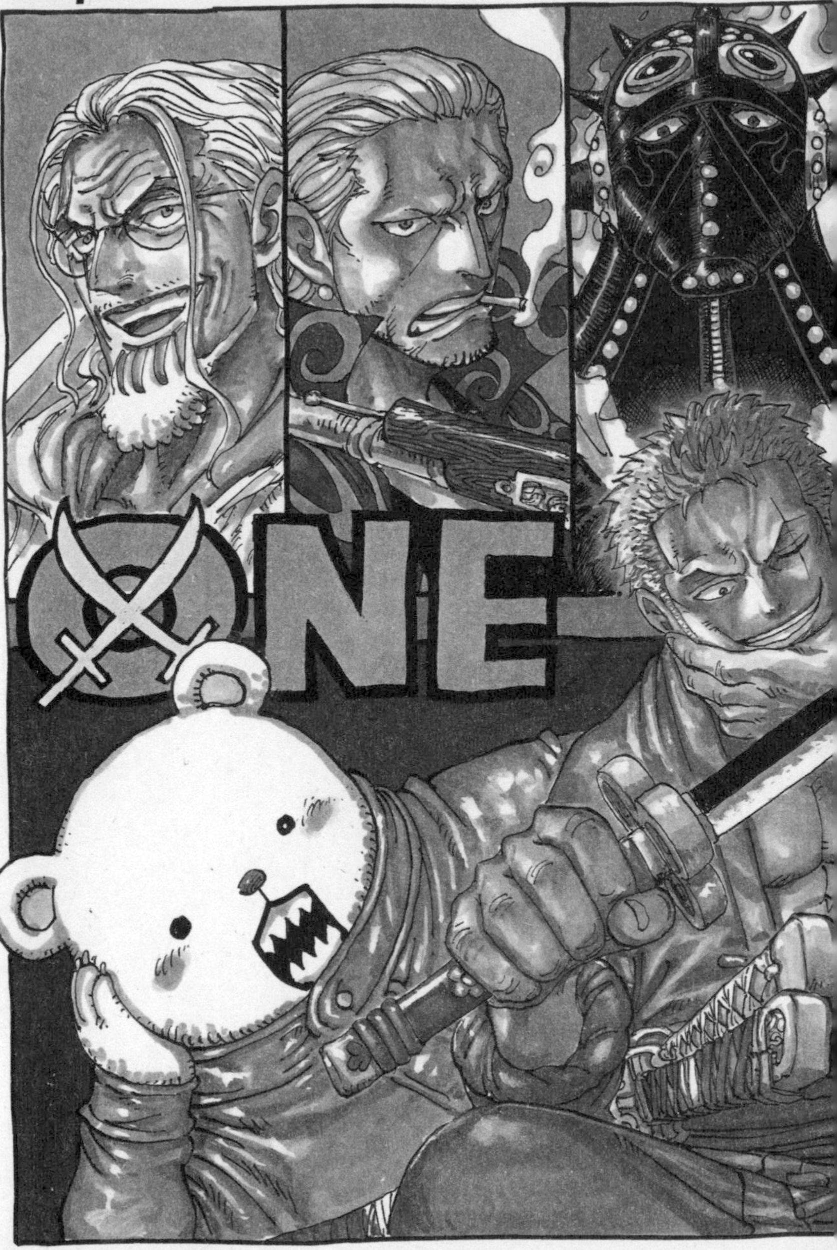
ONE-

vol.102
ONE PIECE

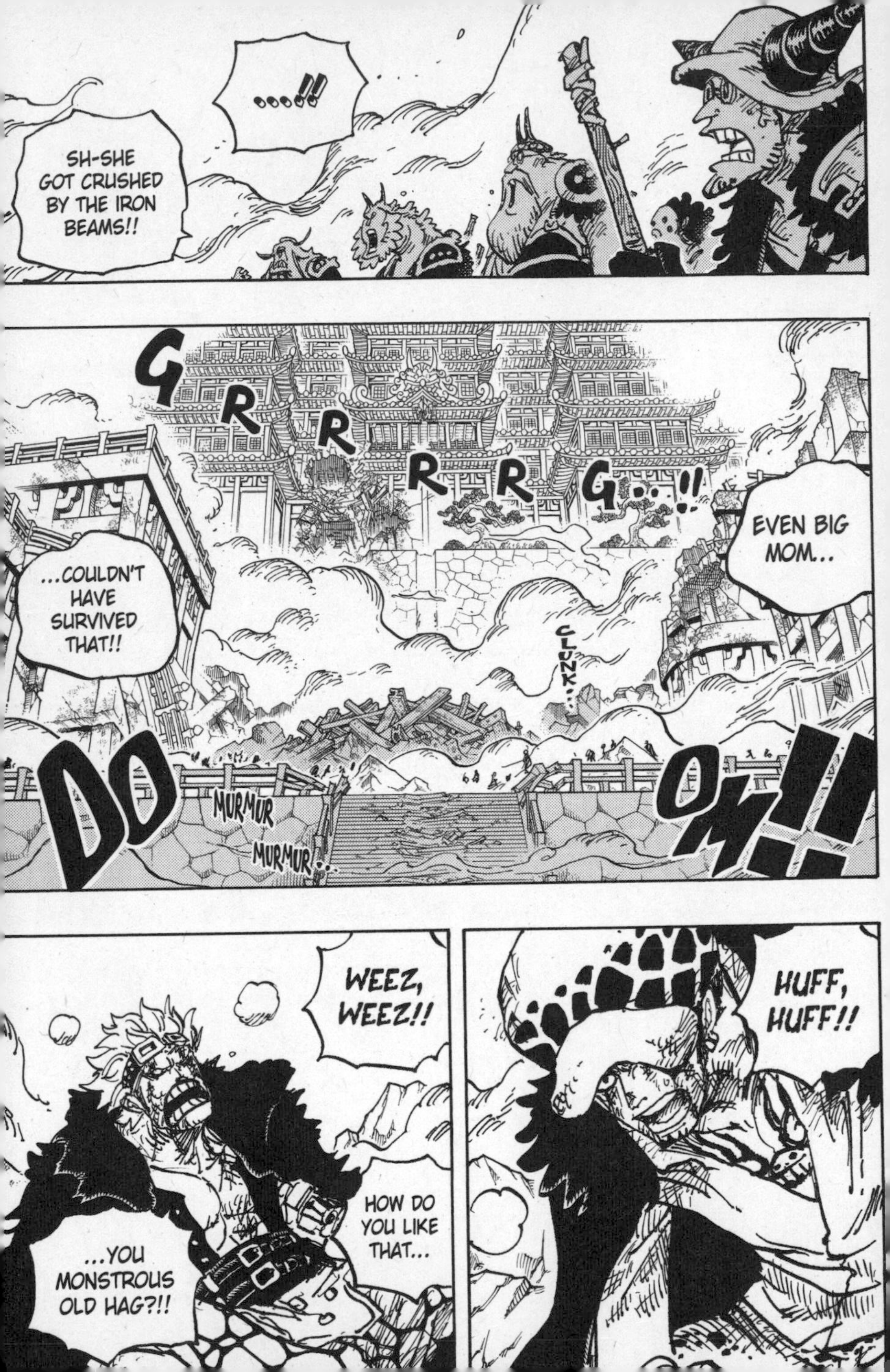
....!!
SH-SHE GOT CRUSHED BY THE IRON BEAMS!!
GRRRRRG..!!
EVEN BIG MOM...
...COULDN'T HAVE SURVIVED THAT!!
CLUNK...
DO
ON!!
MURMUR
MURMUR...
HUFF, HUFF!!
WEEZ, WEEZ!!
HOW DO YOU LIKE THAT...
...YOU MONSTROUS OLD HAG?!!

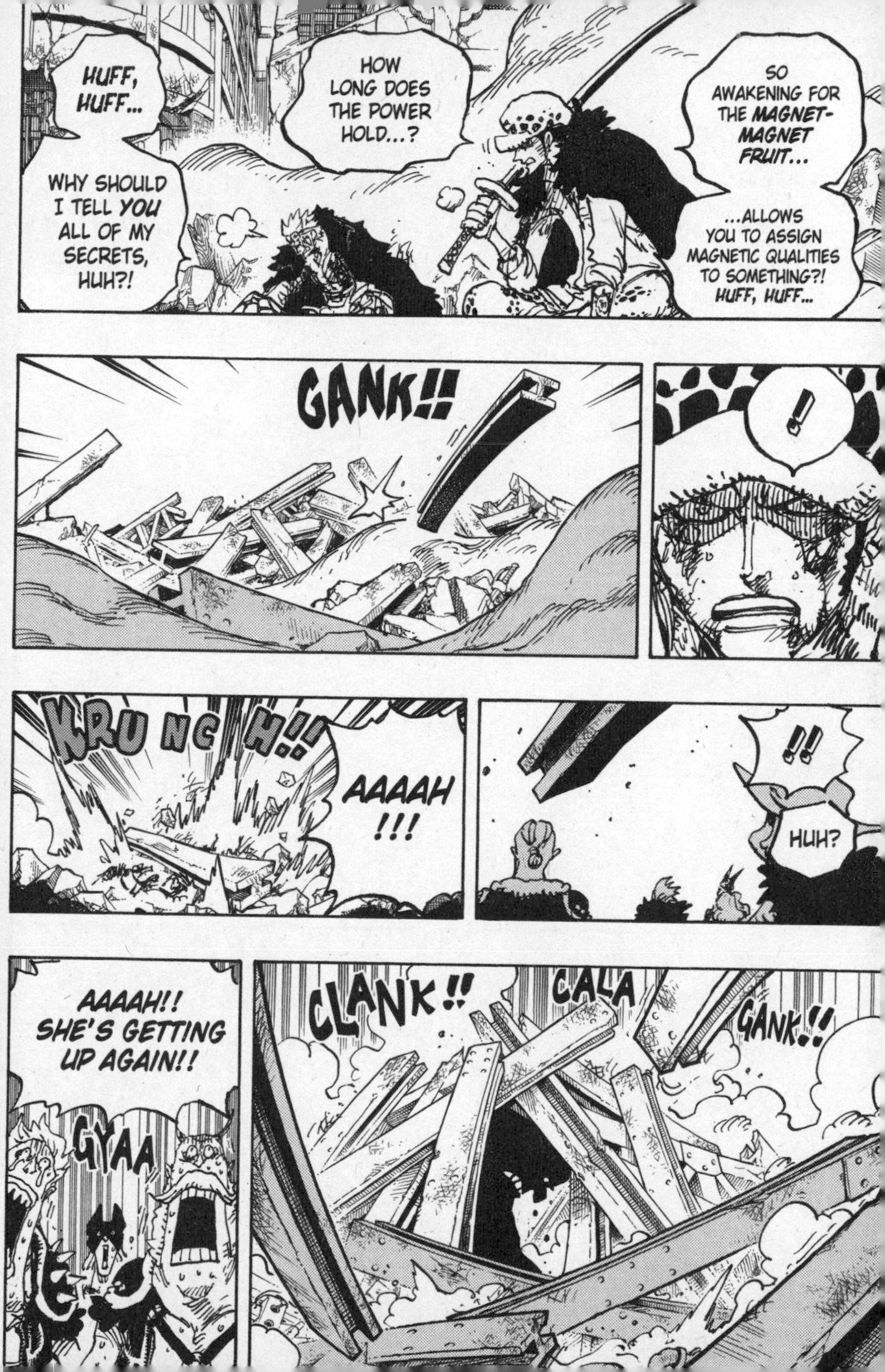
SO AWAKENING FOR THE MAGNET-MAGNET FRUIT...
...ALLOWS YOU TO ASSIGN MAGNETIC QUALITIES TO SOMETHING?! HUFF, HUFF...
HOW LONG DOES THE POWER HOLD...?
HUFF, HUFF...
WHY SHOULD I TELL YOU ALL OF MY SECRETS, HUH?!
!
GANK!!
!!
HUH?
KRUNCH!!
AAAAH!!!
CALA GANK!!
CLANK!!
AAAAH!! SHE'S GETTING UP AGAIN!!
GYAA

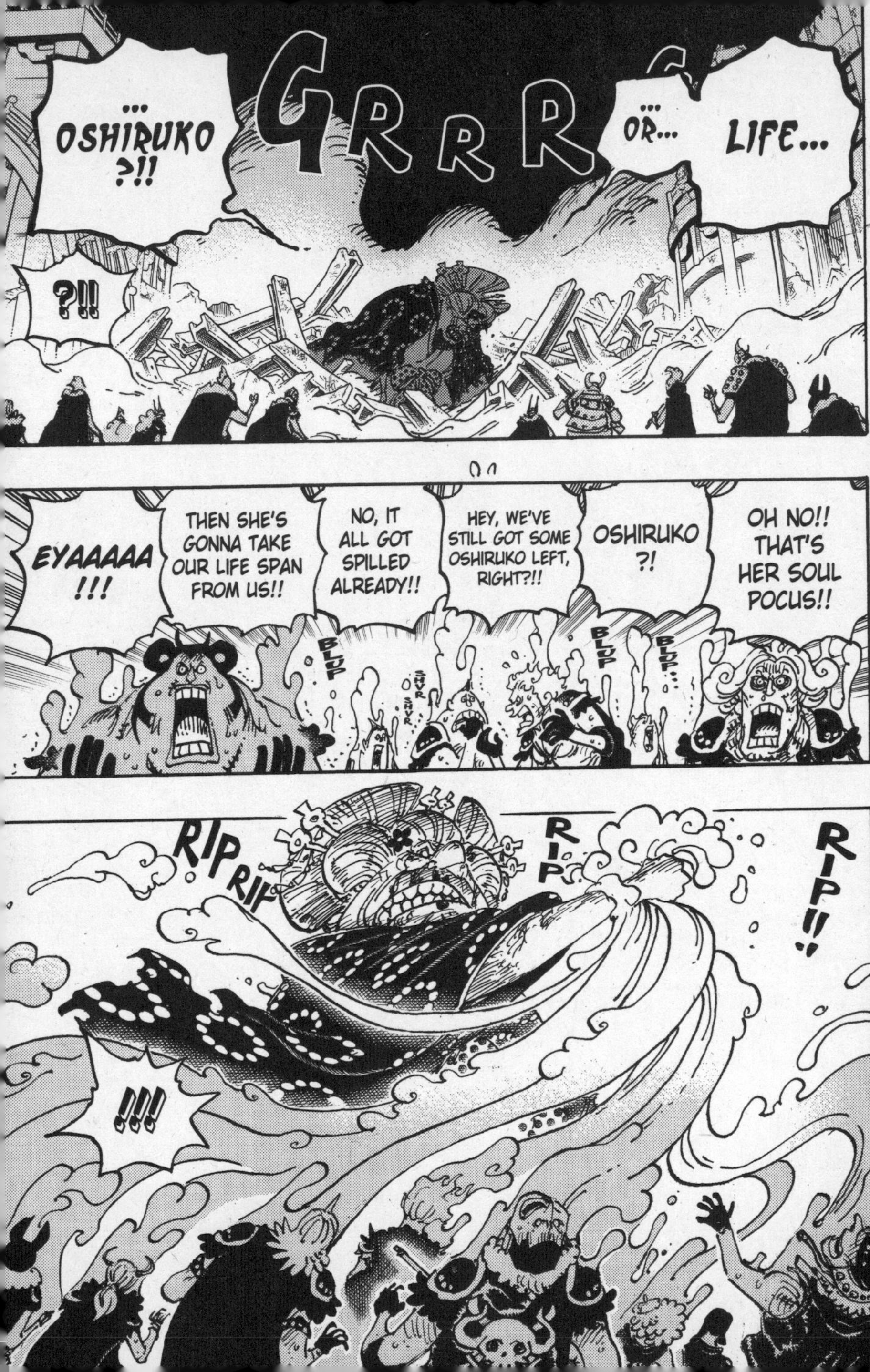

LIFE...
...OR...
GRRR
...OSHIRUKO ?!!
?!!
OH NO!! THAT'S HER SOUL POCUS!!
BLUP
OSHIRUKO ?!
BLUP
HEY, WE'VE STILL GOT SOME OSHIRUKO LEFT, RIGHT?!!
SHVR SHVR
NO, IT ALL GOT SPILLED ALREADY!!
BLUP
THEN SHE'S GONNA TAKE OUR LIFE SPAN FROM US!!
EYAAAAA !!!
RIP!!
RIP
RIP RIP
!!!

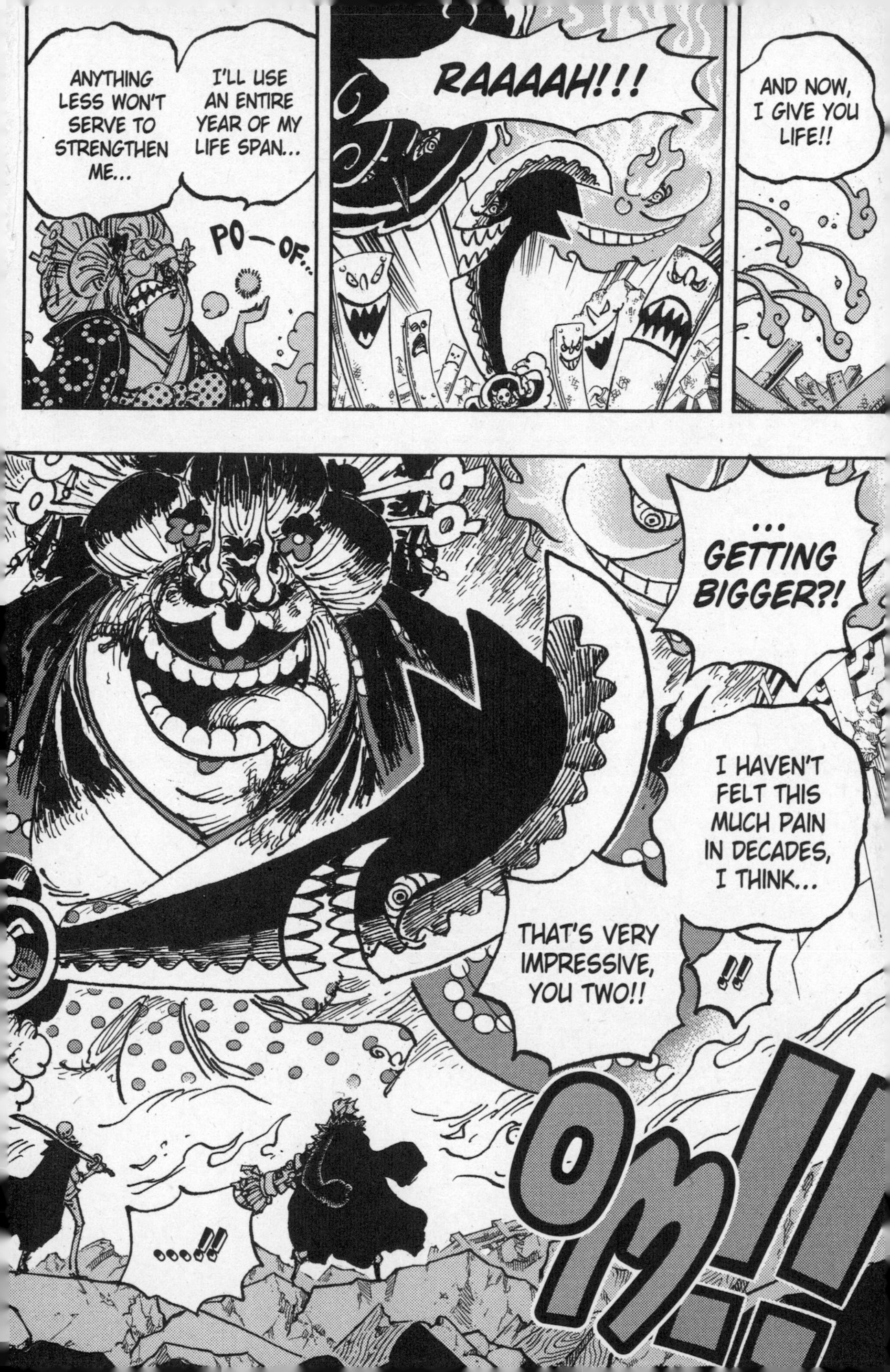
AND NOW, I GIVE YOU LIFE!!
RAAAAH!!!
I'LL USE AN ENTIRE YEAR OF MY LIFE SPAN...
ANYTHING LESS WON'T SERVE TO STRENGTHEN ME...
PO—OF...
...GETTING BIGGER?!
I HAVEN'T FELT THIS MUCH PAIN IN DECADES, I THINK...
THAT'S VERY IMPRESSIVE, YOU TWO!!
!!
....!!

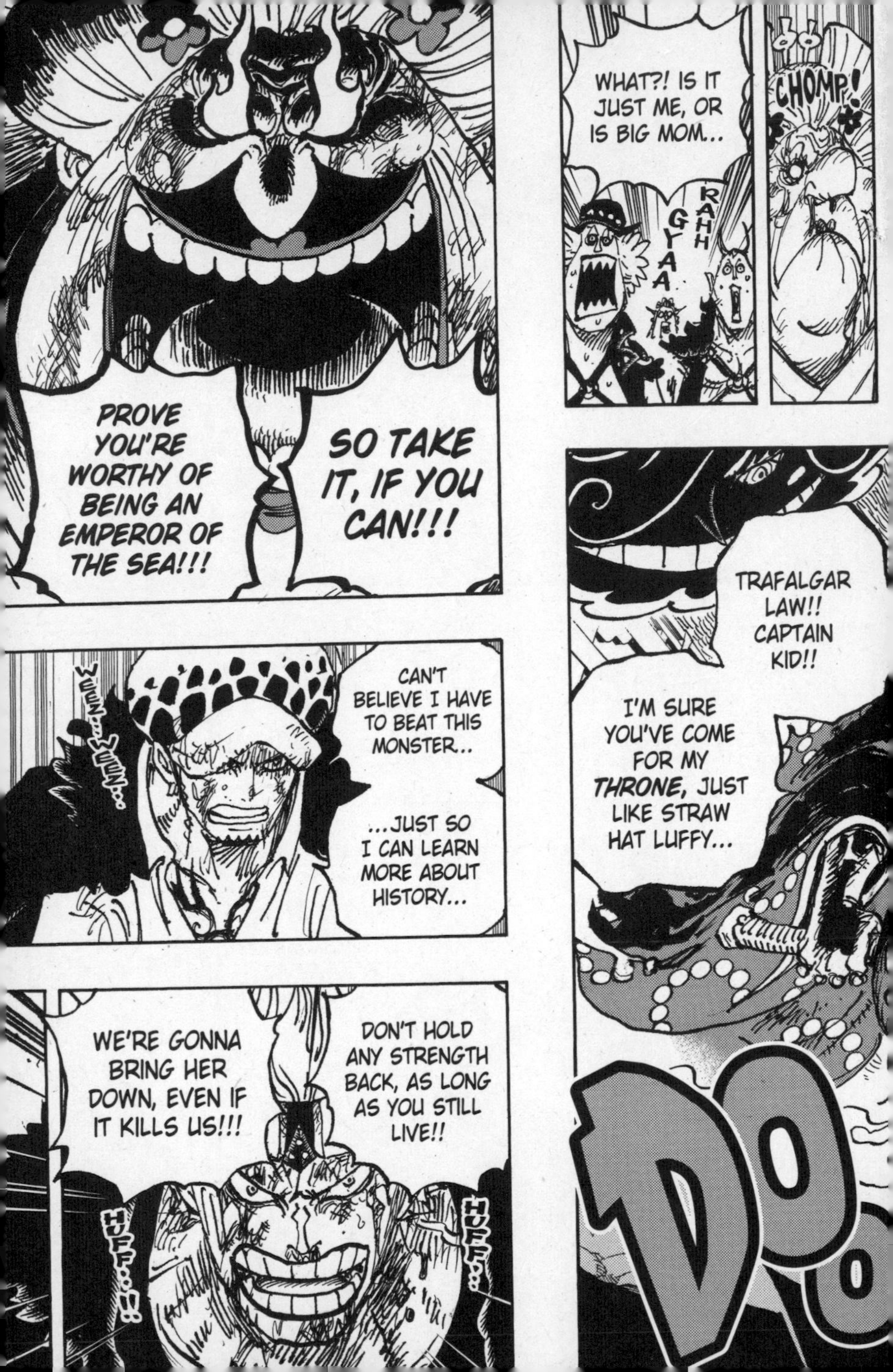
CHOMP!
WHAT?! IS IT JUST ME, OR IS BIG MOM...
RAHH
GYAA
TRAFALGAR LAW!! CAPTAIN KID!!
I'M SURE YOU'VE COME FOR MY *THRONE*, JUST LIKE STRAW HAT LUFFY...
DO
SO TAKE IT, IF YOU CAN!!!
PROVE YOU'RE WORTHY OF BEING AN EMPEROR OF THE SEA!!!
CAN'T BELIEVE I HAVE TO BEAT THIS MONSTER...
...JUST SO I CAN LEARN MORE ABOUT HISTORY...
WEEZ... WEEZ...
DON'T HOLD ANY STRENGTH BACK, AS LONG AS YOU STILL LIVE!!
WE'RE GONNA BRING HER DOWN, EVEN IF IT KILLS US!!!
HUFF...!!
HUFF...

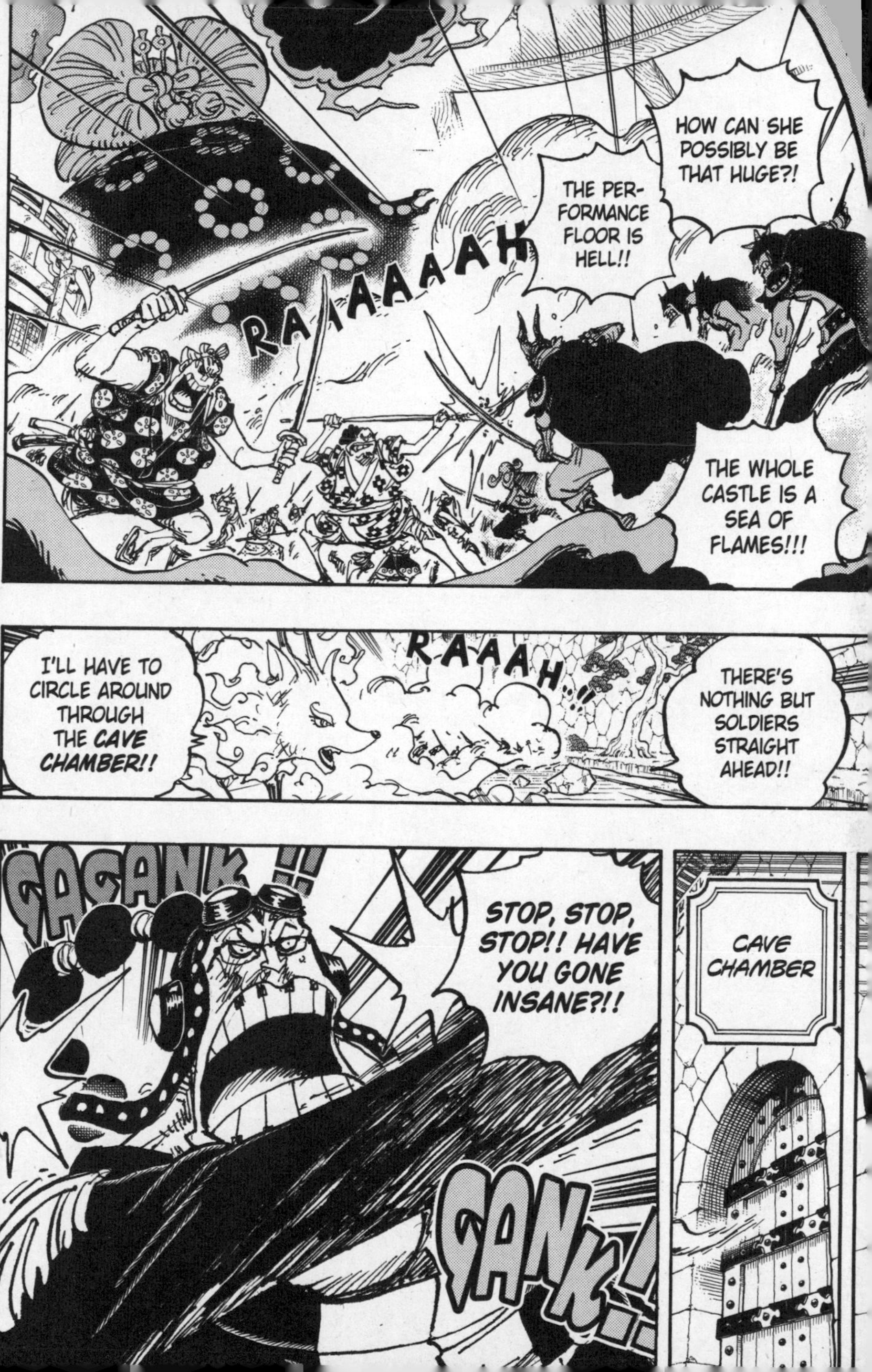
HOW CAN SHE POSSIBLY BE THAT HUGE?!
THE PER-FORMANCE FLOOR IS HELL!!
RAAAAAAH
THE WHOLE CASTLE IS A SEA OF FLAMES!!!
THERE'S NOTHING BUT SOLDIERS STRAIGHT AHEAD!!
RAAAH..!!
I'LL HAVE TO CIRCLE AROUND THROUGH THE CAVE CHAMBER!!
CAVE CHAMBER
GAGANK!!
STOP, STOP, STOP!! HAVE YOU GONE INSANE?!!
GANK..!!

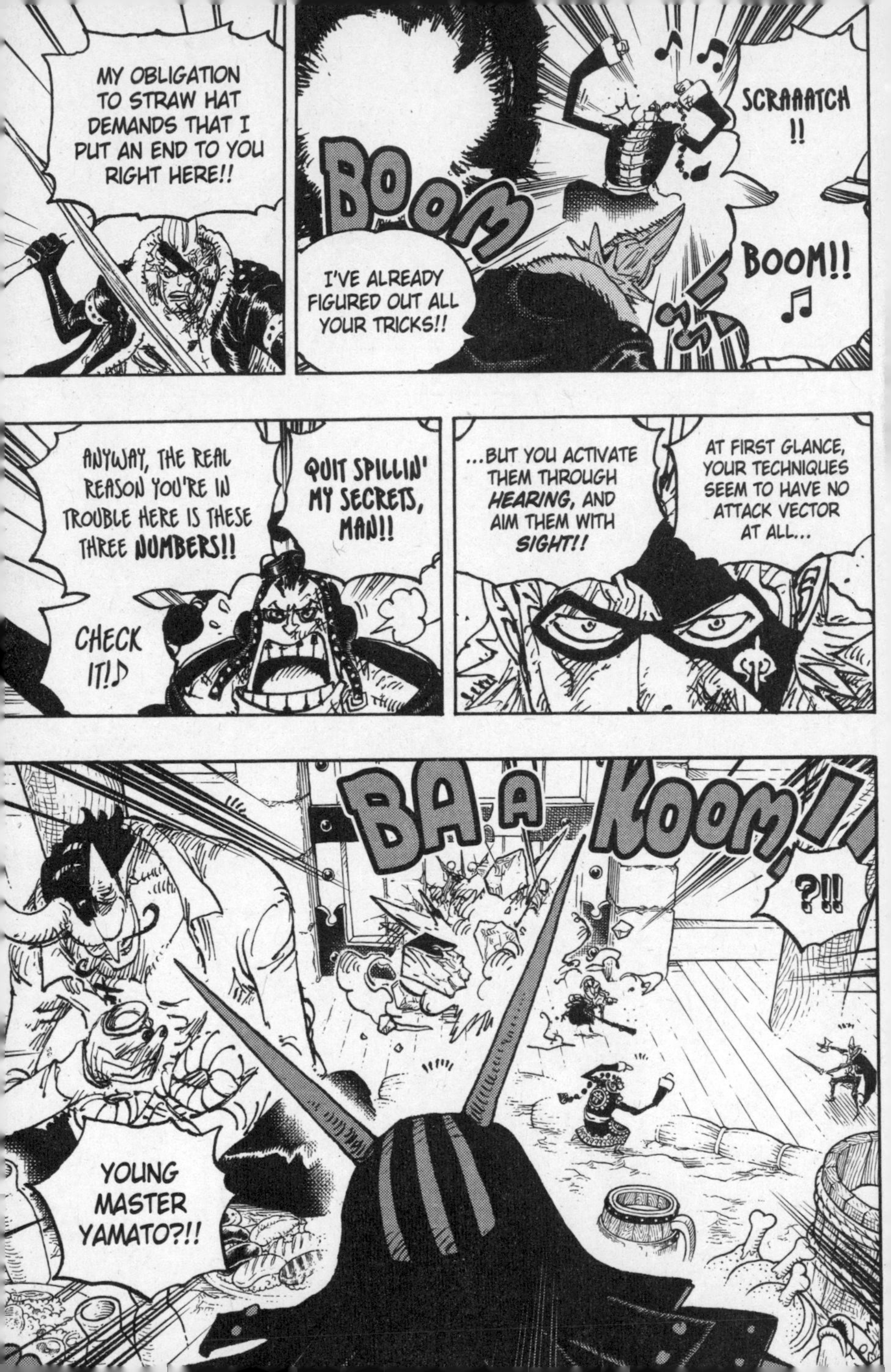
SCRAAATCH !!
BOOM
BOOM!!
I'VE ALREADY FIGURED OUT ALL YOUR TRICKS!!
MY OBLIGATION TO STRAW HAT DEMANDS THAT I PUT AN END TO YOU RIGHT HERE!!
AT FIRST GLANCE, YOUR TECHNIQUES SEEM TO HAVE NO ATTACK VECTOR AT ALL...
...BUT YOU ACTIVATE THEM THROUGH HEARING, AND AIM THEM WITH SIGHT!!
QUIT SPILLIN' MY SECRETS, MAN!!
ANYWAY, THE REAL REASON YOU'RE IN TROUBLE HERE IS THESE THREE NUMBERS!!
CHECK IT!♪
BA A KOOM!!
?!!
YOUNG MASTER YAMATO?!!

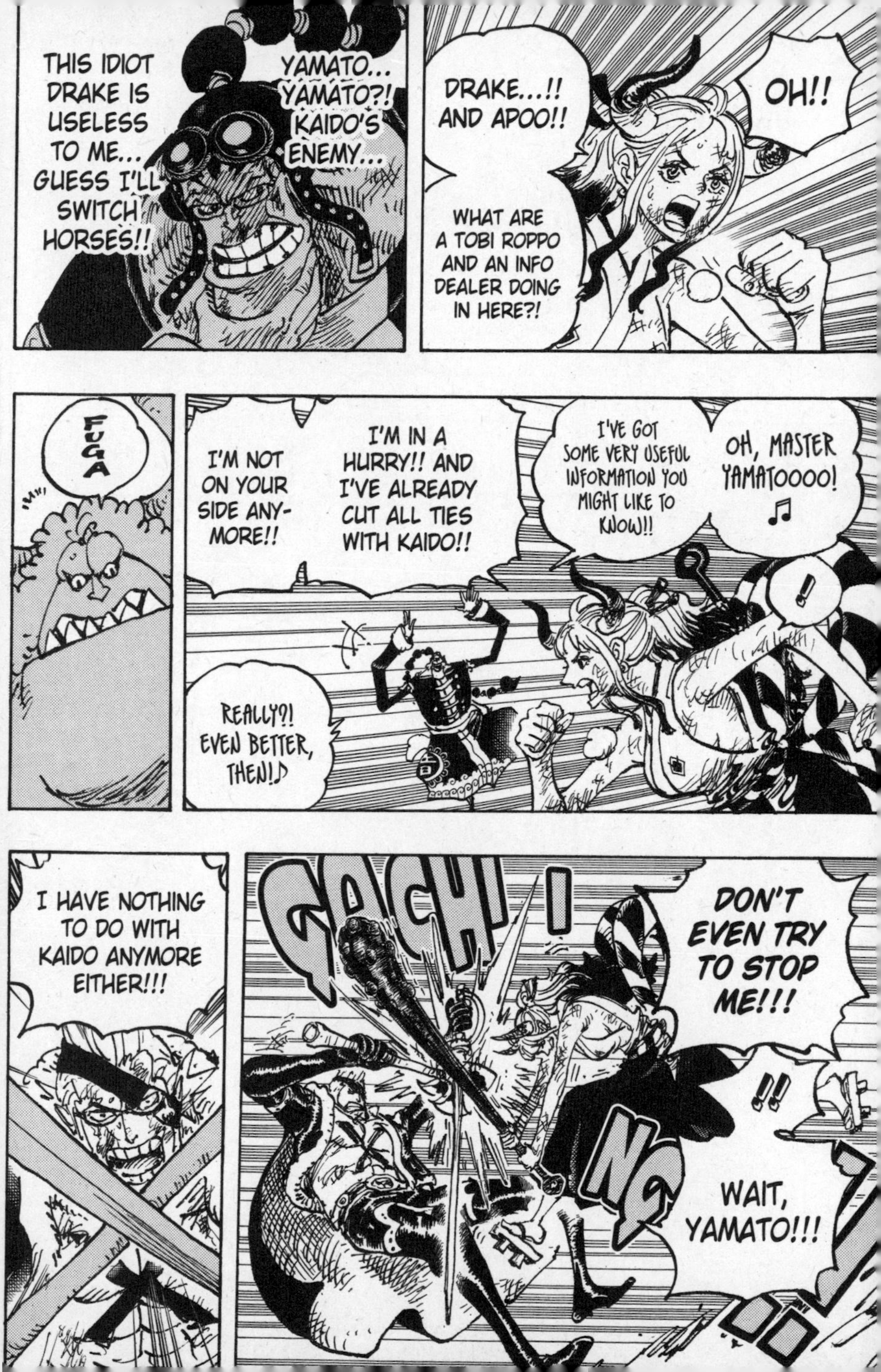
OH!!
DRAKE...!! AND APOO!!
WHAT ARE A TOBI ROPPO AND AN INFO DEALER DOING IN HERE?!
YAMATO... YAMATO?! KAIDO'S ENEMY...
THIS IDIOT DRAKE IS USELESS TO ME... GUESS I'LL SWITCH HORSES!!
OH, MASTER YAMATOOOO! ♫
I'VE GOT SOME VERY USEFUL INFORMATION YOU MIGHT LIKE TO KNOW!!
!
I'M IN A HURRY!! AND I'VE ALREADY CUT ALL TIES WITH KAIDO!!
I'M NOT ON YOUR SIDE ANYMORE!!
REALLY?! EVEN BETTER, THEN!♪
FUGA
DON'T EVEN TRY TO STOP ME!!!
GACHI!
!!
NG
WAIT, YAMATO!!!
I HAVE NOTHING TO DO WITH KAIDO ANYMORE EITHER!!!

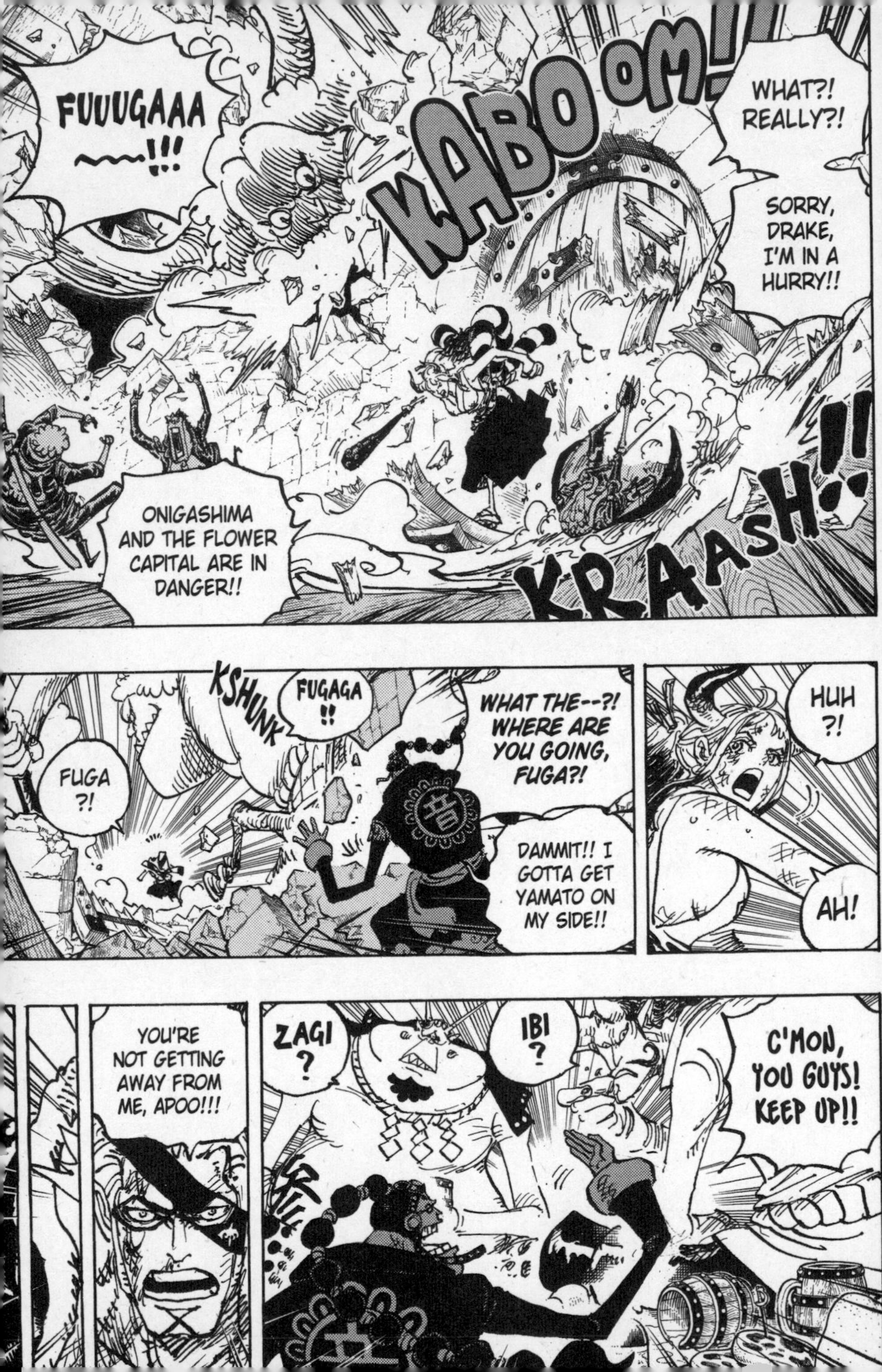
WHAT?! REALLY?!
KABOOM!!
FUUUGAAA ~~~!!!
SORRY, DRAKE, I'M IN A HURRY!!
KRAASH!!
ONIGASHIMA AND THE FLOWER CAPITAL ARE IN DANGER!!
HUH ?!
AH!
WHAT THE--?! WHERE ARE YOU GOING, FUGA?!
FUGAGA !!
KSHUNK
FUGA ?!
DAMMIT!! I GOTTA GET YAMATO ON MY SIDE!!
C'MON, YOU GUYS! KEEP UP!!
IBI ?
ZAGI ?
YOU'RE NOT GETTING AWAY FROM ME, APOO!!!

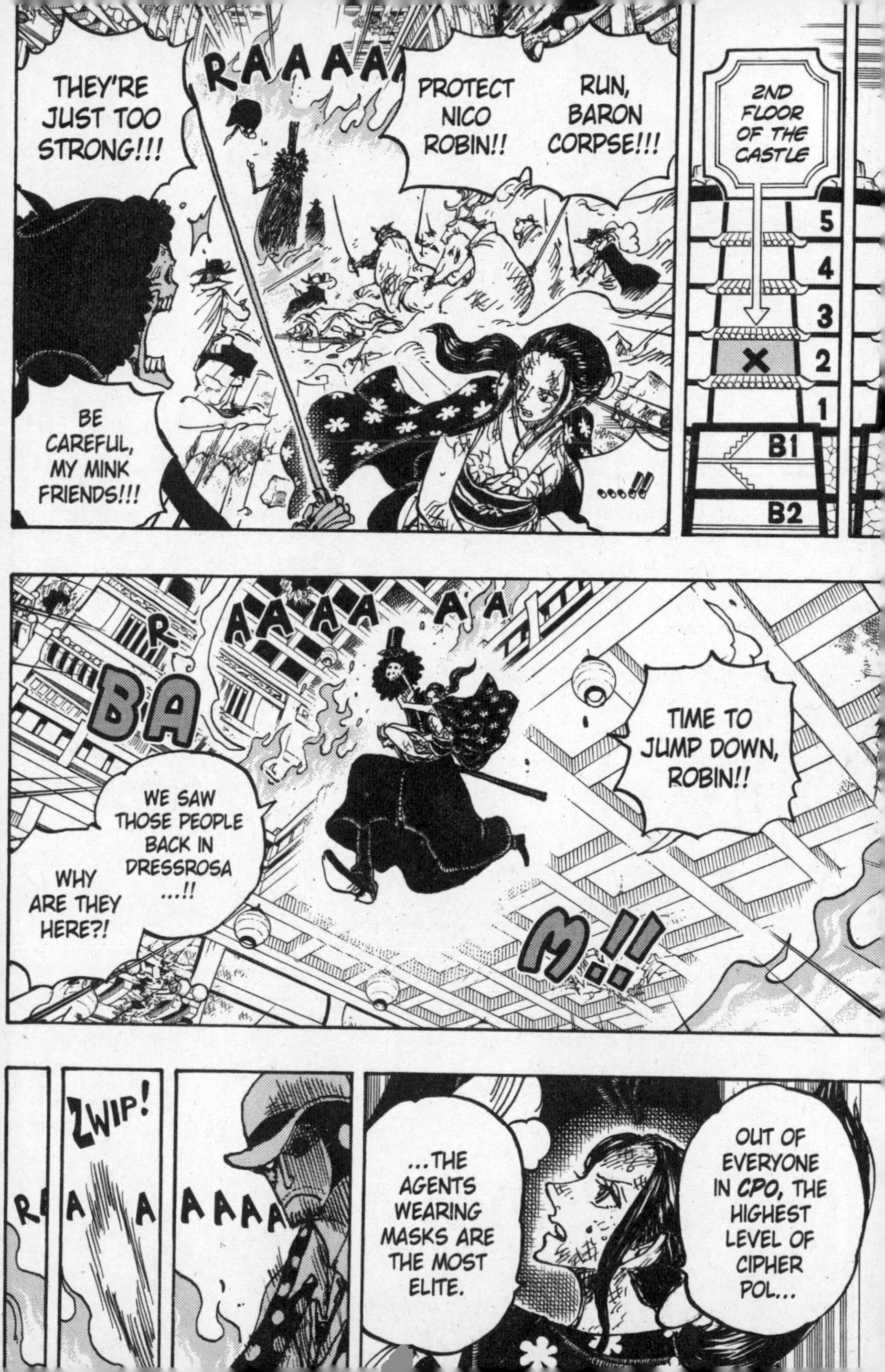
2ND FLOOR OF THE CASTLE
5
4
3
2
1
B1
B2
RUN, BARON CORPSE!!!
PROTECT NICO ROBIN!!
RAAAAA
THEY'RE JUST TOO STRONG!!!
...!!
BE CAREFUL, MY MINK FRIENDS!!!
TIME TO JUMP DOWN, ROBIN!!
RAAAAAA
BA
M!!
WE SAW THOSE PEOPLE BACK IN DRESSROSA ...!!
WHY ARE THEY HERE?!
OUT OF EVERYONE IN CPO, THE HIGHEST LEVEL OF CIPHER POL...
...THE AGENTS WEARING MASKS ARE THE MOST ELITE.
ZWIP!
RAAAAAA

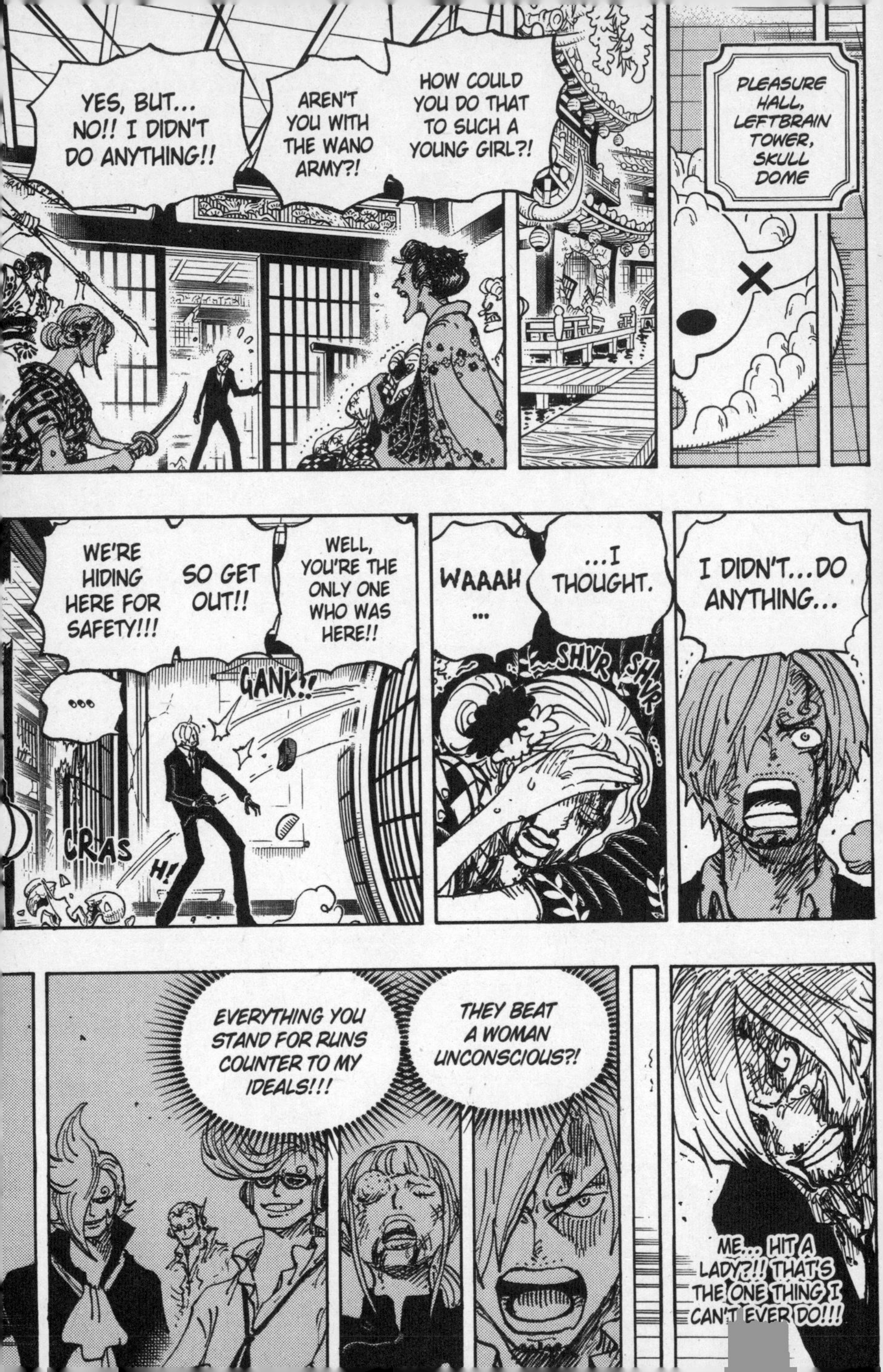
PLEASURE HALL, LEFTBRAIN TOWER, SKULL DOME
HOW COULD YOU DO THAT TO SUCH A YOUNG GIRL?!
AREN'T YOU WITH THE WANO ARMY?!
YES, BUT... NO!! I DIDN'T DO ANYTHING!!
I DIDN'T...DO ANYTHING...
...I THOUGHT.
WAAAH ...
SHVR SHVR
WELL, YOU'RE THE ONLY ONE WHO WAS HERE!!
SO GET OUT!!
WE'RE HIDING HERE FOR SAFETY!!!
GANK!!
...
CRASH!
ME... HIT A LADY?!! THAT'S THE ONE THING I CAN'T EVER DO!!!
THEY BEAT A WOMAN UNCONSCIOUS?!
EVERYTHING YOU STAND FOR RUNS COUNTER TO MY IDEALS!!!

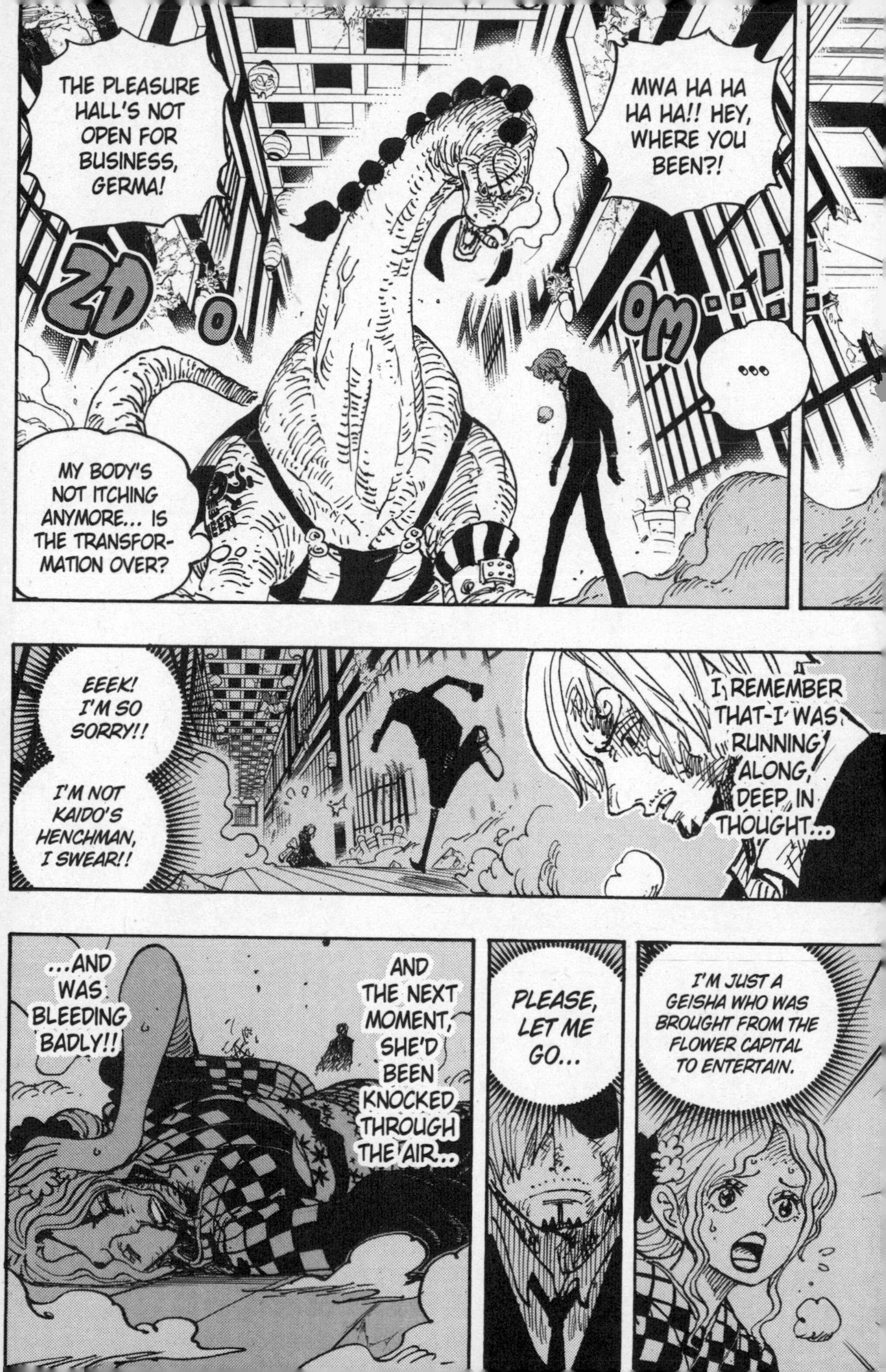
MWA HA HA HA HA!! HEY, WHERE YOU BEEN?!
...
THE PLEASURE HALL'S NOT OPEN FOR BUSINESS, GERMA!
ZDO
OM..!!
MY BODY'S NOT ITCHING ANYMORE... IS THE TRANSFORMATION OVER?
I REMEMBER THAT I WAS RUNNING ALONG, DEEP IN THOUGHT...
EEEK! I'M SO SORRY!!
I'M NOT KAIDO'S HENCHMAN, I SWEAR!!
I'M JUST A GEISHA WHO WAS BROUGHT FROM THE FLOWER CAPITAL TO ENTERTAIN.
PLEASE, LET ME GO...
AND THE NEXT MOMENT, SHE'D BEEN KNOCKED THROUGH THE AIR...
...AND WAS BLEEDING BADLY!!

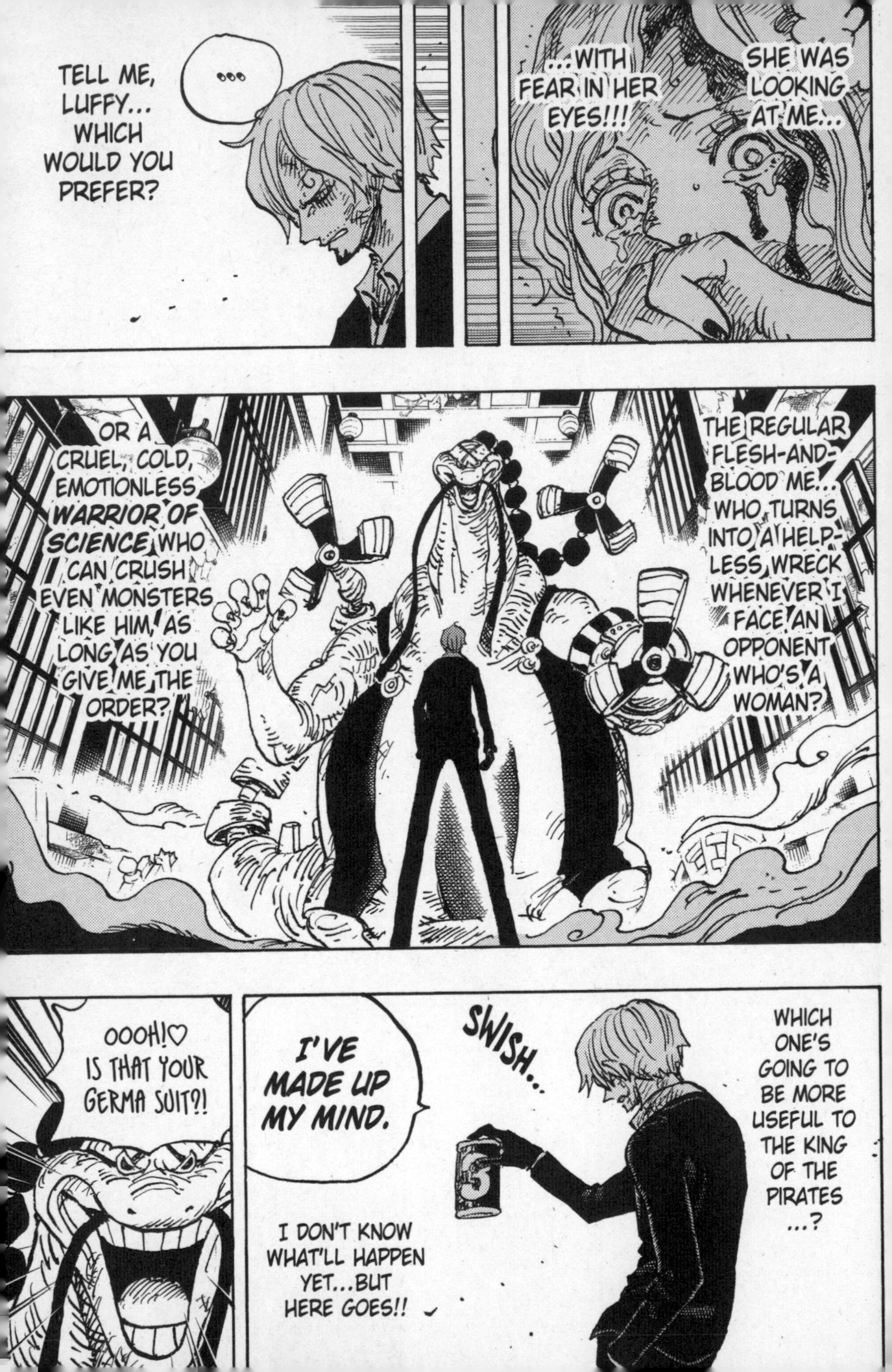
SHE WAS LOOKING AT ME...
...WITH FEAR IN HER EYES!!!
...
TELL ME, LUFFY... WHICH WOULD YOU PREFER?
THE REGULAR FLESH-AND-BLOOD ME... WHO TURNS INTO A HELPLESS WRECK WHENEVER I FACE AN OPPONENT WHO'S A WOMAN?
OR A CRUEL, COLD, EMOTIONLESS WARRIOR OF SCIENCE WHO CAN CRUSH EVEN MONSTERS LIKE HIM, AS LONG AS YOU GIVE ME THE ORDER?
WHICH ONE'S GOING TO BE MORE USEFUL TO THE KING OF THE PIRATES ...?
SWISH...
5
I'VE MADE UP MY MIND.
I DON'T KNOW WHAT'LL HAPPEN YET...BUT HERE GOES!!
OOOH!♡ IS THAT YOUR GERMA SUIT?!

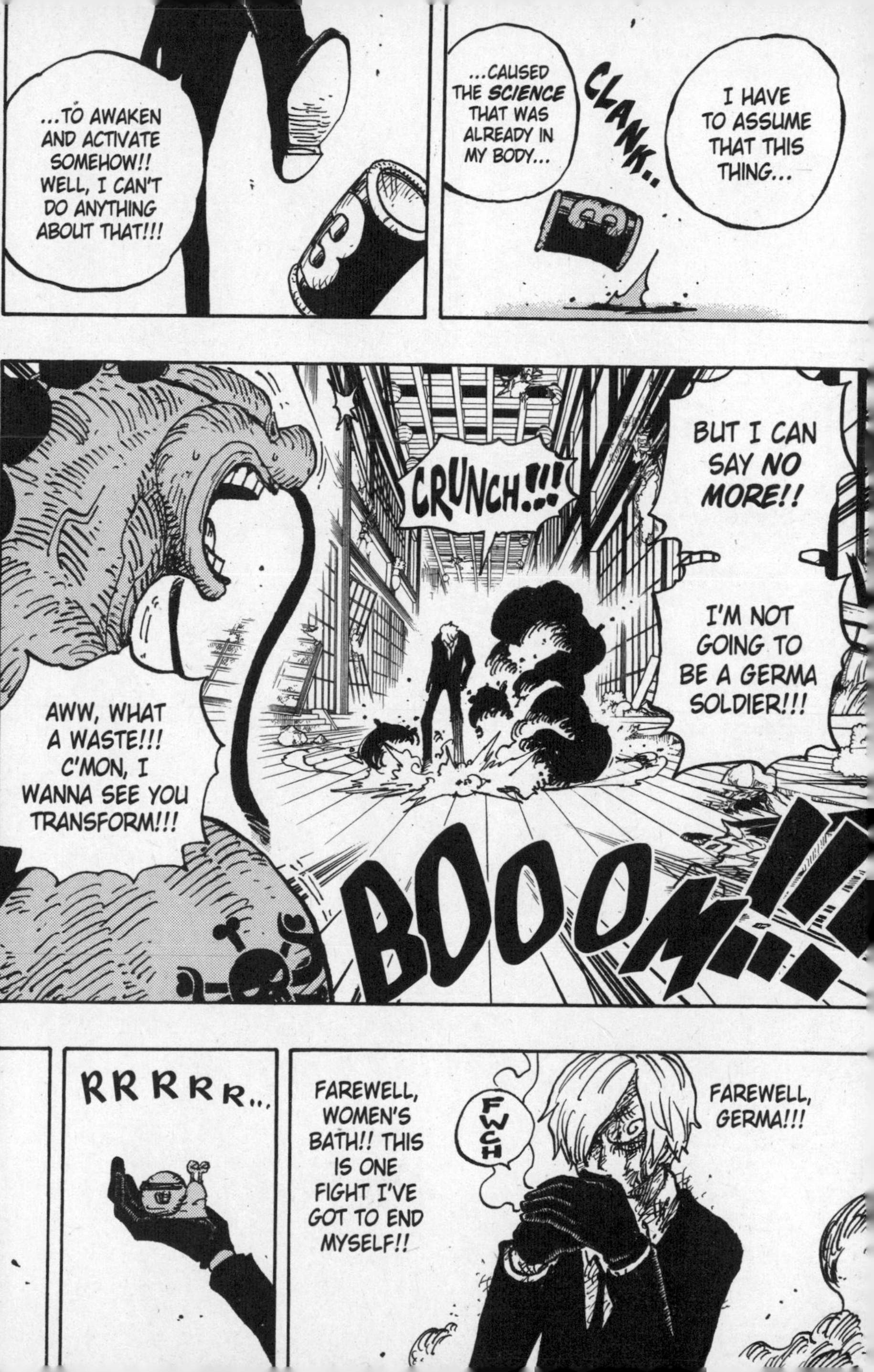
I HAVE TO ASSUME THAT THIS THING...
CLANK..
...CAUSED THE SCIENCE THAT WAS ALREADY IN MY BODY...
...TO AWAKEN AND ACTIVATE SOMEHOW!! WELL, I CAN'T DO ANYTHING ABOUT THAT!!!
BUT I CAN SAY NO MORE!!
I'M NOT GOING TO BE A GERMA SOLDIER!!!
CRUNCH!!!
AWW, WHAT A WASTE!!! C'MON, I WANNA SEE YOU TRANSFORM!!!
BOOOM!!!
FAREWELL, GERMA!!!
FWCH
FAREWELL, WOMEN'S BATH!! THIS IS ONE FIGHT I'VE GOT TO END MYSELF!!
RRRRR...

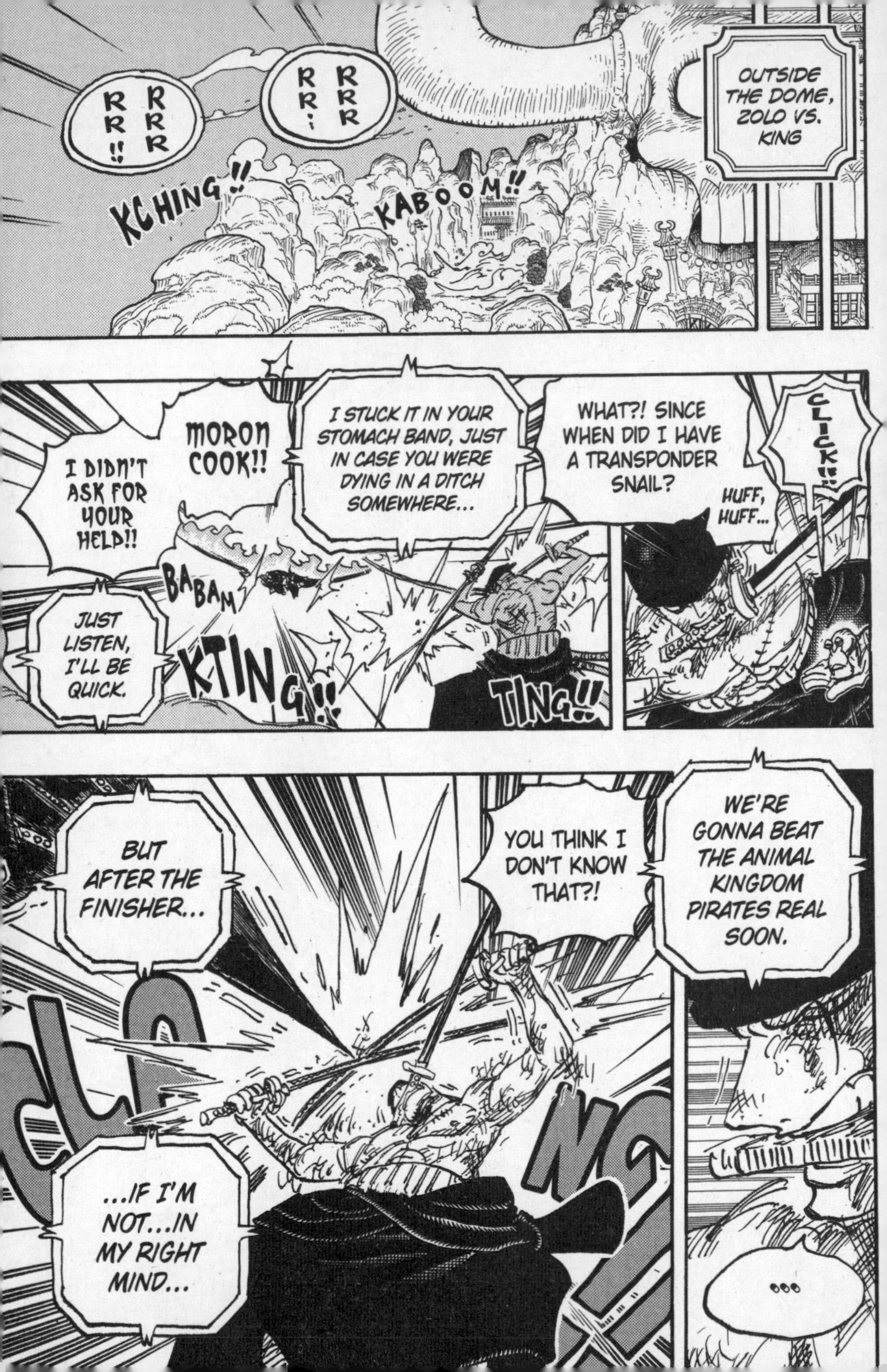
OUTSIDE THE DOME, ZOLO VS. KING
RRRRR
RRRRR!!
KABOOM!!
KCHING!!
CLICK!!
HUFF, HUFF...
WHAT?! SINCE WHEN DID I HAVE A TRANSPONDER SNAIL?
TING!!
I STUCK IT IN YOUR STOMACH BAND, JUST IN CASE YOU WERE DYING IN A DITCH SOMEWHERE...
MORON COOK!!
I DIDN'T ASK FOR YOUR HELP!!
BABAM
KTING!!
JUST LISTEN, I'LL BE QUICK.
WE'RE GONNA BEAT THE ANIMAL KINGDOM PIRATES REAL SOON.
...
YOU THINK I DON'T KNOW THAT?!
BUT AFTER THE FINISHER...
...IF I'M NOT...IN MY RIGHT MIND...

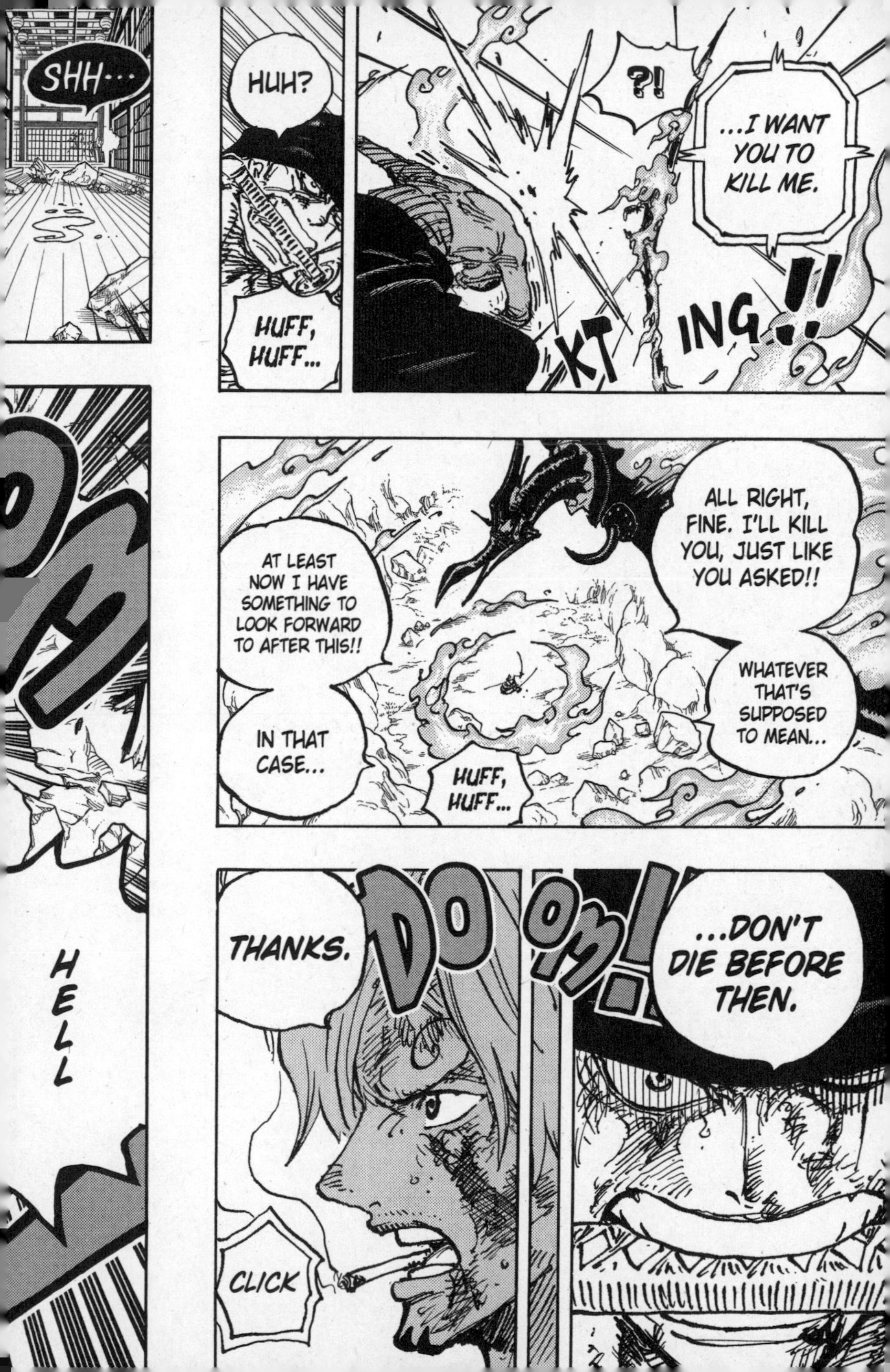
?!
...I WANT YOU TO KILL ME.
KT ING!!
HUH?
HUFF, HUFF...
ALL RIGHT, FINE. I'LL KILL YOU, JUST LIKE YOU ASKED!!
WHATEVER THAT'S SUPPOSED TO MEAN...
AT LEAST NOW I HAVE SOMETHING TO LOOK FORWARD TO AFTER THIS!!
IN THAT CASE...
HUFF, HUFF...
...DON'T DIE BEFORE THEN.
DOOM!!
THANKS.
CLICK
SHH...
HELL

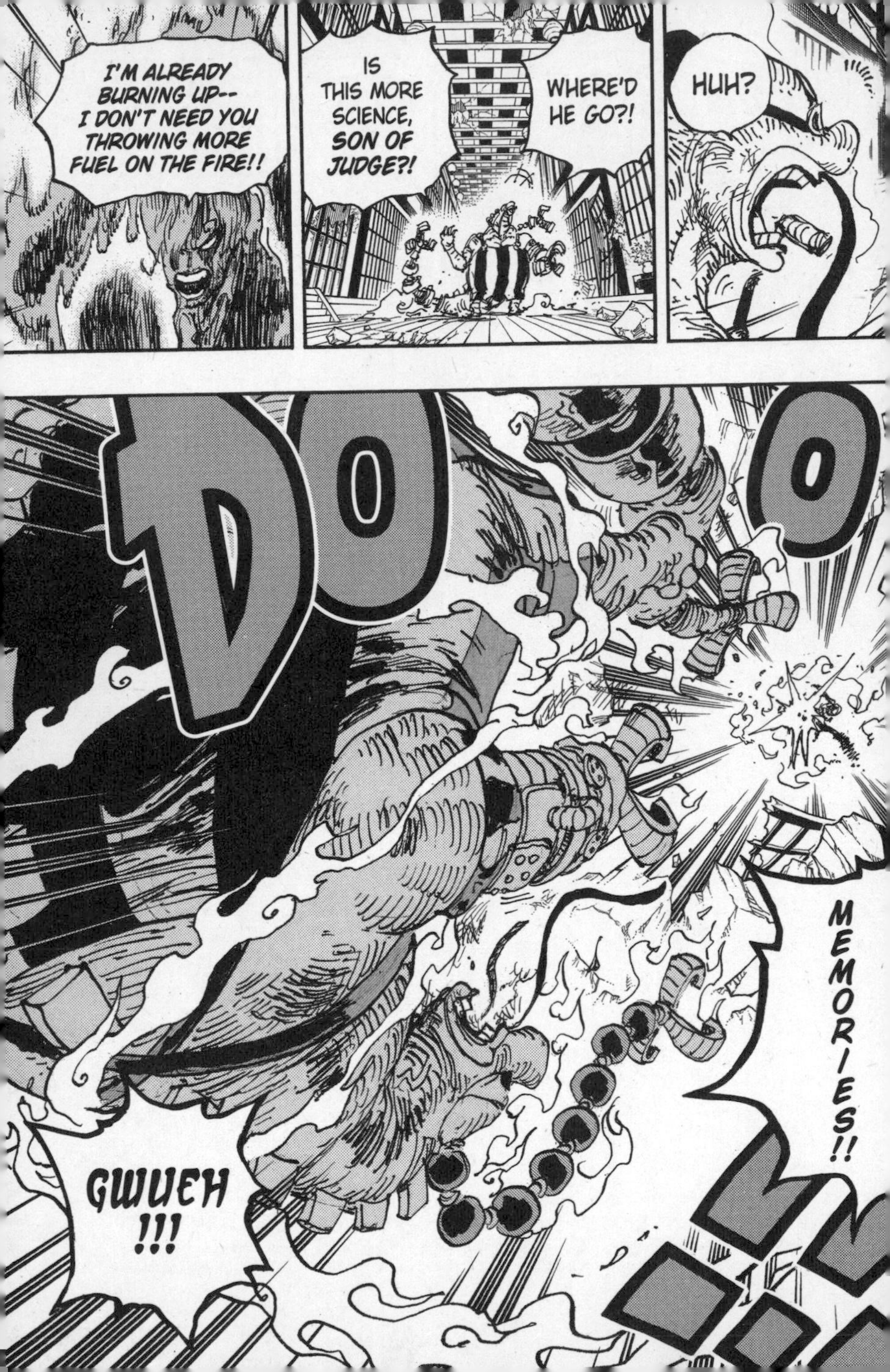
HUH?
WHERE'D HE GO?!
IS THIS MORE SCIENCE, SON OF JUDGE?!
I'M ALREADY BURNING UP-- I DON'T NEED YOU THROWING MORE FUEL ON THE FIRE!!
DOO
MEMORIES!!
GWUEH!!!

SBS Question Corner

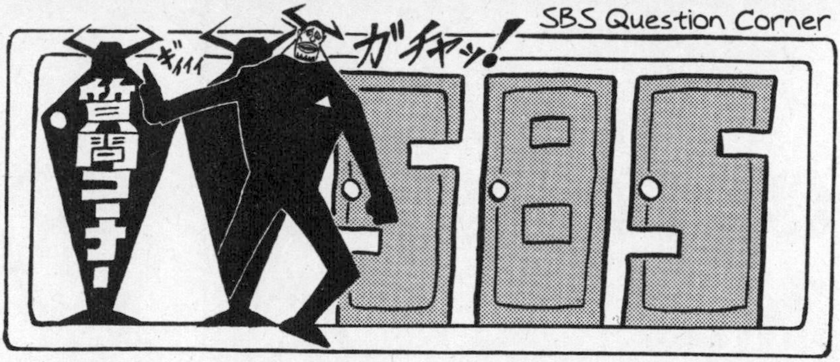
ギィィィ
ガチャッ!
質問コーナー!
SBS

(Hoya, Tokyo)

Q: Please draw the personified versions of Usopp's Black Kabuto and his wide-mouth *(gamaguchi)* bag.

--New Sniper King

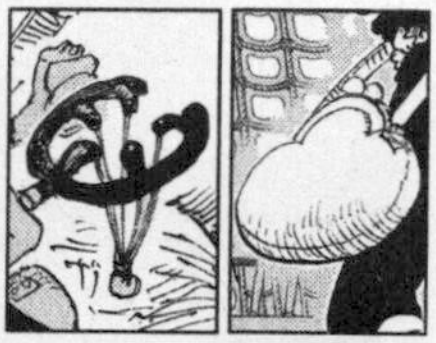

A: Okay, sure.

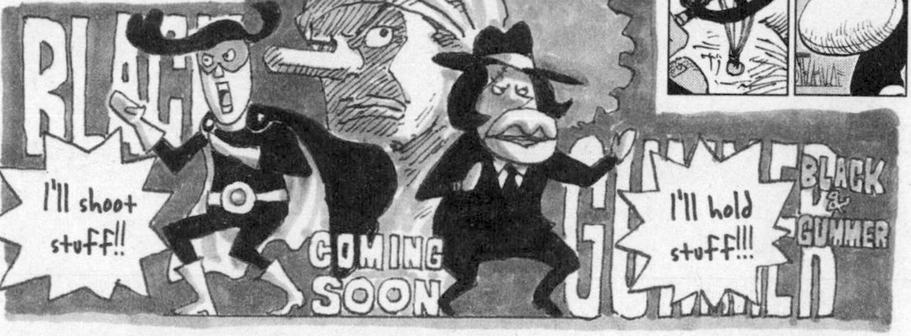
I'll shoot stuff!!
COMING SOON
I'll hold stuff!!!
BLACK & GUMMER

Q: Hello, Odacchi! I want to ask something I've always been curious about. Where did Luffy first hear about the King of the Pirates?

--Masazo

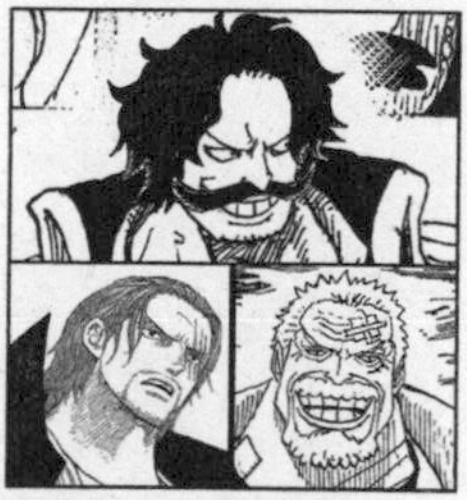

A: He heard that term from Shanks. Of course, Shanks didn't tell Luffy that he was actually on the King of the Pirates' ship. Before meeting Shanks, Garp told Luffy to grow up and join the Navy, but Luffy always wanted to be free and go on adventures, so he felt some resistance to that idea.

Q: Hi, Odacchi! Based on the cover for chapter 1031, should I assume that the No. 2 of the Heart Pirates is Bepo?! This is a surprise to me, because I always assumed it was Penguin, Shachi, and Bepo all together! Is it because Bepo (as Sulong) is the strongest of the three?

--Pudding-ya

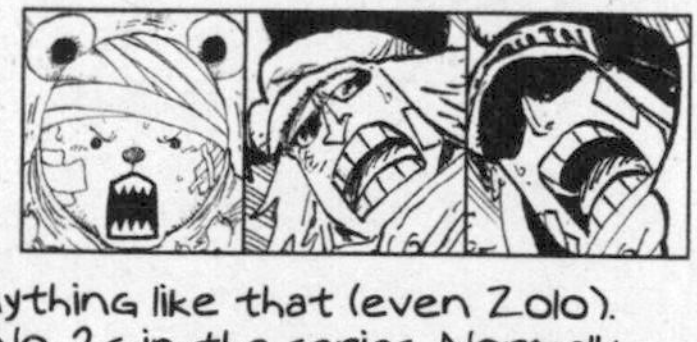

A: That illustration isn't a depiction of the "first mates" of their crews or anything like that (even Zolo). I just decided to pick out some of the No. 2s in the series. Normally Shachi and Penguin would be more reliable leaders, but they've seen Bepo in his Sulong form, and they know they can't beat him.

Chapter 1032:

ODEN'S BELOVED BLADE

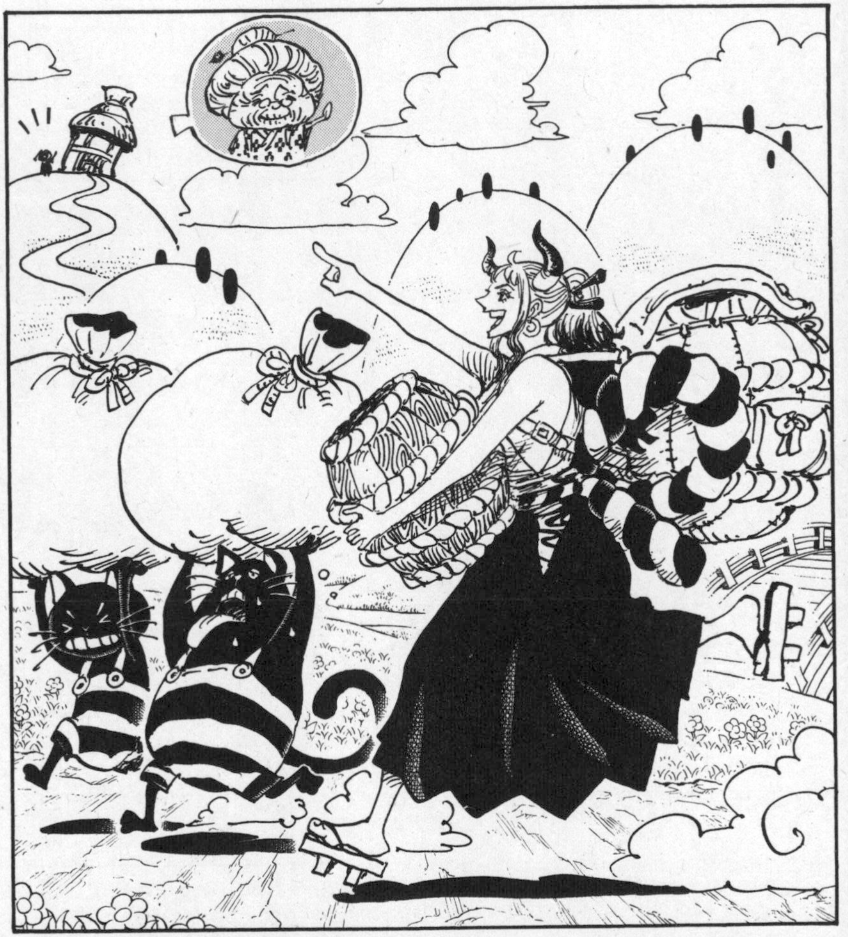

READER REQUEST: "BLACK CATS AND YAMATO MAKING DELIVERIES" BY KOKORO FUKADA

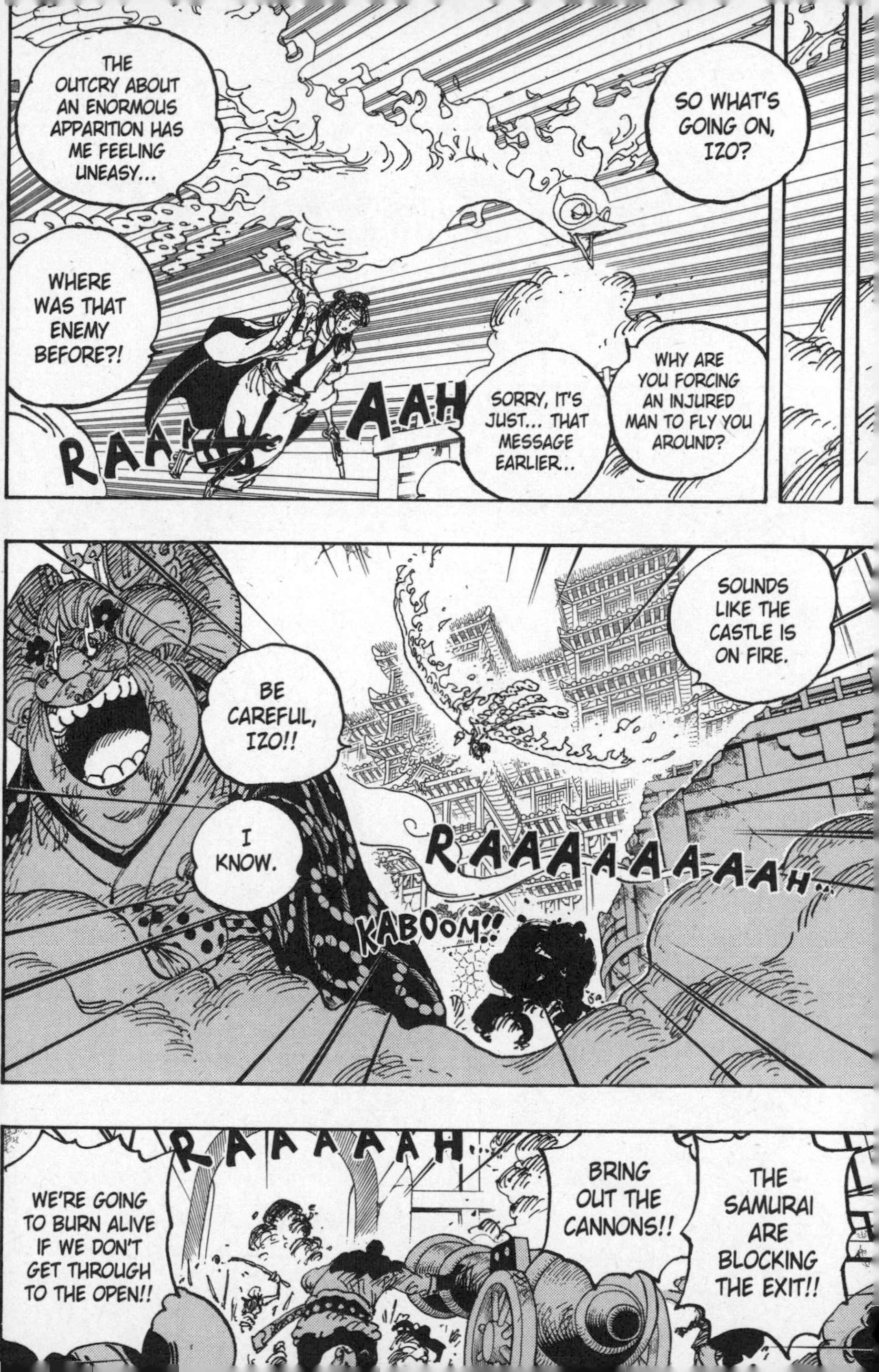
SO WHAT'S GOING ON, IZO?
WHY ARE YOU FORCING AN INJURED MAN TO FLY YOU AROUND?
SORRY, IT'S JUST... THAT MESSAGE EARLIER..
THE OUTCRY ABOUT AN ENORMOUS APPARITION HAS ME FEELING UNEASY...
WHERE WAS THAT ENEMY BEFORE?!
RAA AAH
SOUNDS LIKE THE CASTLE IS ON FIRE.
BE CAREFUL, IZO!!
I KNOW.
RAAAAAAAAH..
KABOOM!!
THE SAMURAI ARE BLOCKING THE EXIT!!
BRING OUT THE CANNONS!!
RAAAAAAH...
WE'RE GOING TO BURN ALIVE IF WE DON'T GET THROUGH TO THE OPEN!!

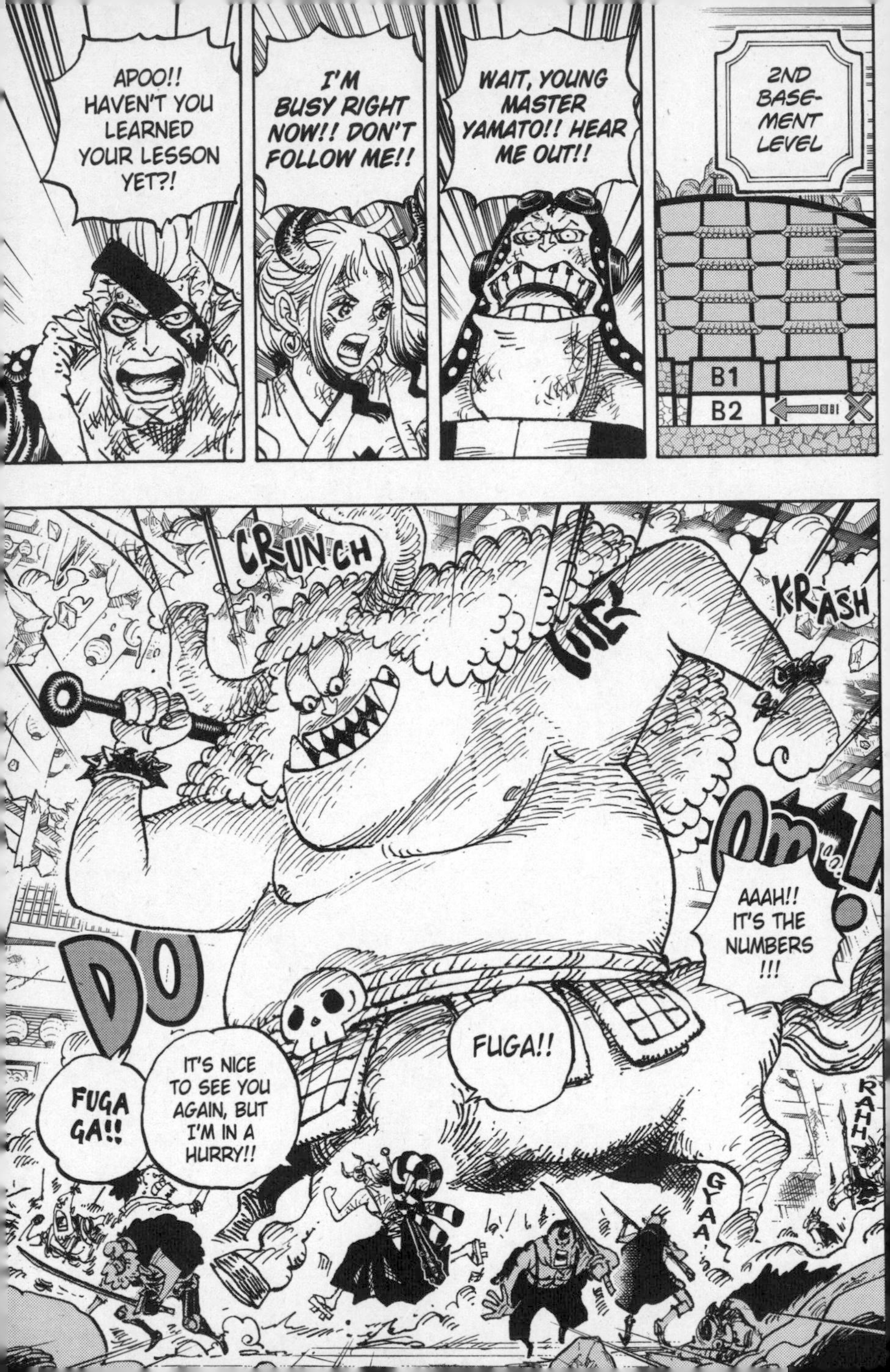
2ND BASEMENT LEVEL
B1
B2
WAIT, YOUNG MASTER YAMATO!! HEAR ME OUT!!
I'M BUSY RIGHT NOW!! DON'T FOLLOW ME!!
APOO!! HAVEN'T YOU LEARNED YOUR LESSON YET?!
KRASH
CRUNCH
AAAH!! IT'S THE NUMBERS!!!
RAHH
FUGA!!
GYAA
DO
IT'S NICE TO SEE YOU AGAIN, BUT I'M IN A HURRY!!
FUGA GA!!

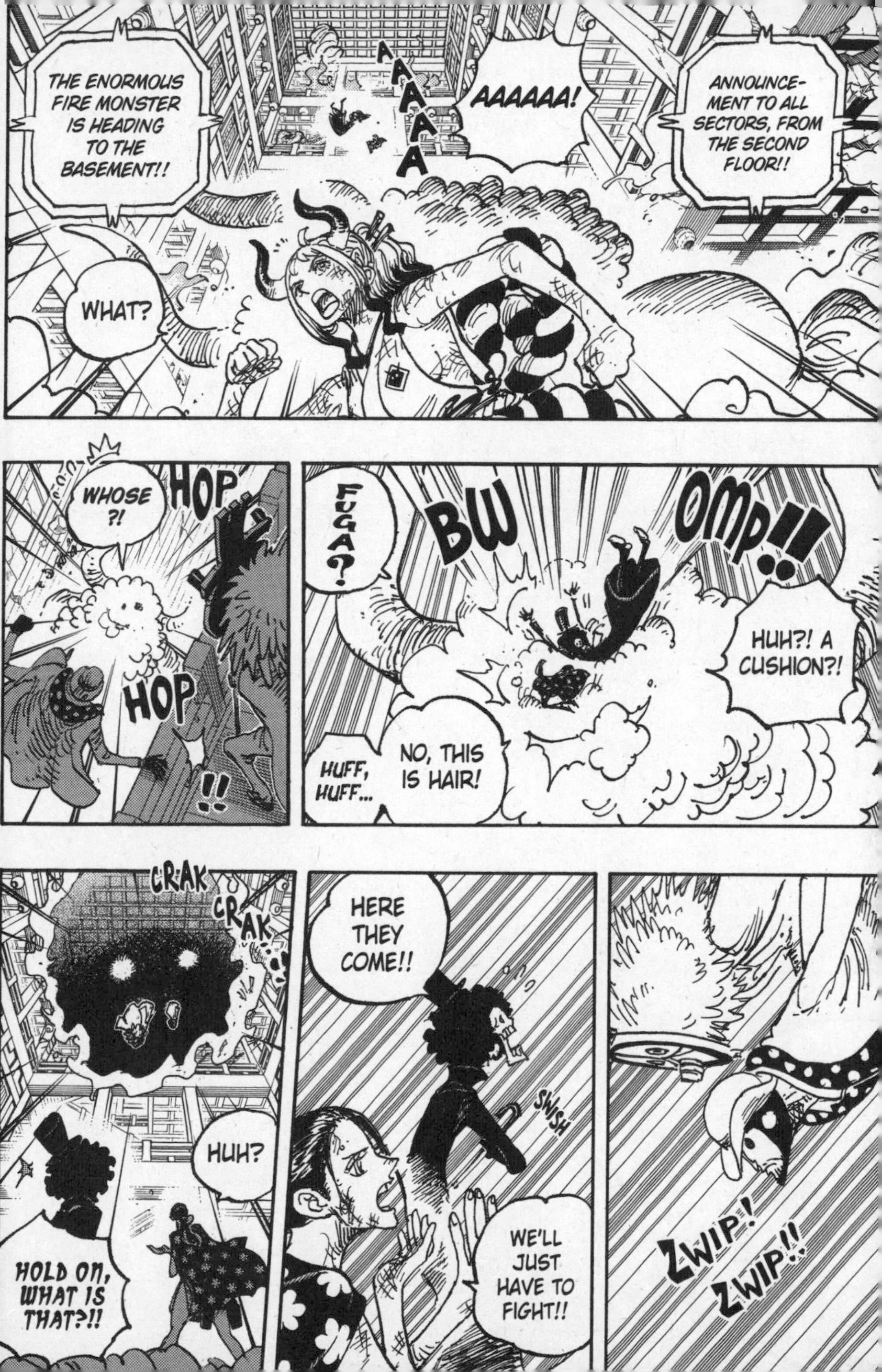
ANNOUNCEMENT TO ALL SECTORS, FROM THE SECOND FLOOR!!
AAAAAA!
AAAAA
THE ENORMOUS FIRE MONSTER IS HEADING TO THE BASEMENT!!
WHAT?
BW
OMP!!
FUGA?
HUH?! A CUSHION?!
NO, THIS IS HAIR!
HUFF, HUFF...
HOP
WHOSE ?!
HOP
!!
ZWIP!
ZWIP!!
HERE THEY COME!!
SWISH
WE'LL JUST HAVE TO FIGHT!!
CRAK
CRAK
HUH?
HOLD ON, WHAT IS THAT?!!

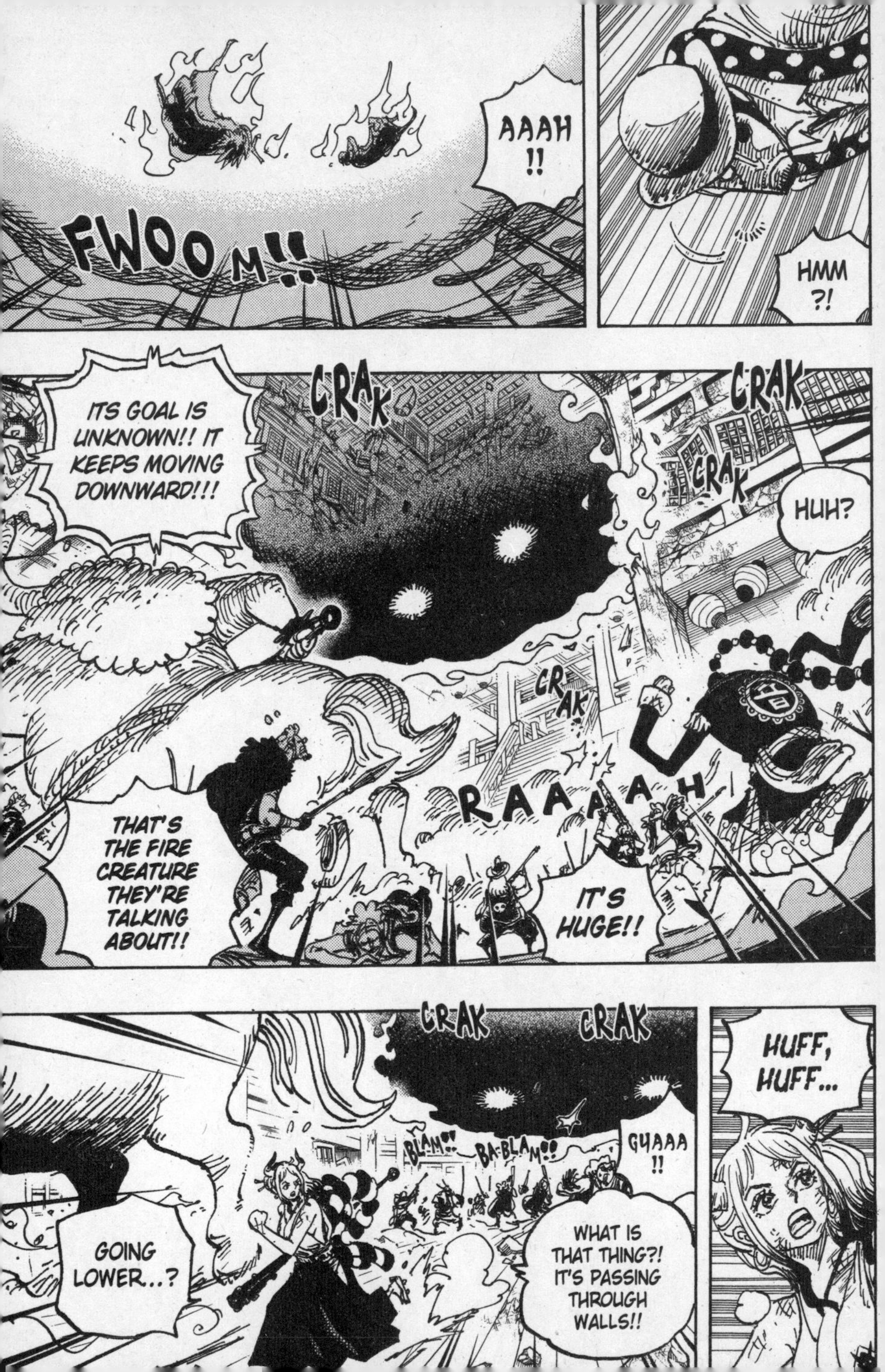
HMM ?!
AAAH !!
FWOOM!!
CRAK
CRAK
CRAK
HUH?
ITS GOAL IS UNKNOWN!! IT KEEPS MOVING DOWNWARD!!!
CRAK
RAAAAAH
IT'S HUGE!!
THAT'S THE FIRE CREATURE THEY'RE TALKING ABOUT!!
HUFF, HUFF...
CRAK
CRAK
GUAAA !!
BA-BLAM!!
BLAM!!
WHAT IS THAT THING?! IT'S PASSING THROUGH WALLS!!
GOING LOWER...?

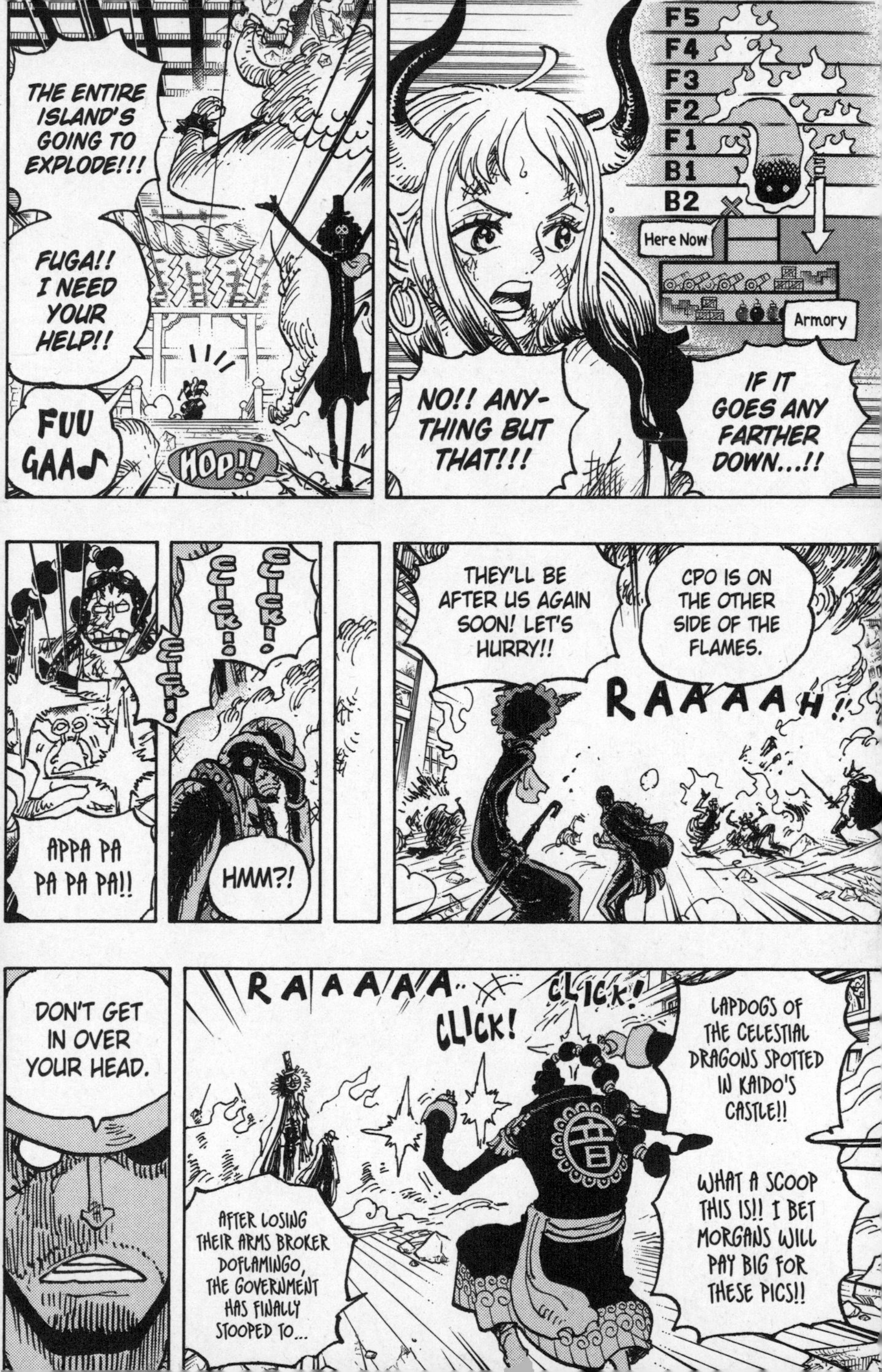
F5
F4
F3
F2
F1
B1
B2
Here Now
Armory
IF IT GOES ANY FARTHER DOWN...!!
NO!! ANYTHING BUT THAT!!!
THE ENTIRE ISLAND'S GOING TO EXPLODE!!!
FUGA!! I NEED YOUR HELP!!
HOP!!
FUU GAA♪
CPO IS ON THE OTHER SIDE OF THE FLAMES.
THEY'LL BE AFTER US AGAIN SOON! LET'S HURRY!!
RAAAAH!!
CLICK!
CLICK!
CLICK!
HMM?!
APPA PA PA PA PA!!
LAPDOGS OF THE CELESTIAL DRAGONS SPOTTED IN KAIDO'S CASTLE!!
CLICK!
CLICK!
RAAAAA
WHAT A SCOOP THIS IS!! I BET MORGANS WILL PAY BIG FOR THESE PICS!!
AFTER LOSING THEIR ARMS BROKER DOFLAMINGO, THE GOVERNMENT HAS FINALLY STOOPED TO...
DON'T GET IN OVER YOUR HEAD.

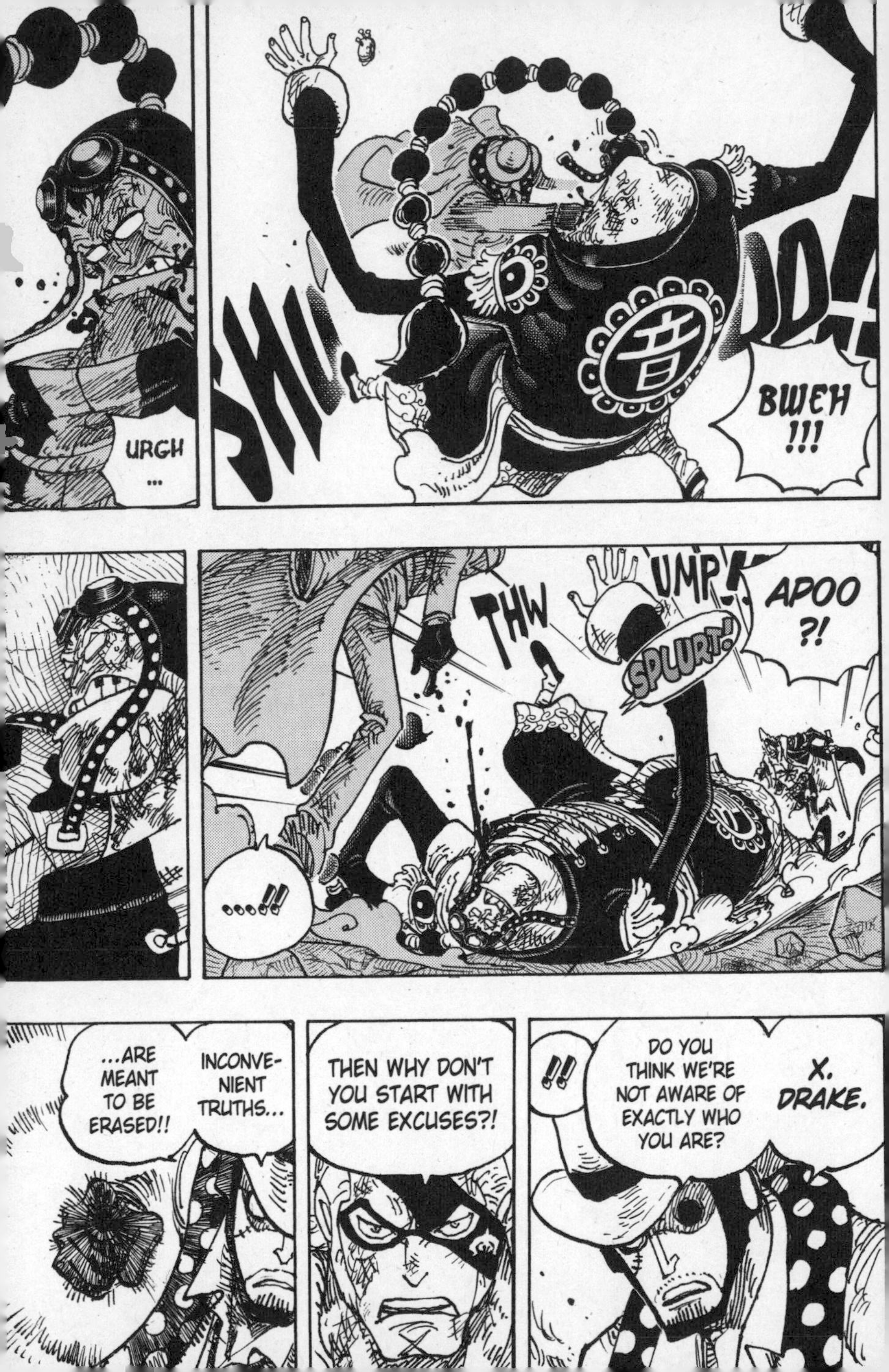
DA!
BWEH!!!
SHU
URGH...
APOO?!
THW
UMP!!
SPLURT!
...!!
X. DRAKE.
DO YOU THINK WE'RE NOT AWARE OF EXACTLY WHO YOU ARE?
!!
THEN WHY DON'T YOU START WITH SOME EXCUSES?!
INCONVENIENT TRUTHS...
...ARE MEANT TO BE ERASED!!

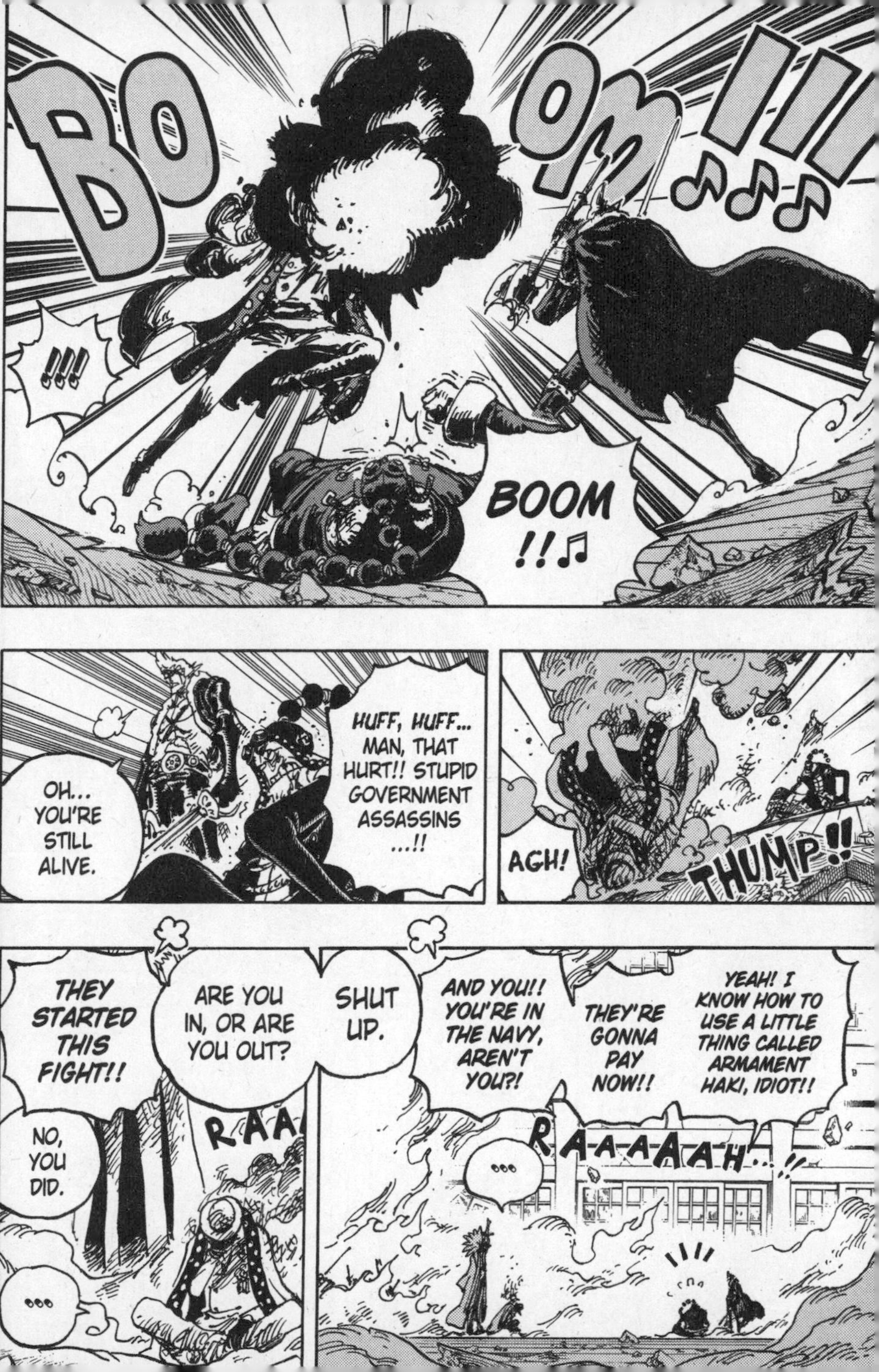
BOOOM!!! ♪♪♪
BOOM !!♪
!!!
AGH!
THUMP!!
HUFF, HUFF... MAN, THAT HURT!! STUPID GOVERNMENT ASSASSINS ...!!
OH... YOU'RE STILL ALIVE.
YEAH! I KNOW HOW TO USE A LITTLE THING CALLED ARMAMENT HAKI, IDIOT!!
THEY'RE GONNA PAY NOW!!
AND YOU!! YOU'RE IN THE NAVY, AREN'T YOU?!
SHUT UP.
RAAAAAAH...!!
...
ARE YOU IN, OR ARE YOU OUT?
THEY STARTED THIS FIGHT!!
RAA
NO, YOU DID.
...

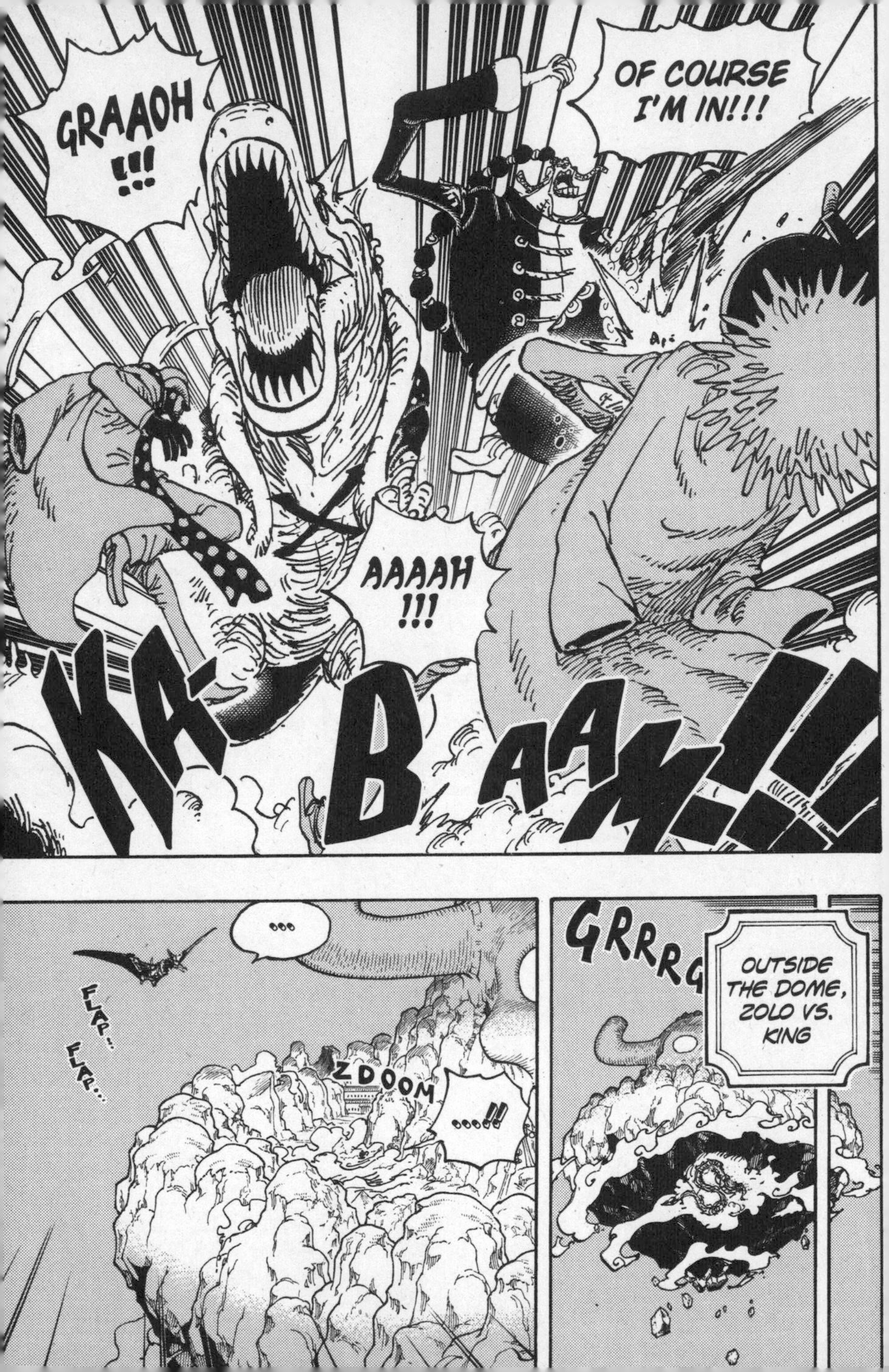
OF COURSE I'M IN!!!
GRAAOH!!!
AAAAH!!!
KA-BAAM!!!
GRRRG
OUTSIDE THE DOME, ZOLO VS. KING
...
FLAP!! FLAP...
ZDOOM
....!!

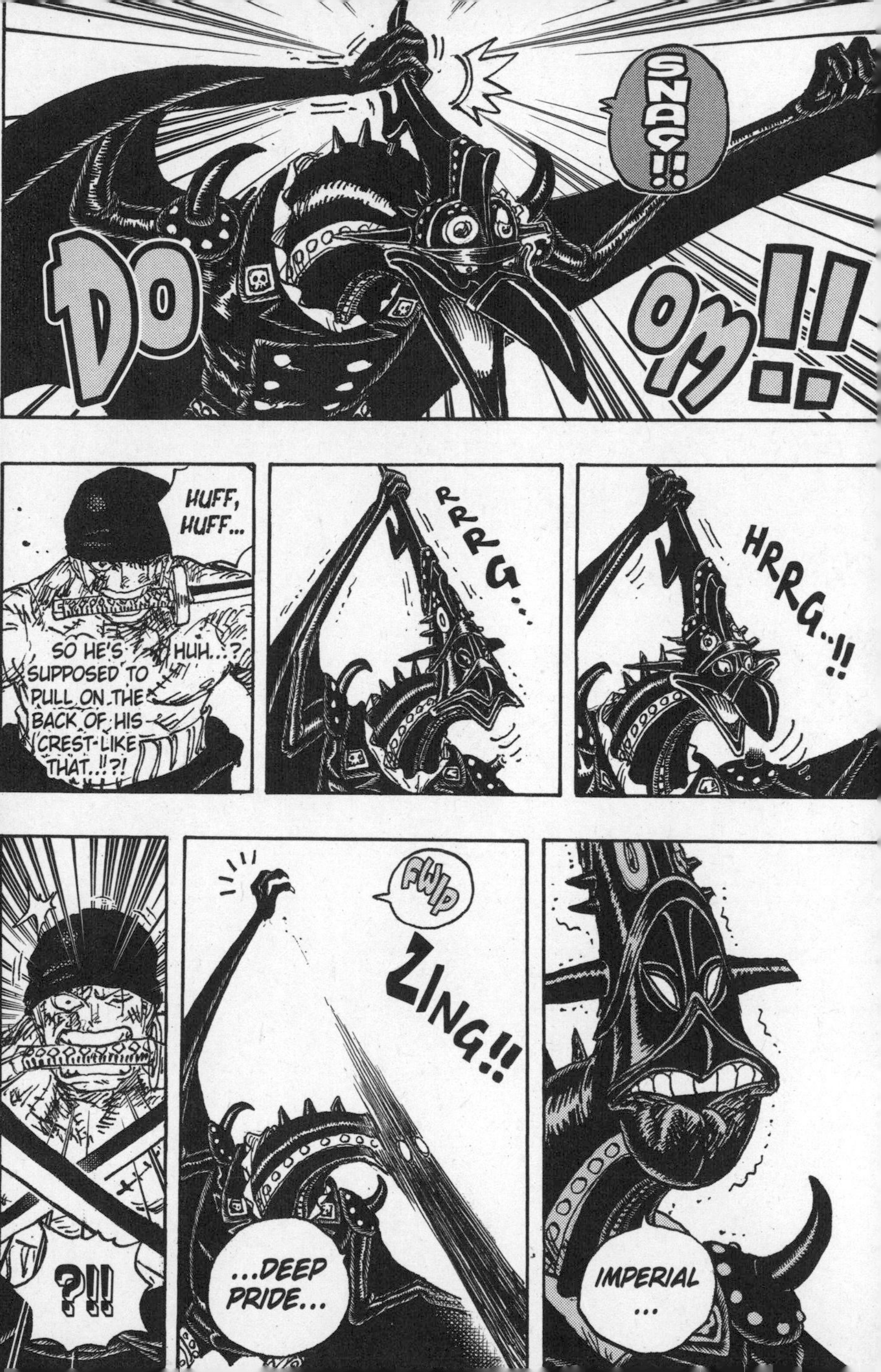
SNAG!!
DO OM!!
HRRG...!!
RRRG...
HUFF, HUFF...
HUH...?
SO HE'S SUPPOSED TO PULL ON THE BACK OF HIS CREST-LIKE THAT...!?!
IMPERIAL ...
FWIP
ZING!!
...DEEP PRIDE...
?!!

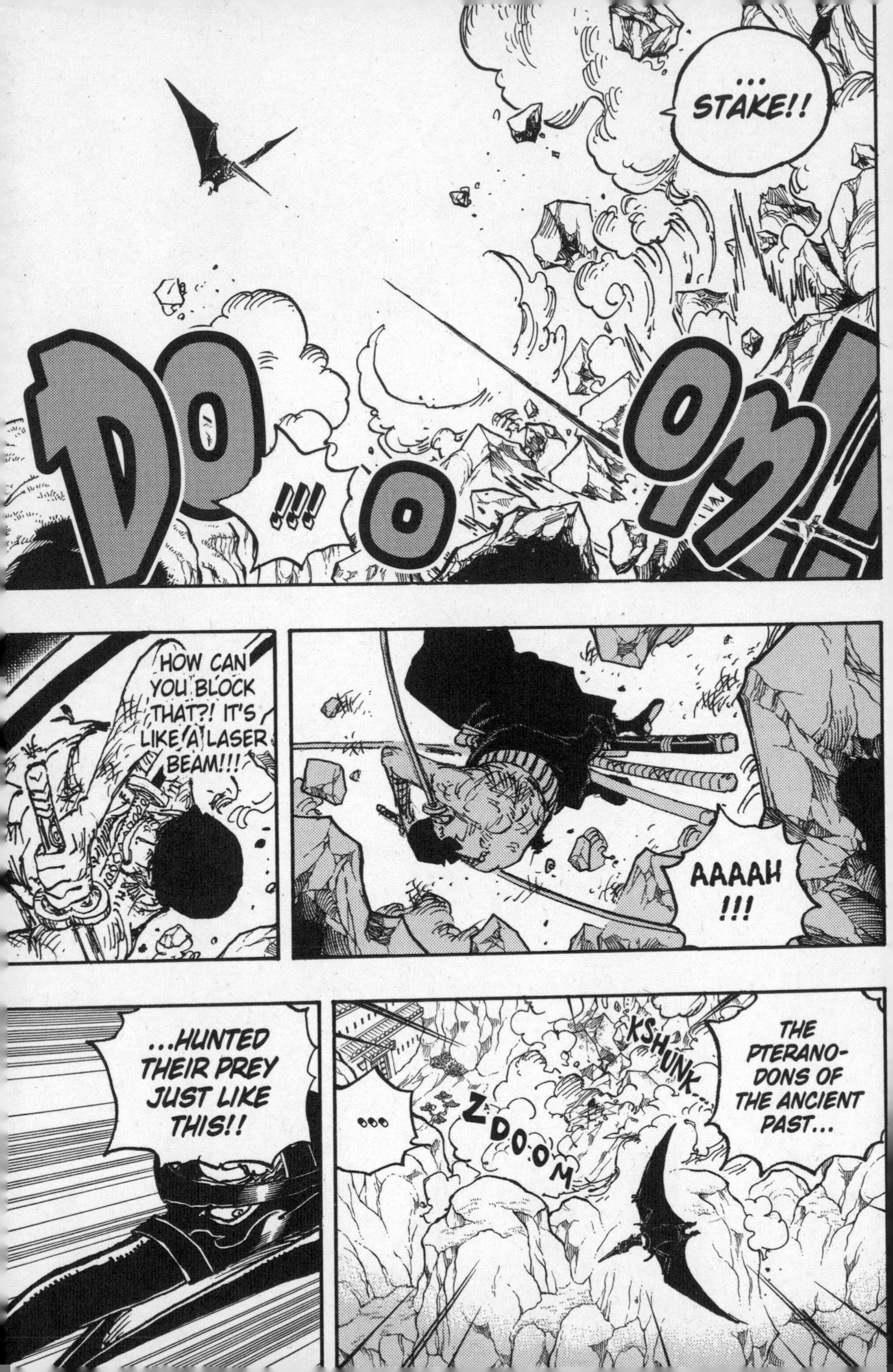
...STAKE!!
DOOOM!!!
AAAAH!!!
HOW CAN YOU BLOCK THAT?! IT'S LIKE A LASER BEAM!!!
THE PTERANO-DONS OF THE ANCIENT PAST...
KSHUNK
ZDOOM
...
...HUNTED THEIR PREY JUST LIKE THIS!!

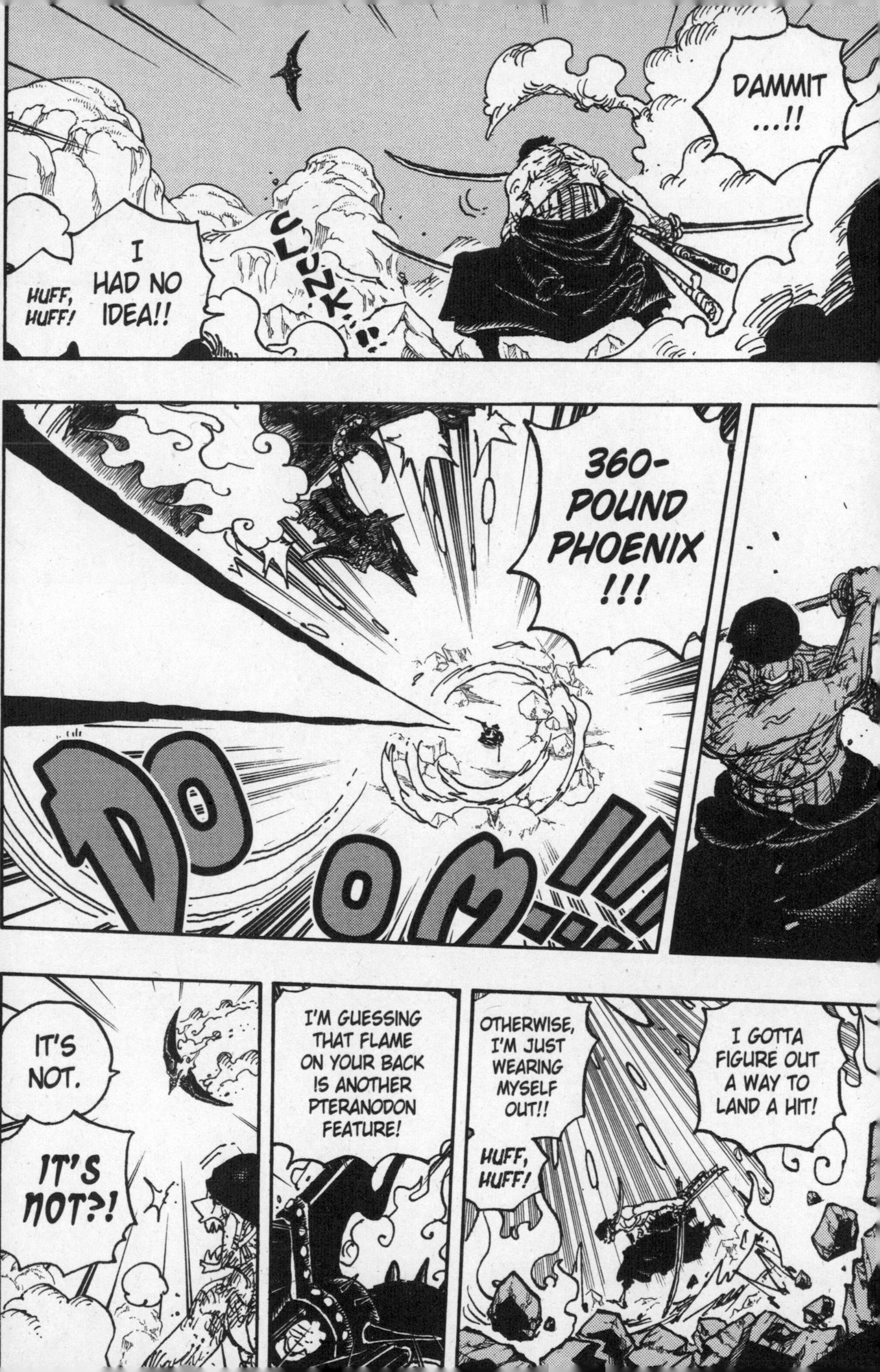
DAMMIT ...!!
CLUNK!!
I HAD NO IDEA!!
HUFF, HUFF!
360-POUND PHOENIX!!!
DOOM!!
I GOTTA FIGURE OUT A WAY TO LAND A HIT!
OTHERWISE, I'M JUST WEARING MYSELF OUT!!
HUFF, HUFF!
I'M GUESSING THAT FLAME ON YOUR BACK IS ANOTHER PTERANODON FEATURE!
IT'S NOT.
IT'S NOT?!

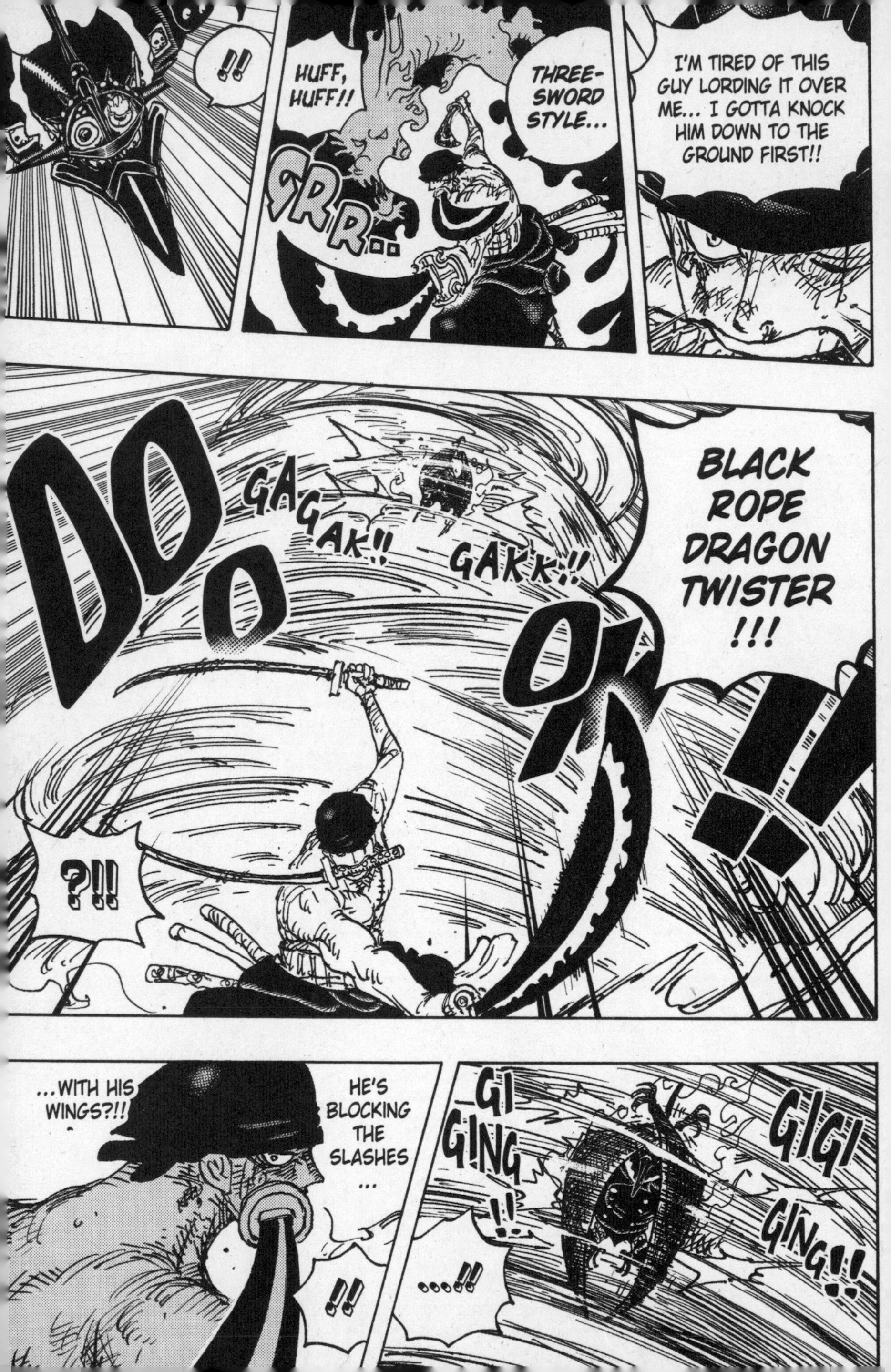
I'M TIRED OF THIS GUY LORDING IT OVER ME... I GOTTA KNOCK HIM DOWN TO THE GROUND FIRST!!
THREE-SWORD STYLE...
HUFF, HUFF!!
GRR...
!!
BLACK ROPE DRAGON TWISTER!!!
DOOO!!
GAKK!!
GAGAK!!
?!!
GIGI GING!!
GI GING!!
...!!
HE'S BLOCKING THE SLASHES...
...WITH HIS WINGS?!!
!!

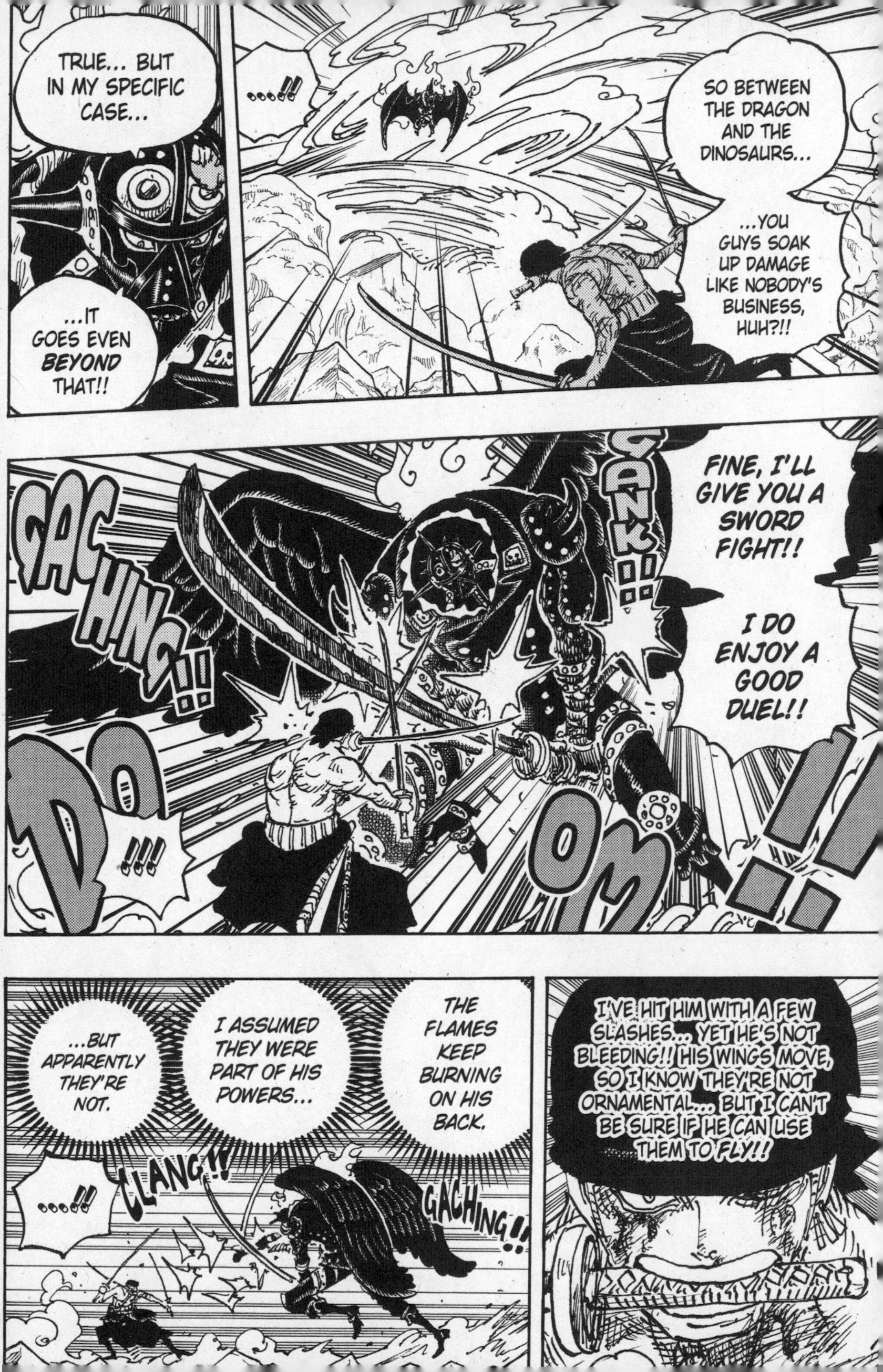
SO BETWEEN THE DRAGON AND THE DINOSAURS...
...YOU GUYS SOAK UP DAMAGE LIKE NOBODY'S BUSINESS, HUH?!!
...!!
TRUE... BUT IN MY SPECIFIC CASE...
...IT GOES EVEN BEYOND THAT!!
FINE, I'LL GIVE YOU A SWORD FIGHT!!
I DO ENJOY A GOOD DUEL!!
ANK!!
GAC HING!!
DO!!!
OM!!
I'VE HIT HIM WITH A FEW SLASHES... YET HE'S NOT BLEEDING!! HIS WINGS MOVE, SO I KNOW THEY'RE NOT ORNAMENTAL... BUT I CAN'T BE SURE IF HE CAN USE THEM TO FLY!!
THE FLAMES KEEP BURNING ON HIS BACK.
I ASSUMED THEY WERE PART OF HIS POWERS...
...BUT APPARENTLY THEY'RE NOT.
GACHING!!
CLANG!!
...!!

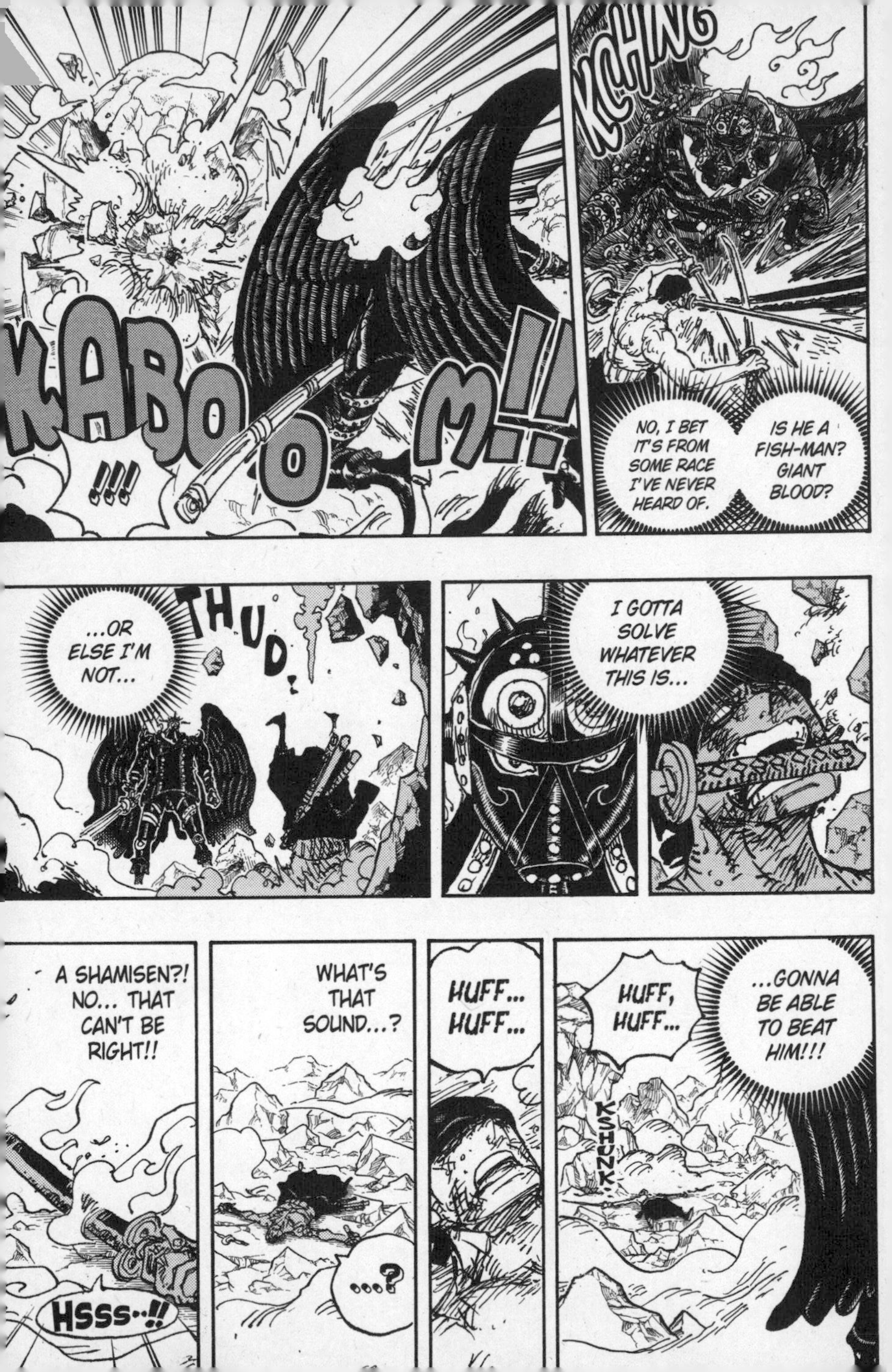
KCHING
IS HE A FISH-MAN? GIANT BLOOD?
NO, I BET IT'S FROM SOME RACE I'VE NEVER HEARD OF.
KABOOOM!!
!!!
I GOTTA SOLVE WHATEVER THIS IS...
THUD
...OR ELSE I'M NOT...
...GONNA BE ABLE TO BEAT HIM!!!
HUFF, HUFF...
KSHUNK
HUFF... HUFF...
WHAT'S THAT SOUND...?
...?
A SHAMISEN?! NO... THAT CAN'T BE RIGHT!!
HSSS..!!

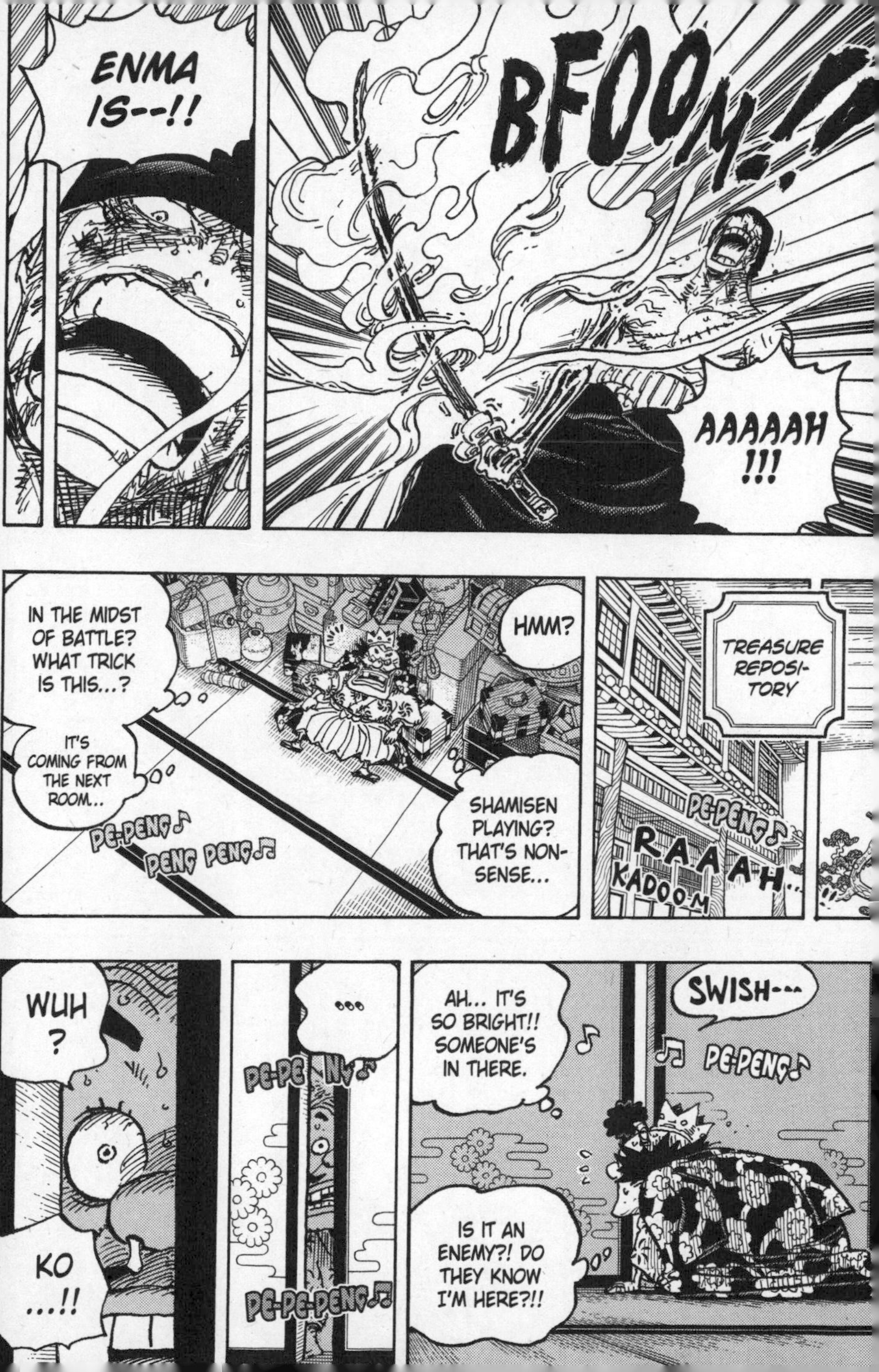

BFOOM!!
AAAAAH!!!
ENMA IS--!!
!!
TREASURE REPOSITORY
PE-PENG
RAAAAH..
KADOOM
HMM?
SHAMISEN PLAYING? THAT'S NONSENSE...
IN THE MIDST OF BATTLE? WHAT TRICK IS THIS...?
IT'S COMING FROM THE NEXT ROOM..
PE-PENG
PENG PENG
SWISH---
PE-PENG
AH... IT'S SO BRIGHT!! SOMEONE'S IN THERE.
IS IT AN ENEMY?! DO THEY KNOW I'M HERE?!!
...
PE-PE-N
PE-PE-PENG
WUH?
KO...!!

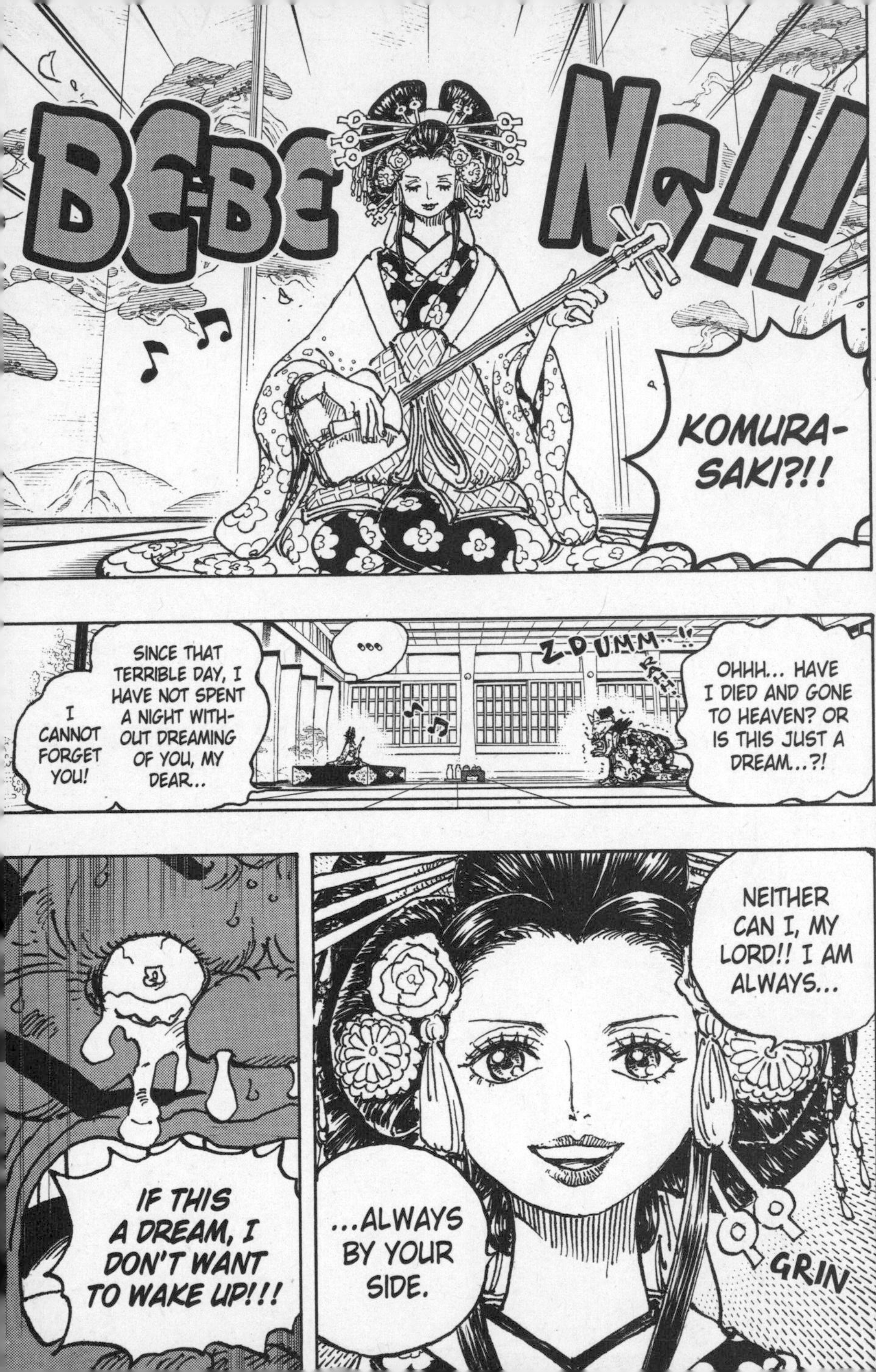
BE-BE
NG!!
KOMURA-SAKI?!!
OHHH... HAVE I DIED AND GONE TO HEAVEN? OR IS THIS JUST A DREAM..?!
ZDUMM !!
...
SINCE THAT TERRIBLE DAY, I HAVE NOT SPENT A NIGHT WITH-OUT DREAMING OF YOU, MY DEAR..
I CANNOT FORGET YOU!
NEITHER CAN I, MY LORD!! I AM ALWAYS...
...ALWAYS BY YOUR SIDE.
GRIN
IF THIS A DREAM, I DON'T WANT TO WAKE UP!!!

SBS Question Corner

(Kaiden, Miyagi)

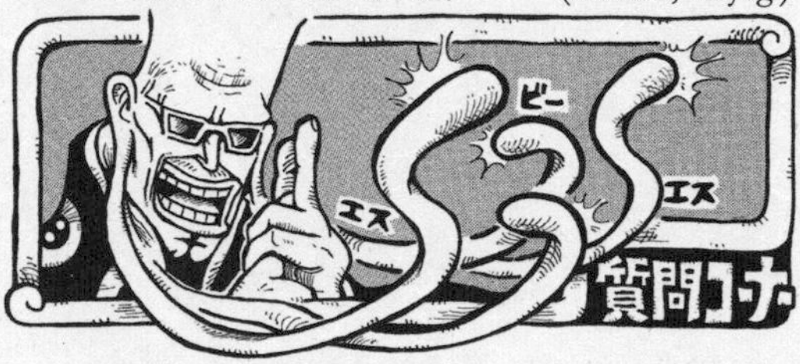

Q: Kid and Killer are so awesome! You've drawn other members of the Kid Pirates here and there too. Can you give us their names?

--Kotaro

A: Sure. These are just my original rough sketches, and it's not even all of them. There are 31 members of the Kid Pirates. You don't have to memorize these!

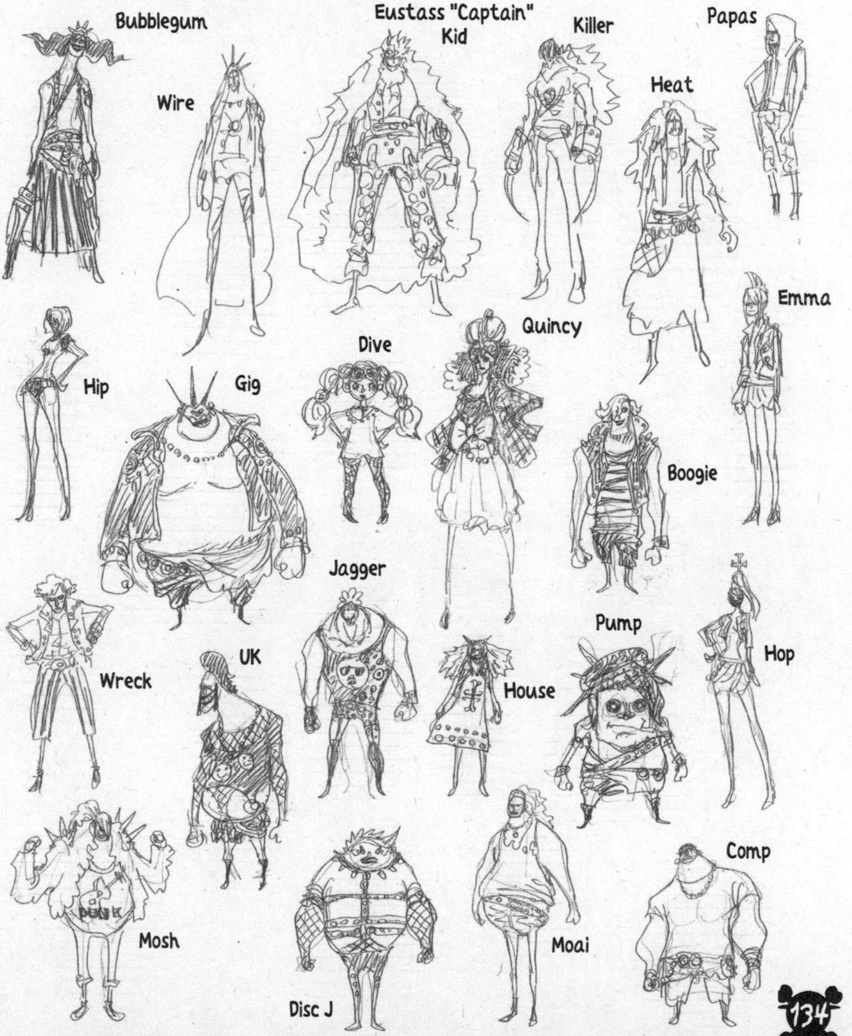

Bubblegum
Wire
Eustass "Captain" Kid
Killer
Heat
Papas
Emma
Quincy
Dive
Hip
Gig
Boogie
Jagger
Pump
Hop
Wreck
UK
House
PUNK
Mosh
Disc J
Moai
Comp

Chapter 1033:
SHIMOTSUKI KOZABURO

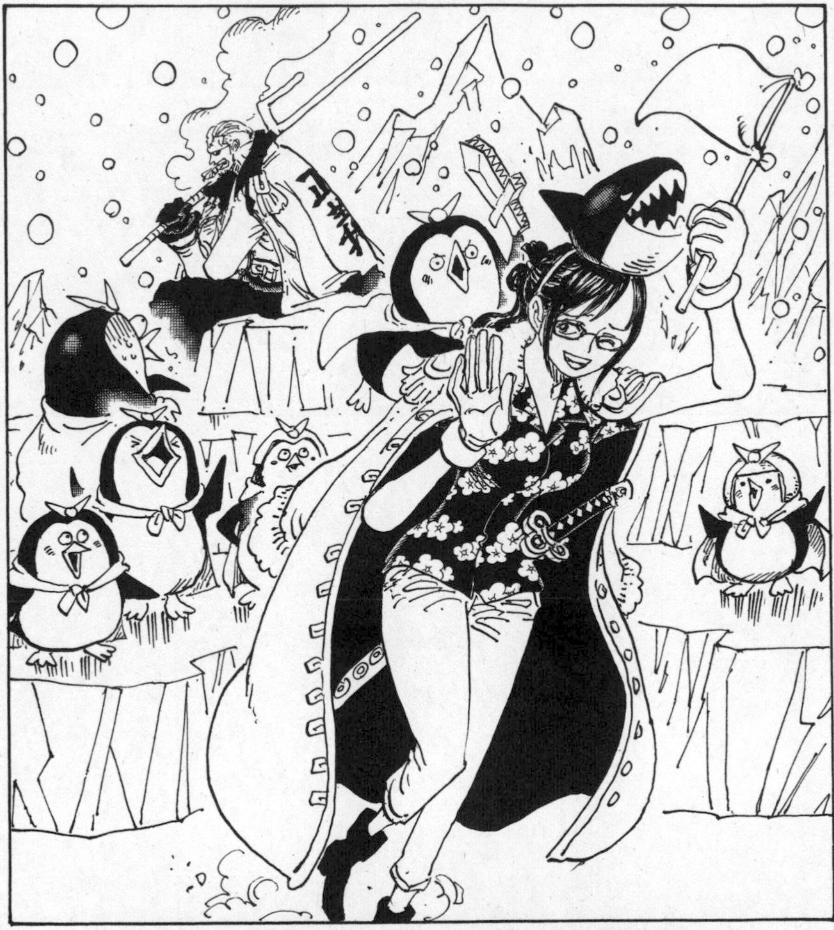

READER REQUEST: "TASHIGI DRESSED AS A BAD GUY, GETTING DEFEATED BY BABY PENGUINS PLAYING HEROES" BY SODASUSU

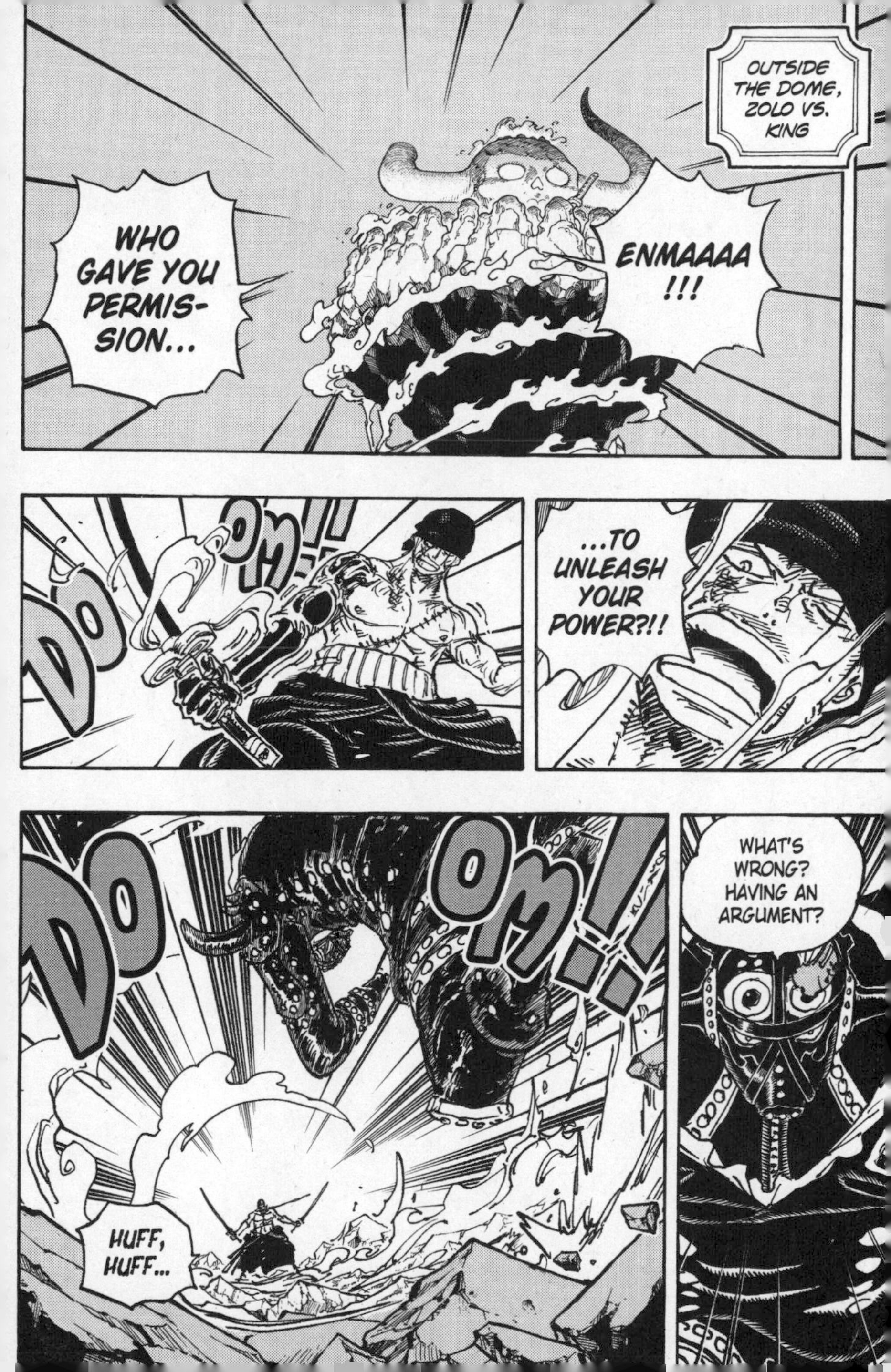
OUTSIDE THE DOME, ZOLO VS. KING
ENMAAAA!!!
WHO GAVE YOU PERMISSION...
...TO UNLEASH YOUR POWER?!!
DOOM!!
WHAT'S WRONG? HAVING AN ARGUMENT?
DOOM!!
HUFF, HUFF...

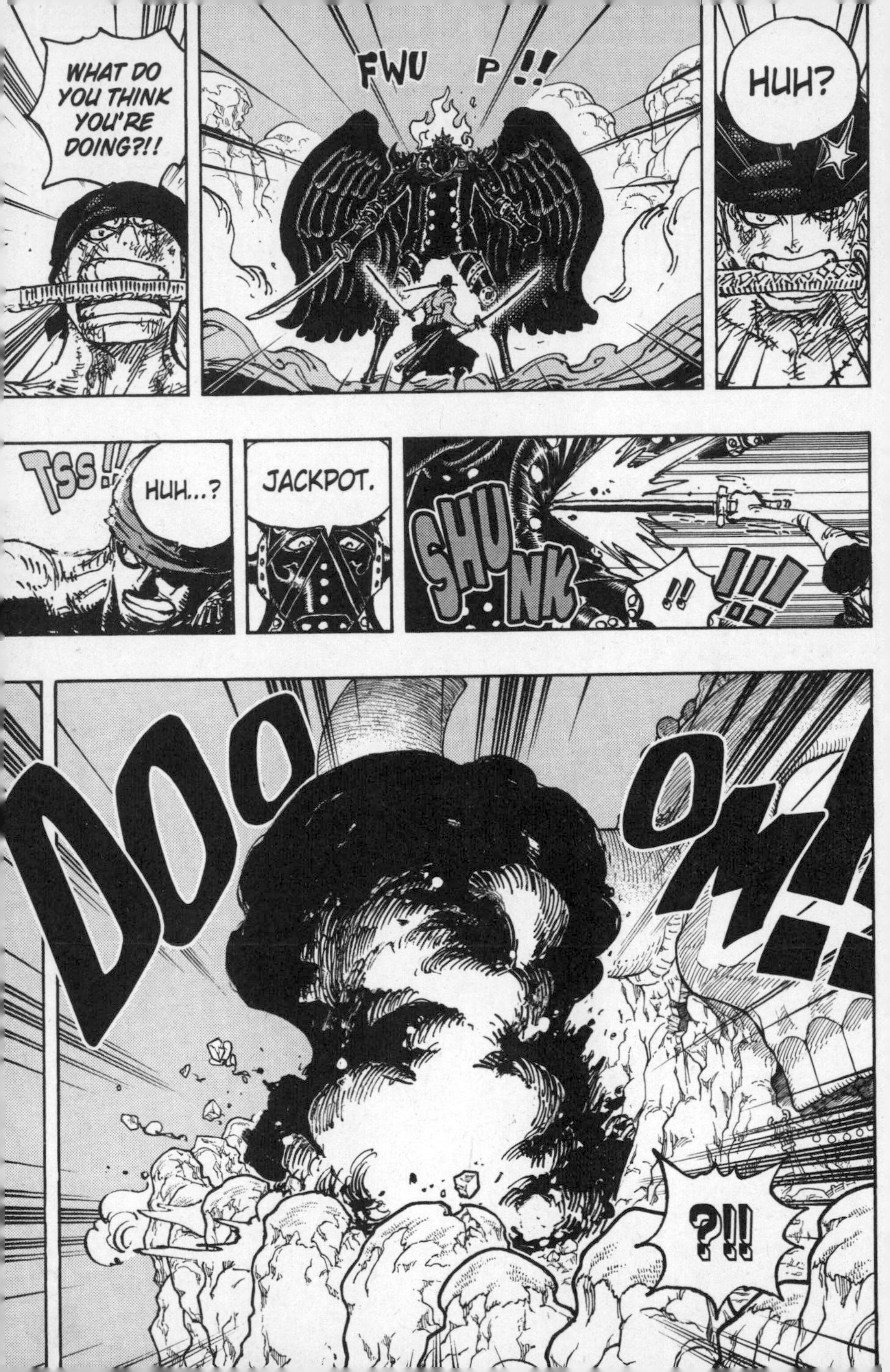
HUH?
FWU P!!
WHAT DO YOU THINK YOU'RE DOING?!!
SHUNK
!!!
!!
JACKPOT.
TSS!!
HUH...?
DOOOM!!
?!!

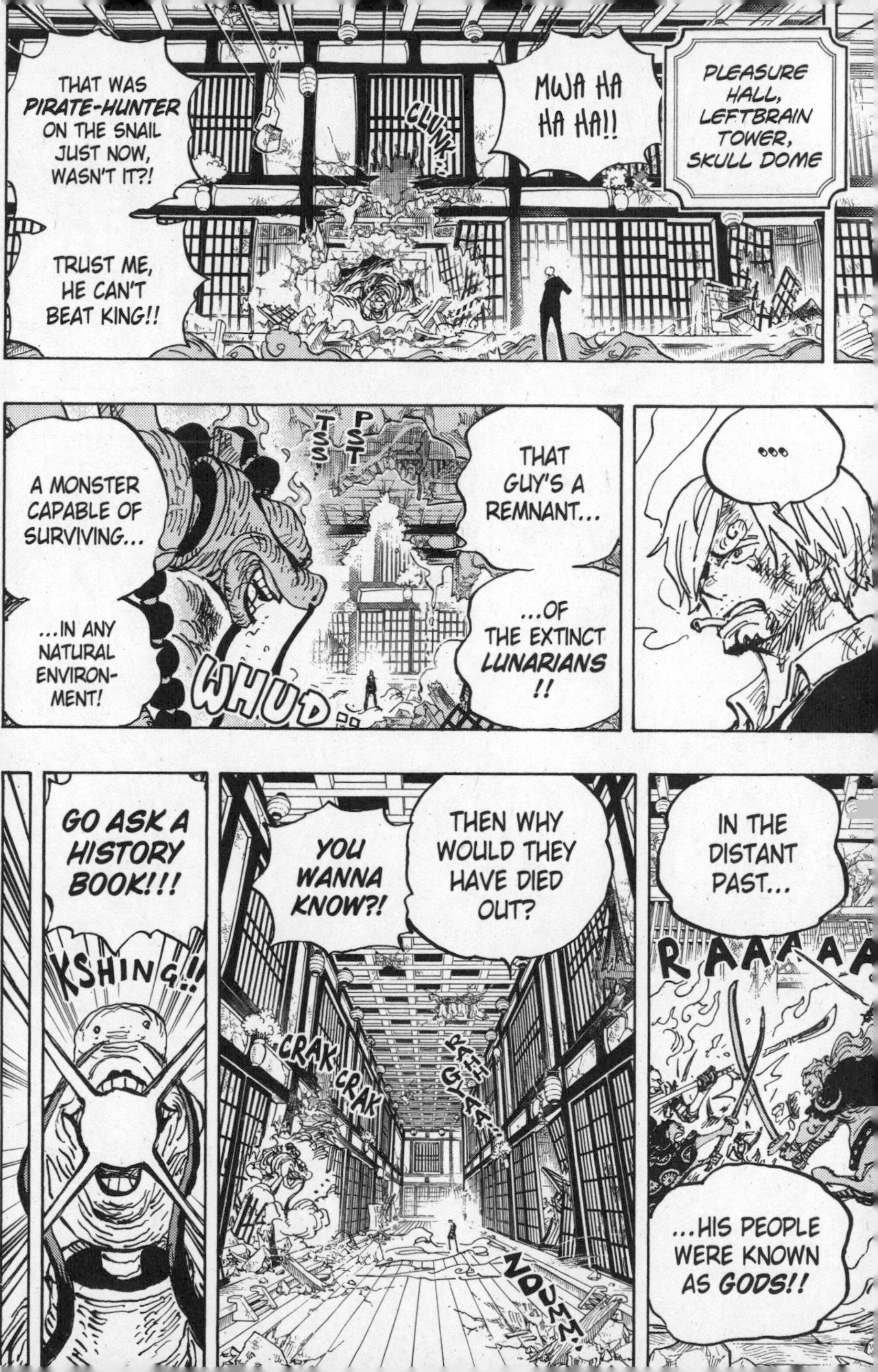
PLEASURE HALL, LEFTBRAIN TOWER, SKULL DOME
MWA HA HA HA!!
CLUNK
THAT WAS PIRATE-HUNTER ON THE SNAIL JUST NOW, WASN'T IT?!
TRUST ME, HE CAN'T BEAT KING!!
...
THAT GUY'S A REMNANT...
...OF THE EXTINCT LUNARIANS!!
PST
TSS
A MONSTER CAPABLE OF SURVIVING...
...IN ANY NATURAL ENVIRONMENT!
WHUD
IN THE DISTANT PAST...
RAAAAA
...HIS PEOPLE WERE KNOWN AS GODS!!
THEN WHY WOULD THEY HAVE DIED OUT?
YOU WANNA KNOW?!
CRAK
CRAK
RAHHGYAA
NDUMM
GO ASK A HISTORY BOOK!!!
KSHING!!

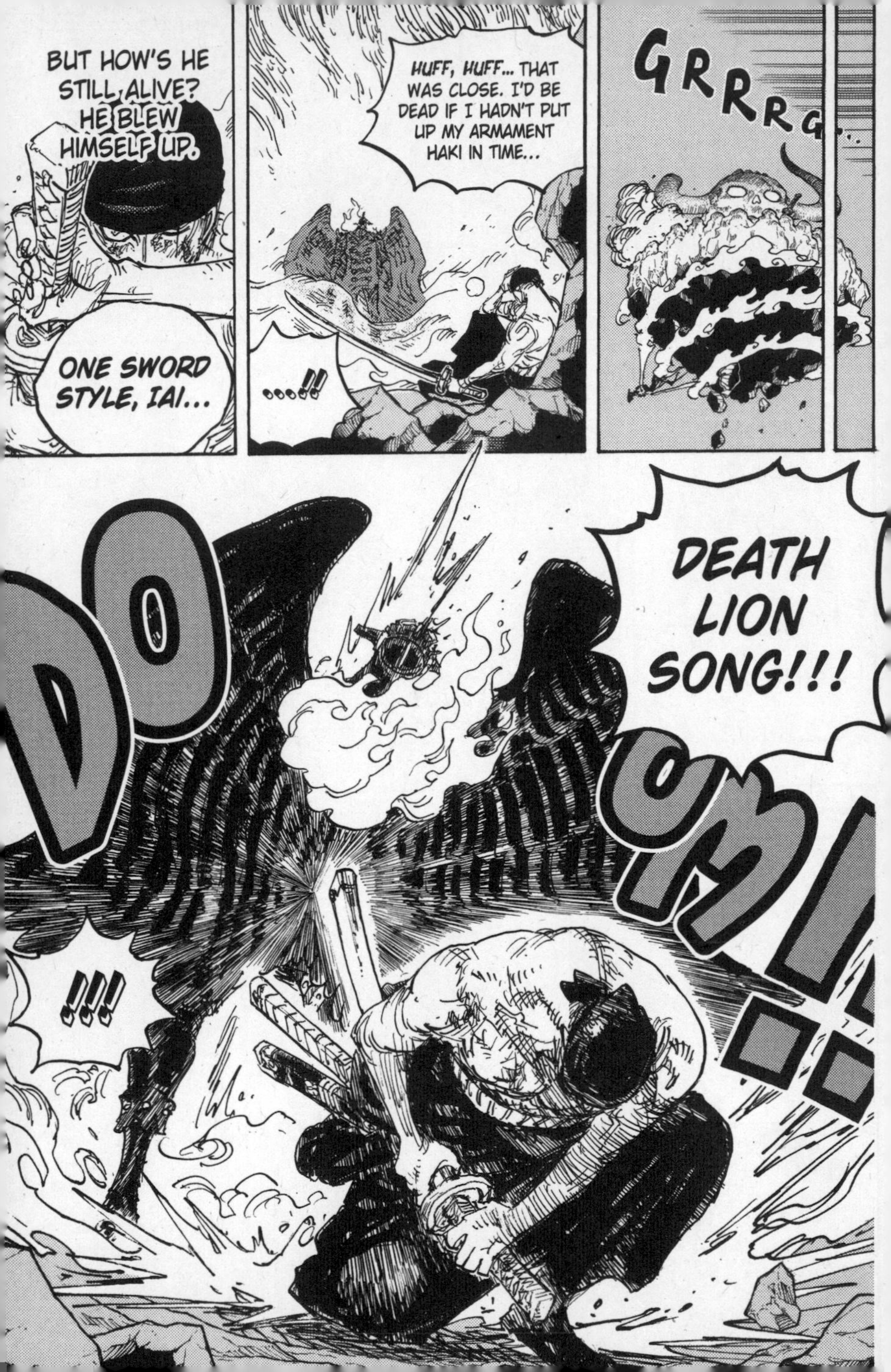
GRRRRG...
HUFF, HUFF... THAT WAS CLOSE. I'D BE DEAD IF I HADN'T PUT UP MY ARMAMENT HAKI IN TIME...
....!!
BUT HOW'S HE STILL ALIVE? HE BLEW HIMSELF UP.
ONE SWORD STYLE, IAI...
DEATH LION SONG!!!
DOOM!!
!!!

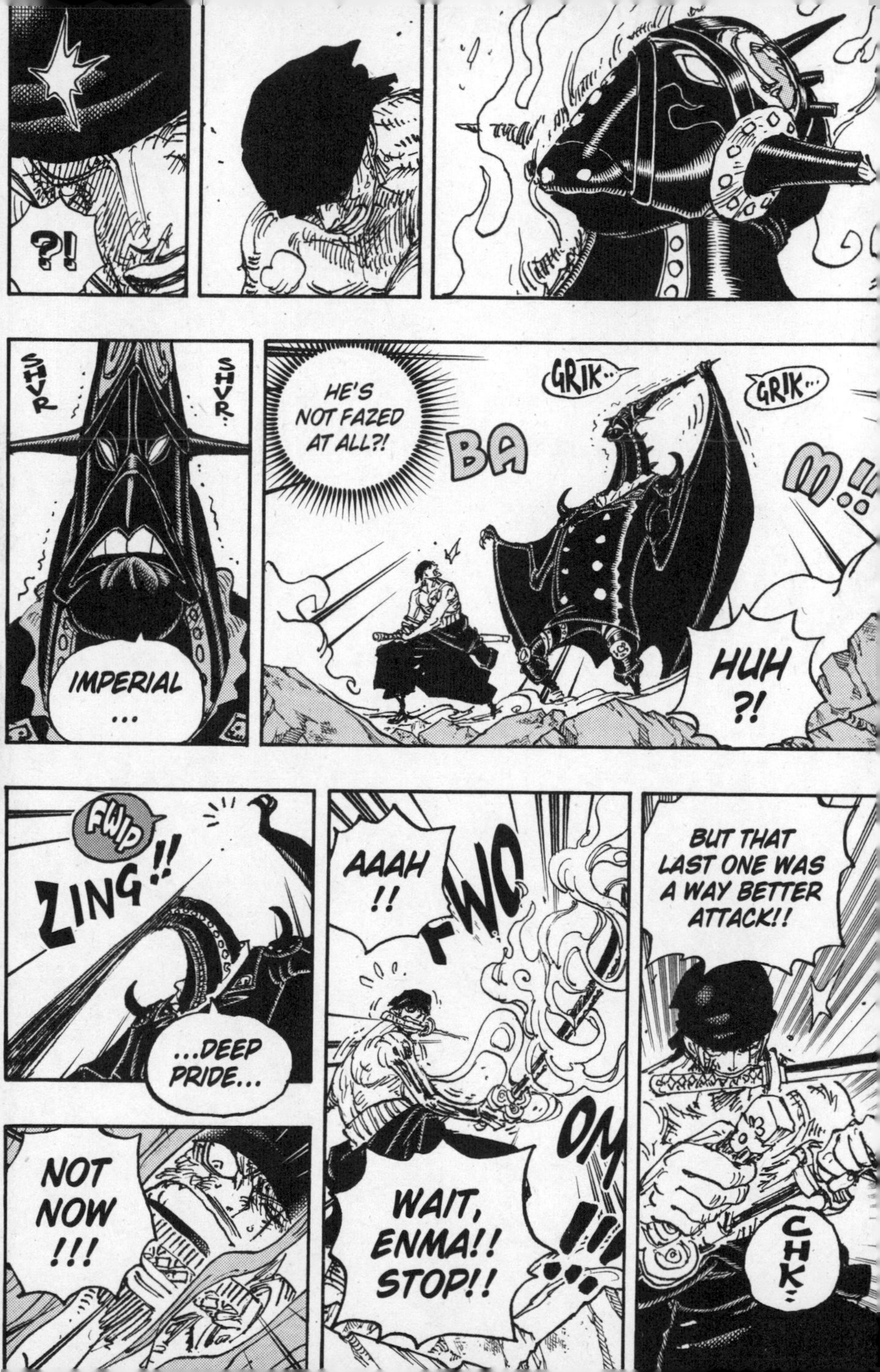
?!
GRIK...
M!!
GRIK...
HE'S NOT FAZED AT ALL?!
BA
HUH?!
SHVR
SHVR
IMPERIAL...
BUT THAT LAST ONE WAS A WAY BETTER ATTACK!!
CHK
AAAH!!
FWO
OM
!!!
WAIT, ENMA!! STOP!!
FWIP
ZING!!
...DEEP PRIDE...
NOT NOW!!!

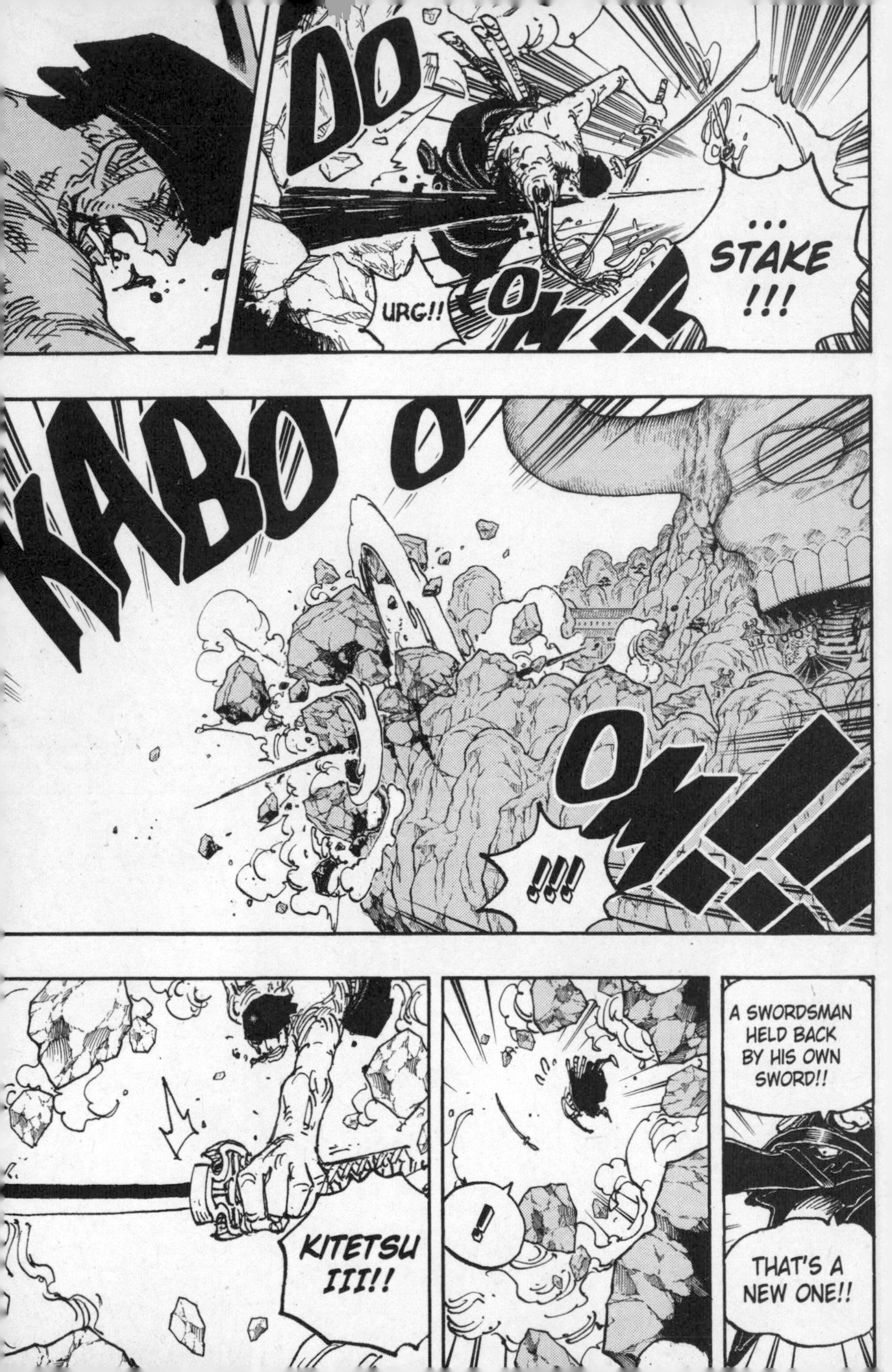
...STAKE !!!
DO
OM!!
URG!!
KABOOO
OM!!!
!!!
A SWORDSMAN HELD BACK BY HIS OWN SWORD!!
THAT'S A NEW ONE!!
!
KITETSU III!!

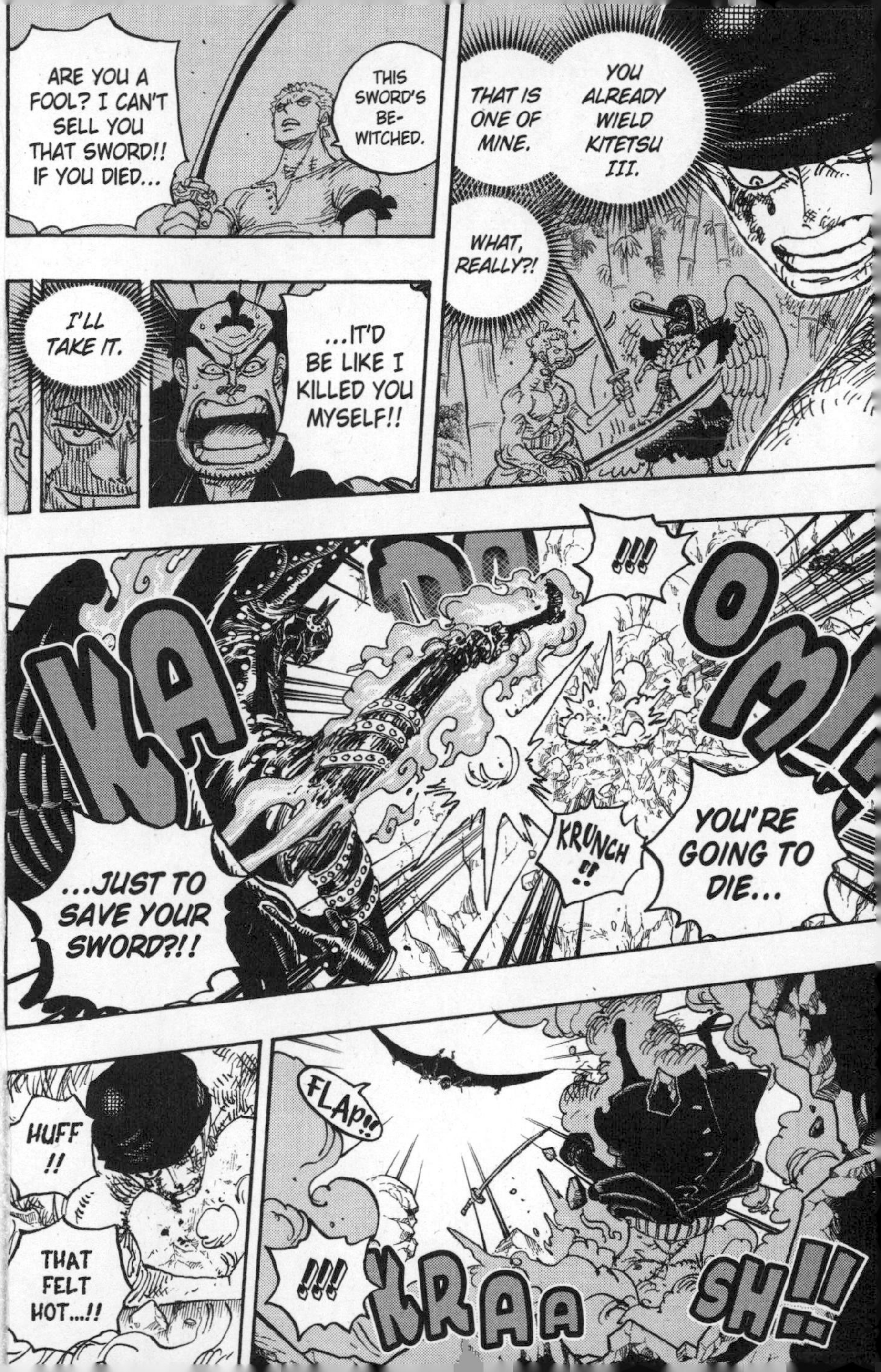
YOU ALREADY WIELD KITETSU III.
THAT IS ONE OF MINE.
WHAT, REALLY?!
THIS SWORD'S BE-WITCHED.
ARE YOU A FOOL? I CAN'T SELL YOU THAT SWORD!! IF YOU DIED...
...IT'D BE LIKE I KILLED YOU MYSELF!!
I'LL TAKE IT.
YOU'RE GOING TO DIE...
!!!
KRUNCH!!
KA
...JUST TO SAVE YOUR SWORD?!!
FLAP!!
!!!
KRAASH!!
HUFF!!
THAT FELT HOT...!!

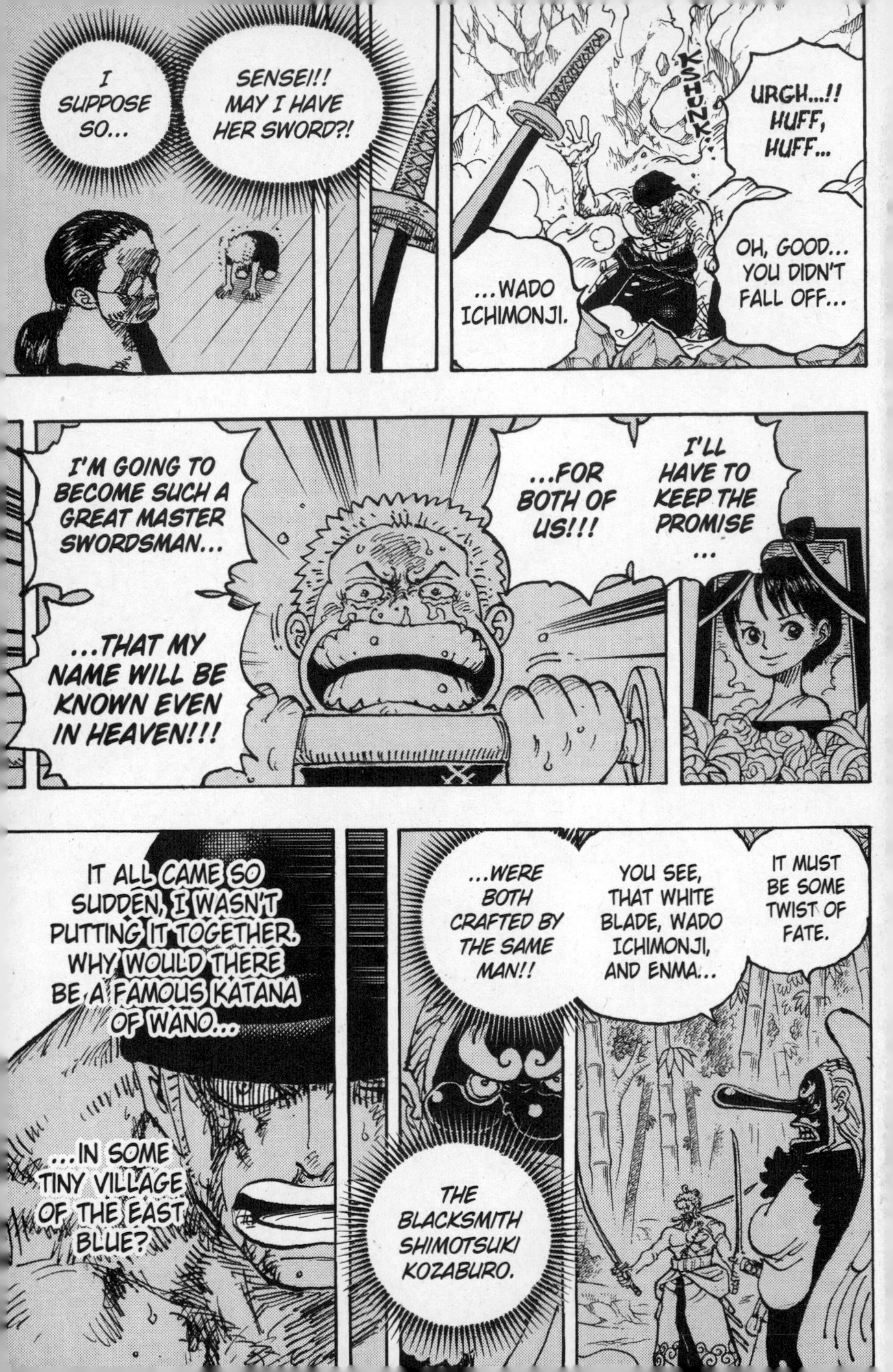
KSHUNK
URGH...!! HUFF, HUFF...
OH, GOOD... YOU DIDN'T FALL OFF...
...WADO ICHIMONJI.
SENSEI!! MAY I HAVE HER SWORD?!
I SUPPOSE SO...
I'LL HAVE TO KEEP THE PROMISE...
...FOR BOTH OF US!!!
I'M GOING TO BECOME SUCH A GREAT MASTER SWORDSMAN...
...THAT MY NAME WILL BE KNOWN EVEN IN HEAVEN!!!
IT MUST BE SOME TWIST OF FATE.
YOU SEE, THAT WHITE BLADE, WADO ICHIMONJI, AND ENMA...
...WERE BOTH CRAFTED BY THE SAME MAN!!
THE BLACKSMITH SHIMOTSUKI KOZABURO.
IT ALL CAME SO SUDDEN, I WASN'T PUTTING IT TOGETHER. WHY WOULD THERE BE A FAMOUS KATANA OF WANO...
...IN SOME TINY VILLAGE OF THE EAST BLUE?

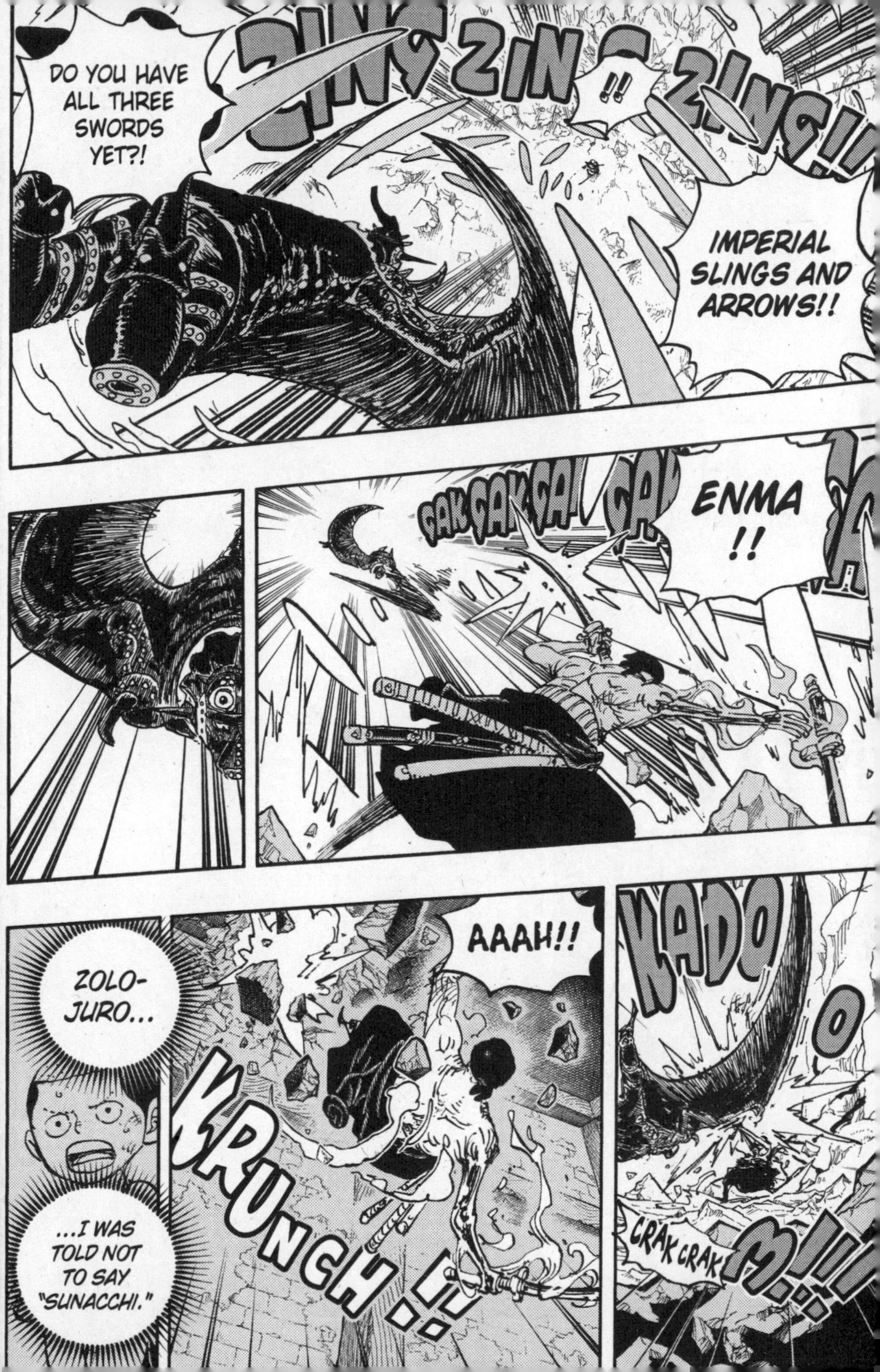
ZING!!
!!
IMPERIAL SLINGS AND ARROWS!!
ZIN
DO YOU HAVE ALL THREE SWORDS YET?!
ENMA !!
GAK GAK
KADO O
M!!!
CRAK CRAK
AAAH!!
KRUNCH!!
ZOLO-JURO...
...I WAS TOLD NOT TO SAY "SUNACCHI."

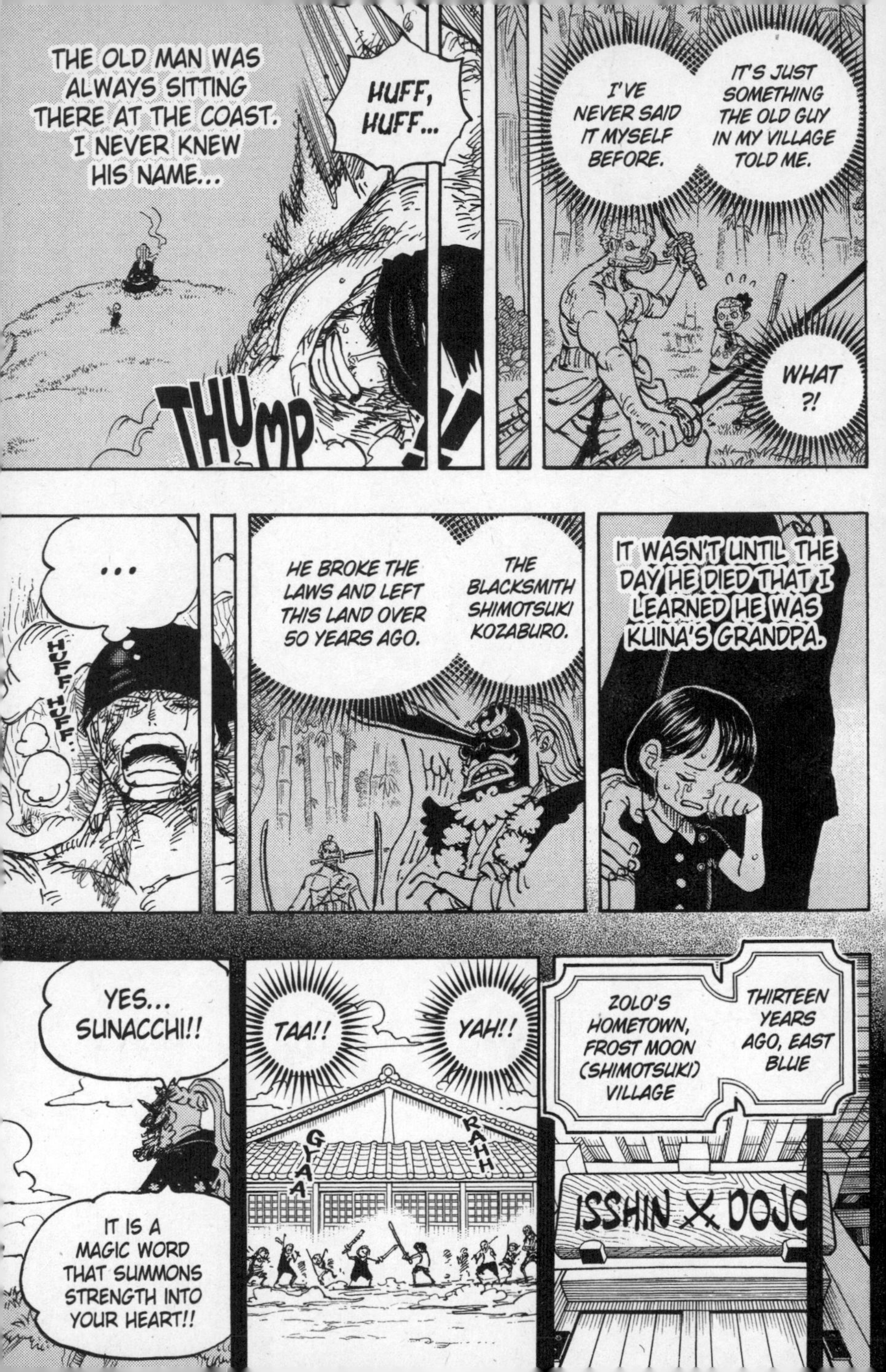
IT'S JUST SOMETHING THE OLD GUY IN MY VILLAGE TOLD ME.
I'VE NEVER SAID IT MYSELF BEFORE.
WHAT ?!
HUFF, HUFF...
THUMP
THE OLD MAN WAS ALWAYS SITTING THERE AT THE COAST. I NEVER KNEW HIS NAME...
IT WASN'T UNTIL THE DAY HE DIED THAT I LEARNED HE WAS KUINA'S GRANDPA.
THE BLACKSMITH SHIMOTSUKI KOZABURO.
HE BROKE THE LAWS AND LEFT THIS LAND OVER 50 YEARS AGO.
...
HUFF HUFF...
THIRTEEN YEARS AGO, EAST BLUE
ZOLO'S HOMETOWN, FROST MOON (SHIMOTSUKI) VILLAGE
ISSHIN DOJO
YAH!!
RAHH
TAA!!
GYAA
YES... SUNACCHI!!
IT IS A MAGIC WORD THAT SUMMONS STRENGTH INTO YOUR HEART!!

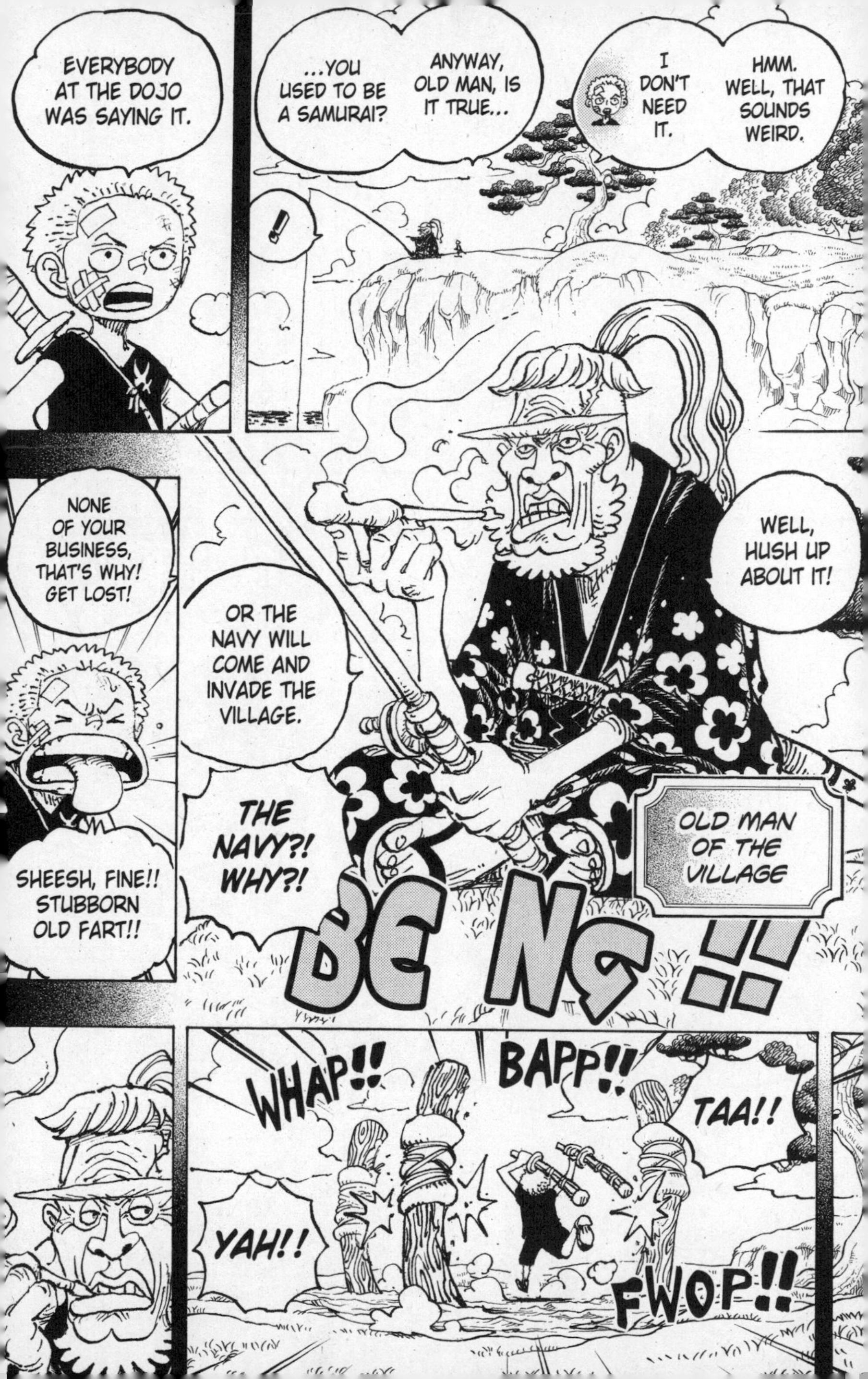
HMM. WELL, THAT SOUNDS WEIRD.
I DON'T NEED IT.
ANYWAY, OLD MAN, IS IT TRUE...
...YOU USED TO BE A SAMURAI?
!
EVERYBODY AT THE DOJO WAS SAYING IT.
WELL, HUSH UP ABOUT IT!
OR THE NAVY WILL COME AND INVADE THE VILLAGE.
OLD MAN OF THE VILLAGE
BENG!!
THE NAVY?! WHY?!
NONE OF YOUR BUSINESS, THAT'S WHY! GET LOST!
SHEESH, FINE!! STUBBORN OLD FART!!
TAA!!
BAPP!!
WHAP!!
YAH!!
FWOP!!

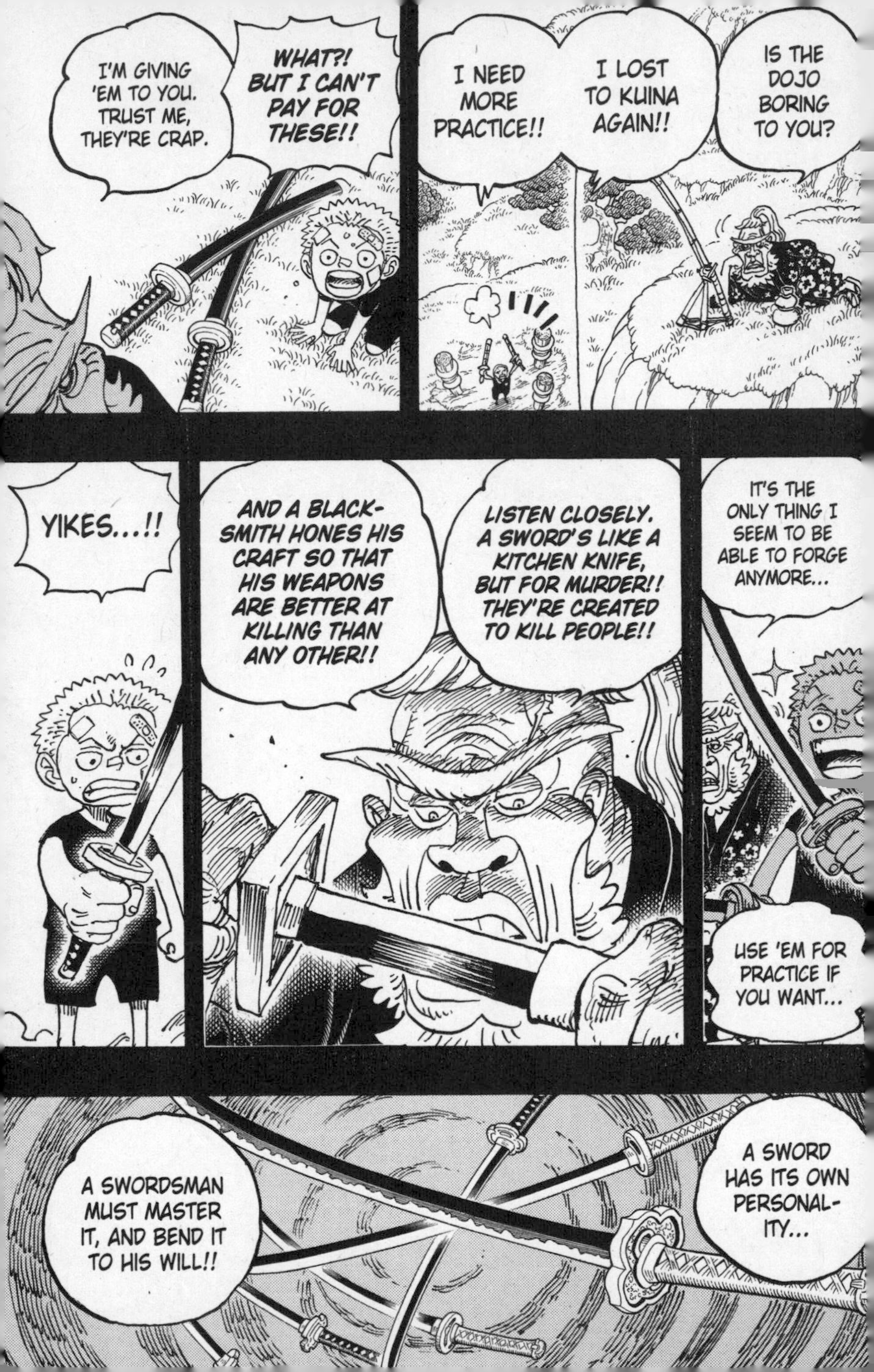
IS THE DOJO BORING TO YOU?
I LOST TO KUINA AGAIN!!
I NEED MORE PRACTICE!!
WHAT?! BUT I CAN'T PAY FOR THESE!!
I'M GIVING 'EM TO YOU. TRUST ME, THEY'RE CRAP.
IT'S THE ONLY THING I SEEM TO BE ABLE TO FORGE ANYMORE...
USE 'EM FOR PRACTICE IF YOU WANT...
LISTEN CLOSELY. A SWORD'S LIKE A KITCHEN KNIFE, BUT FOR MURDER!! THEY'RE CREATED TO KILL PEOPLE!!
AND A BLACK-SMITH HONES HIS CRAFT SO THAT HIS WEAPONS ARE BETTER AT KILLING THAN ANY OTHER!!
YIKES...!!
A SWORD HAS ITS OWN PERSONAL-ITY...
A SWORDSMAN MUST MASTER IT, AND BEND IT TO HIS WILL!!

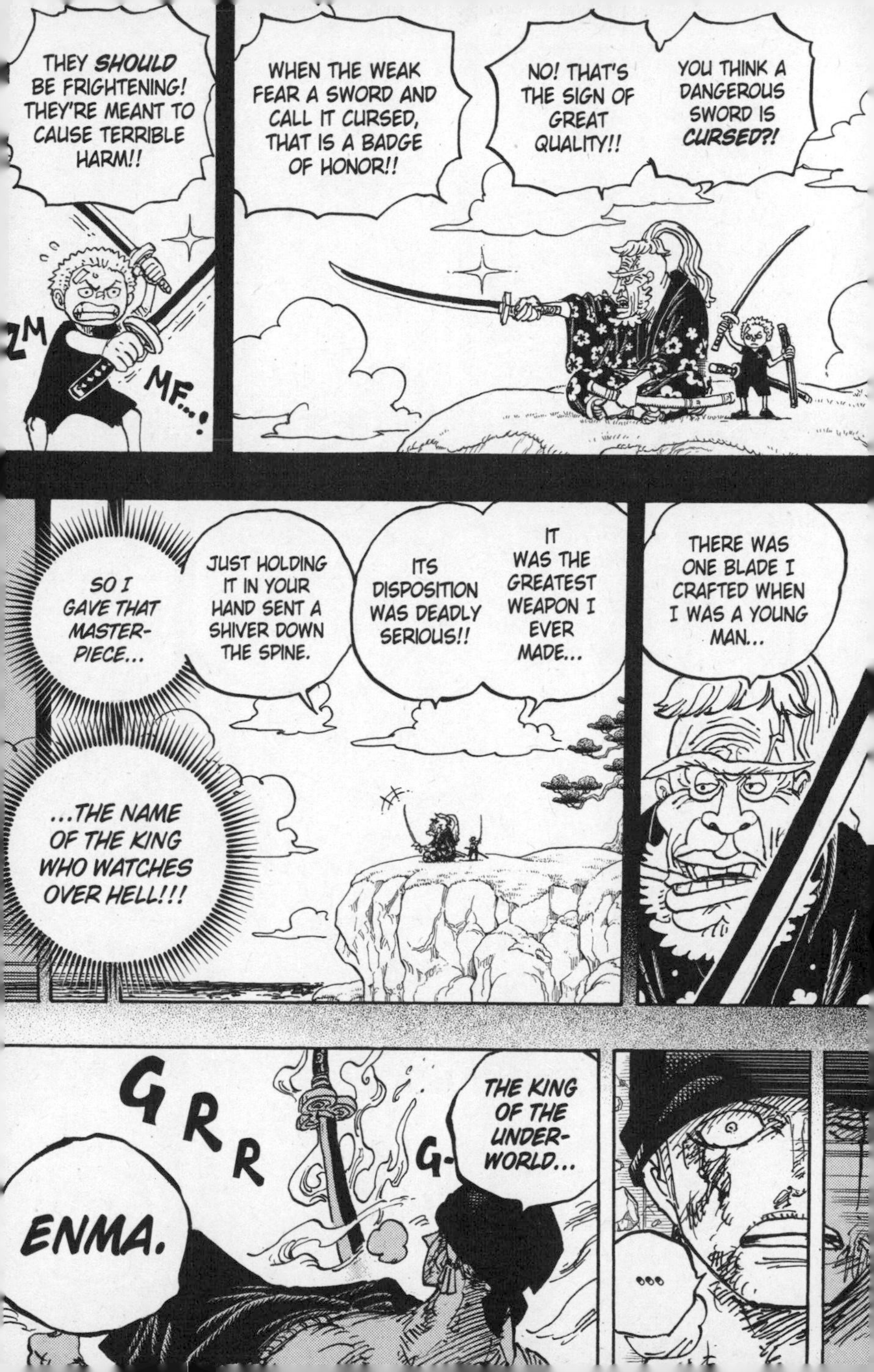
YOU THINK A DANGEROUS SWORD IS CURSED?!
NO! THAT'S THE SIGN OF GREAT QUALITY!!
WHEN THE WEAK FEAR A SWORD AND CALL IT CURSED, THAT IS A BADGE OF HONOR!!
THEY SHOULD BE FRIGHTENING! THEY'RE MEANT TO CAUSE TERRIBLE HARM!!
ZM
MF...!
THERE WAS ONE BLADE I CRAFTED WHEN I WAS A YOUNG MAN...
IT WAS THE GREATEST WEAPON I EVER MADE...
ITS DISPOSITION WAS DEADLY SERIOUS!!
JUST HOLDING IT IN YOUR HAND SENT A SHIVER DOWN THE SPINE.
SO I GAVE THAT MASTER-PIECE...
...THE NAME OF THE KING WHO WATCHES OVER HELL!!!
...
THE KING OF THE UNDER-WORLD...
GRRRG-
ENMA.

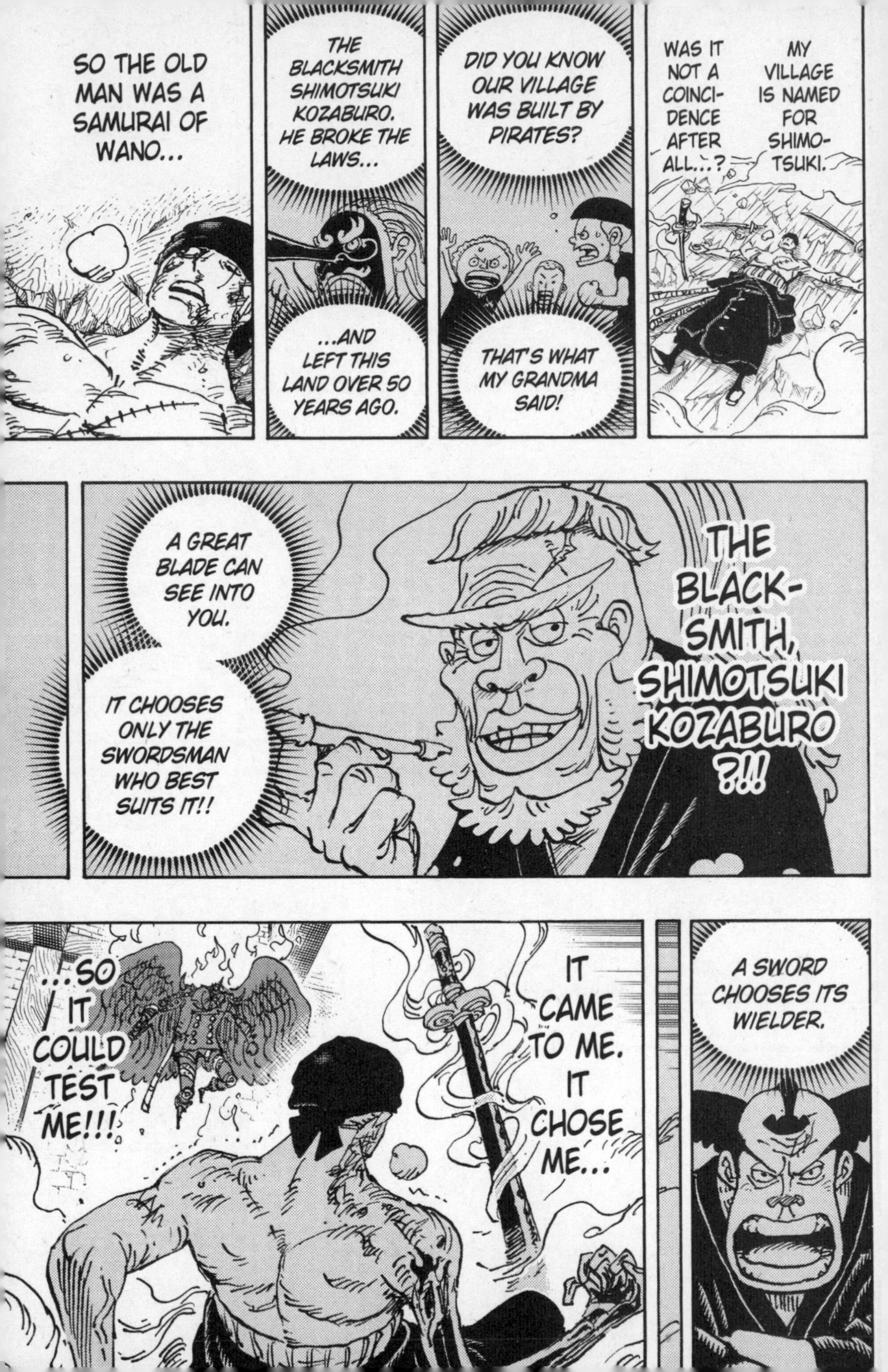
MY VILLAGE IS NAMED FOR SHIMOTSUKI.
WAS IT NOT A COINCIDENCE AFTER ALL...?
DID YOU KNOW OUR VILLAGE WAS BUILT BY PIRATES?
THAT'S WHAT MY GRANDMA SAID!
THE BLACKSMITH SHIMOTSUKI KOZABURO. HE BROKE THE LAWS...
...AND LEFT THIS LAND OVER 50 YEARS AGO.
SO THE OLD MAN WAS A SAMURAI OF WANO...
THE BLACKSMITH, SHIMOTSUKI KOZABURO?!!
A GREAT BLADE CAN SEE INTO YOU.
IT CHOOSES ONLY THE SWORDSMAN WHO BEST SUITS IT!!
A SWORD CHOOSES ITS WIELDER.
IT CAME TO ME. IT CHOSE ME...
...SO IT COULD TEST ME!!!

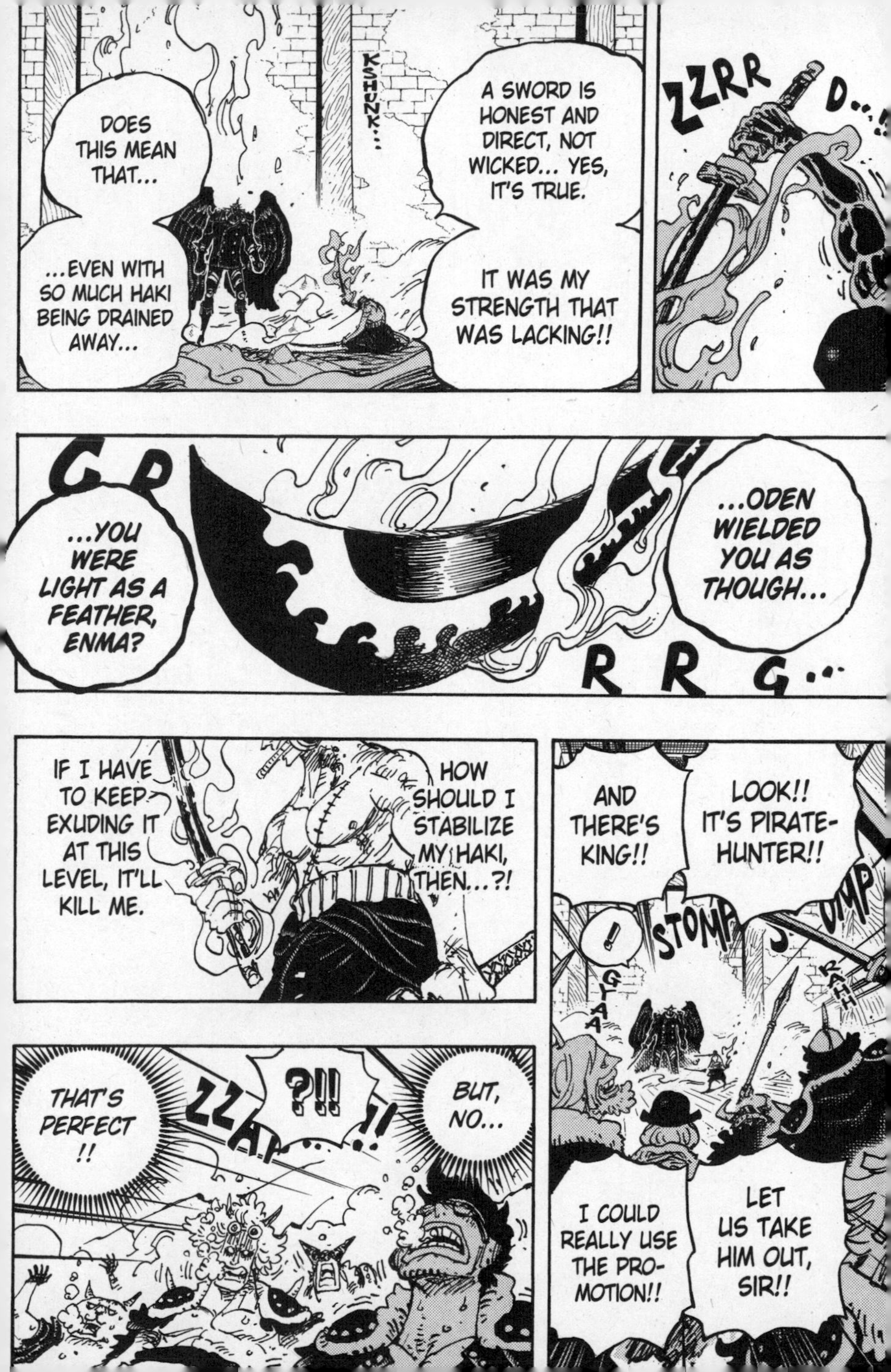
ZZRR D...!!
A SWORD IS HONEST AND DIRECT, NOT WICKED... YES, IT'S TRUE.
IT WAS MY STRENGTH THAT WAS LACKING!!
KSHUNK...
DOES THIS MEAN THAT...
...EVEN WITH SO MUCH HAKI BEING DRAINED AWAY...
...ODEN WIELDED YOU AS THOUGH...
...YOU WERE LIGHT AS A FEATHER, ENMA?
GRRRRG...
LOOK!! IT'S PIRATE-HUNTER!!
AND THERE'S KING!!
STOMP
!
GYAA
RAHH
LET US TAKE HIM OUT, SIR!!
I COULD REALLY USE THE PRO-MOTION!!
HOW SHOULD I STABILIZE MY HAKI, THEN...?!
IF I HAVE TO KEEP EXUDING IT AT THIS LEVEL, IT'LL KILL ME.
BUT, NO...
?!!
THAT'S PERFECT!!

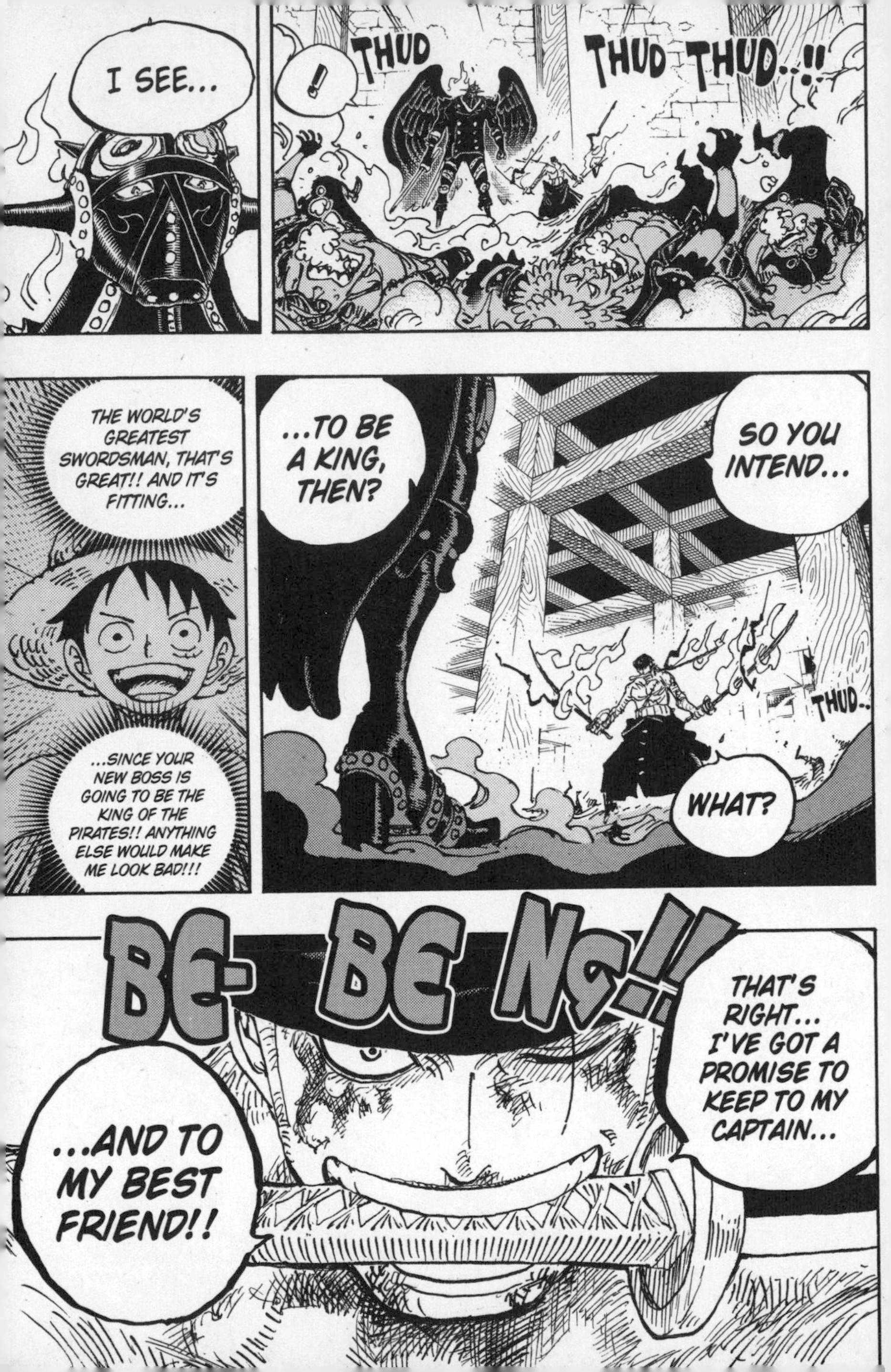
THUD THUD..!!
THUD
!
I SEE...
SO YOU INTEND...
...TO BE A KING, THEN?
THUD..
WHAT?
THE WORLD'S GREATEST SWORDSMAN, THAT'S GREAT!! AND IT'S FITTING...
...SINCE YOUR NEW BOSS IS GOING TO BE THE KING OF THE PIRATES!! ANYTHING ELSE WOULD MAKE ME LOOK BAD!!!
BE-BE NG!!
THAT'S RIGHT... I'VE GOT A PROMISE TO KEEP TO MY CAPTAIN...
...AND TO MY BEST FRIEND!!

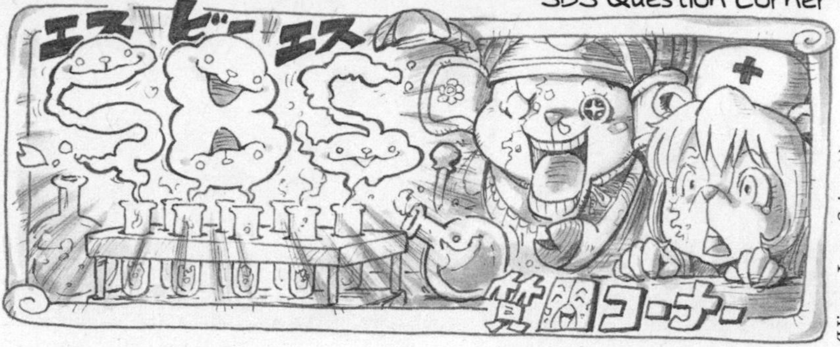
エスビーエス
質問コーナー

(Hippo Iron, Saitama)

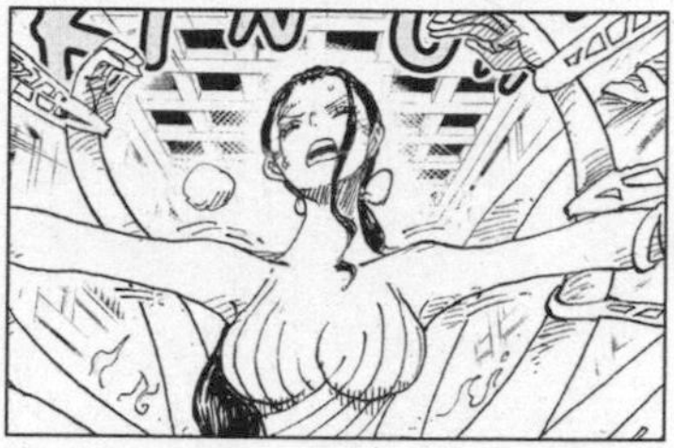

A: Okay! Previously, I asked all of you to explain what those lines were on Robin's chest when she was in Gigante Fleur form. You sent in many answers, so here's a selection!!

Q: Are those the lone scars that Robin ever suffered, from the time that she whooped my butt?

--Leo from the Cleave

Q: They must be **vaccine** lines, to protect against **obscene** thoughts!!

--Tamaemon

Q: Oh, those are Demonio Lines. You know how people get that pulsing blue vein when they're angry? This is a warning sign that if you make her any angrier, she'll go Demonio Fleur!!

--Daichi Kuriki

Q: What if those aren't her boobs at all? What if they're just onions?

--Eeyan

A: Very interesting!! Thank you for these fascinating comments, as well as the many others we don't have room for! So, which one will be selected as the official answer? *Drrrrururururum!!* Take it away, Robin!!

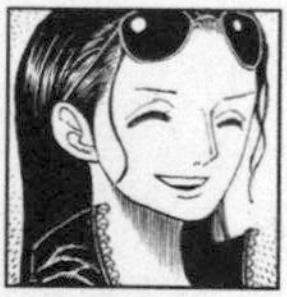

Robin: **They're onions.♡ Hee hee hee!**

A: They were onions!!! They weren't her chest at all!!

Q: Hello, Odacchi!! What's with the endless parade of boob questions in the SBS Segment these days? Do guys think about anything other than boobs?! It made me so sad when an entire page of volume 100 was nothing but a boob festival. It's like, are we all supposed to be perverts or something?!
So, Odacchi, were you aware that what we ladies want to know is…

Zolo's bust size!!! Tell us now!!!

--Roromiki

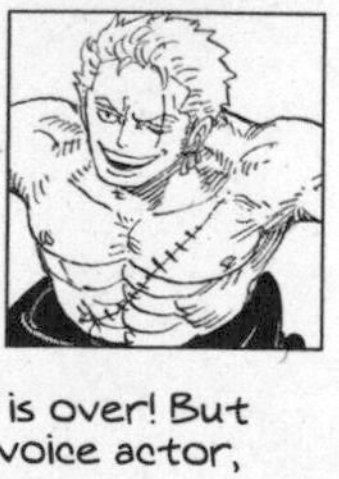

A: We got a girl pervert here!!! It's over! This segment is all over! Dammit! How should I know Zolo's bust size?! About 110 cm (43.3 in) or something? This SBS is over! But we still have another SBS section coming up with Jimbei's voice actor, Mr. Hoki! (See pg. 168)

Chapter 1034:
SANJI VS. QUEEN

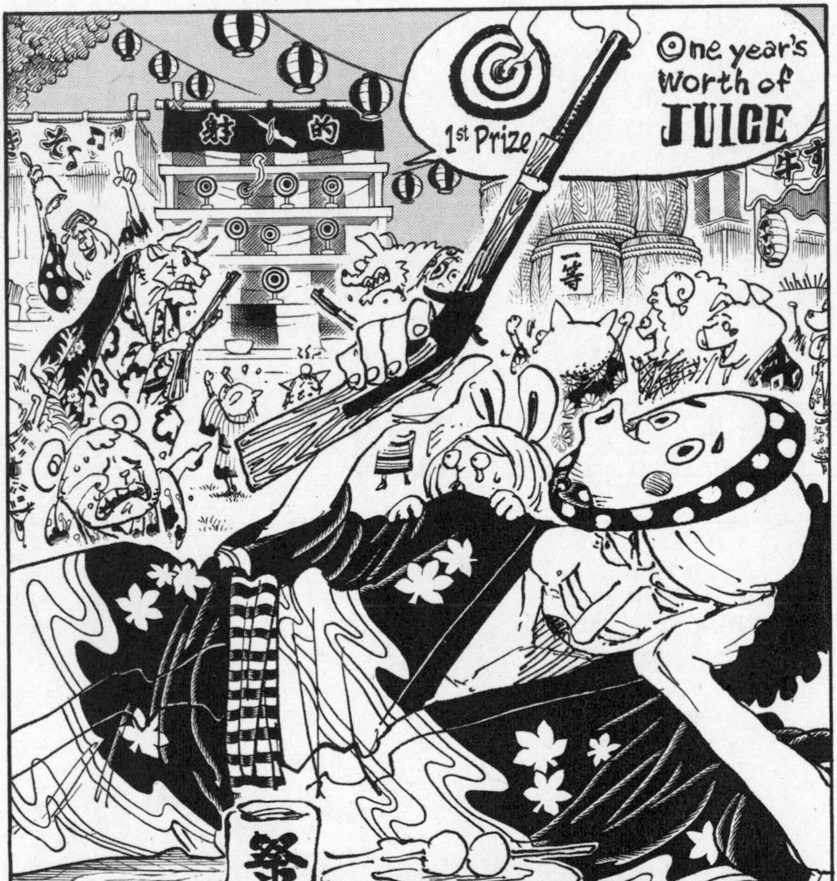

1st Prize
One year's worth of JUICE

READER REQUEST: "USOPP WINNING PRIZES FOR THE CHILDREN AT THE FESTIVAL SHOOTING GAME " BY EBI

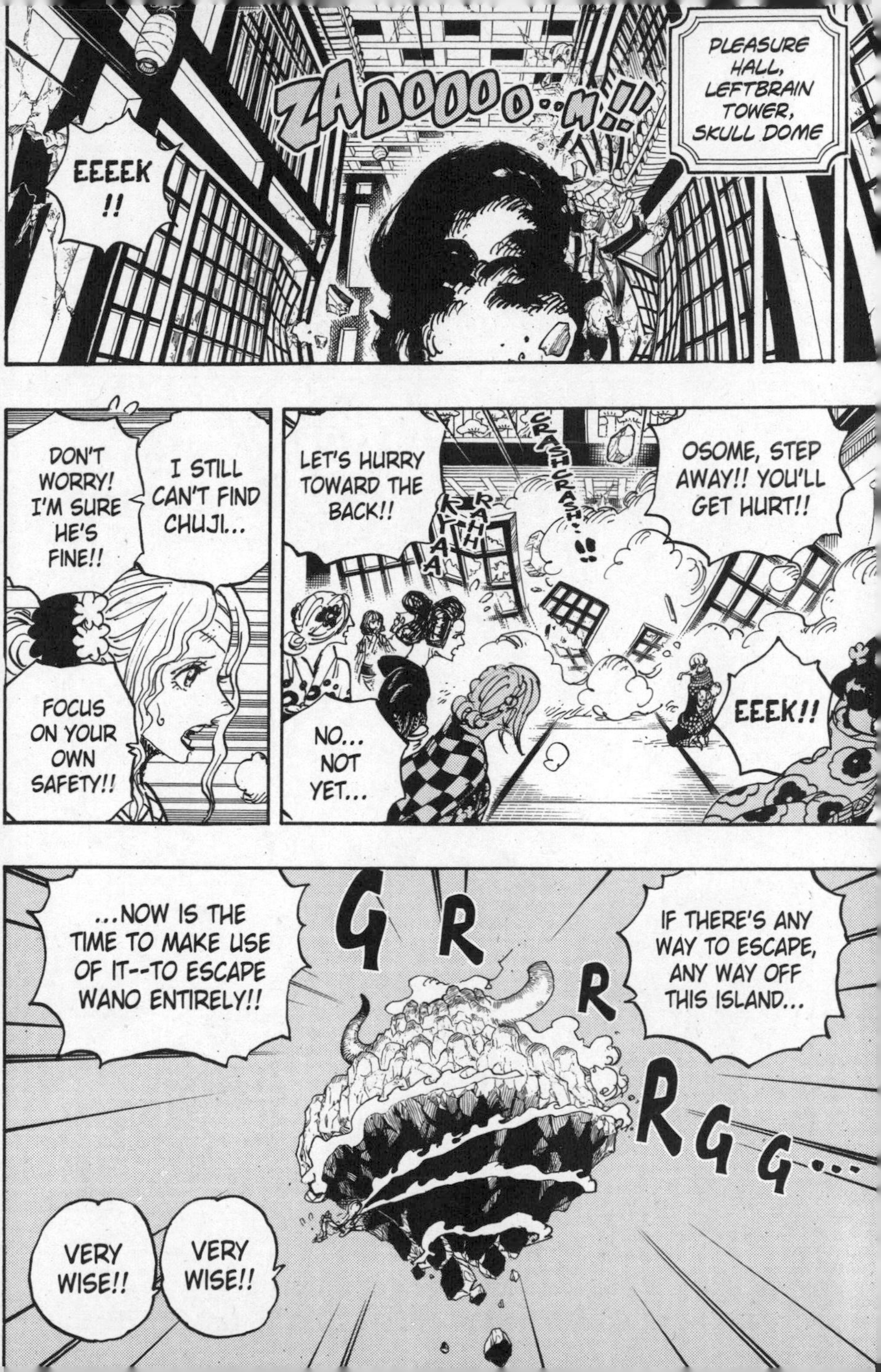
PLEASURE HALL, LEFTBRAIN TOWER, SKULL DOME
ZADOOOO..M!!
EEEEK !!
OSOME, STEP AWAY!! YOU'LL GET HURT!!
EEEK!!
CRASHCRASH..!!
RAHHH
KYAAA
LET'S HURRY TOWARD THE BACK!!
NO... NOT YET...
I STILL CAN'T FIND CHUJI...
DON'T WORRY! I'M SURE HE'S FINE!!
FOCUS ON YOUR OWN SAFETY!!
IF THERE'S ANY WAY TO ESCAPE, ANY WAY OFF THIS ISLAND...
...NOW IS THE TIME TO MAKE USE OF IT--TO ESCAPE WANO ENTIRELY!!
GRRRRGGG...
VERY WISE!!
VERY WISE!!

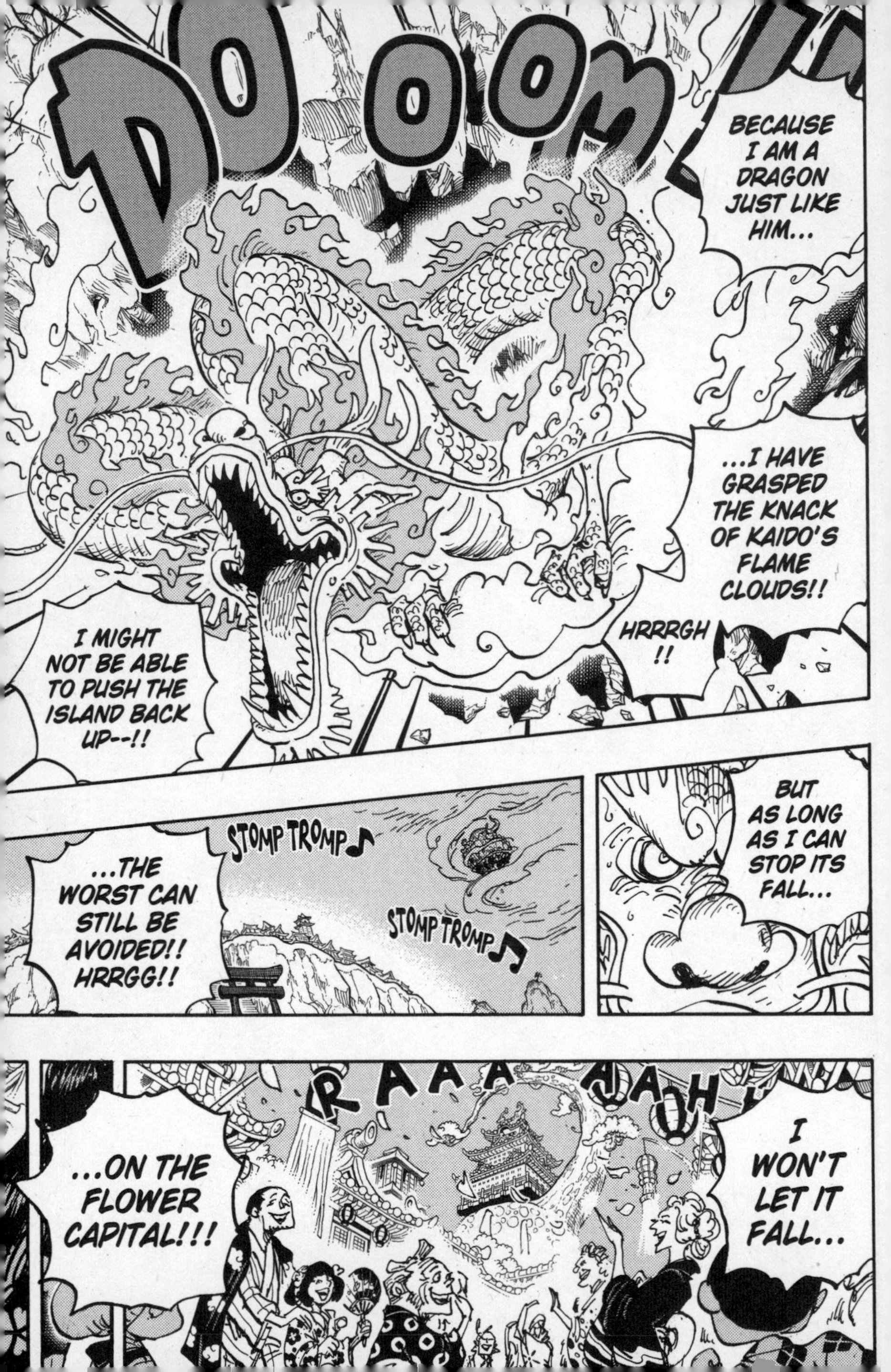
DOOOM
BECAUSE I AM A DRAGON JUST LIKE HIM...
...I HAVE GRASPED THE KNACK OF KAIDO'S FLAME CLOUDS!!
HRRRGH!!
I MIGHT NOT BE ABLE TO PUSH THE ISLAND BACK UP--!!
BUT AS LONG AS I CAN STOP ITS FALL...
STOMP TROMP♪
STOMP TROMP♪
...THE WORST CAN STILL BE AVOIDED!! HRRGG!!
I WON'T LET IT FALL...
RAAAAAH
...ON THE FLOWER CAPITAL!!!

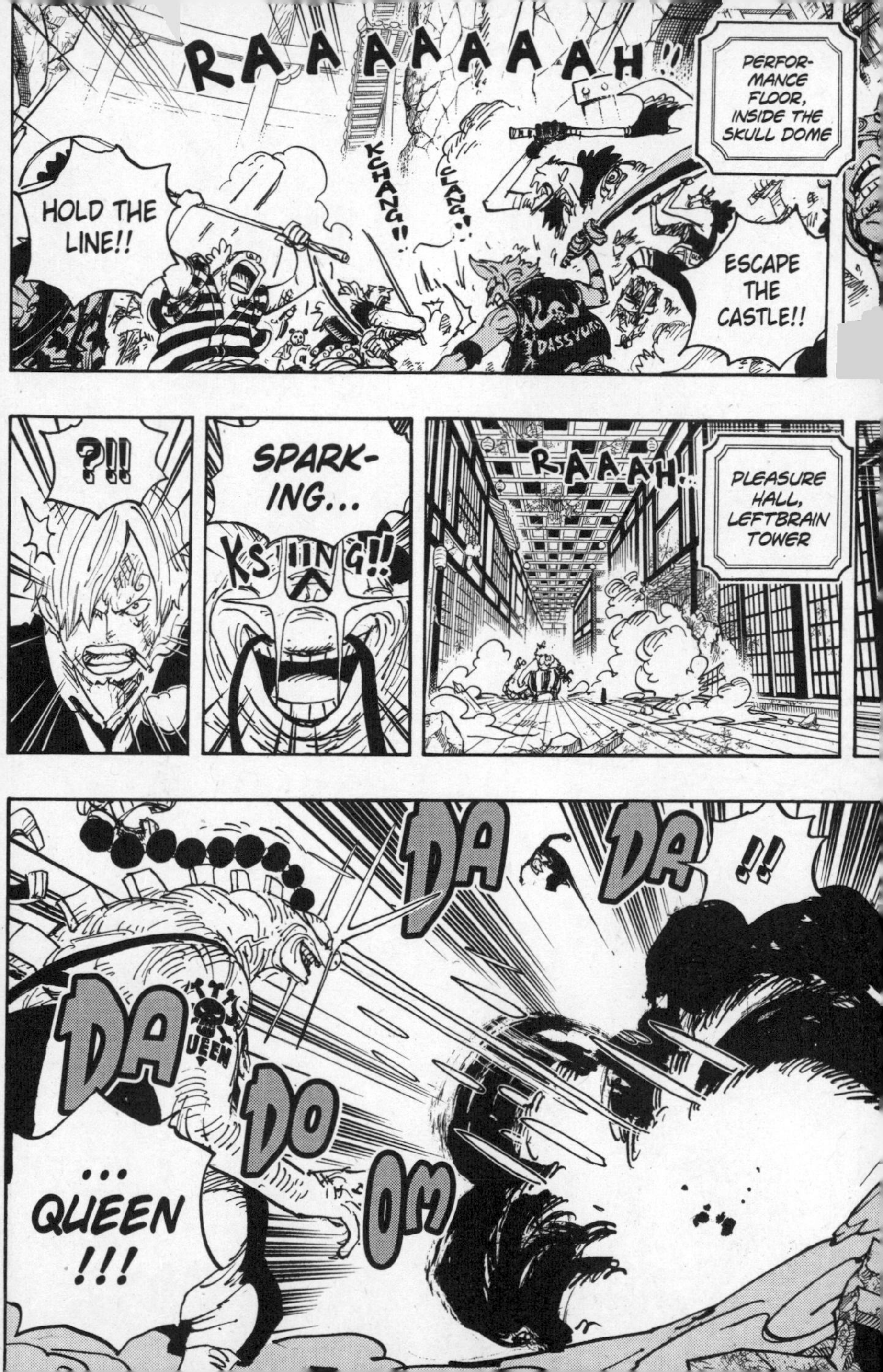
PERFOR-
MANCE
FLOOR,
INSIDE THE
SKULL DOME
RAAAAAAAH!!
ESCAPE
THE
CASTLE!!
CLANG!!
KCHANG!!
HOLD THE
LINE!!
PLEASURE
HALL,
LEFTBRAIN
TOWER
RAAAH...
SPARK-
ING...
KS IING!!
?!!
DA DA!!
DA DO OM
...
QUEEN
!!!

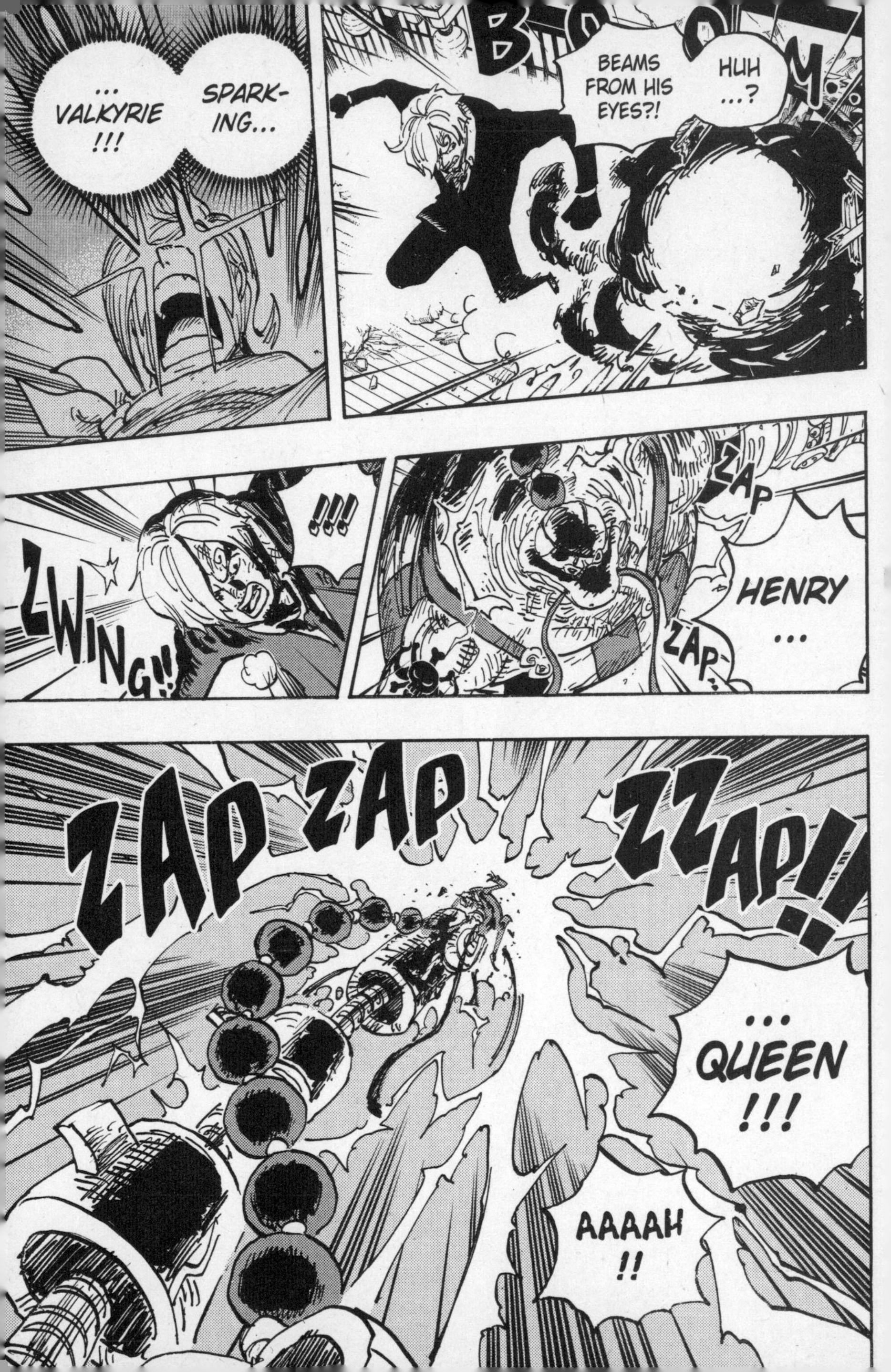
HUH ...?
BEAMS FROM HIS EYES?!
SPARK-ING...
... VALKYRIE !!!
ZAP
HENRY ...
ZAP
!!!
ZWING!!
ZAP ZAP ZZAP!!
... QUEEN !!!
AAAAH !!

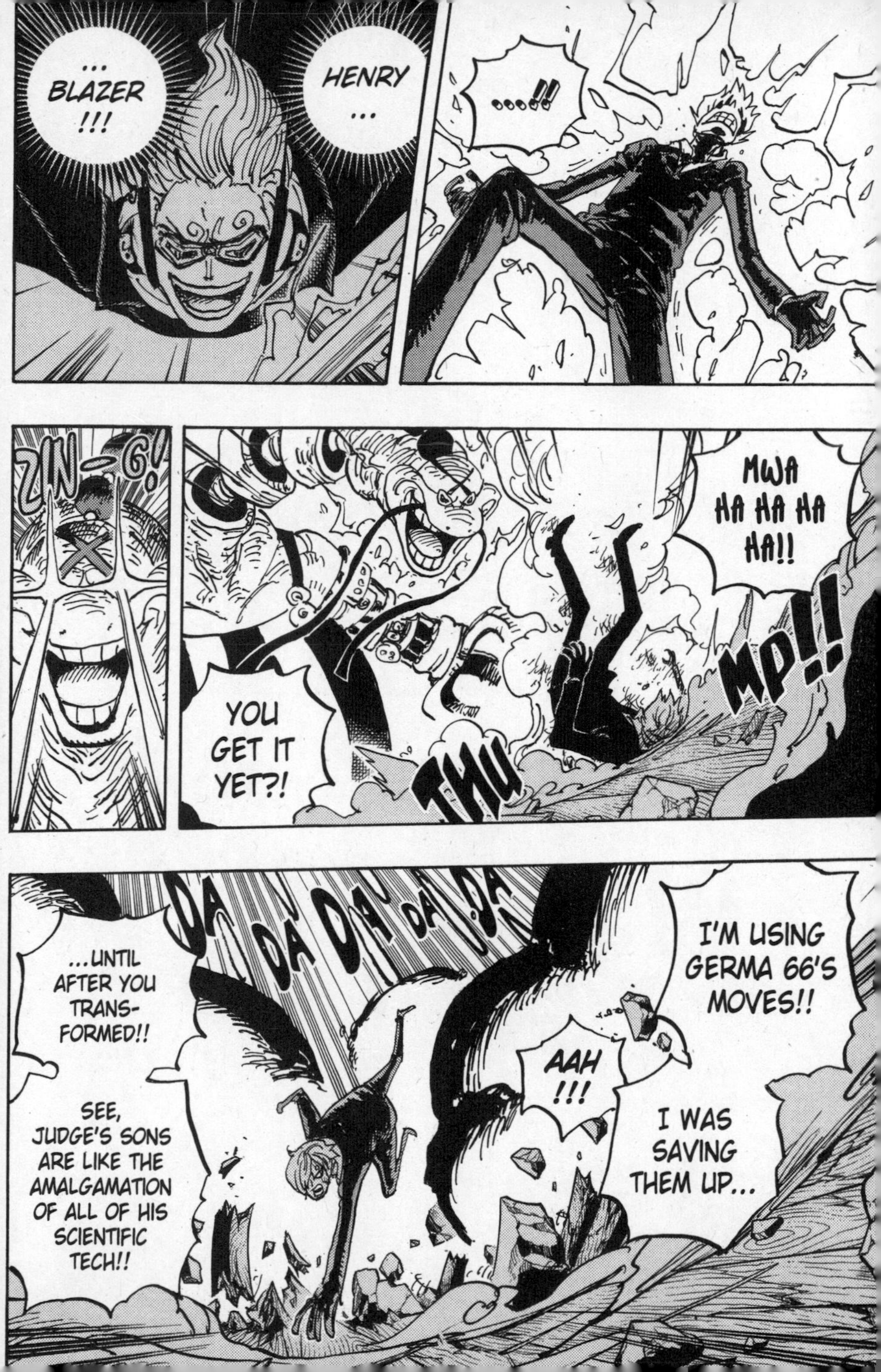
....!!
HENRY ...
... BLAZER !!!
MWA HA HA HA HA!!
THUMP!!
YOU GET IT YET?!
ZIN-G!
I'M USING GERMA 66'S MOVES!!
I WAS SAVING THEM UP...
AAH !!!
DA DA DA DA DA
...UNTIL AFTER YOU TRANS-FORMED!!
SEE, JUDGE'S SONS ARE LIKE THE AMALGAMATION OF ALL OF HIS SCIENTIFIC TECH!!

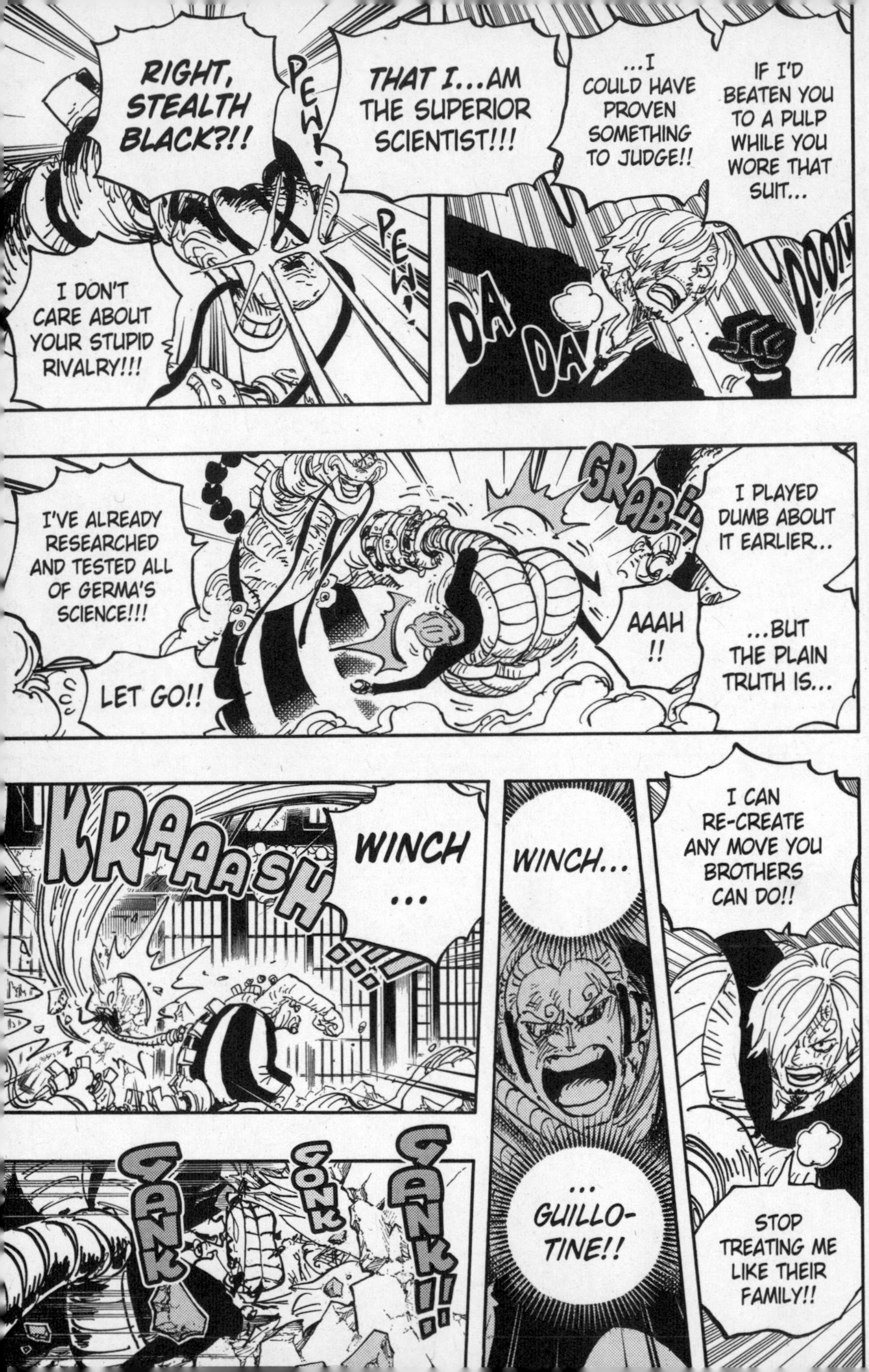
IF I'D BEATEN YOU TO A PULP WHILE YOU WORE THAT SUIT...
...I COULD HAVE PROVEN SOMETHING TO JUDGE!!
DOOM
DA
DA
THAT I...AM THE SUPERIOR SCIENTIST!!!
RIGHT, STEALTH BLACK?!!
PEW!
PEW!
I DON'T CARE ABOUT YOUR STUPID RIVALRY!!!
I PLAYED DUMB ABOUT IT EARLIER...
...BUT THE PLAIN TRUTH IS...
GRAB!!
AAAH!!
I'VE ALREADY RESEARCHED AND TESTED ALL OF GERMA'S SCIENCE!!!
LET GO!!
I CAN RE-CREATE ANY MOVE YOU BROTHERS CAN DO!!
STOP TREATING ME LIKE THEIR FAMILY!!
WINCH...
...GUILLO-TINE!!
WINCH ...
KRAAASH!!
GANK!!
GONK
GANK

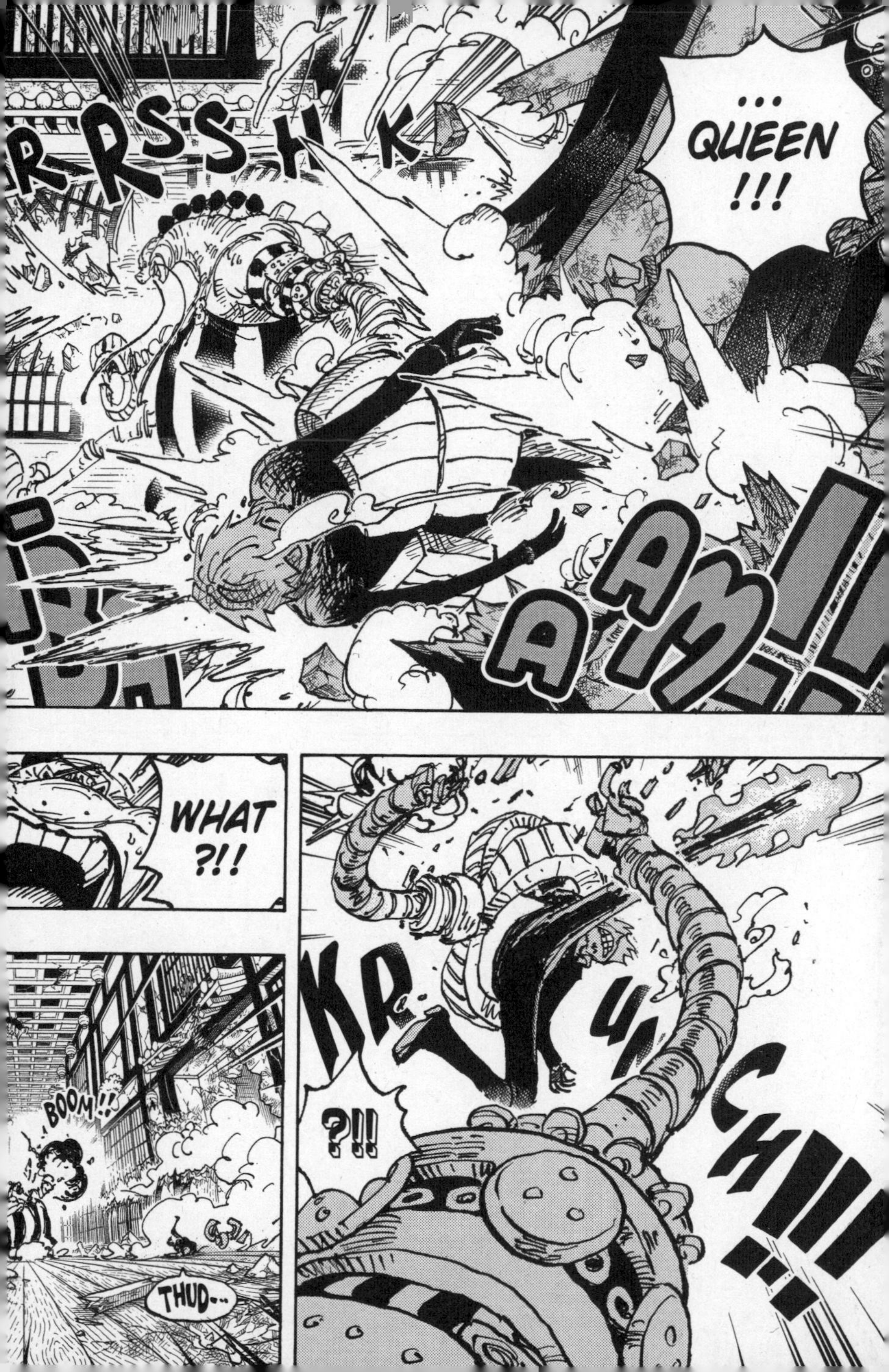

... QUEEN !!!
RRSSHK
AAM!!
KRUNCH!!
?!!
WHAT ?!!
BOOM!!
THUD...

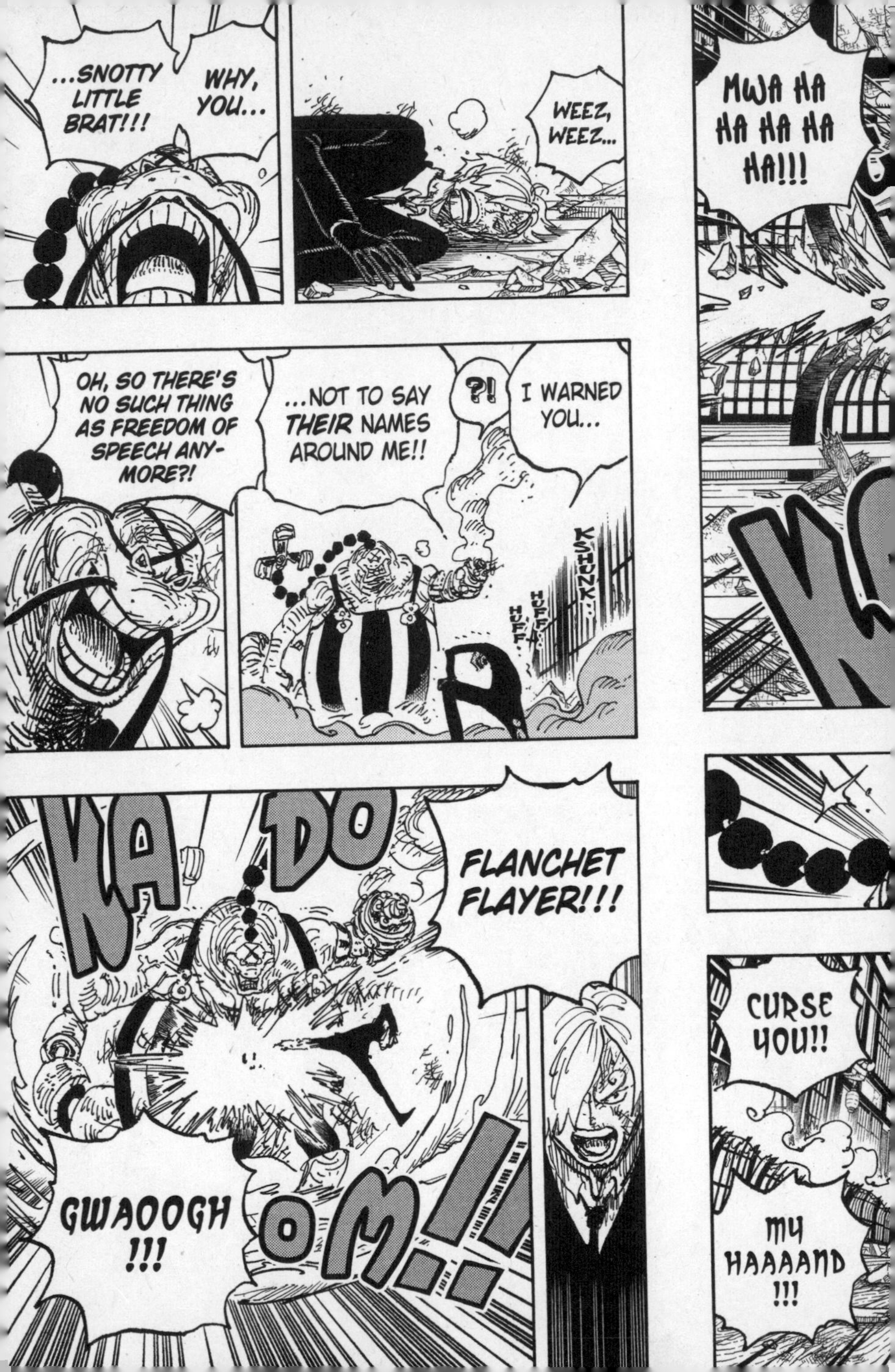
MWA HA HA HA HA HA!!!
CURSE YOU!!
MY HAAAAND!!!
WEEZ, WEEZ...
WHY, YOU...
...SNOTTY LITTLE BRAT!!!
I WARNED YOU...
?!
...NOT TO SAY THEIR NAMES AROUND ME!!
KSHUNK...
HUFF HUFF
OH, SO THERE'S NO SUCH THING AS FREEDOM OF SPEECH ANY-MORE?!
FLANCHET FLAYER!!!
KA DO OM!!
GWAOOGH!!!

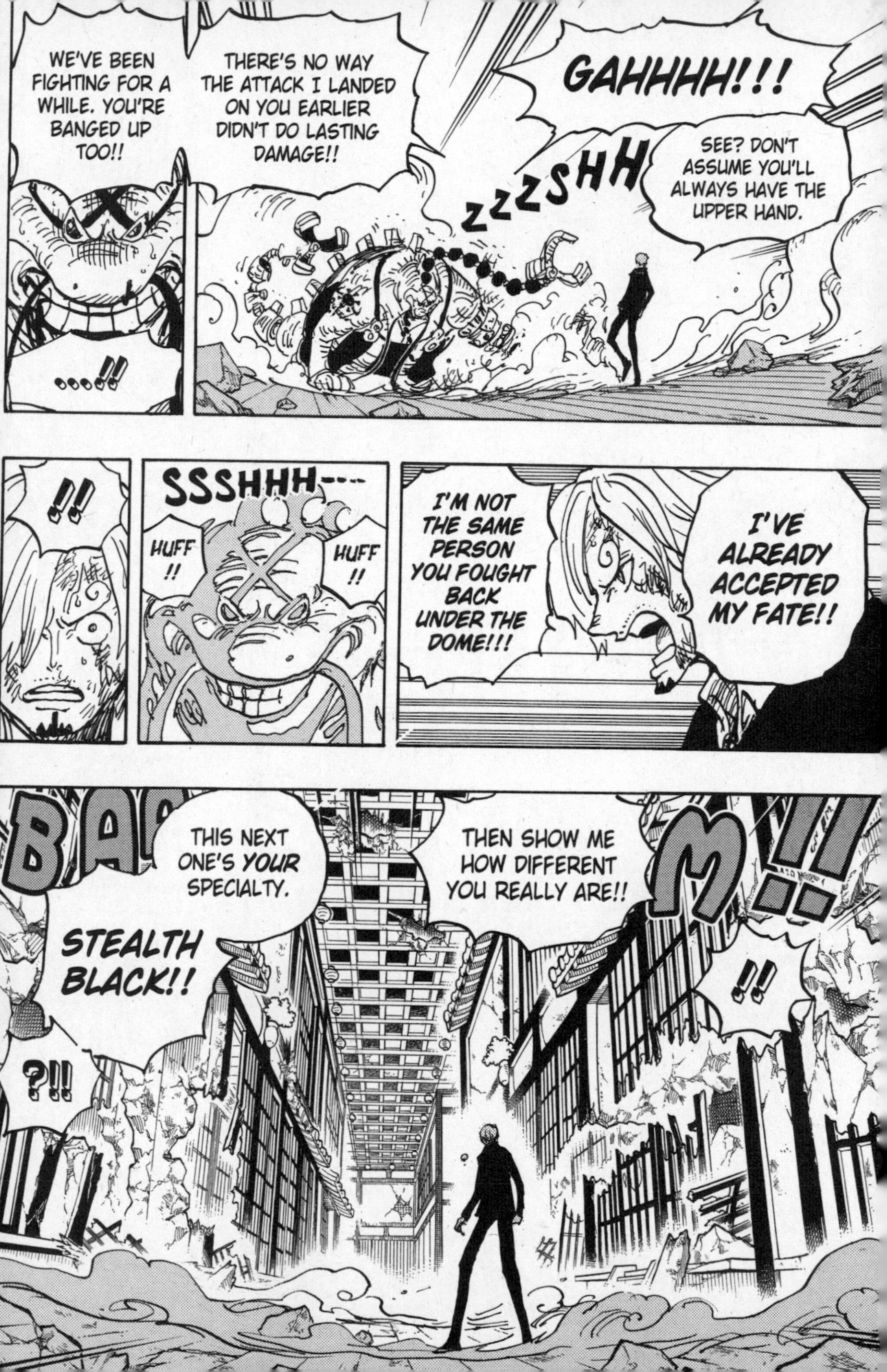
GAHHHH!!!
SEE? DON'T ASSUME YOU'LL ALWAYS HAVE THE UPPER HAND.
ZZZZSHH
THERE'S NO WAY THE ATTACK I LANDED ON YOU EARLIER DIDN'T DO LASTING DAMAGE!!
WE'VE BEEN FIGHTING FOR A WHILE. YOU'RE BANGED UP TOO!!
....!!
I'VE ALREADY ACCEPTED MY FATE!!
I'M NOT THE SAME PERSON YOU FOUGHT BACK UNDER THE DOME!!!
SSSHHH---
HUFF !!
HUFF !!
!!
BAAM!!
THEN SHOW ME HOW DIFFERENT YOU REALLY ARE!!
THIS NEXT ONE'S YOUR SPECIALTY.
!!
STEALTH BLACK!!
?!!

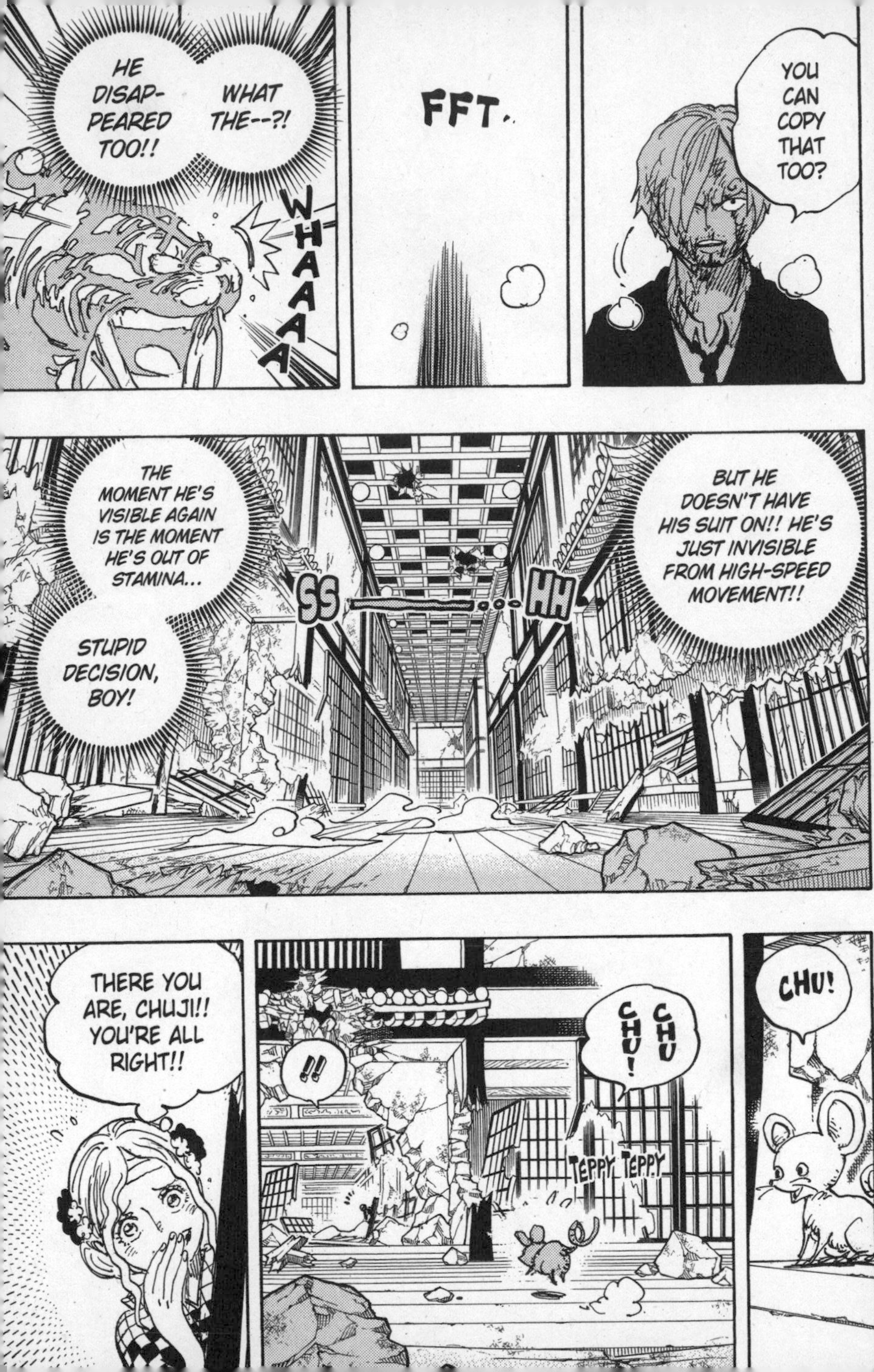
YOU CAN COPY THAT TOO?
FFT.
WHAT THE--?!
HE DISAP-PEARED TOO!!
WHAAAAA
BUT HE DOESN'T HAVE HIS SUIT ON!! HE'S JUST INVISIBLE FROM HIGH-SPEED MOVEMENT!!
SS---...HH
THE MOMENT HE'S VISIBLE AGAIN IS THE MOMENT HE'S OUT OF STAMINA...
STUPID DECISION, BOY!
CHU!
CHU CHU!
!!
TEPPY TEPPY
THERE YOU ARE, CHUJI!! YOU'RE ALL RIGHT!!

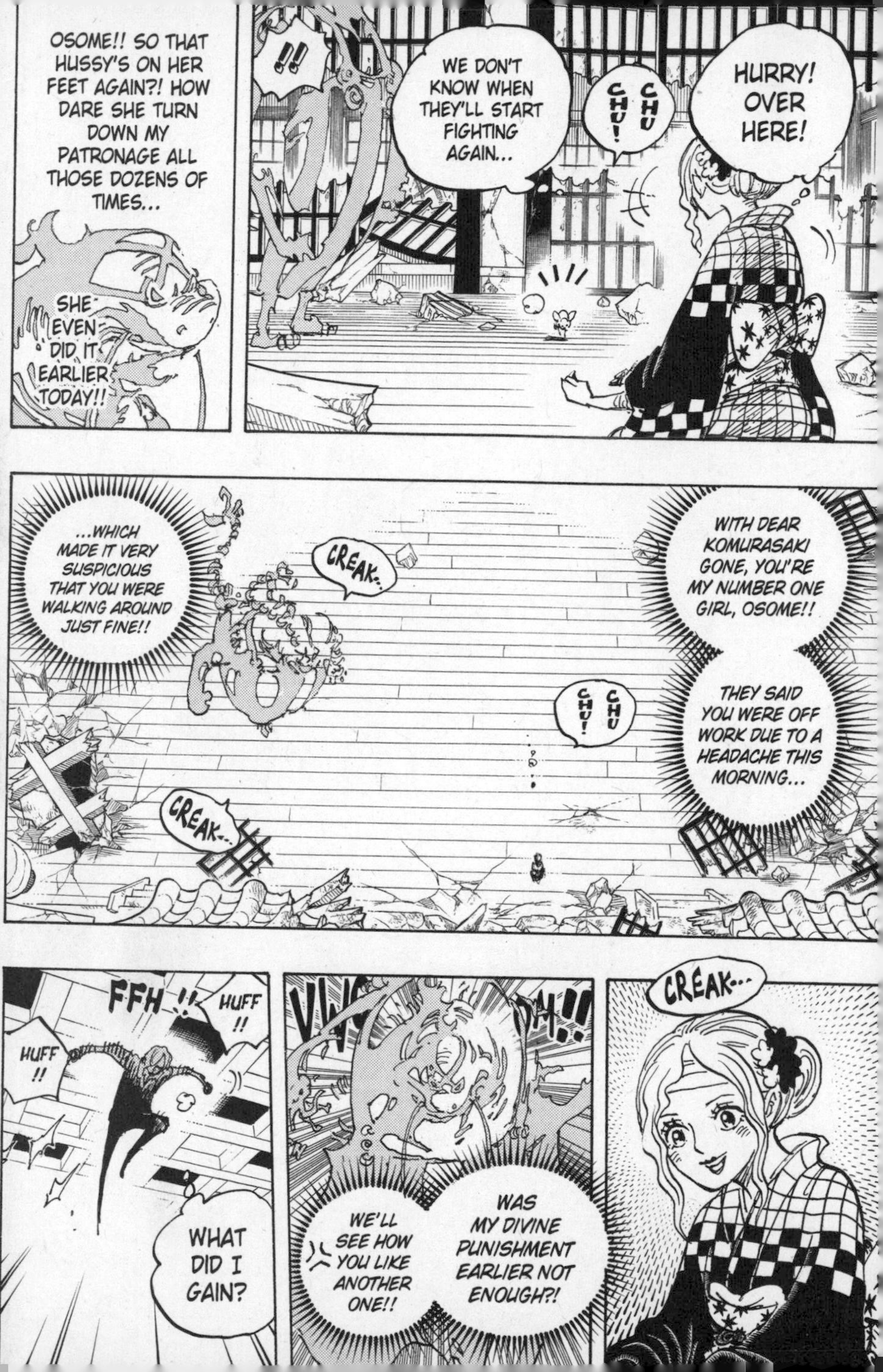
HURRY! OVER HERE!
CHU CHU!
WE DON'T KNOW WHEN THEY'LL START FIGHTING AGAIN...
!!
OSOME!! SO THAT HUSSY'S ON HER FEET AGAIN?! HOW DARE SHE TURN DOWN MY PATRONAGE ALL THOSE DOZENS OF TIMES...
SHE EVEN DID IT EARLIER TODAY!!
WITH DEAR KOMURASAKI GONE, YOU'RE MY NUMBER ONE GIRL, OSOME!!
THEY SAID YOU WERE OFF WORK DUE TO A HEADACHE THIS MORNING...
CHU CHU!
CREAK...
...WHICH MADE IT VERY SUSPICIOUS THAT YOU WERE WALKING AROUND JUST FINE!!
CREAK...
CREAK...
WAS MY DIVINE PUNISHMENT EARLIER NOT ENOUGH?!
WE'LL SEE HOW YOU LIKE ANOTHER ONE!!
FFH!!
HUFF!!
HUFF!!
WHAT DID I GAIN?

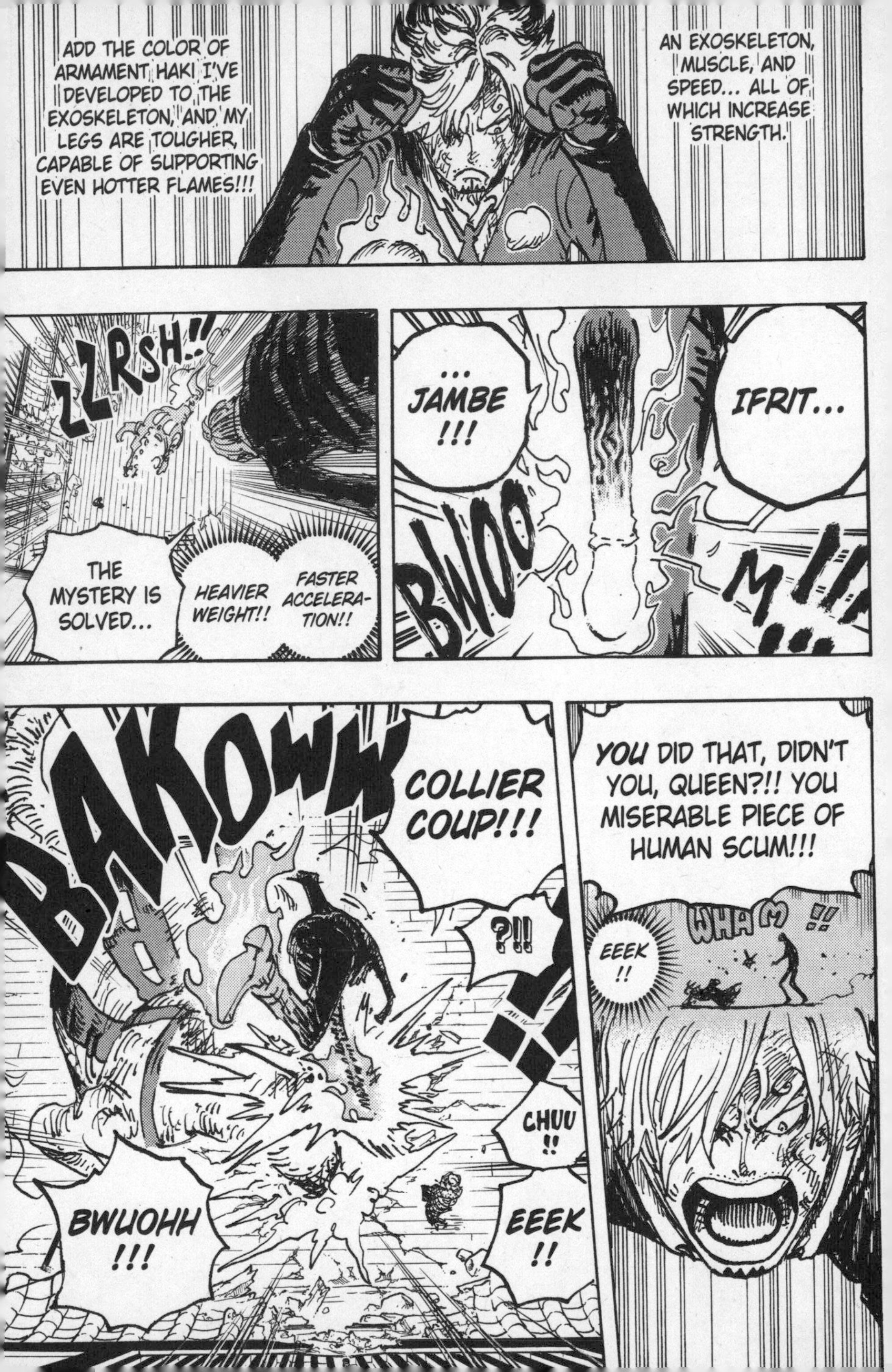
AN EXOSKELETON, MUSCLE, AND SPEED... ALL OF WHICH INCREASE STRENGTH.
ADD THE COLOR OF ARMAMENT HAKI I'VE DEVELOPED TO THE EXOSKELETON, AND MY LEGS ARE TOUGHER, CAPABLE OF SUPPORTING EVEN HOTTER FLAMES!!!
IFRIT...
...JAMBE!!!
BWOOM!!!...
ZZRSH!!
FASTER ACCELERATION!!
HEAVIER WEIGHT!!
THE MYSTERY IS SOLVED...
YOU DID THAT, DIDN'T YOU, QUEEN?!! YOU MISERABLE PIECE OF HUMAN SCUM!!!
WHAM!!
EEEK!!
COLLIER COUP!!!
BAKOWW
?!!
CHUU!!
EEEK!!
BWUOHH!!!

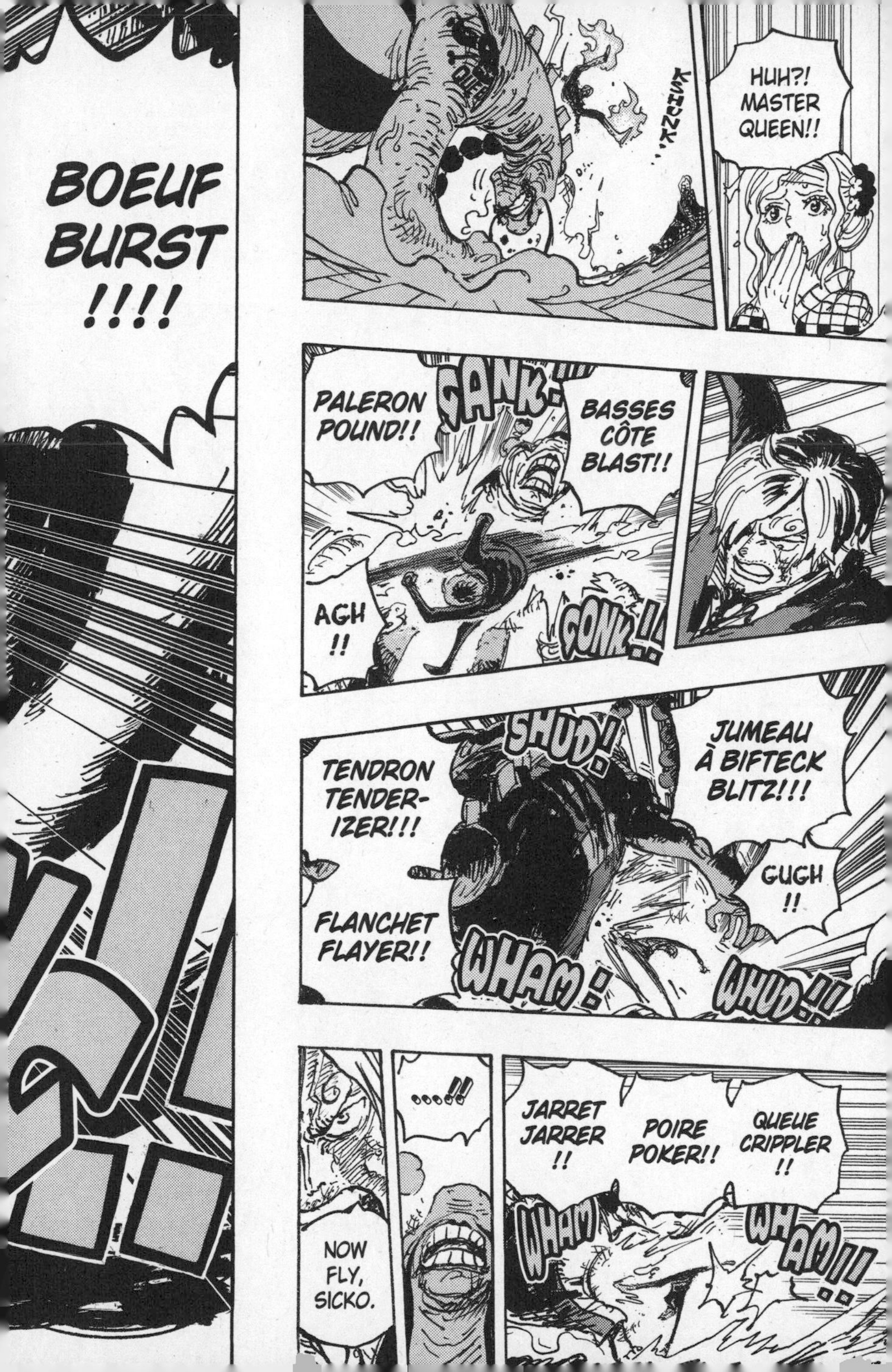
HUH?! MASTER QUEEN!!
KSHUNK...
BASSES CÔTE BLAST!!
GANK!!
PALERON POUND!!
GONK!!
AGH!!
JUMEAU À BIFTECK BLITZ!!!
SHUD!
TENDRON TENDER-IZER!!!
GUGH!!
FLANCHET FLAYER!!
WHUD!!
WHAM!
QUEUE CRIPPLER!!
POIRE POKER!!
JARRET JARRER!!
WHAM!!
WHAM
....!!
NOW FLY, SICKO.
BOEUF BURST!!!!

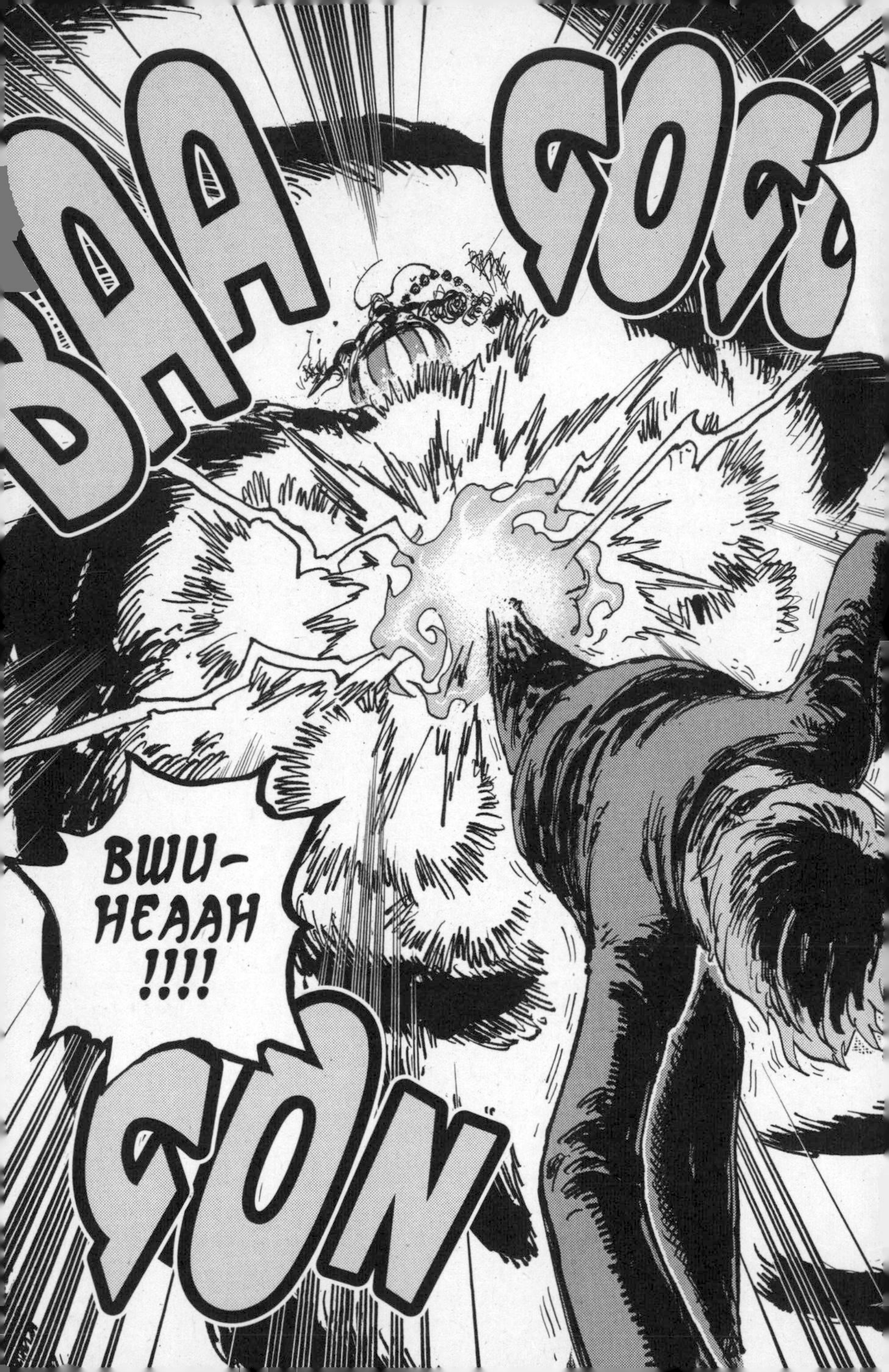
BWU-
HEAAH
!!!!

Jimbei's Voice Actor!!

SBS Question Corner

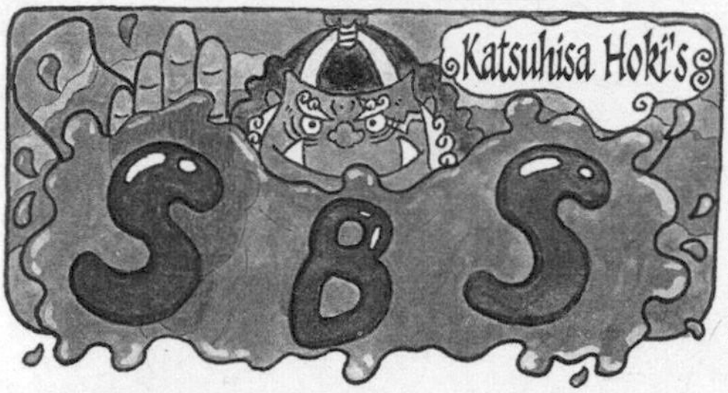
Katsuhisa Hoki's
SBS

(Kashiki, Tochigi)

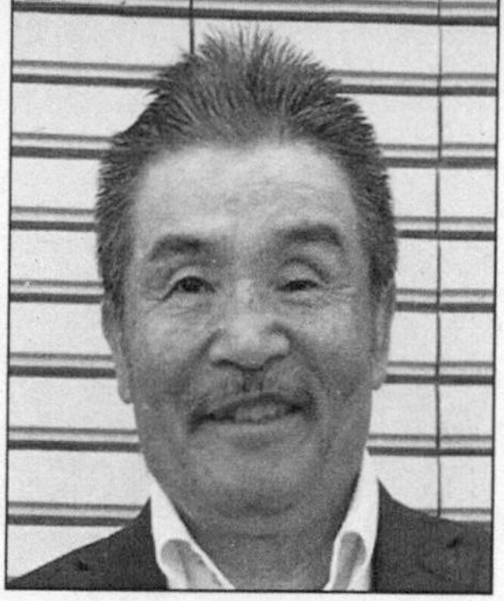

H.T.E.!! (Hi There Everybody)

At last it has returned: **Voice Actor SBS!** It's been so long. Ten years, in fact! We started this with Luffy's actor Mayumi Tanaka in volume 52, all the way through Brook's actor Cho in volume 64, but now that Jimbei's officially joined as the tenth crewmate, you readers have requested its return! So let's do this!

We've got our trusty helmsman, **the Japanese voice of Jimbei, a truly chivalrous gentleman, Katsuhisa Hoki in the house!!**

O (Oda): Well, here's Mr. Hoki. Give the folks an introduction!

H (Hoki): **Men~~♪ of the sea~~~♫ are all brotherrrrs~~~♫**

O: Whoa, whoa, whoa! He's singing, folks, he's singing!! No, I meant introduce yourself! We get that you're proud of your singing voice!

H: **Oh, you do? Care to join me? Men of the sea~~~♪**

O: **Okay, you can stop now!! We're not getting anywhere!!**

H: **I am Katsuhisa Hoki, part of the crew at last. Be-beng!!**

O: Be-beng, indeed. I've kept you waiting for so long. Kept the readers waiting too! Well, we've taken up enough time with this, so let's go! It's the SBS Corner. Do you know what SBS stands for?

H: **(S)ending (B)ig (S)mooches!!**

O: Of course we'll do that, but no! I should have known you'd get all goofy...

H: **(S)top (C)alling me (S)enile!!**

O: Geez, take it easy!! And that says "SCS"!! Okay, we're out of time. Take it away!! Here's your letters!! (*thump*)

H: **I've got this!!**

Katsuhisa Hoki's SBS segment continues on p. 186!! ☞

Chapter 1035:
ZOLO VS. KING

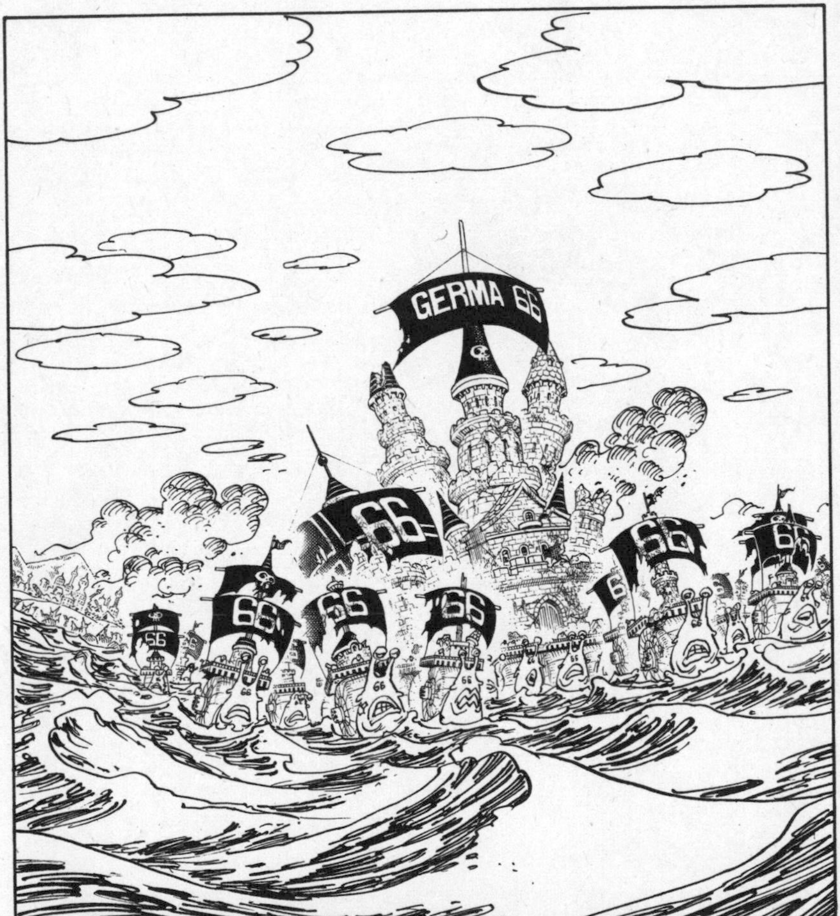
GERMA 66

LIMITED COVER SERIES, NO. 25, VOL. 1:
"ESCAPE WHOLE CAKE ISLAND!"

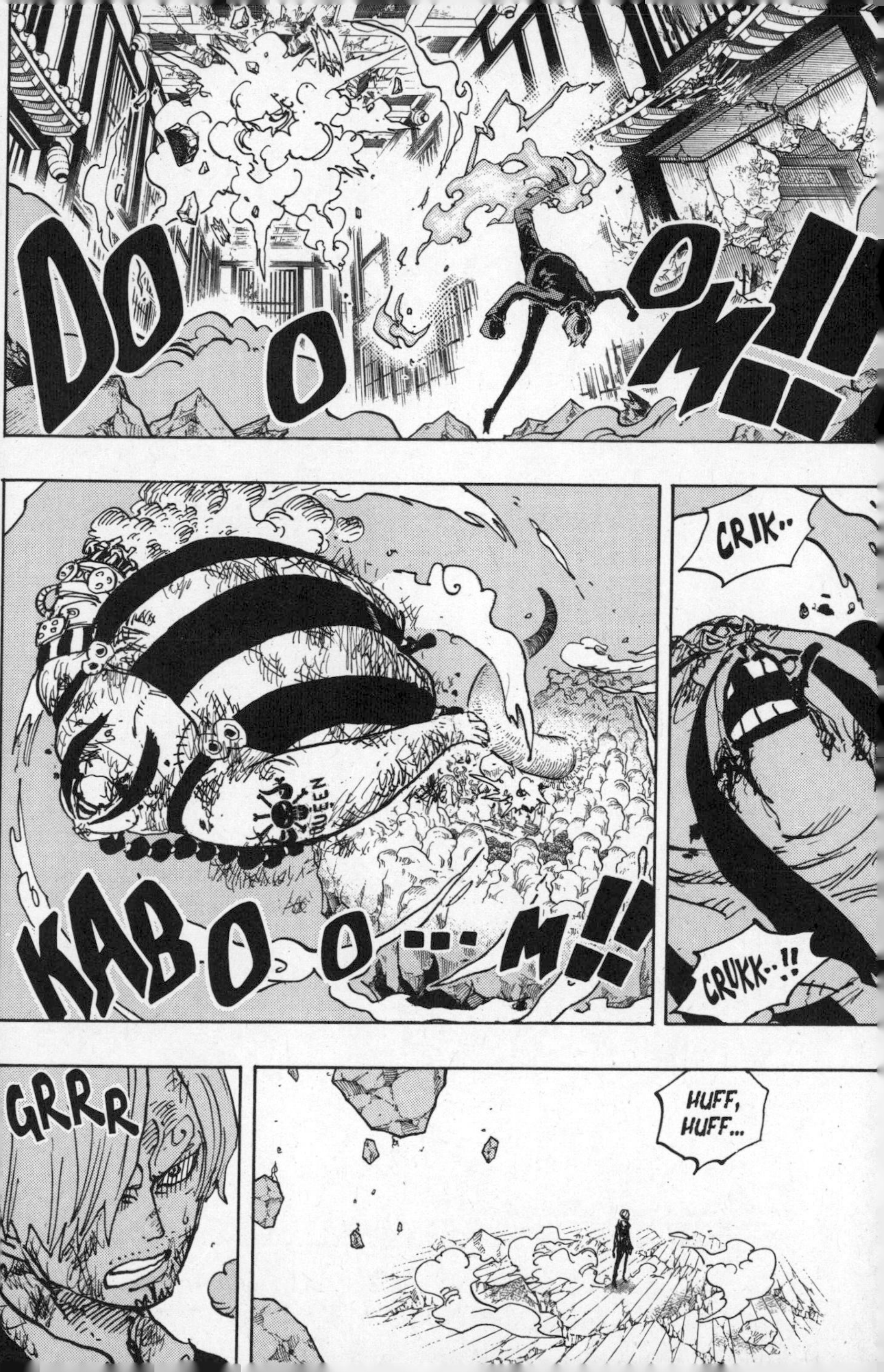
DOOOM!!
CRIK..
CRUKK..!!
KABOO...M!!
HUFF, HUFF...
GRRR

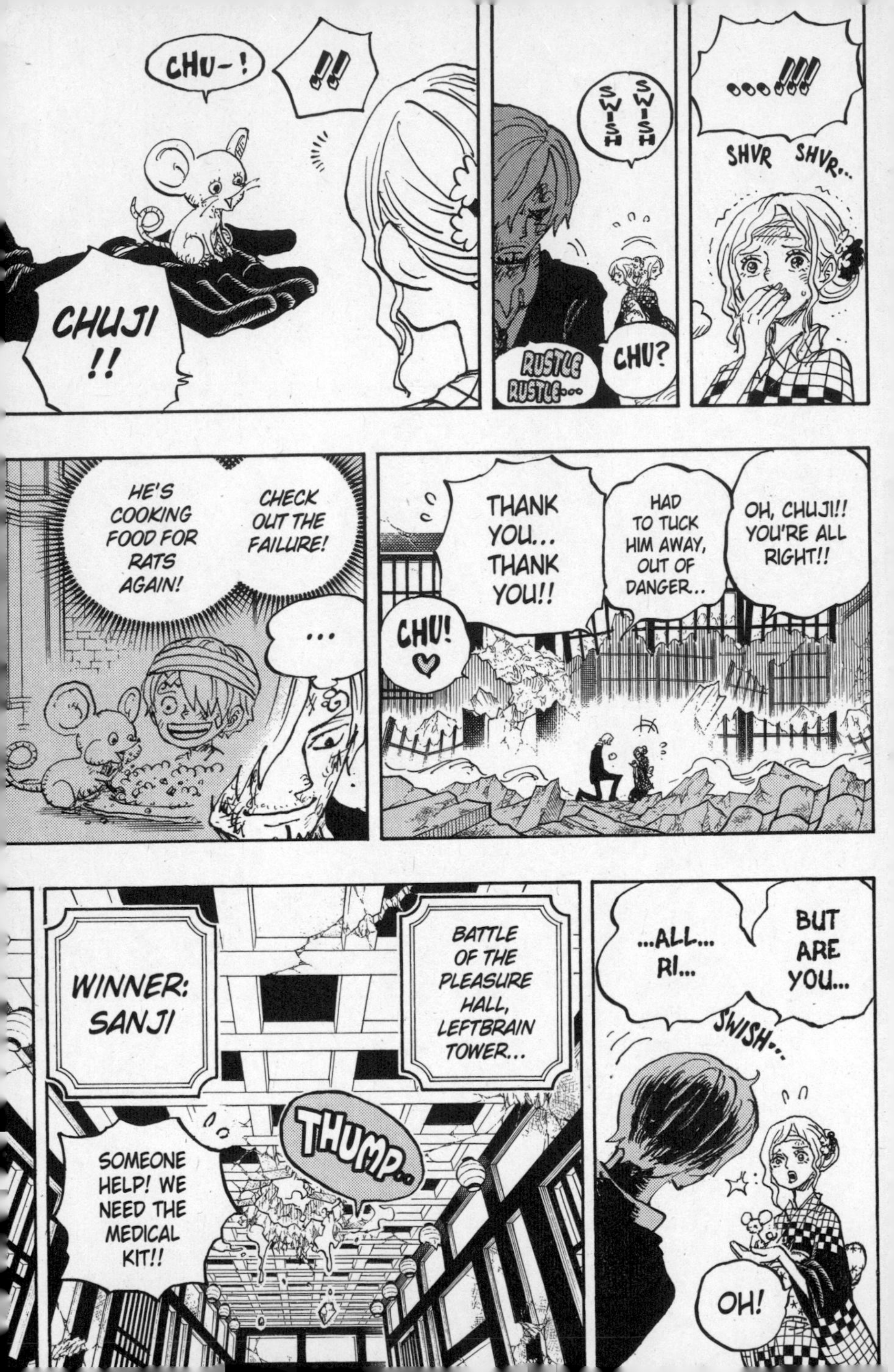
...!!!
SHVR SHVR...
SWISH SWISH
CHU?
RUSTLE RUSTLE...
!!
CHU-!
CHUJI !!
OH, CHUJI!! YOU'RE ALL RIGHT!!
HAD TO TUCK HIM AWAY, OUT OF DANGER...
THANK YOU... THANK YOU!!
CHU! ♥
CHECK OUT THE FAILURE!
HE'S COOKING FOOD FOR RATS AGAIN!
...
BUT ARE YOU...
...ALL... RI...
SWISH...
OH!
BATTLE OF THE PLEASURE HALL, LEFTBRAIN TOWER...
WINNER: SANJI
THUMP..
SOMEONE HELP! WE NEED THE MEDICAL KIT!!

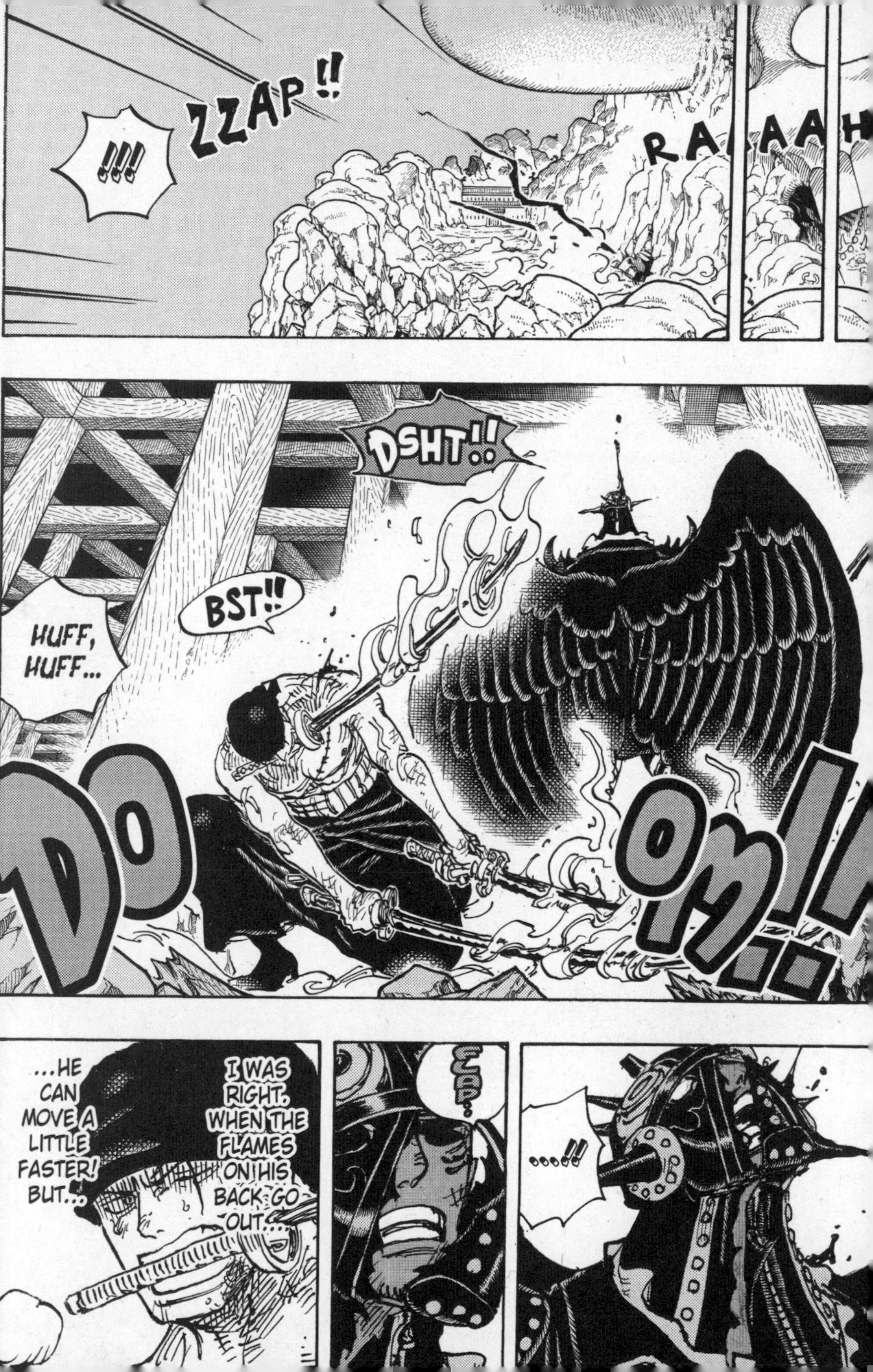
RAAAH
ZZAP!!
!!!
DSHT!!
BST!!
HUFF, HUFF...
DOOM!!
...!!
I WAS RIGHT. WHEN THE FLAMES ON HIS BACK GO OUT...
...HE CAN MOVE A LITTLE FASTER! BUT...

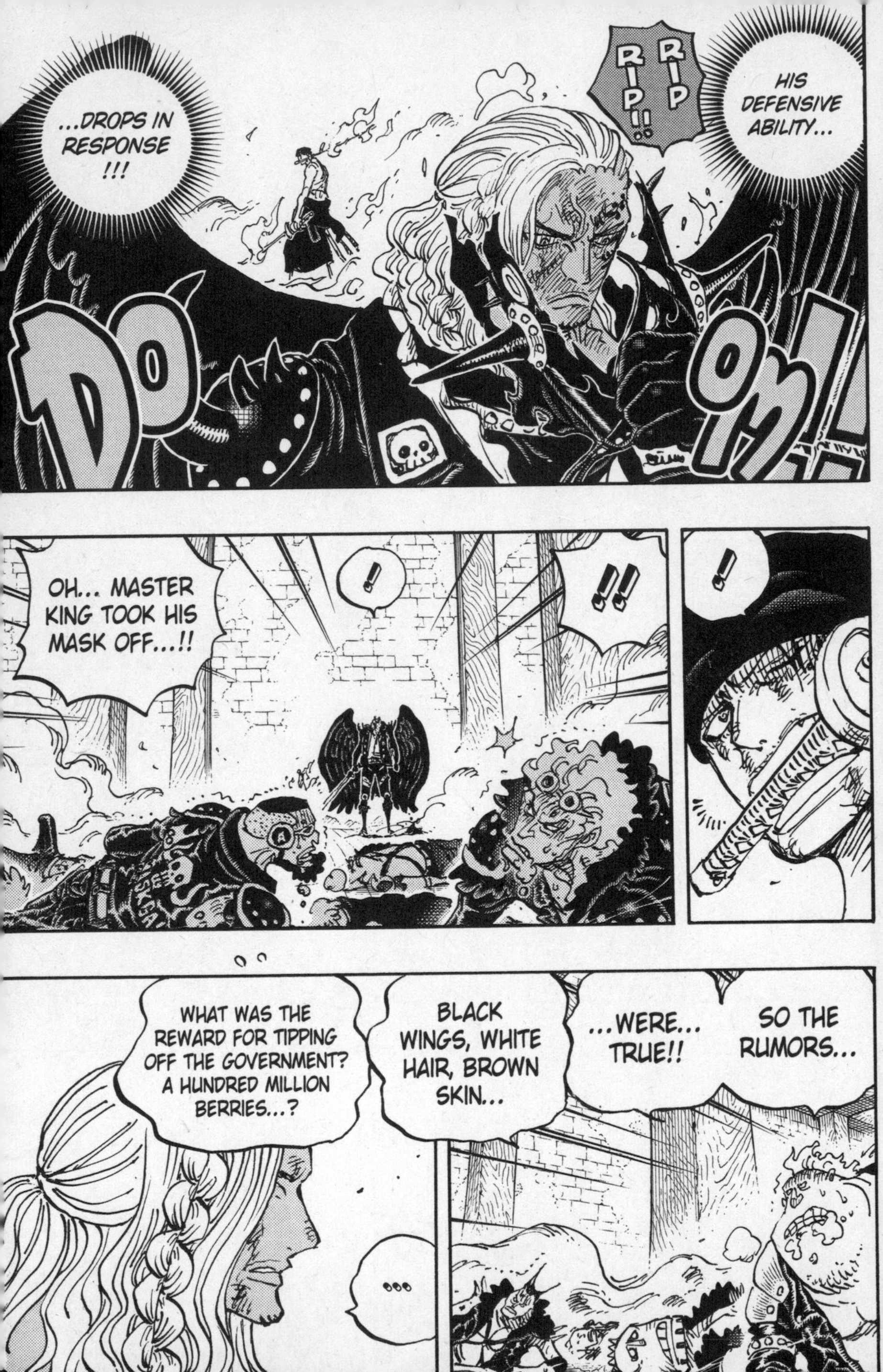
HIS DEFENSIVE ABILITY...
RIP RIP!!
...DROPS IN RESPONSE !!!
DOOM!!
!
!!
!
OH... MASTER KING TOOK HIS MASK OFF...!!
SO THE RUMORS...
...WERE... TRUE!!
BLACK WINGS, WHITE HAIR, BROWN SKIN...
WHAT WAS THE REWARD FOR TIPPING OFF THE GOVERNMENT? A HUNDRED MILLION BERRIES...?
...

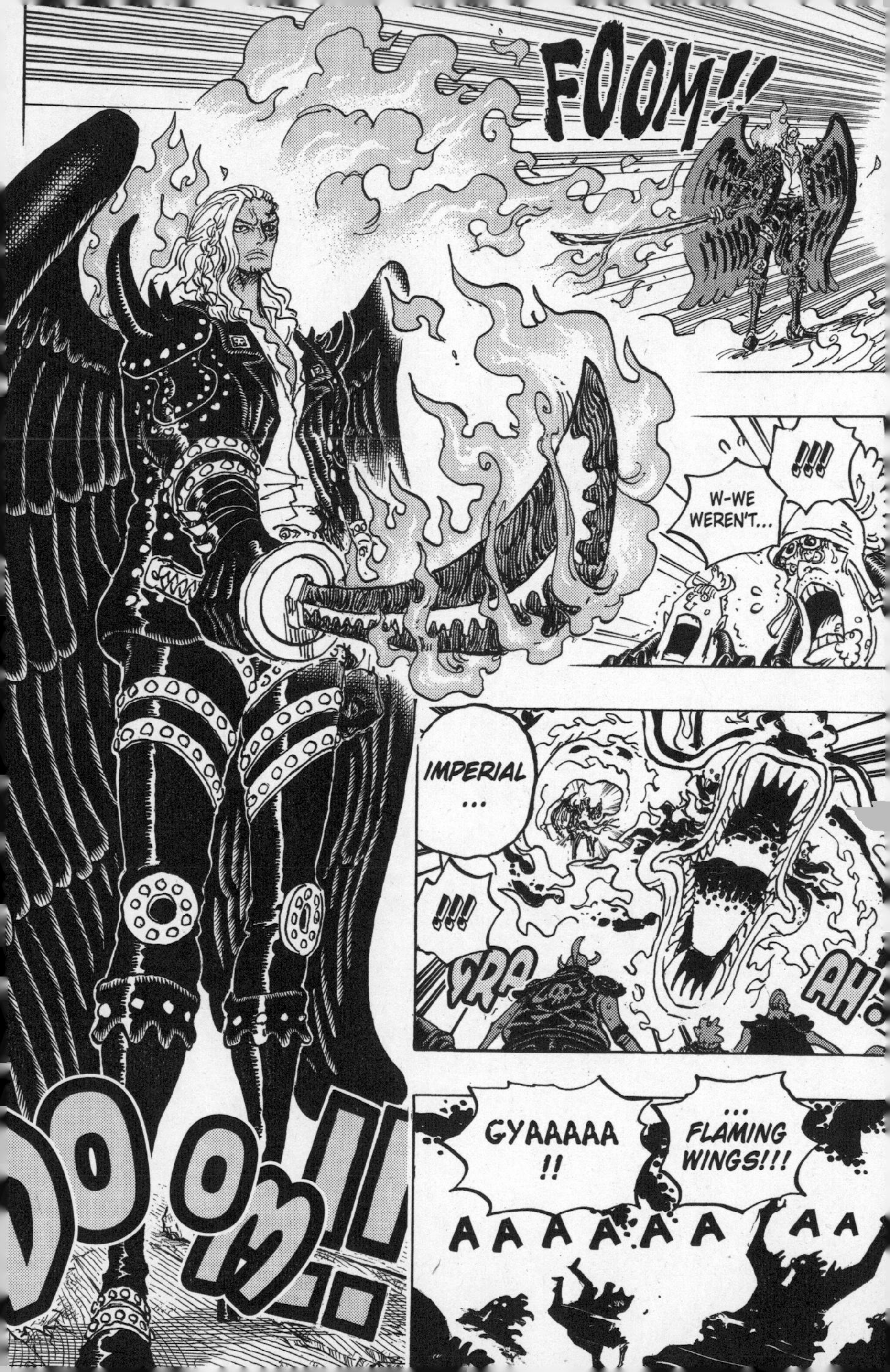
FOOM!!
!!!
W-WE WEREN'T...
IMPERIAL ...
AH!
!!!
VRA
... FLAMING WINGS!!!
GYAAAAA !!
AAAAAAAAA

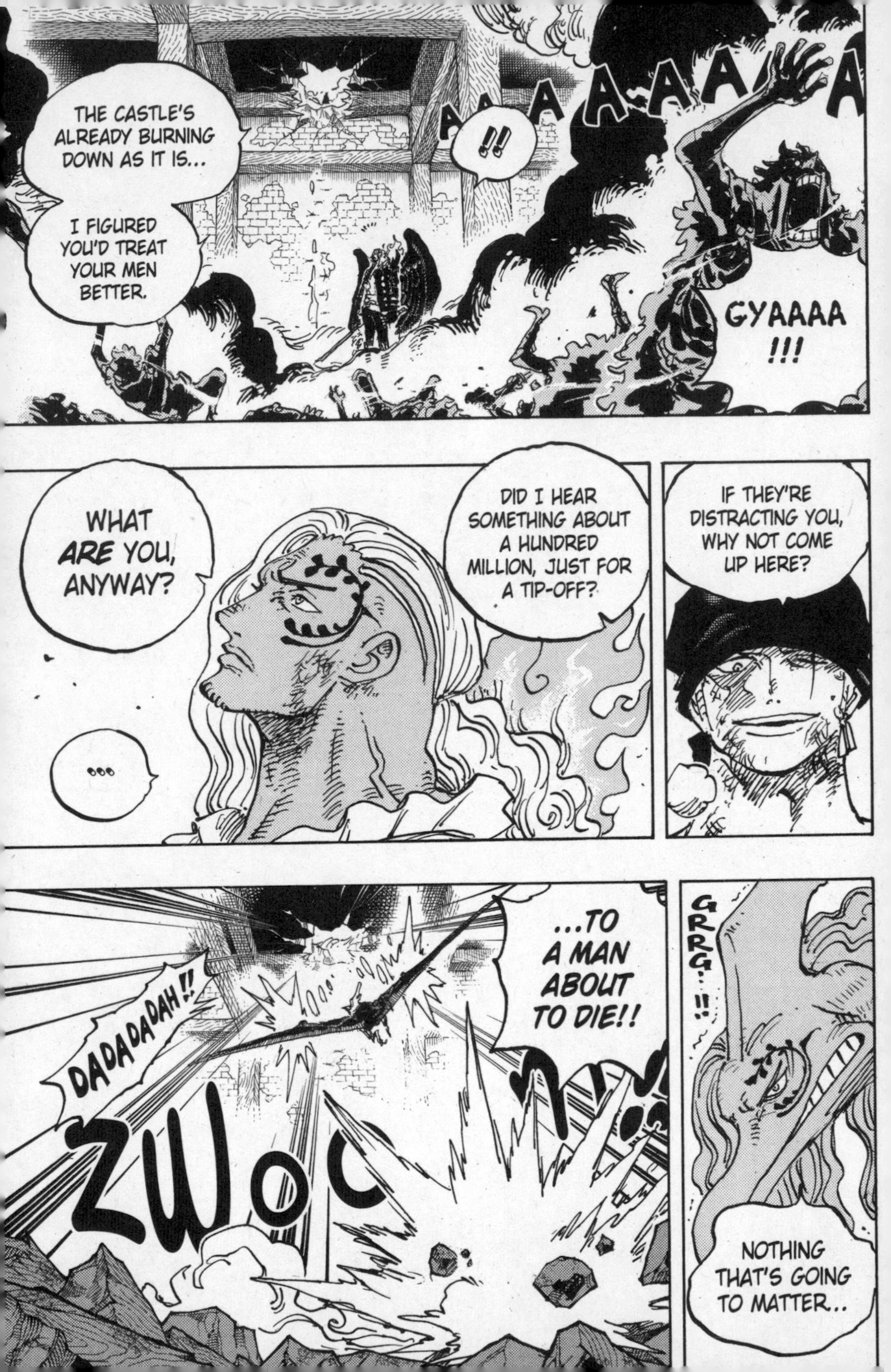
AAAAAAA
GYAAAA!!!
!!
THE CASTLE'S ALREADY BURNING DOWN AS IT IS...
I FIGURED YOU'D TREAT YOUR MEN BETTER.
IF THEY'RE DISTRACTING YOU, WHY NOT COME UP HERE?
DID I HEAR SOMETHING ABOUT A HUNDRED MILLION, JUST FOR A TIP-OFF?
WHAT *ARE* YOU, ANYWAY?
...
GRRG..!!
NOTHING THAT'S GOING TO MATTER...
...TO A MAN ABOUT TO DIE!!
DADADADAH!!
ZWOC

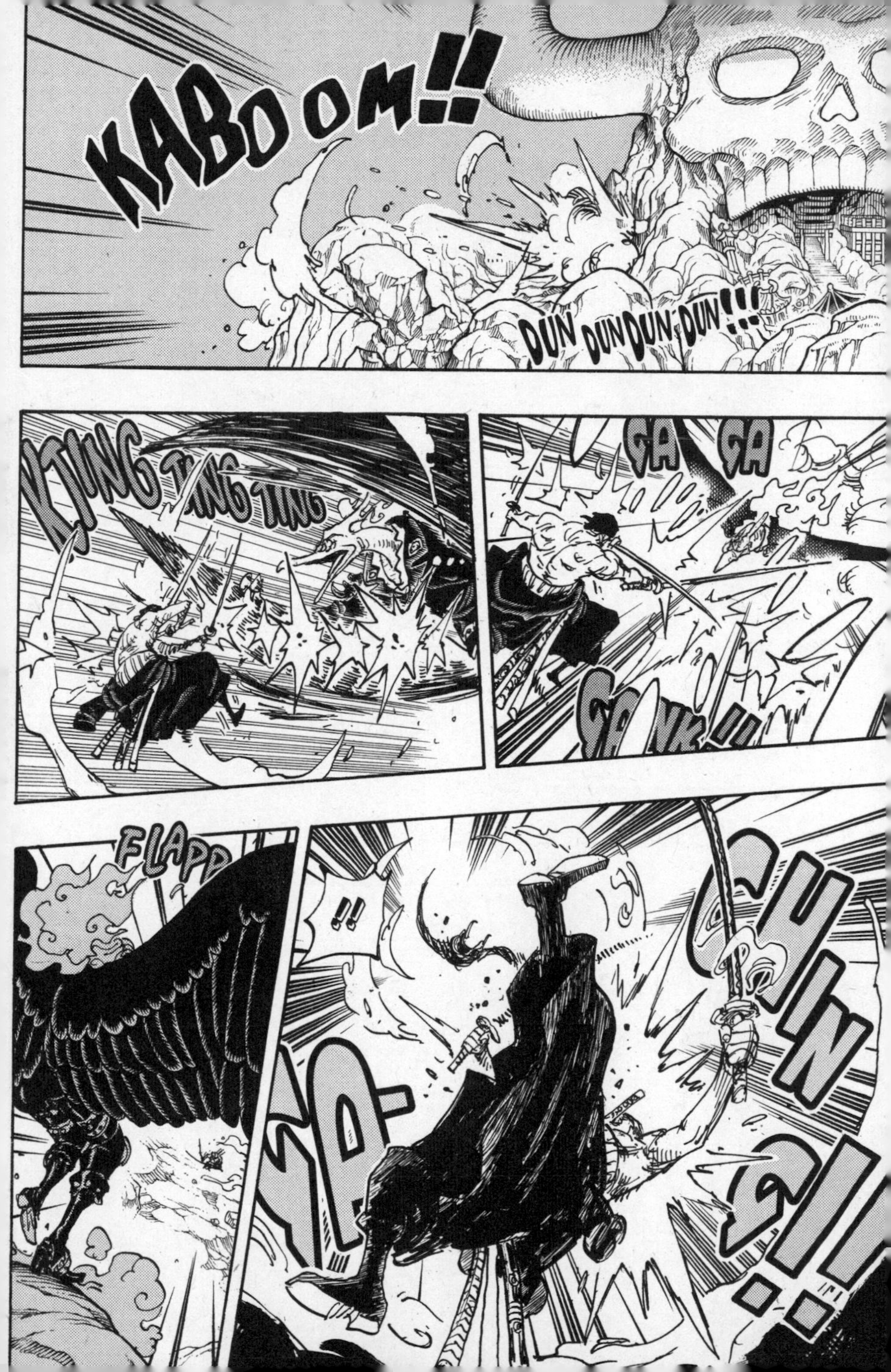
KABOOM!!
DUN DUN DUN DUN!!!
GA GA
GONK!!!
KTING TING TING TING
CHUIN!!
!!
FLAPP

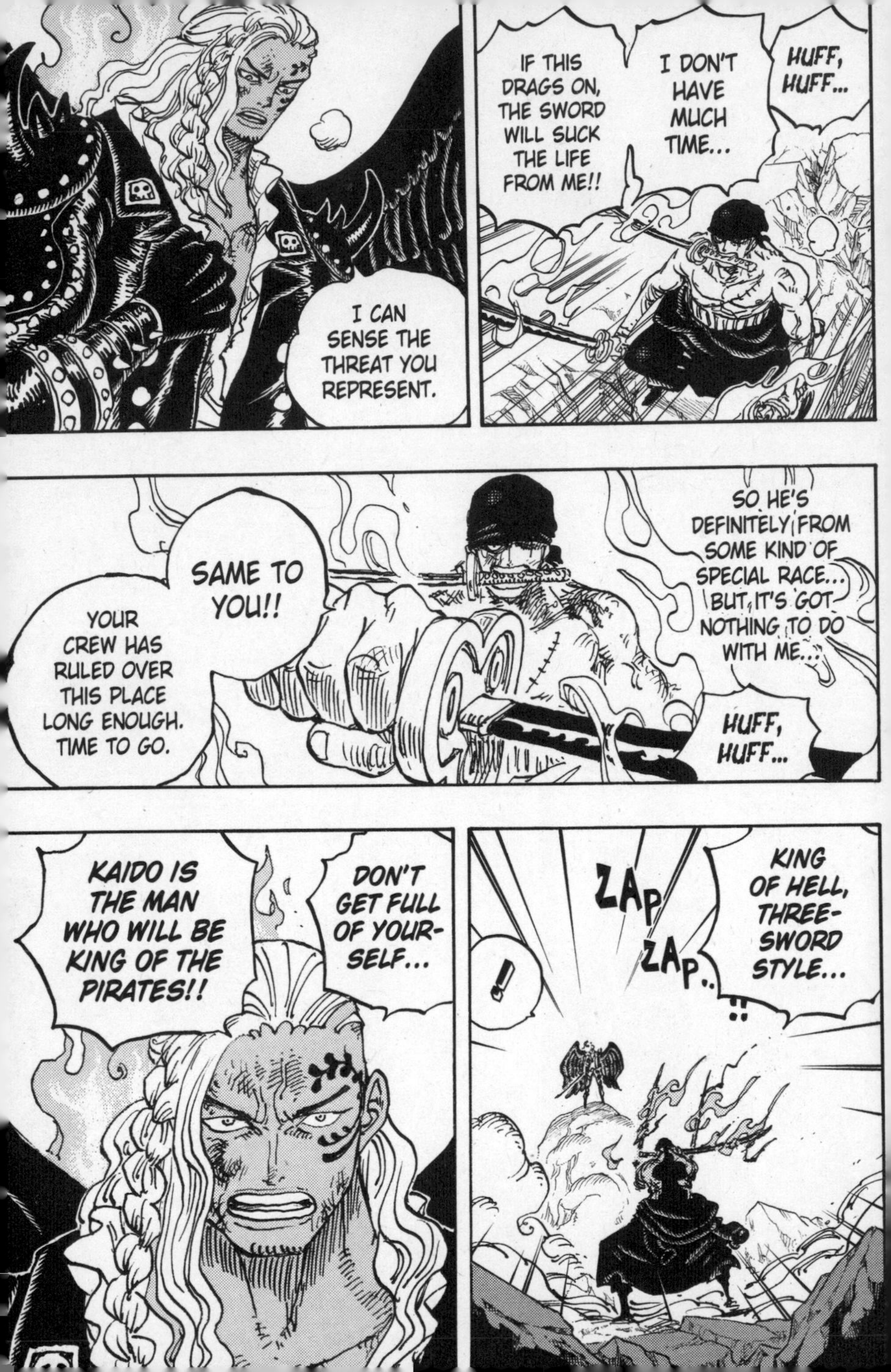
HUFF, HUFF...
I DON'T HAVE MUCH TIME...
IF THIS DRAGS ON, THE SWORD WILL SUCK THE LIFE FROM ME!!
I CAN SENSE THE THREAT YOU REPRESENT.
SO HE'S DEFINITELY FROM SOME KIND OF SPECIAL RACE... BUT IT'S GOT NOTHING TO DO WITH ME...
HUFF, HUFF...
SAME TO YOU!!
YOUR CREW HAS RULED OVER THIS PLACE LONG ENOUGH. TIME TO GO.
KING OF HELL, THREE-SWORD STYLE...
!!
ZAP
ZAP..
!
DON'T GET FULL OF YOURSELF...
KAIDO IS THE MAN WHO WILL BE KING OF THE PIRATES!!

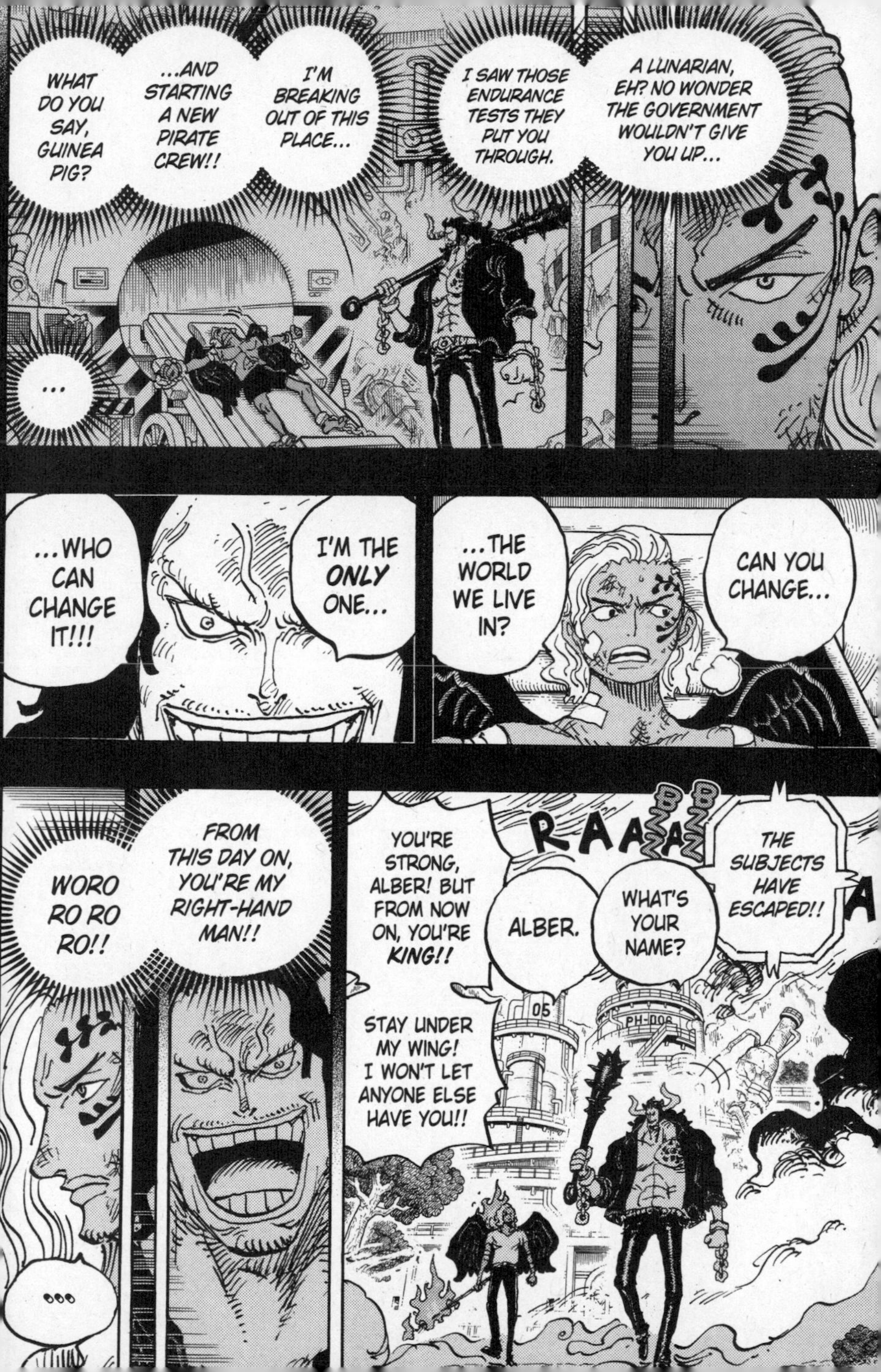
A LUNARIAN, EH? NO WONDER THE GOVERNMENT WOULDN'T GIVE YOU UP...
I SAW THOSE ENDURANCE TESTS THEY PUT YOU THROUGH.
I'M BREAKING OUT OF THIS PLACE...
...AND STARTING A NEW PIRATE CREW!!
WHAT DO YOU SAY, GUINEA PIG?
...
CAN YOU CHANGE...
...THE WORLD WE LIVE IN?
I'M THE *ONLY* ONE...
...WHO CAN CHANGE IT!!!
RAAA
THE SUBJECTS HAVE ESCAPED!!
WHAT'S YOUR NAME?
ALBER.
YOU'RE STRONG, ALBER! BUT FROM NOW ON, YOU'RE *KING!!*
05
PH-006
STAY UNDER MY WING! I WON'T LET ANYONE ELSE HAVE YOU!!
FROM THIS DAY ON, YOU'RE MY RIGHT-HAND MAN!!
WORO RO RO RO!!
...

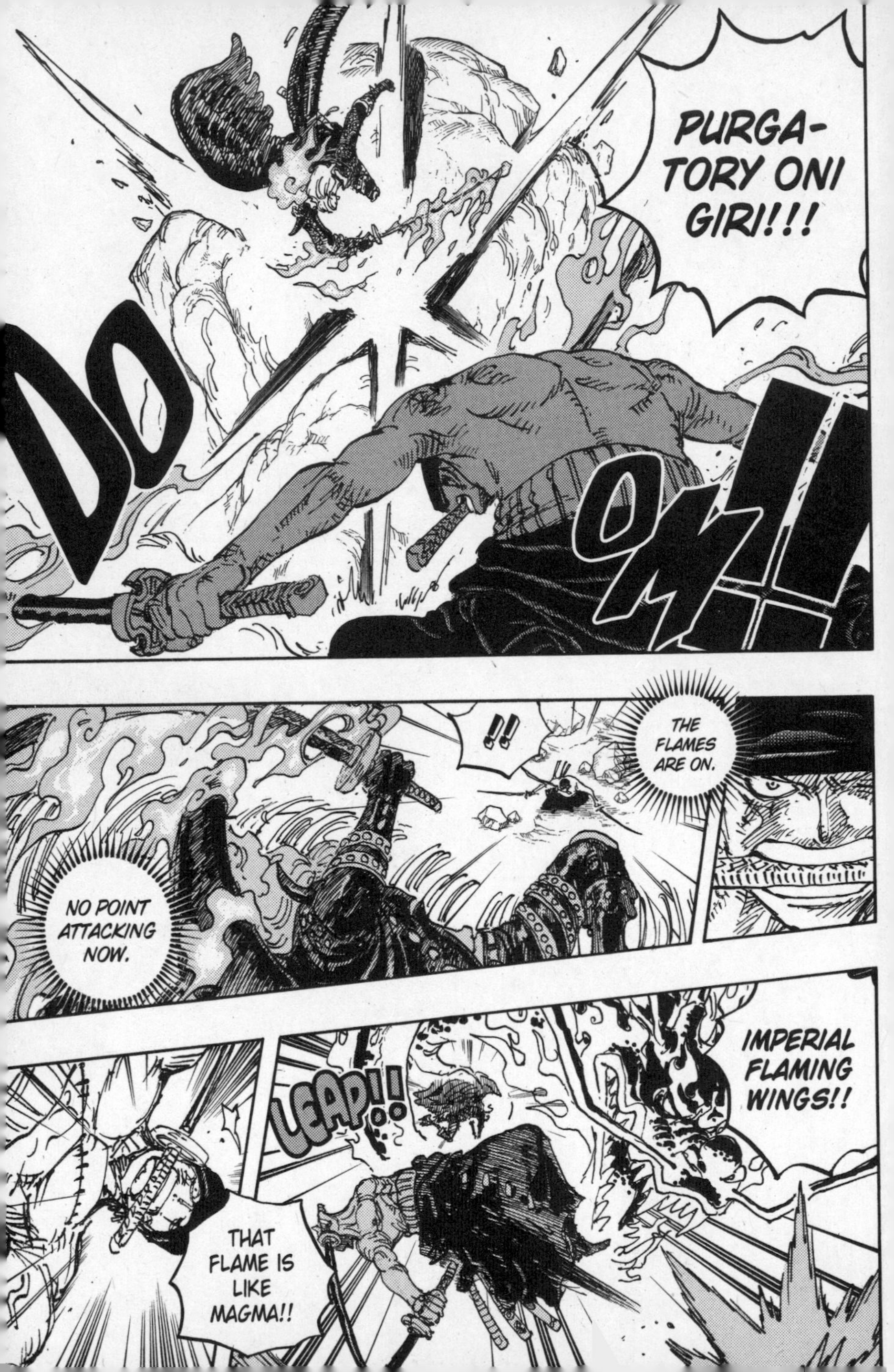
PURGA-
TORY ONI
GIRI!!!
DO
OM!!
!!
THE FLAMES ARE ON.
NO POINT ATTACKING NOW.
IMPERIAL FLAMING WINGS!!
LEAP!!
THAT FLAME IS LIKE MAGMA!!

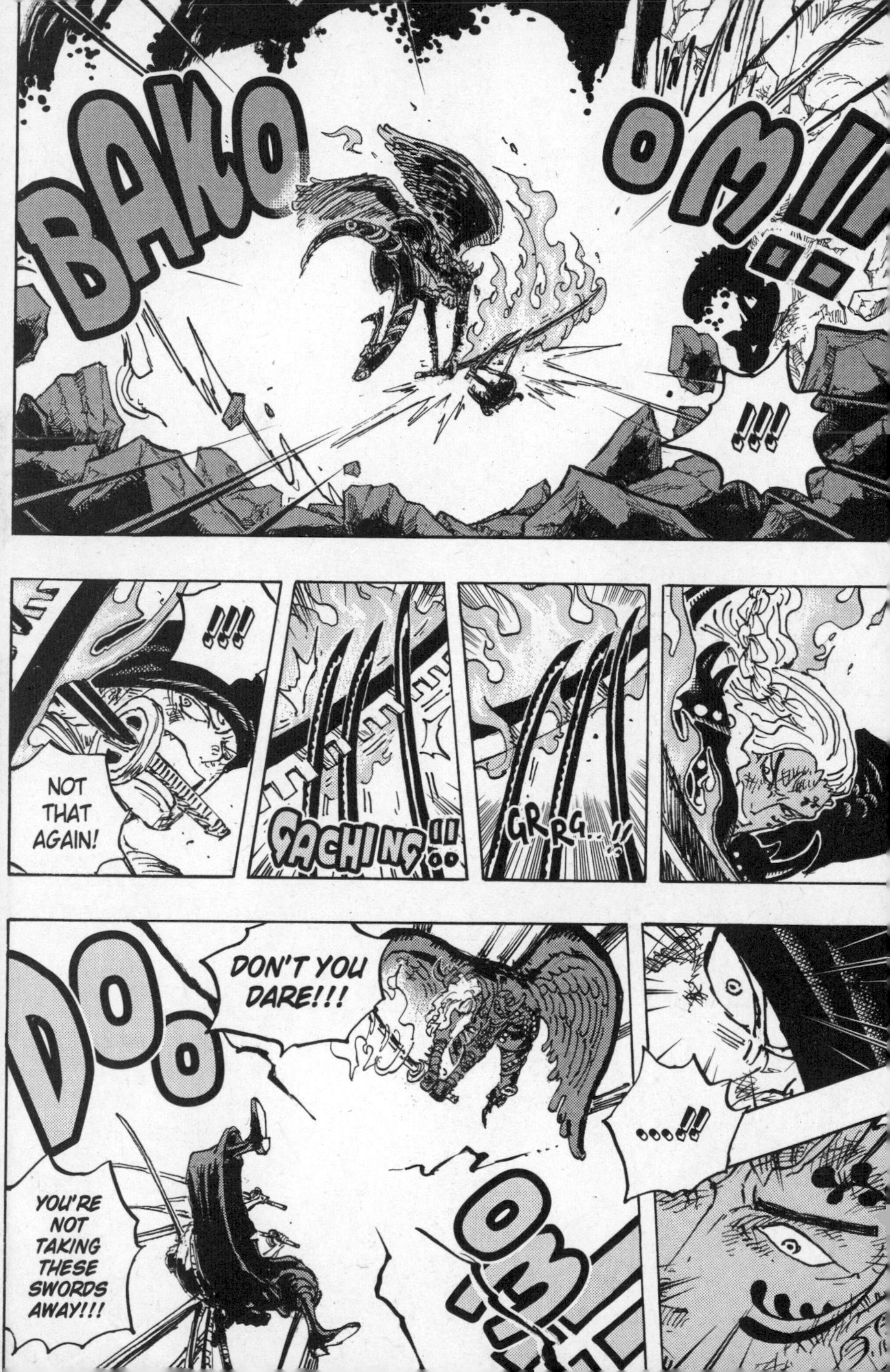
BAKOOM!!
!!!
GRRG..!!
GACHING!!
!!!
NOT THAT AGAIN!
....!!
DON'T YOU DARE!!!
DOOOM
YOU'RE NOT TAKING THESE SWORDS AWAY!!!

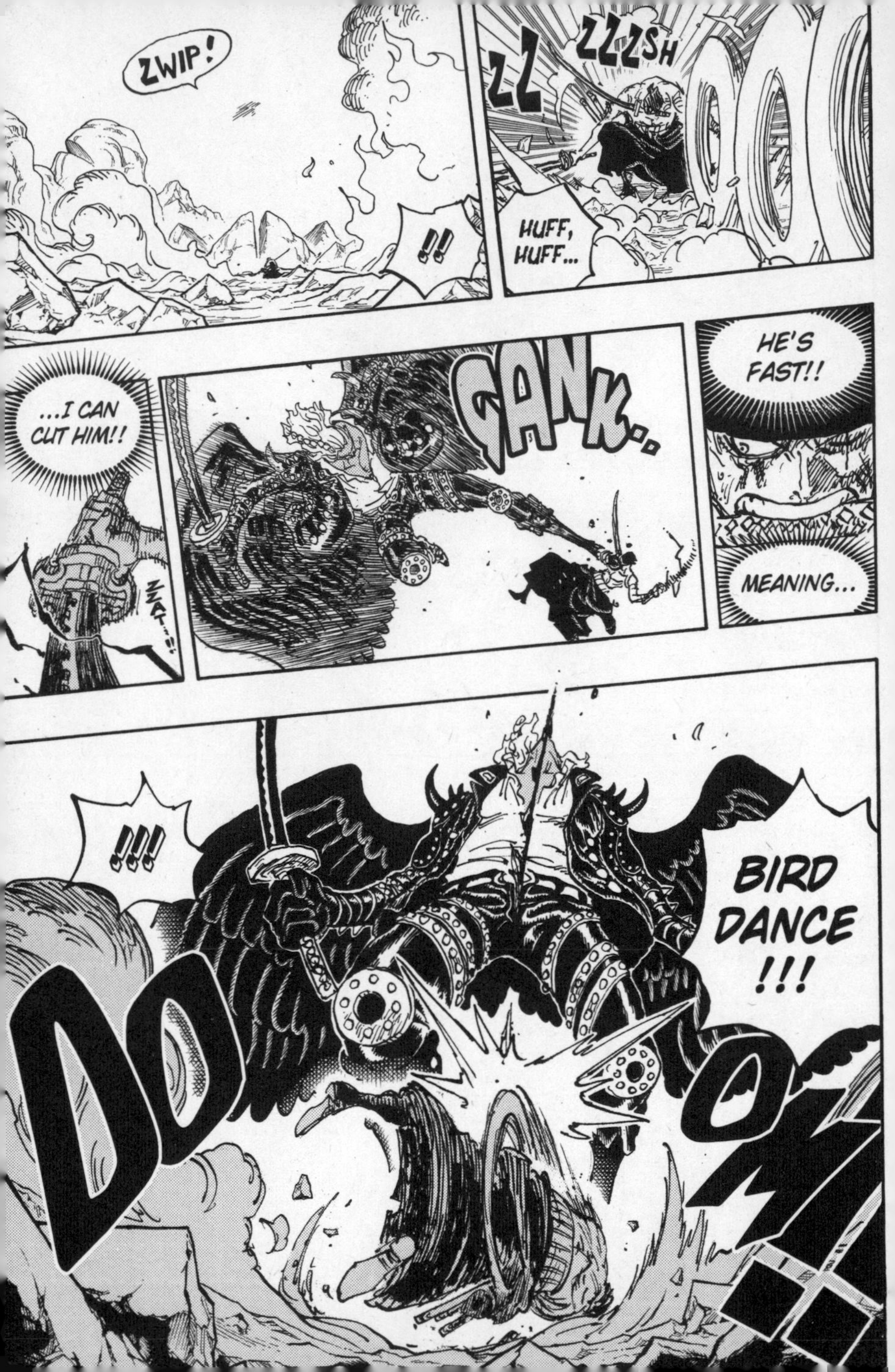
ZZZZZSH
HUFF, HUFF...
ZWIP!
!!
HE'S FAST!!
MEANING...
GANK..
...I CAN CUT HIM!!
ZZAT..!!
BIRD DANCE!!!
!!!
DOOM

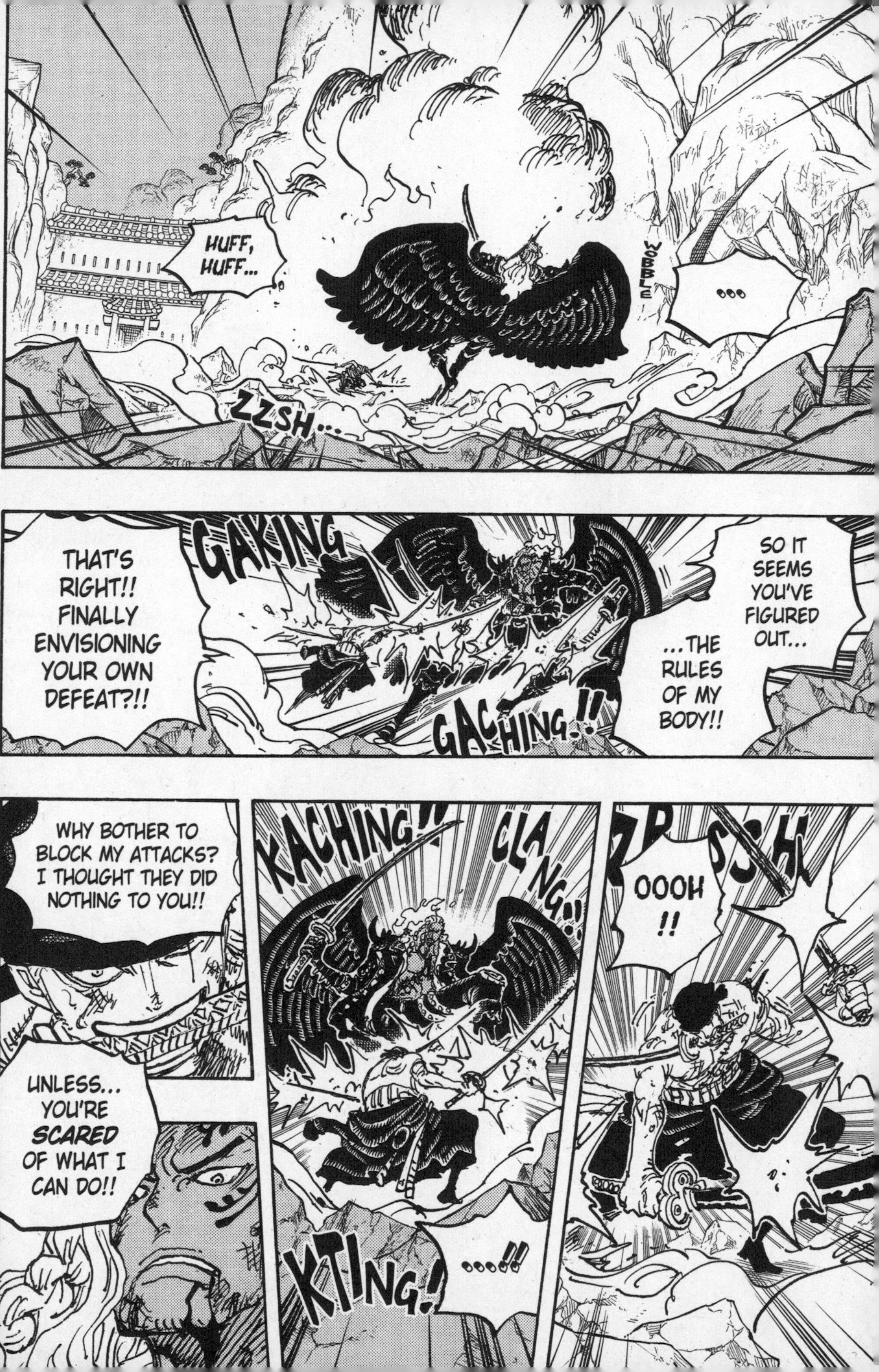
...
WOBBLE
HUFF, HUFF...
ZZSH...
SO IT SEEMS YOU'VE FIGURED OUT...
...THE RULES OF MY BODY!!
GAKING
GACHING!!
THAT'S RIGHT!! FINALLY ENVISIONING YOUR OWN DEFEAT?!!
OOOH !!
KACHING!!
CLANG!!
KTING!!
...!!
WHY BOTHER TO BLOCK MY ATTACKS? I THOUGHT THEY DID NOTHING TO YOU!!
UNLESS... YOU'RE *SCARED* OF WHAT I CAN DO!!

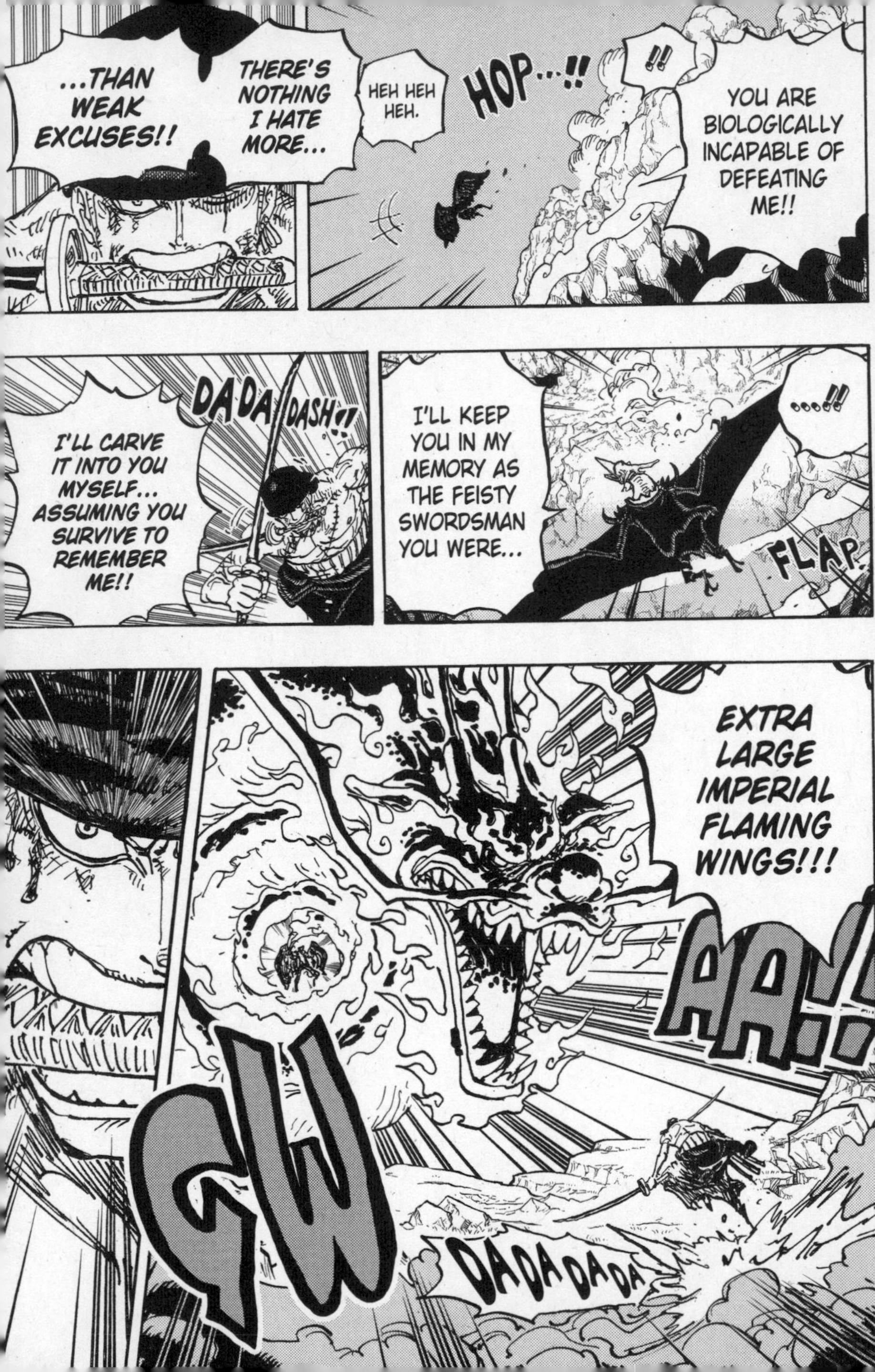
!!
YOU ARE BIOLOGICALLY INCAPABLE OF DEFEATING ME!!
HOP...!!
HEH HEH HEH.
THERE'S NOTHING I HATE MORE...
...THAN WEAK EXCUSES!!
...!!
I'LL KEEP YOU IN MY MEMORY AS THE FEISTY SWORDSMAN YOU WERE...
FLAP
DADA DASH!!
I'LL CARVE IT INTO YOU MYSELF... ASSUMING YOU SURVIVE TO REMEMBER ME!!
EXTRA LARGE IMPERIAL FLAMING WINGS!!!
AA!!
GW
DADADADA

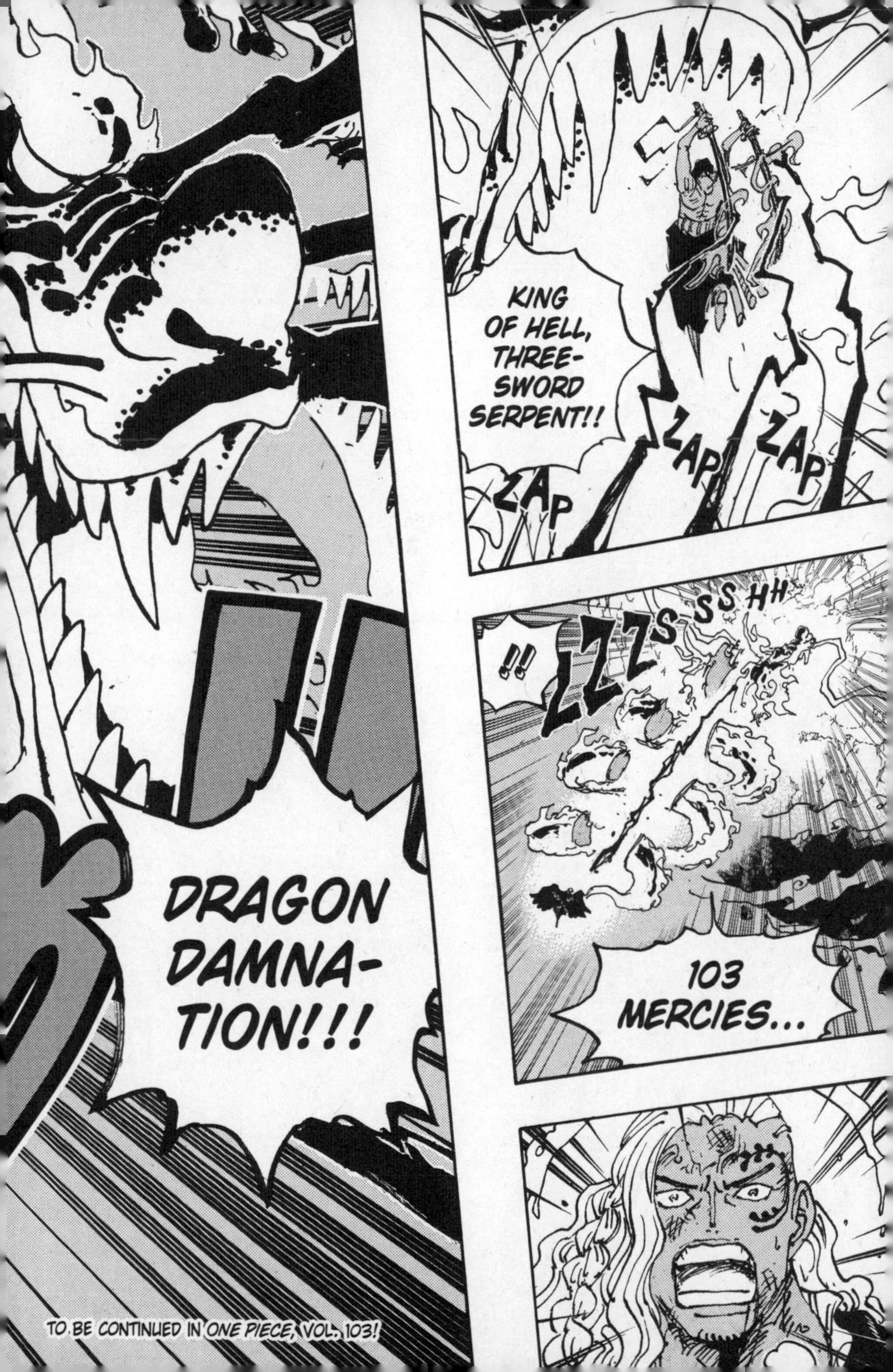
KING OF HELL, THREE-SWORD SERPENT!!
ZAP
ZAP
ZAP
!!
ZZZSSSHH
103 MERCIES...
DRAGON DAMNATION!!!

TO BE CONTINUED IN ONE PIECE, VOL. 103!

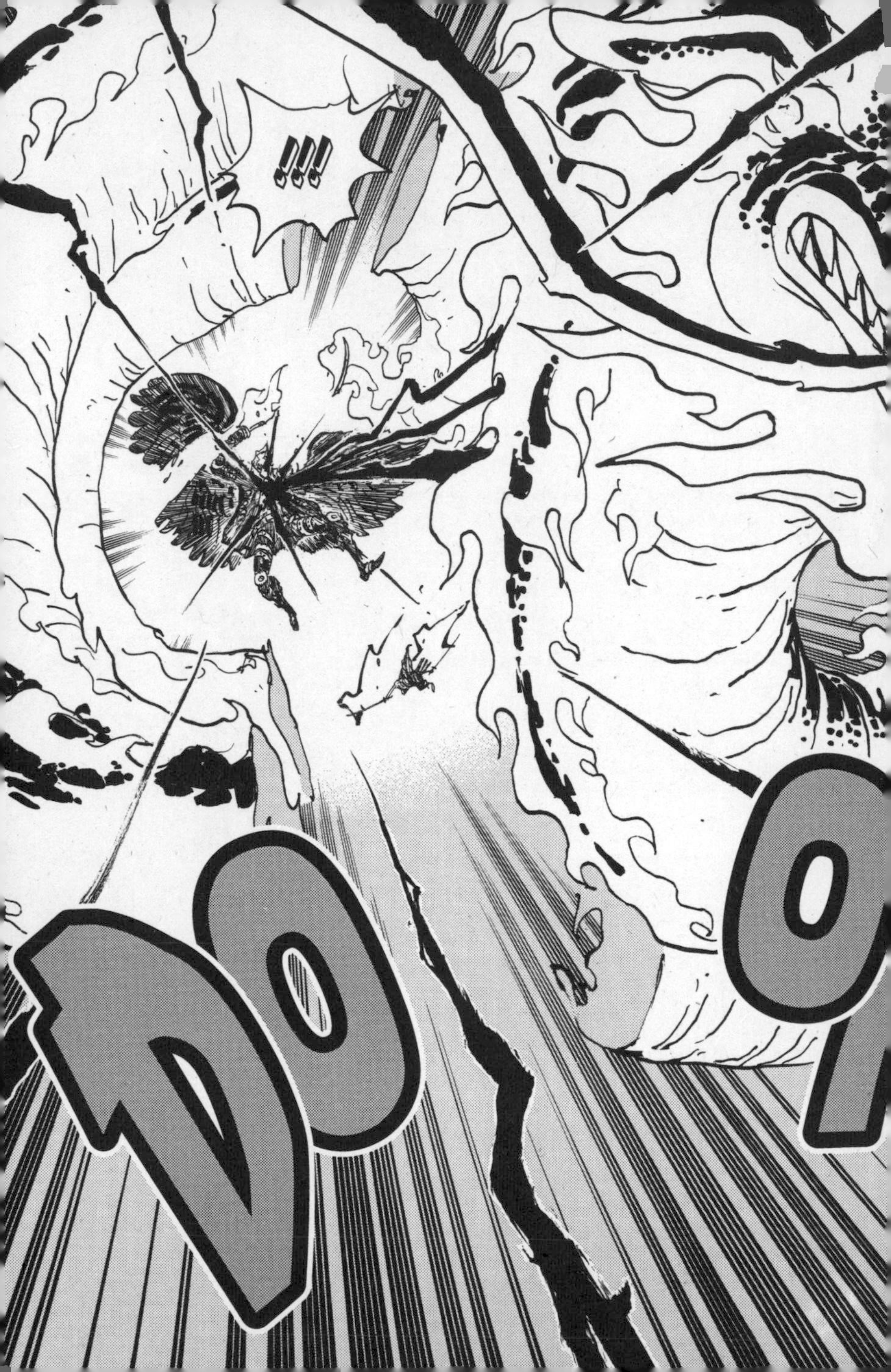
!!!
DOO

It's our helmsman, Katsuhisa Hoki's...

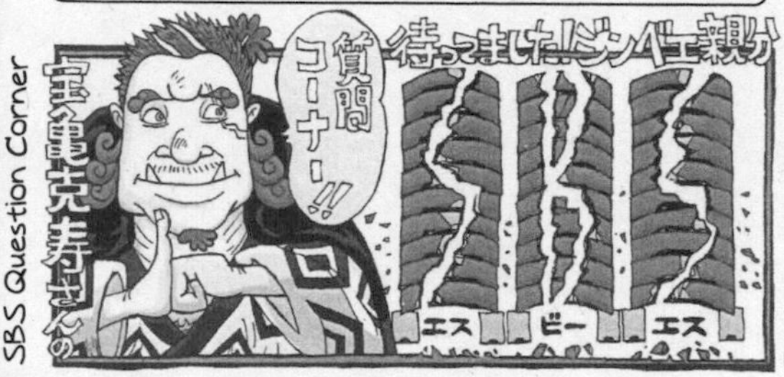
SBS Question Corner
宝亀克寿さんの
質問コーナー!!
待ってました!ジンベエ親分
SBS
エス ビー エス

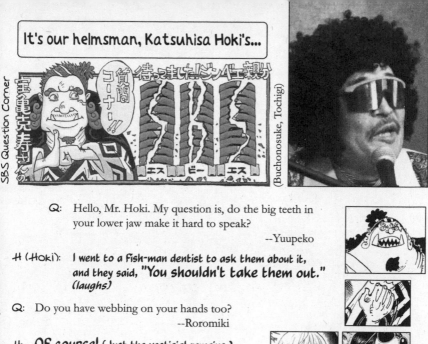

(Buchonosuke, Tochigi)

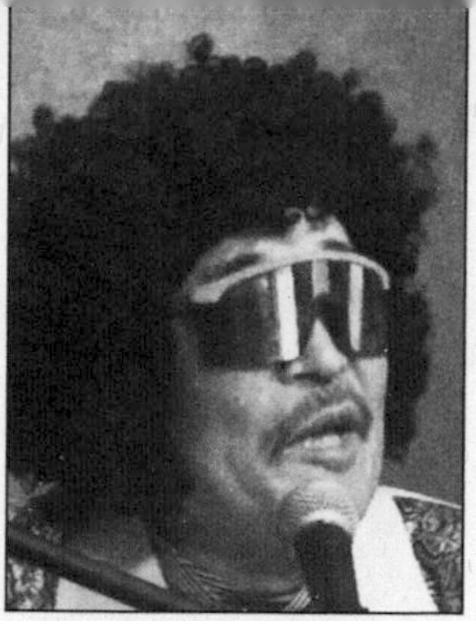

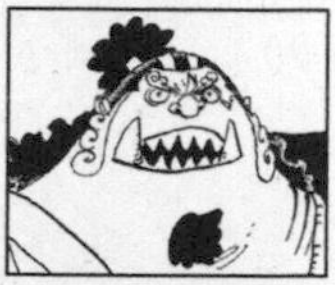

Q: Hello, Mr. Hoki. My question is, do the big teeth in your lower jaw make it hard to speak?

--Yuupeko

H (Hoki): **I went to a fish-man dentist to ask them about it, and they said, "You shouldn't take them out." *(laughs)***

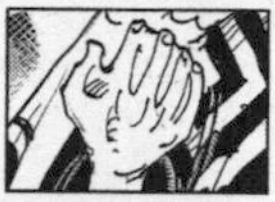

Q: Do you have webbing on your hands too?

--Roromiki

H: **Of course! (Just the vestigial remains.) Doesn't everyone?**

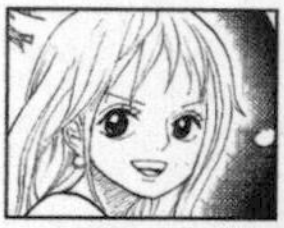

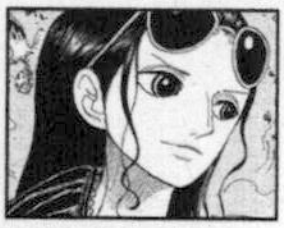

Q: Which one is your type--Nami or Robin?

--Roromiki

H: **Robin. She seems like she knows a lot about fish-men.**

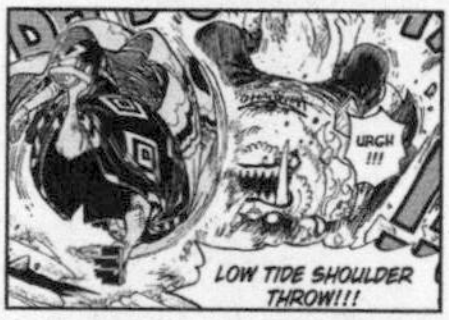
URGH !!!
LOW TIDE SHOULDER THROW!!!

Q: Have you ever practiced any kind of martial art?

--Ramen-maru

H: **I've done judo since I was in the 3rd grade. I'm a black belt!**

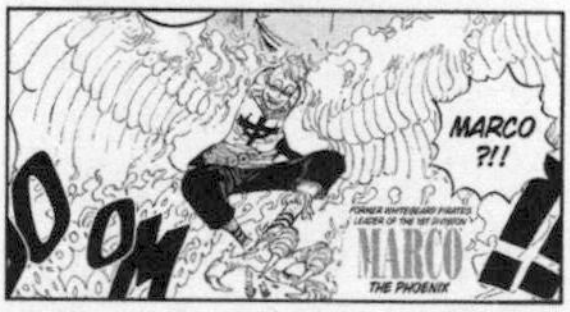
MARCO ?!!
FORMER WHITEBEARD PIRATES LEADER OF THE 1ST DIVISION
MARCO
THE PHOENIX

Q: Mr. Hoki, if Jimbei ate a Devil Fruit, which fruit would it be?

--420 Land

H: **Because a fish-man can live on land or in the water, I think he should get the Bird-Bird Fruit! But it would hurt too much not to be able to swim!**

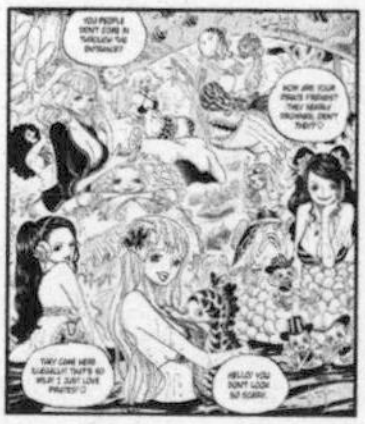

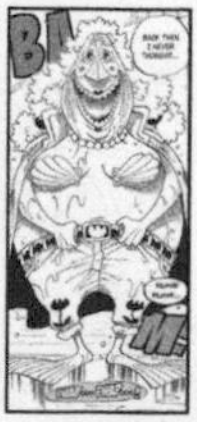

Q: Do you love mermaids too, Mr. Hoki?

--Match and Takeshi

H: **I like pretty mermaids. *(laughs)***

Q: What's your favorite kind of fish?

--Match and Takeshi

H: **I like blackthroat seaperch! It's delicious!**

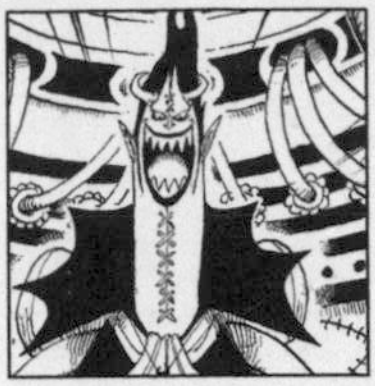

Q: Jimbei or Moria: which character is harder to act?

--Ryota Ehara

(*Note: Hoki also plays the role of Gecko Moria.)

H: **Jimbei! He's had a life of many twists and turns, ups and downs.**

Q: Draw a picture of Jimbei without looking at the paper.

--Yuupeko

H:

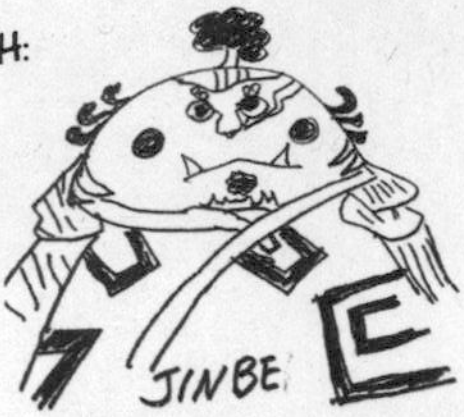
JINBE

Q: If you could describe Jimbei with a *yojijukugo* (four-kanji poetic phrase) which would it be?

--Ikeda

H: **Gashinshotan! (Undergoing extreme hardship to achieve your goal.)**

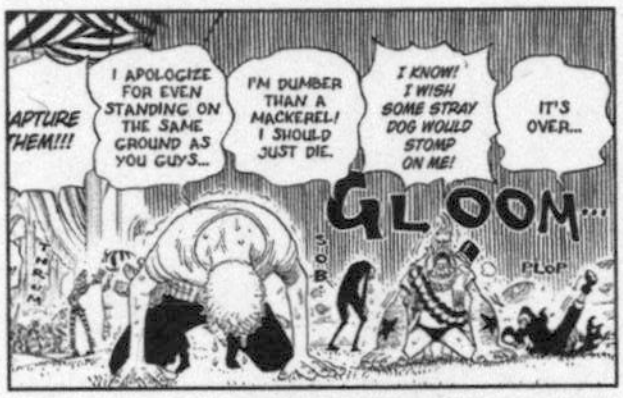
IT'S OVER...
I KNOW! I WISH SOME STRAY DOG WOULD STOMP ON ME!
I'M DUMBER THAN A MACKEREL! I SHOULD JUST DIE.
I APOLOGIZE FOR EVEN STANDING ON THE SAME GROUND AS YOU GUYS...
APTURE THEM!!!
GLOOM...
SOB
PLOP

Q: I can't even pick up my pen, because I don't know if I'm worthy of asking Mr. Hoki a question… Take this! Negative Hollow!!

--Occhi

H: **Oooh… I'm sorry for playing a fish-man, even though I almost drowned when I was in kindergarten.**

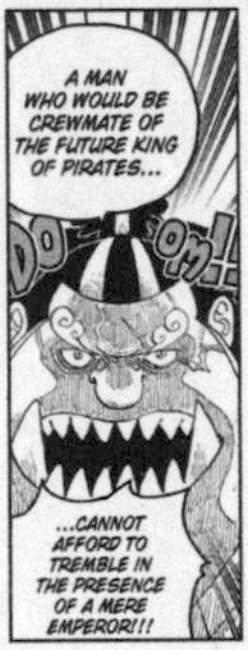
A MAN WHO WOULD BE CREWMATE OF THE FUTURE KING OF PIRATES...
...CANNOT AFFORD TO TREMBLE IN THE PRESENCE OF A MERE EMPEROR!!!

Q: What's your favorite Jimbei line and scene?!

--Occhi

H: **It's the scene where Jimbei returns the ritual cup of sake! "A man who would be crewmate of the future King of Pirates cannot afford to tremble in the presence of a mere Emperor!!!"**

Q: In the volume 99 SBS, it was revealed that Jimbei's best dish is "seared bonito tuna"! Do you have a specialty you like to make?

--Shiba

H: **Stir-fried vegetables, vegetable ramen. I made these a lot when I was young!**

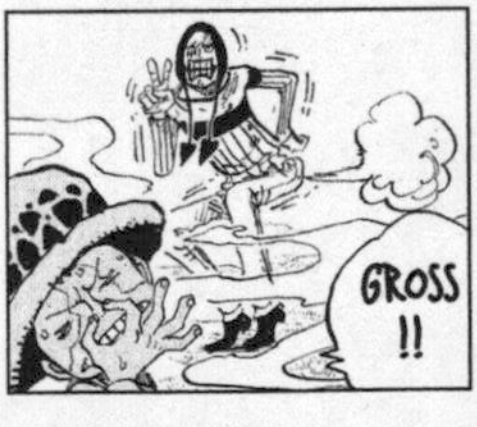
GROSS !!

Q: What powers do you have, Mr. Hoki? Tell us!!

--Yo D

H: **I've got the Toot-Toot Fruit! They call me Tootankhamun because my farts turn people into mummies…**

O (Oda): Okay! Thank you for that, Mr. Hoki. Our time is up! Toot-Toot Fruit, I mean, really... Everybody knows you can't knock someone unconscious with a fa... urk!! That smells... flop!!

H: **Oh! Odacchi!! Uh-oh, there's no pulse. Well, uh... everybody split! So long!!**

O: Don't leave me here!!

COMING NEXT VOLUME:

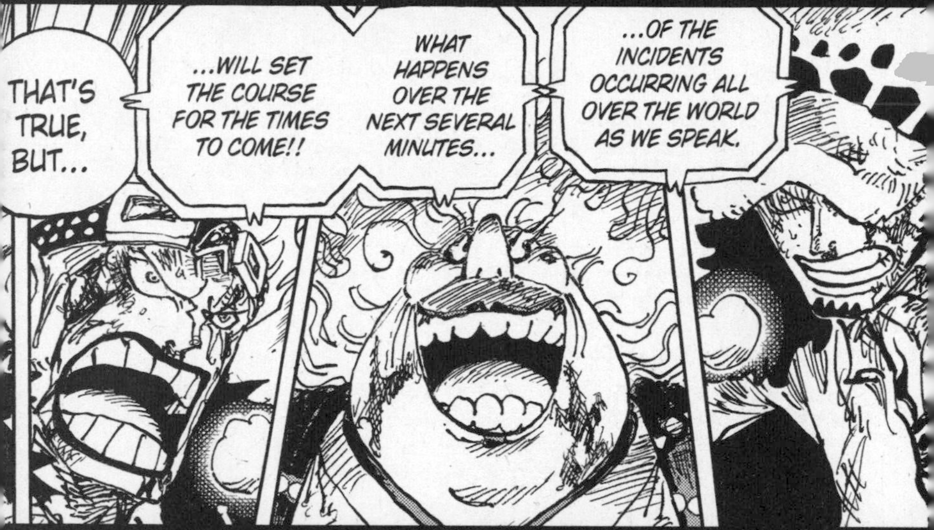
...OF THE INCIDENTS OCCURRING ALL OVER THE WORLD AS WE SPEAK.
WHAT HAPPENS OVER THE NEXT SEVERAL MINUTES...
...WILL SET THE COURSE FOR THE TIMES TO COME!!
THAT'S TRUE, BUT...

Zolo unleashes everything he has against King, but will it be enough? Elsewhere, Luffy vs. Kaido round two is underway and already out of control. Luffy is going to have to transcend to another level if he hopes to win this fight!

ON SALE JULY 2023!

尾田栄一郎

In the Edo period, "it" was sold as fertilizer for crops. And the "it" from people who ate fine food was sold at a premium, while the "it" from the poor or criminals was cheap. Even "it" has ranks of quality.

The age-old question is "Which would you rather eat it-flavored curry, or curry-flavored it?"

But the question you should ask in response is, "Whose 'it' are we talking about?"

Anyway... Man, I wish the PTA liked me!!!

Here's volume 102. Enjoy!!!

-Eiichiro Oda, 2022

Eiichiro Oda began his manga career at the age of 17, when his one-shot cowboy manga **Wanted!** won second place in the coveted Tezuka manga awards. Oda went on to work as an assistant to some of the biggest manga artists in the industry, including Nobuhiro Watsuki, before winning the Hop Step Award for new artists. His pirate adventure **One Piece**, which debuted in **Weekly Shonen Jump** in 1997, quickly became one of the most popular manga in Japan.

ONE PIECE VOL. 102
WANO PART 13

SHONEN JUMP Edition

STORY AND ART BY EIICHIRO ODA

Translation/Stephen Paul
Touch-Up Art & Lettering/Vanessa Satone
Design/Yukiko Whitley
Editor/Alexis Kirsch

Printed in the U.S.A.

Published by VIZ Media, LLC
P.O. Box 77010
San Francisco, CA 94107

10 9 8 7 6 5 4 3 2 1
First printing, April 2023

viz.com